AIRWAYS SYSTEM

GOLF / NEW HORIZONS

Joe McCarthy

GOLF

Pan Am's Guide to Golf Courses Round the World

REVISED EDITION

G E N E S A R A Z E N *with* P E T E R McL E A N

Thomas Y. Crowell Company / New York / Established 1834

EW HORIZONS

This book was made possible through the cooperation and assistance of many individuals and agencies interested in golfing throughout the world, and of Pan Am's employees and agents in countries where golf is played. Special recognition is accorded to Hal Power of the Shell Oil Company for providing many of the photographs, to Frank Jaster for editorial aid, and to Mel Diamond of *Golf Digest* for his editorial assistance and for supplying the "Places to Play" list in the appendix.

INTRODUCTION

by ALLAN BROWN, *U.S.G.A. Official*

For the golfer who is searching for new courses to conquer there are now unlimited opportunities for adventure on the fairways of the world. Even the most distant courses are only a few hours away by Pan Am jets.

Wherever the English have colonized, they have introduced golf. This also is true of the French and Belgians, particularly where they have developed mining properties and plantations in remote areas. The golf clubs maintained by these interests provide recreational centers for members of the supervisory staff and their families. Many of these clubs welcome guests. In recent years an increasing number of Americans have been investing money in foreign resorts in which golf is the focal attraction.

I have played golf on many of these courses and have some fond recollections as a reward for my efforts. For example, I shall never forget the signs on the golf courses of Northern Rhodesia and the Belgian Congo: "Elephant Have the Right of Way," "Beware of Snakes and Crocodiles," and "Caution—You Are in Wild Animal Country."

Unusual features will help me always to remember certain courses:

> The black sand (greens) of Ndola; the caddie house made of cornstalks at Kilemba Mines; the breathtaking scenery of the course near Jao Jao in the Argentine Andes; the green located in the middle of an ancient race track in Goma; the termite-proof concrete tees at the Mombasa Golf Club; the hexagonal clubhouse at Mnazi Mnoza Sports Club in Zanzibar; the shadows of the great pyramids near the eighteenth green at Cairo's Mena House Golf Course.

One of the strangest sights was the small volcanic tee markers emitting steam and sulfurous fumes at the Rotorua Golf Club in New Zealand. They gave me the impression I was playing in Hades.

In Queenstown, New Zealand, I borrowed the key to the local golf club from the leading sports shop and enjoyed the unique experience of having a nine-hole course entirely to myself.

On an island in the Tonga group, the golf course was built around a temple—convenient for appealing to the Deity when negotiating a particularly difficult putt.

I also recall the care with which I followed the borrowed ball at the Longwood Golf Course on the island of St. Helena, because the fourteen playing members had only nine golf balls among them.

I remember the old barefooted caddie on a golf course near São Paulo, Brazil, who made small wagers on the players. He would give his favorites an assist by picking up balls in the rough with his toes and depositing them on the fairway without any of the players being aware of the transfer. Shortly after this, however, a sign was posted in the caddie house: "Caddies must wear shoes."

The land on which one private golf course in Uruguay is located is owned by the city of Montevideo. On one occasion the mayor of the city declared the course closed to its members on Sunday and opened to the public as a park. Eighteen guards, one to each green, were employed to keep the picnickers from damaging the putting surface. On Monday, what I thought was a ball in a trap turned out to be a hard-boiled egg left over from the previous day's outing.

I recall the difficulty of concentrating when putting on a green in Switzerland while the tinkle of cowbells in the valley far below blended with the echo of a yodeler high in the Alps.

There is plenty of opportunity for adventure on the golf courses of the world, but it is advisable for the touring golfer to do some planning with Pam Am or his travel agent in advance.

In general there are three classes of golf courses: private clubs similar to the private clubs in the United States, public courses which are state-owned or controlled by the local community, and resort courses that are part of the recreational facilities of a hotel.

It is most advisable to have letters of introduction to the private clubs, although membership cards of well-known clubs sometimes will be honored. Advance reservation at the hotels also is recommended, particularly at the more popular resorts during the height of their season.

It is also well to check with the clubs regarding the most convenient time to play the course. In Peru and Chile, for example, the courses are closed on Monday, the day for watering them. This does not mean turning on a sprinkling system. It means opening the gates of an irrigation system and flooding the course.

There are certain days when caddies are not available. Many courses do not have caddies but provide tote carts instead. Very few have electric or gas-driven carts for the golfers. Club and local tournaments also are held from time to time, making it necessary to close courses to visitors.

It is most advisable for visitors to conform to the customs of the country and to the local rules of the club. Many foreign clubs do not allow either men or women to wear Bermuda shorts, and some clubs do not allow women in slacks. Many clubs also have special rules affecting play by visitors on holidays and weekends.

Mode of play should be taken into consideration, too. Many golfers in the British Isles and elsewhere play a Scotch foursome, in which two balls are used, and partners play alternate shots. Such matches are played at about the same speed as a twosome. When a golfer is playing a four-ball match or if he is inclined to play slowly, he should always let the faster match through.

Tipping is another problem. It is always wise to ask the caddie master what the prevailing rate is for fees, so as not to overtip and thus cause embarrassment to regular members.

In some of the more remote areas, taxis are extremely scarce. To be assured of transportation back from the club to the hotel, it is best to make arrangements in advance for the return trip.

Another suggestion to the traveling golfer is to brush up on his foreign language. It is always much more interesting and enjoyable to be able to converse with people in their native tongue.

Last, but by no means least, be courteous and considerate of other golfers. The visiting golfer is not only a guest, he is also an "ambassador" from his own country. He should not forget that the grand game of golf has given him the opportunity to enjoy these foreign courses. By leaving a good impression, the Americans who follow will be welcome.

CONTENTS

EUROPE

Austria

Austria is the land of the Alps, and the golf courses are no exception. Half of the dozen courses now operating are above 2,500 feet, and nearly all are within view of the snow-capped Alpine horizons.

Golf here has been called golf-in-the-rough because the architects have left the natural land features totally intact. There are no artificial hazards on the courses—in fact, almost no sand traps—and don't look for meticulous grooming. The style is completely *au naturel*.

Variety is infinite, stretching from lakeside links at Dellach to the Alpine hillsides of Kitzbuehel, where the fairways are 2,700 feet above the valley floor. For those who like the mountain air but lack the endurance of a mountain goat, the nine-hole course at Innsbruck-Igls is nearly 3,000 feet up on a plateau where there is very little incline. For the gambler, the country club at Vienna is on the grounds of the Freudenau Race Track, and there are casinos not far from the courses at Salzburg, Bad Gastein, and Kitzbuehel. For the health addict, Bad Gastein is a world-famous spa.

The golf season in Austria runs from April through November except in Vienna, where braver souls brace themselves with a bit of local plum brandy called slivovitz and play throughout the winter. The hotels and guest houses are inexpensive, immaculate, and atmospheric, and the Bavarian brews and selection of weiners and wursts will do a great deal for a mountain-fostered appetite, but little for the waistline. The local people are delightful, generous hosts, and will make the traveling golfer's stay in this storybook land most comfortable.

SEASON: April through November.

HOW TO GET THERE: By Pan Am Jet Clipper, 11 hours (elapsed time) to Vienna from New York via London and Frankfurt. By ship, 5 to 9 days to Le Havre, France, then 21 to 24 hours by train to Vienna. Western Austria is most easily reached by

1

Pan Am to Munich and thence a 2½-hour train ride to either Innsbruck or Salzburg. Austrian Airlines provides frequent service by connecting with Pan Am in many European cities. There is also daily air service to Salzburg, Innsbruck, Graz, Linz, and Klagenfurt.

GOLF EQUIPMENT: American equipment available at reasonable prices.

LANGUAGE: German is the official language, but English is widely understood.

TIME: Six hours later than U.S. Eastern Standard Time.

Golf and Country Club Salzburg

LOCATION: Salzburg-Klesheim (3 miles from Salzburg). COURSE SIZE: 9 holes; 2,815 yards; par 35. AVAILABILITY TO VISITORS: Visitors welcome. GREEN FEES: Per day, $2; Saturdays and Sundays, $2.80 daily; per week, $9.20. CADDIE FEES: 50¢ for each 9 holes. GOLF CLUB RENTALS: 40¢ per round. GOLF CART RENTALS: 40¢ per round. MOTORIZED GOLF CART RENTALS: Not available. LESSONS: $3 per hour. CLUBHOUSE FACILITIES: Restaurant, bar, swimming pool, and tennis. The clubhouse is an eighteenth-century castle. Gambling casino located in town. RECOMMENDED ACCOMMODATIONS: Salzburg: Hotel Osterreichischer Hof, Hotel Golden Hirsh, Hotel Europe, Dr. Wührer's Haus Gastein.

Golf and Country Club Schloss Fuschl

LOCATION: Fuschl (about 8 miles from Salzburg). COURSE SIZE: 9 holes; par 3. AVAILABILITY TO VISITORS: Visitors welcome. GREEN FEES: $2 per day. CADDIE FEES: 40¢ per round. GOLF CLUB RENTALS: Available. GOLF CART RENTALS: Available. MOTORIZED GOLF CART RENTALS: Not available. LESSONS: $2.40 per hour. CLUBHOUSE FACILITIES: Available. RECOMMENDED ACCOMMODATIONS: Schlosshotel Fuschl.

Golf Club Achensee

LOCATION: Pertisau am Achensee (5- to 10-minute walk from Pertisau). COURSE SIZE: 9 holes; 2,032 yards; par 35. AVAILABILITY TO VISITORS: Visitors welcome. GREEN FEES: Per day, $1.60; per week,

$8; per month, $20. CADDIE FEES: 40¢ for each 9 holes. GOLF CLUB RENTALS: $1.20 per day. GOLF CART RENTALS: Not available. MOTORIZED GOLF CART RENTALS: Not available. LESSONS: $2 per hour. CLUBHOUSE FACILITIES: Not available, but tennis courts, boating, fishing, and hunting are all close by. RECOMMENDED ACCOMMODATIONS: Hotel Karlwirt (near course), Hotel Alpenhof, Hotel Fuerstenhaus, Hotel Pfandler, Hotel Reiser, Strand Hotel.

Golf Club Gastein

LOCATION: Kurverwaltung (½ mile from Bad Gastein). COURSE SIZE: 9 holes; 3,087 yards; par 37. AVAILABILITY TO VISITORS: Visitors welcome. GREEN FEES: Weekdays, $2.40; Saturdays and Sundays, $2.80 daily; per week, $12. CADDIE FEES: Available. GOLF CLUB RENTALS: Available. GOLF CART RENTALS: Available. MOTORIZED GOLF CART RENTALS: Not available. LESSONS: $2.40 per hour. CLUBHOUSE FACILITIES: Restaurant and bar. Complete health spa facilities as well as gambling casino located in town. RECOMMENDED ACCOMMODATIONS: Hotel Astoria, Grand Hotel de l'Europe, Hotel der Kaiserhof, Bellevue Parc Hotel, Hotel Elizabethparc, Grand Hotel Gasteinerhof.

Golf-Club Innsbruck-Igls

LOCATION: Innsbruck-Igls (1 mile from Igls, 3 miles from Innsbruck by car or on local electric railway). COURSE SIZE: 9 holes, 18 different tees; 5,250 yards; par 68. AVAILABILITY TO VISITORS: Visitors welcome. GREEN FEES: Weekdays, $2.40; weekends, $3.50 per day; per week, $14; per month, $32. CADDIE FEES: $1–$1.25 per 18 holes. GOLF CLUB RENTALS: 80¢ per half day; $1.35 per day. GOLF CART RENTALS: 80¢ per half day; $1.35 per day. MOTORIZED GOLF CART RENTALS: Not available. LESSONS: $3 per hour. CLUBHOUSE FACILITIES: Restaurant and bar. RECOMMENDED ACCOMMODATIONS: Igls: Golfhotel Iglerhof, Hotel Maximilian, Sporthaus Igls, Hotel Pension Sperberegg. Innsbruck: Hotel Europa, Hotel Tyrol.

Golf Club Kitzbuehel-Mittersill

LOCATION: ½ mile from Kitzbuehel. COURSE SIZE: 9 holes; 3,215 yards; par 36. AVAILABILITY TO VISITORS: Visitors welcome. GREEN

FEES: Weekdays, $2; weekends, $2.40 per day; per week, $11. CADDIE FEES: 80¢ for 9 holes; $1.20 for 18 holes. GOLF CLUB RENTALS: $1 per day. GOLF CART RENTALS: 40¢ per day. MOTORIZED GOLF CART RENTALS: Not available. LESSONS: $2.40 per hour. CLUBHOUSE FACILITIES: Restaurant, bar, and lockers. RECOMMENDED ACCOMMODATIONS: Kitzbuehel: Sporthaus Hinterbrau, Gartenhotel Tennerhof, Hotel Hirzingerhof, Schloss Hotel Kaps, Grand Hotel, Hotel Guido Reish, Sporthotel E. Reish, Hotel Goldener Greiff, Hotel Toni Seiler.

Golf Club Linz

LOCATION: 3 miles from the center of Linz. COURSE SIZE: 9 holes; 2,850 yards; par 35. AVAILABILITY TO VISITORS: Visitors welcome. GREEN FEES: $2.40 daily. CADDIE FEES: 40¢ each 9 holes. GOLF CLUB RENTALS: 80¢ per day. GOLF CART RENTALS: Not available. MOTORIZED GOLF CART RENTALS: Not available. LESSONS: $2 per hour. CLUBHOUSE FACILITIES: Bar only. RECOMMENDED ACCOMMODATIONS: Linz: Parkhotel, Hotel Schwechater Hof, Hotel Schwarzer Bär, Hotel Achlietner.

Golf Club Semmering

LOCATION: Semmering (50 miles south of Vienna). COURSE SIZE: 9 holes; 2,085 yards; par 31. AVAILABILITY TO VISITORS: Visitors welcome. GREEN FEES: Per day, $2; per week, $8; per month, $24; per season, $60. CADDIE FEES: 30¢ to 60¢ per hour. GOLF CLUB RENTALS: 60¢ per round. GOLF CART RENTALS: 20¢ per round. MOTORIZED GOLF CART RENTALS: Not available. LESSONS: $2 per hour. CLUBHOUSE FACILITIES: Restaurant and bar. RECOMMENDED ACCOMMODATIONS: Südbahnhotel Semmering (on course).

Golf Club Wien

LOCATION: Vienna (10 minutes from the center of town by car; 40 minutes by tram). On the grounds of the Freudenau Race Track. COURSE SIZE: 18 holes; 5,922 yards; par 71. AVAILABILITY TO VISITORS: Unlimited for members of acknowledged clubs. GREEN FEES: Weekdays, $2; weekends, $3 per day; per month, $24. CADDIE FEES: $1.20, plus 40¢ tip per round. GOLF CLUB RENTALS: $1.20 with cart. GOLF CART RENTALS: 40¢ per day. MOTORIZED GOLF CART RENTALS: Not available. LESSONS: $3 per hour. CLUBHOUSE FACILITIES: Restaurant, bar, and locker rooms. Opposite the golf course there is a riding stable where one of Dobbin's descendants can be rented for a gallop through the woods. RECOMMENDED ACCOMMODATIONS: Hotel Bristol, Hotel Imperial, Hotel Sacher, Hotel Vienna Intercontinental.

Kärntner Golf Club

LOCATION: Dellach am Wörther See (9 miles from Klagenfurt). COURSE SIZE: 9 holes; 3,022 yards; par 35. AVAILABILITY TO VISITORS: Visitors welcome. GREEN FEES: Per day, $1.60, except July and August, $2 per day; per week, $9.20, except July and August, $12 per week; season, $105. CADDIE FEES: $1.25 per 18-hole round. GOLF CLUB RENTALS: $1.20 per day. GOLF CART RENTALS: 40¢ per 18-hole round. MOTORIZED GOLF CART RENTALS: Not available. LESSONS: $2.40 per hour. CLUBHOUSE FACILITIES: Bar and restaurant. RECOMMENDED ACCOMMODATIONS: Dellach: Golf Hotel (near course), Hotel Lamplhof. Velden (4 miles): Schlosshotel, Hotel Mosslacher, Hotel Excelsior.

Salzkammergut Golf Club

LOCATION: Bad Ischel (4 miles from Bad Ischel; 5 miles from St. Wolfgang). COURSE SIZE: 9 holes; 3,003 yards; par 35. AVAILABILITY TO VISITORS: Visitors welcome. GREEN FEES: Daily, $2, except during July and August, $2.40; per week, $10; per month, $35. CADDIE FEES: 35¢ per 9-hole round; 65¢ per 18-hole round. GOLF CLUB RENTALS: Available. GOLF CART RENTALS: $1 per day. MOTORIZED GOLF CART RENTALS: Not available. LESSONS: $2.40 per hour. CLUBHOUSE FACILITIES: Restaurant and bar. Bad Ischel has its own mountain accessible by a gondola cable railway rising to 4,640 feet, and offering an excellent view of the Alps. RECOMMENDED ACCOMMODATIONS: Aigen-Voglhub: Haus Voglhub (near course). Bad Ischel: Hotel Post.

Steirmaerkische Golf-Club

LOCATION: Murhof bei Frohnleiten, a short ride from Graz. COURSE SIZE: 9 holes; 3,150 yards; par 36. AVAILABILITY TO VISITORS: Always welcome. GREEN FEES: $2 daily; $8 per week. CADDIE FEES: 50¢ per 9-hole round. GOLF CLUB RENTALS: Available. GOLF CART RENTALS: Available. MOTORIZED GOLF CART RENTALS: Not available. LESSONS: $2.40 per hour. CLUBHOUSE FACILITIES: Restaurant, bar, and full changing facilities available. RECOMMENDED ACCOMMODATIONS: Accommodations excellent in the clubhouse.

Belgium and Luxembourg

Belgium, the most densely populated country in Europe, has more than 9½ million people in an area the size of Maryland. Nevertheless, the Belgians have found room to build ten fine courses to accommodate 3,000 local players and overseas guests comfortably.

The countryside of Belgium is heavily wooded, and the golf courses are no exception. Nurtured by plenty of rain and moderate year-round temperatures, forest pines curl tightly around narrow fairways that demand accurate shots from tee to green. While the greens are usually open, the Belgians have a habit of cross-bunkering the fairways to add to the already difficult test.

One of the most exciting days of the golfer's visit to Belgium will be his tour around the 18-hole Royal Golf Club les Buttes Blanches. An attractive layout of almost 6,400 yards, Les Buttes Blanches will test his skill as a golfer Belgian style. Each hole offers its own particular brand of hazards, both natural and man-made. He'll have to be accurate all the time or suffer the consequences resulting from out-of-bounds errors, trees that screen greens, and yawning sand traps. On the scorecard, the par-3 eighth hole looks easy. But when stepping up to the tee, look toward the green. Six well-planned traps lurk about the green in wait for the imperfect shot. There just isn't an easy hole on the entire course.

Across the border in Luxembourg, the Grand-Ducal golf course—the only one in that country—has followed the tight Belgian style. The course here is even narrower than those found to the north, and any shot hit off the fairway invariably demands a penalty. Only 6,000 yards long, the Grand-Ducal is a test of accuracy rather than power. On many tees an iron will prove a wiser choice than a wood. The greens are large, but huge traps dot the fairways and sprawling evergreens and birches often make approach shots difficult. Even when the greens are reached in regulation, two putts through their subtle undulations are not automatic. A good score here attests to a finely controlled game.

Belgium is used to tourists, having hosted a world's fair in 1958. The local women who usually caddie here are good guides to the courses and excellent hostesses in this charming country. Luxembourg, not as well known to tourists, is no less beautiful and offers a quiet and relaxing interlude to the often hurried traveler.

SEASON: April to October.

HOW TO GET THERE: By Pan Am Jet Clipper, from New York to Brussels, 7½ hours (elapsed time). Fare from airport into Brussels, is 50¢ by bus, about $4 by taxi, including tip. By ship, 5 to 11 days to Antwerp.

GOLF EQUIPMENT: American equipment available.

LANGUAGE: French and Flemish official languages; English widely understood.

TIME: Six hours later than U.S. Eastern Standard Time.

Golf Club du Château Royal d'Ardennes

LOCATION: Houyet (about 9 miles from Dinant by car). COURSE SIZE: 18 holes; 5,308 yards; par 68. AVAILABILITY TO VISITORS: Visitors welcome. GREEN FEES: $2 per day. CADDIE FEES: $1.50 per round. GOLF CART RENTALS: Not available. LESSONS: $2.50 per hour. CLUBHOUSE FACILITIES: Restaurant and bar. RECOMMENDED ACCOMMODATIONS: Dinant: Hôtel des Postes.

Golf Club Grand-Ducal de Luxembourg

LOCATION: Luxembourg (about 4 miles from center of Luxembourg). COURSE SIZE: 18 holes; 6,059 yards; par 72. AVAILABILITY TO VISITORS: Visitors welcome. GREEN FEES: Weekdays, $2; weekends, $3 per day; per week, $8; two weeks, $14; per month, $20; season: $70, men; $50, women. CADDIE FEES: $1.20 per round. GOLF CLUB RENTALS: Available. GOLF CART RENTALS: 60¢ per day. LESSONS: $2.50 per hour. CLUBHOUSE FACILITIES: Restaurant and bar. RECOMMENDED ACCOMMODATIONS: Hôtel Reno, Hôtel Brasseur, Hôtel Kons, Hôtel Alfa.

The clubhouse of Royal Golf Club de Belgique.

Royal Golf Club de Belgique

LOCATION: Tervueren (about 6 miles from Brussels). COURSE SIZE: 18 holes; 6,638 yards; par 74. Also 9 holes; 2,075 yards; par 33. AVAILABILITY TO VISITORS: Play is limited. On Saturday and Sunday guests must be accompanied by a member; inquire ahead for reservations. GREEN FEES: Weekdays, $2; Saturdays and Sundays, $5 a day; weekends, $8. CADDIE FEES: $2 per round. GOLF CLUB RENTALS: Available through caddie master. GOLF CART RENTALS: 40¢ per round. MOTORIZED GOLF CART RENTALS: Not available. LESSONS: $3 per hour. CLUBHOUSE FACILITIES: Restaurant and bar. RECOMMENDED ACCOMMODATIONS: Tervueren: Hôtel Beau Soleil. Brussels: Hôtel Westbury, Hôtel Hilton, Hôtel Metropole, Hôtel Amigo, and Hôtel Palace.

Royal Golf Club des Fagnes

LOCATION: Balmoral-Spa (3 miles from Spa). COURSE SIZE: 18 holes; 6,353 yards; par 74. AVAILABILITY TO VISITORS: Visitors welcome. GREEN FEES: $3.60 per day; $15 per week; two weeks, $24.

CADDIE FEES: $2 per round. GOLF CLUB RENTALS: 80¢ per round. GOLF CART RENTALS: 40¢ per day. MOTORIZED GOLF CART RENTALS: Not available. LESSONS: $3 per hour plus balls, 60¢. CLUBHOUSE FACILITIES: Restaurant and bar. RECOMMENDED ACCOMMODATIONS: Balmoral-Spa: Golf Hôtel (near course), Hôtel Annette and Lubin, Pension les Clematites. Bois à Spa: Hôtel Château-Sous-Bois. Tiège: Hôtel la Charmille.

Royal Golf Club d'Ostende

LOCATION: Coq s/mer (7 miles from Ostende). COURSE SIZE: 18 holes; 5,889 yards; par 70. AVAILABILITY TO VISITORS: Visitors welcome. GREEN FEES: Daily, $3; per week, $12; two weeks, $18; per month, $30. CADDIE FEES: $2 per round. GOLF CLUB RENTALS: Not available. GOLF CART RENTALS: Not available. MOTORIZED GOLF CART RENTALS: Not available. LESSONS: $3 per half hour. CLUBHOUSE FACILITIES: Restaurant and bar. RECOMMENDED ACCOMMODATIONS: Coq s/mer: Golf Hôtel, Hôtel Astoria, Hôtel Joli Bois, Hôtel Belle-Vue (all near course).

Royal Golf Club du Hainaut

LOCATION: Erbisoeul (about 4 miles from Mons, close to the French border). COURSE SIZE: 18 holes; 5,958 yards; par 71. AVAILABILITY TO VISITORS: Visitors welcome. GREEN FEES: Daily, $2; Saturdays and Sundays, $3.50 a day; per week, $10; per month, $20. CADDIE FEES: $1.20 per round. GOLF CLUB RENTALS: Not available. GOLF CART RENTALS: Not available. MOTORIZED GOLF CART RENTALS: Not available. LESSONS: Not available. CLUBHOUSE FACILITIES: Restaurant and bar. RECOMMENDED ACCOMMODATIONS: Hôtel Terminus.

Royal Golf Club du Sart-Tilman

LOCATION: Ougrée (about 6 miles from Liège by car). COURSE SIZE: 18 holes; 6,545 yards; par 74. AVAILABILITY TO VISITORS: Visitors welcome. GREEN FEES: Weekdays, $2; weekends, $2.50 per day; per week, $12; per month, $30. CADDIE FEES: $1.50 per round. GOLF CLUB RENTALS: Not available. MOTORIZED GOLF CART RENTALS: Not available. LESSONS: $2.50–$3.00 per hour. CLUBHOUSE FACILITIES: Restaurant and bar. RECOMMENDED ACCOMMODATIONS: Hôtel du Casino

Tilff (near course), Palace Hôtel-Chaufontaine. Liège: Hôtel du Suede, Hôtel de la Couronne.

Royal Golf Club les Buttes Blanches

LOCATION: Latem Saint Martin (10 minutes by car from Ghent). COURSE SIZE: 18 holes; 6,390 yards; par 73. AVAILABILITY TO VISITORS: Visitors welcome. GREEN FEES: Weekdays, $2; weekends, $3 per day; per week, $10. CADDIE FEES: $2 per round. GOLF CLUB RENTALS: Available. GOLF CART RENTALS: Available. MOTORIZED GOLF CART RENTALS: Not available. LESSONS: $4 per hour. CLUBHOUSE FACILITIES: Restaurant and bar. RECOMMENDED ACCOMMODATIONS: Deurle: Hôtel St. Cristoffle.

Royal Waterloo Golf Club

LOCATION: Ohain (about 15 miles from Brussels by car). COURSE SIZE: 18 holes; 6,310 yards; par 74. 18 holes; 5,090 yards; par 69.

Shell's Wonderful World of Golf

Hearty Belgian caddies are expert advisers on course conditions and club choice.

AVAILABILITY TO VISITORS: Limited play permitted; inquire ahead. GREEN FEES: Weekdays, $3; weekends, $5.50 per day; two weeks, $20; per month, $30; three months, $60. CADDIE FEES: $2 per round. GOLF CLUB RENTALS: $1 per round. GOLF CART RENTALS: $1 per round. MOTORIZED GOLF CART RENTALS: Not available. LESSONS: $4 per round. CLUBHOUSE FACILITIES: Restaurant and bar. RECOMMENDED ACCOMMODATIONS: Brussels: Hôtel Metropole, Hôtel Palace, Hôtel Hilton, Hôtel Amigo, and Hôtel Westbury.

Royal Zoute Golf Course

LOCATION: Knokke-le-Zoute (on the North Sea near the Dutch border). COURSE SIZE: 18 holes; 6,626 yards; par 74. AVAILABILITY TO VISITORS: Limited play permitted; inquire ahead. GREEN FEES: Weekdays, $3; weekends, $5 per day; per week, $12; two weeks, $18; per month, $30. CADDIE FEES: $1.50 per round. GOLF CLUB RENTALS: Not available. GOLF CART RENTALS: Not available. MOTORIZED GOLF CART RENTALS: Not available. LESSONS: $3 per hour. CLUBHOUSE FACILITIES: Restaurant and bar. Gambling casino in town. RECOMMENDED ACCOMMODATIONS: Memling Hotel (near course), La Reserve.

England and Northern Ireland

This is golfers' paradise. Nowhere else in the world will the traveling golfer meet such a variety of challenges in a relatively compact area. And seldom will he find championship golf courses as inexpensive. There are more than 1,200 golf courses in Great Britain and all but a handful are available to visitors from other countries—many at green fees of less than $1.00.

A golfing trip through Britain is like a walk through the pages of golf history. The venerable Old Course of the Royal and Ancient Club of St. Andrews in Scotland is generally regarded as the birthplace of the game, although the Dutch still insist on their earlier claims. But the fact that the Scotch and the English were chiefly responsible for the growth and development of the game cannot be disputed. And many of the courses that stimulated this growth still stand—some after many centuries—and still present the same bedeviling challenge that intrigued pioneer golfers.

Royal Lytham and St. Anne's Golf Club has for centuries been considered a landmark of golf. Although the English coast is not visible from the course, the sand dunes definitely do affect play on the course. There are sand traps wherever the golfer turns—two hundred of them in all. Right next to Lytham-St. Anne's is the Royal Birkdale Golf Club where the British Open has been played several times. Its roughs are very sandy and willows offer unusual obstacles.

The visiting golfer will soon realize that pitting himself against the physical characteristics of the country is the primary challenge that golf in Britain offers. The most important element is the wind. Since a large number of English courses are at the seaside, they are constantly buffeted by the winds that sweep and swirl in from the

Golfers' map of Great Britain.

ocean in constantly changing directions. Indeed, it is quite possible on many of these courses for the golfer to play a complete round and have the wind in his face from start to finish. To meet these conditions, the golfer has the choice of playing the smaller British ball, rather than the larger American one. Most golfers will select the smaller ball for playing in the wind since it does not have the high climb of the American ball and will be less affected by a crosswind. It will also run farther on the fairway. But there are definite disadvantages to using the small ball, such as the increased probability of a sharp hook or slice resulting from a faulty swing.

Another surprise for the visiting golfer in England is the condition of the fairways. Because of the smaller British ball, a much finer grass is used on the fairways and the growth is neither so heavy nor so plush as in the United States. Also, because of the constant dampness, it is not necessary for English clubs to water their fairways. The result is that a golf ball, large or small, will get more roll than on a U.S. fairway. The problem comes on the approach to the green. Because the turf is so hard, it is difficult for even the most expert golfer to place his shot and make it stick where he wants it to go. On the other hand, the less skilled golfer will find that it is much easier for him to pitch his ball onto the green from within 25 yards and roll it close to the hole.

Putting is much easier than in most parts of the United States. The greens are very tight and there is hardly any course in England where the grain of the grass will affect the direction of a putt.

The more experienced golfer who has followed the play at the British Open from year to year has heard about the roughs that border the fairways of British golf courses. Advice to the visiting golfer: stay away from them! The best golfers in the world have yet to come out unscathed from the roughs of Walton Heath, Woodhall Spa, Wentworth, and the other great courses that use these ruthless yet natural embellishments as guardians of their pars.

Although there are some notable exceptions, most British golf courses are not country clubs. The emphasis is on golf, not on social activities. The clubhouse, generally speaking, is designed along conservative lines—functional, but not luxurious. The choice of golf courses in Great Britain is simply a matter of preference in terms of time and place. There are courses to suit every golfer's taste throughout the country.

The visiting golfer should be prepared for quick changes in the weather—wet-weather gear and plenty of sweaters are essential. But above all, the visiting golfer should be prepared for one of the greatest experiences of his golfing life.

SEASON: March to November.

HOW TO GET THERE: By Pan American Jet Clipper 6½ hours from New York or Boston. Service also from Atlanta, New Orleans, Philadelphia, Baltimore–Washington, Dallas, and Houston; direct from Chicago, 7¾ hours, or via Detroit. Jet Clippers fly from the U.S. West Coast via the polar route in 9½ hours. Clippers serve Glasgow through Prestwick Airport. By ship, about 5 days.

GOLF EQUIPMENT: American equipment available.

TIME: Six hours later than U.S. Eastern Standard Time.

Berkshire Golf Club

LOCATION: Ascot, Berkshire (2 miles from Bagshot railroad station by taxi). COURSE SIZE: Red Course: 18 holes; 6,379 yards; par 74. Blue Course: 18 holes; 6,244 yards; par 73. AVAILABILITY TO VISITORS: Visitors welcome; must be accompanied by a member on weekends and holidays. GREEN FEES: $2.80 per round. CADDIE FEES: Only by previous arrangement. GOLF CLUB RENTALS: Not available. GOLF CART RENTALS: Not available. MOTORIZED GOLF CART RENTALS: Not available. LESSONS: By appointment. CLUBHOUSE FACILITIES: Restaurant and bar available (lunch only). RECOMMENDED ACCOMMODATIONS: Ascot: Berystede Hotel, Royal Foresters Hotel.

Formby Golf Club

LOCATION: Freshfield, Lancashire (¼ mile from Freshfield railroad station; 13 miles from Liverpool). COURSE SIZE: 18 holes; 6,803 yards; par 74. AVAILABILITY TO VISITORS: Visitors welcome. GREEN FEES: Weekdays, $1.40; weekends, $2.80 per day. CADDIE FEES: $1.75 per round, single. GOLF CLUB RENTALS: Not available. GOLF CART RENTALS: Not available. MOTORIZED GOLF CART RENTALS: Not available. LESSONS: Available by appointment. CLUBHOUSE FACILITIES: Restaurant and bar available. RECOMMENDED ACCOMMODATIONS: Limited rooms in the clubhouse for guests. Palace Hotel, Birkdale.

Little Aston Golf Club

LOCATION: Streetly, Sutton Coldfield, Staffordshire (1½ miles from the Streetly railroad station; 9 miles from Birmingham). COURSE SIZE: 18 holes; 6,700 yards; par 74. AVAILABILITY TO VISITORS: Visitors permitted limited play. Ladies may not play on Saturdays; on Sundays and bank holidays they may play only after 2:30 P.M. GREEN FEES: Weekdays, $2.10 (70¢ if playing with a member); weekends, $3.50

($1.40 if playing with a member). CADDIE FEES: Caddies not available. GOLF CLUB RENTALS: Not available. GOLF CART RENTALS: 30¢ per round. MOTORIZED GOLF CART RENTALS: Not available. LESSONS: Available by appointment; $2.80 per hour. CLUBHOUSE FACILITIES: Restaurant and bar available. RECOMMENDED ACCOMMODATIONS: Walmley, Sutton Coldfield: Penns Hall Hotel.

Moor Park Golf Club

LOCATION: Rickmansworth, Moor Park, Hertfordshire (1 mile by taxi from Moor Park railway station). COURSE SIZE: High Course: 18 holes; 6,602 yards; par 73. AVAILABILITY TO VISITORS: Visitors welcome with a letter from home club. GREEN FEES: Weekdays, $2.10; weekends, $4.20 per day (fees are one-half this amount if playing with a member). CADDIE FEES: $1.75 per round, single. GOLF CLUB RENTALS: Not available. GOLF CART RENTALS: Not available. MOTORIZED GOLF CART RENTALS: Not available. LESSONS: Available by appointment. CLUBHOUSE FACILITIES: Restaurant and bar available. RECOMMENDED ACCOMMODATIONS: Park View Hotel, Hotel White Bear.

North Hants Golf Club

LOCATION: Minley Road, Fleet, Hampshire (a mile ride from the station by taxi; 5 miles from Aldershot; about 35 miles from London). COURSE SIZE: 18 holes; 6,392 yards; par 72. AVAILABILITY TO VISITORS: Visitors permitted limited play. GREEN FEES: Weekdays, $1.40; weekends, $4.20 per day; per week, $5.90; per month, $11.80. CADDIE FEES: $4.20 per round; limited number available. GOLF CLUB RENTALS: Limited number available; price by arrangement. GOLF CART RENTALS: 30¢ per round. MOTORIZED GOLF CART RENTALS: Not available. LESSONS: Available by appointment; $1.40 per half hour. CLUBHOUSE FACILITIES: Restaurant and bar available. RECOMMENDED ACCOMMODATIONS: Lismoyne Hotel.

Princes Golf Club

LOCATION: Sandwich, Kent (2½-mile taxi ride from Sandwich station; 15 miles from Dover). COURSE SIZE: Blue Course: 18 holes; 6,681 yards; par 74. Red Course: 9 holes; 3,277 yards; par 36. AVAILABILITY TO VISITORS: Visitors welcome when introduced by a member

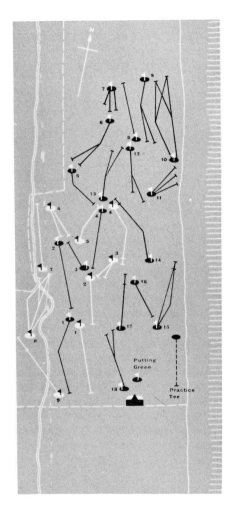

Layout of the course at
Princes Golf Club.

or letter. GREEN FEES: Weekdays, $2.80; weekends, $4.20 per day;
per week, $11.20; two weeks, $19.60; per month, $28. CADDIE FEES:
$2.10 per 18-hole round, single. GOLF CLUB RENTALS: Available. GOLF
CART RENTALS: 30¢ per round. MOTORIZED GOLF CART RENTALS: Not
available. LESSONS: Available by appointment, $1.75 per hour. CLUB-
HOUSE FACILITIES: Restaurant and bar available. RECOMMENDED AC-
COMMODATIONS: Sandwich Bay, Kent: Guilford Hotel (near course),
Bell Hotel.

Royal Birkdale Golf Club

LOCATION: Waterloo Road, Southport, Lancashire (¼ mile from Hillside railroad station; about 20 miles from Liverpool). COURSE SIZE: 18 holes; 6,844 yards; par 74. AVAILABILITY TO VISITORS: Visitors welcome; however, ladies may not play Saturdays until after 4:30 P.M. or on Sundays unless playing with a gentleman. GREEN FEES: Weekdays, $1.40; weekends, $2.80 per day; per week, $8.90. CADDIE FEES: $1.40 per round, single. GOLF CLUB RENTALS: Not available. GOLF CART RENTALS: Not available. MOTORIZED GOLF CART RENTALS: Not available. LESSONS: Available by appointment. CLUBHOUSE FACILITIES: Restaurant and bar available. RECOMMENDED ACCOMMODATIONS: Southport: Hotel Prince of Wales, Palace Hotel, Scarisbrick Hotel.

Royal Cinque Ports Golf Club

LOCATION: Golf Road, Deal, Kent (1½ miles by taxi from Deal railroad station; 5 miles from Dover). COURSE SIZE: 18 holes; 6,384 yards; par 72. AVAILABILITY TO VISITORS: Visitors permitted limited play with a letter from home club. GREEN FEES: Weekdays, $2.80; weekends, $4.20 per day. CADDIE FEES: $1.75 per round, single. GOLF CLUB RENTALS: $1 per round. GOLF CART RENTALS: 30¢ per round. MOTORIZED GOLF CART RENTALS: Not available. LESSONS: Available by appointment, $1.75 per half hour. CLUBHOUSE FACILITIES: Restaurant and bar available. RECOMMENDED ACCOMMODATIONS: Deal: Royal Hotel (near course), Queens Hotel, Black Horse Hotel, Star and Garter Hotel. Sandwich Bay: Guilford.

Royal County Down Golf Club

LOCATION: New Castle, County Down, Northern Ireland. COURSE SIZE: 18 holes; 6,647 yards; par 74. 18 holes; 4,079 yards; par 63. AVAILABILITY TO VISITORS: Allowed limited play; inquire at the office of the club secretary in advance (tel. 33 14). GREEN FEES: Big course: weekdays, $1.25; weekends, $2.80 per day; per week, $6.25; two weeks, $10; per month, $14. Small course: weekdays, 85¢; Saturdays and Sundays, $1 per day; per week, $3.50; two weeks, $5.60; per month, $8.40. CADDIE FEES: $1.70 per round. GOLF CLUB RENTALS: 70¢ per round. GOLF CART RENTALS: 35¢ per day. MOTORIZED GOLF

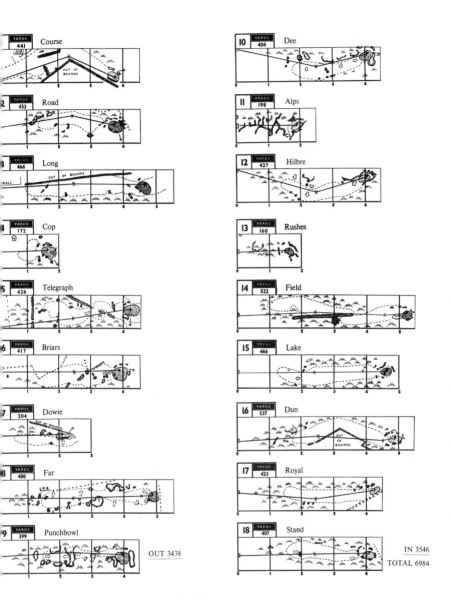

#	YARDS	Name		#	YARDS	Name
1	441	Course		10	406	Dee
2	433	Road		11	198	Alps
3	466	Long		12	427	Hilbre
4	172	Cop		13	160	Rushes
5	426	Telegraph		14	522	Field
6	417	Briars		15	466	Lake
7	204	Dowie		16	537	Dun
8	480	Far		17	423	Royal
9	399	Punchbowl		18	407	Stand

OUT 3438

IN 3546
TOTAL 6984

Plan of the Royal Liverpool Golf Club.

CART RENTALS: Not available. LESSONS: 70¢ per half hour. CLUBHOUSE FACILITIES: Restaurant and bar available to guests of members only. RECOMMENDED ACCOMMODATIONS: Slieve Donard Hotel.

Royal Liverpool Golf Club

LOCATION: Meols Drive, Hoylake, Cheshire (less than ½ mile by taxi from the Hoylake station). COURSE SIZE: 18 holes; 6,673 yards; par 75. AVAILABILITY TO VISITORS: Visitors allowed limited play; Sunday play allowed. GREEN FEES: Weekdays, $2.80; weekends, $4.20 per day; per week, $8.40; two weeks, $14; per month, $22.40; three months, $33.60. CADDIE FEES: $1.40 per round, single. GOLF CLUB RENTALS: Not available. GOLF CART RENTALS: 30¢ per round. MOTORIZED GOLF CART RENTALS: Not available. LESSONS: $1 per half hour. CLUBHOUSE FACILITIES: Restaurant, bar, and all facilities available. RECOMMENDED ACCOMMODATIONS: Hoylake: Stanley Hotel, The Quadrant (near course), King's Gap Court Hotel. New Brighton: Victoria Hotel.

Royal Lytham and St. Anne's Golf Club

LOCATION: St. Anne's on the Sea, Lancashire (1 mile by taxi from St. Anne's station; 5 miles from Blackpool). COURSE SIZE: 18 holes; 6,657 yards; par 74. AVAILABILITY TO VISITORS: Visitors welcome with letter from home club. GREEN FEES: Weekdays, $2.80 per day or $2.10 per round; weekends, $4.20 per day or $2.80 per round; five days, $8.40; per week, $14. CADDIE FEES: $1.75 per round, single. GOLF CLUB RENTALS: Available but limited. GOLF CART RENTALS: 20¢ per round. MOTORIZED GOLF CART RENTALS: Not available. LESSONS: Available by appointment. CLUBHOUSE FACILITIES: Restaurant and bar available. RECOMMENDED ACCOMMODATIONS: St. Anne's on the Sea: Hotel Majestic, Princess Hotel, Promenade, Westmoreland Hotel, Orchard Road. Lytham: Clifton Arms Hotel. There is also a dormitory at the club (gentlemen only).

Royal Mid-Surrey Golf Club

LOCATION: Old Deer Park, Richmond, Surrey (1 mile from Richmond station by taxi; 8 miles from the London city limits). COURSE SIZE: 18 holes; 6,380 yards; par 73. AVAILABILITY TO VISITORS: Visitors welcome weekdays only; must be introduced by a member. GREEN

FEES: Weekdays, $2.80 per round. CADDIE FEES: By arrangement. GOLF CLUB RENTALS: Not available. GOLF CART RENTALS: Available. MOTORIZED GOLF CART RENTALS: Not available. LESSONS: Available by appointment. CLUBHOUSE FACILITIES: Restaurant and bar available. RECOMMENDED ACCOMMODATIONS: Richmond: Richmond Hill Hotel, The Morshead.

Royal North Devon Golf Course

LOCATION: Westward Ho, Bideford, Devonshire (2 miles from Bideford station). COURSE SIZE: 18 holes; 6,540 yards; par 71. AVAILABILITY TO VISITORS: Visitors welcome. GREEN FEES: Per day, $1.75; per week, $5.60; two weeks, $8.40; per month, $11.20; season, $29.40. CADDIE FEES: $1.40 per round, single. GOLF CLUB RENTALS: 50¢ per round. GOLF CART RENTALS: 30¢ per day. MOTORIZED GOLF CART RENTALS: Not available. LESSONS: Available by appointment, $1.40 per half hour. CLUBHOUSE FACILITIES: Restaurant and bar available. RECOMMENDED ACCOMMODATIONS: Westward Ho: Dormy House. Bideford: New Inn Hotel, Durant House, Atlanta Hotel.

Royal Portrush Golf Club

LOCATION: County Antrim, Northern Ireland (by taxi, 2 miles from the Portrush station; 65 miles north of Belfast on the North Channel). COURSE SIZE: Dunluce Course: 18 holes; 6,842 yards; par 74. Valley Course: 18 holes; 6,641 yards; par 73. Short Course: 9 holes. AVAILABILITY TO VISITORS: Visitors welcome. GREEN FEES: Dunluce Course: Weekdays, $1.40; weekends, $2.80 per day; per week, $6.30; two weeks, $10.50; season, $35. Valley Course: Weekdays, 85¢; weekends, $1.40 per day; per week, $4.20; two weeks, $7. Short Course, 20¢ per round. CADDIE FEES: $1.50 per round, single. GOLF CLUB RENTALS: Not available. GOLF CART RENTALS: 30¢ per round. MOTORIZED GOLF CART RENTALS: Not available. LESSONS: Available by appointment, $1 per half hour. CLUBHOUSE FACILITIES: Restaurant and bar available. RECOMMENDED ACCOMMODATIONS: Portrush: Skerry Bhan Hotel, Northern Counties Hotel.

Royal St. Georges Golf Club

LOCATION: Sandwich, Kent (1½-mile taxi ride from the Sandwich station; 14 miles from Dover). COURSE SIZE: 18 holes; 6,748 yards;

par 74. AVAILABILITY TO VISITORS: Visitors permitted limited play when introduced by a letter or a member; inquire ahead. GREEN FEES: $2.10 per day. CADDIE FEES: $1.40 per round, single. GOLF CLUB RENTALS: Not available. GOLF CART RENTALS: Not available. MOTORIZED GOLF CART RENTALS: Not available. LESSONS: By appointment. CLUBHOUSE FACILITIES: Restaurant and bar available. RECOMMENDED ACCOMMODATIONS: Sandwich Bay: Guilford Hotel, Bell Hotel.

Selsdon Park Golf Club

LOCATION: Sanderstead, Surrey, London (1 mile by taxi from the Sanderstead station). COURSE SIZE: 18 holes; 6,405 yards; par 71. AVAILABILITY TO VISITORS: Visitors welcome. GREEN FEES: Weekdays, 70¢; Saturdays, $1; Sundays, $2.10. CADDIE FEES: Limited number of caddies available; inquire in advance. GOLF CLUB RENTALS: Not available. GOLF CART RENTALS: Available by arrangement. MOTORIZED GOLF CART RENTALS: Not available. LESSONS: Available by apointment. CLUBHOUSE FACILITIES: Restaurant and bar available. RECOMMENDED ACCOMMODATIONS: Selsdon Park Hotel.

South Herts Golf Club

LOCATION: Links Drive, Totteridge, Hertfordshire (½ mile by taxi from Totteridge station; 8 miles from London). COURSE SIZE: 18 holes; 6,412 yards; par 72. AVAILABILITY TO VISITORS: Visitors welcome when introduced by member or letter; Sunday play permitted only when accompanied by a member. GREEN FEES: Weekdays, $2.10; weekends, $2.80 per day; per month, $7. CADDIE FEES: By arrangement. GOLF CLUB RENTALS: 70¢ per round. GOLF CART RENTALS: 30¢ per round. MOTORIZED GOLF CART RENTALS: Not available. LESSONS: Available by appointment, $2.80 per hour. CLUBHOUSE FACILITIES: Restaurant and bar available. RECOMMENDED ACCOMMODATIONS: Hendon: Hendon Hall Hotel.

Southport and Ainsdale Golf Club

LOCATION: Liverpool Road, Ainsdale, Lancashire (½ mile from Ainsdale station; 17 miles from Liverpool). COURSE SIZE: 18 holes; 6,625 yards; par 73. AVAILABILITY TO VISITORS: Visitors welcome. GREEN FEES: Weekdays, $1.40; weekends, $2.80 per day. CADDIE FEES:

$1.05 per round, single. GOLF CLUB RENTALS: 35¢ per round. GOLF CART RENTALS: 20¢ per round. MOTORIZED GOLF CART RENTALS: Not available. LESSONS: Available by appointment. CLUBHOUSE FACILITIES: Restaurant and bar available. RECOMMENDED ACCOMMODATIONS: Southport: Hotel Prince of Wales, Palace Hotel, Scarisbrick Hotel.

Sunningdale Golf Club

LOCATION: Sunningdale, Berkshire (23 miles from London; within walking distance of the Sunningdale rail station). COURSE SIZE: Old Course: 18 holes; 6,348 yards; par 72. New Course: 18 holes; 6,487 yards; par 73. AVAILABILITY TO VISITORS: Visitors welcome; however, arrangements should be made in advance. GREEN FEES: Weekdays, $2.80. CADDIE FEES: $1.40 per round, single. GOLF CLUB RENTALS: Not available. GOLF CART RENTALS: Not available. MOTORIZED GOLF

Clubhouse and putting green at Sunningdale Golf Club.

Shell's Wonderful World of Golf

Pub near Sunningdale offers excellent English brews for a nineteenth-hole refresher.

CART RENTALS: Not available. LESSONS: By appointment. CLUBHOUSE FACILITIES: Restaurant and bar available. RECOMMENDED ACCOMMODATIONS: Sunningdale Hotel. Ascot: Berystede Hotel, Royal Foresters Hotel.

Walton Heath Golf Club

LOCATION: Tadworth, Surrey (½ mile from the Tadworth station). COURSE SIZE: Old Course: 18 holes; 6,735 yards; par 74. New Course: 18 holes; 6,516 yards; par 73. AVAILABILITY TO VISITORS: Visitors permitted limited play when introduced by a member or letter; inquire ahead. GREEN FEES: Weekdays, $2.10; weekends, $2.80 per day; two weeks, $8.40; per month, $8.80. CADDIE FEES: $4.90 per day. GOLF CLUB RENTALS: Available. GOLF CART RENTALS: 30¢ per round. MOTORIZED GOLF CART RENTALS: Not available. LESSONS: Available by appointment, $1.40 per round. CLUBHOUSE FACILITIES: Restaurant and bar available. RECOMMENDED ACCOMMODATIONS: Dorking: Burford Bridge Hotel. Epsom: Drift Bridge Hotel. Reigate: Reigate Hotel.

Wentworth Club

LOCATION: Virginia Water, Surrey (1½ miles by taxi from the Virginia Water station; 21 miles southwest of London off route A. 30). COURSE SIZE: West Course (Burma Road): 18 holes; 6,936 yards; par 75. East Course: 18 holes; 6,209 yards; par 72. Short Course: 9 holes; 1,743 yards; par 32. AVAILABILITY TO VISITORS: Visitors permitted limited play when introduced by a member or a letter; make advance arrangements. GREEN FEES: Monday through Saturday, $3.20; Sunday, $4.20. CADDIE FEES: $2.80 per round, single. GOLF CLUB RENTALS: Available. GOLF CART RENTALS: 30¢ per round. MOTORIZED GOLF CART RENTALS: Not available. LESSONS: By appointment. CLUBHOUSE FACILITIES: Restaurant and bar available. RECOMMENDED ACCOMMODATIONS: Egham: Great Fosters Hotel. Ascot: Berystede Hotel.

Plan of the courses at Wentworth Club.

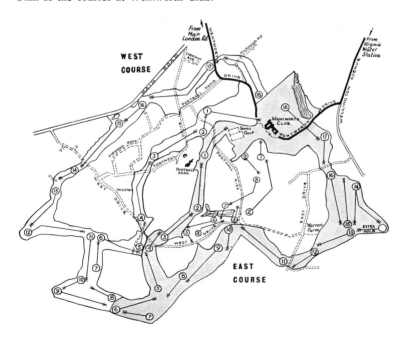

Playing in London rain.

Worthing Golf Club

LOCATION: Links Road, Worthing, Sussex (2 miles by taxi from Worthing Central station; 58 miles from London). COURSE SIZE: Lower Course: 18 holes; 6,270 yards; par 71. Upper Course: 18 holes; 5,046 yards; par 69. AVAILABILITY TO VISITORS: Visitors welcome. GREEN FEES: Lower Course: weekdays, $1.75; weekends, $2.80 per day; per week, $8.40; two weeks, $14; per month, $19.60. Upper Course: weekdays, $2.80; weekends, $2.10 per day; per week, $7; two weeks, $11.20; per month, $15.40. CADDIE FEES: $2.10 per round, single. GOLF CLUB RENTALS: 70¢ per round. GOLF CART RENTALS: 30¢ per round. MOTORIZED GOLF CART RENTALS: Not available. LESSONS: By appointment, $1.40 per half hour. CLUBHOUSE FACILITIES: Restaurant and bar available. RECOMMENDED ACCOMMODATIONS: Worthing: Warnes Hotel, Beach Hotel, Chatsworth Hotel. Findon: Findon Manor Hotel, Gun Hotel.

France and Monte Carlo

The golfer who wants to play a variety of courses while vacationing in Europe should certainly make France a stop. But he should also prepare for some departure from the bargain prices of other European countries. By European standards, golf in France is comparatively expensive, especially on weekends and holidays when most clubs prefer to keep their courses reasonably free of tourist traffic for the convenience of their members.

Golf is not as popular in France as it is elsewhere on the Continent. The reasons are basic. The game did not make its appearance in France until the twentieth century, and two wars fought on French soil during this period did not help the sport's growth. During World War II, the Germans converted many golf courses into farms to provide rations for their troops; other courses were stripped of their timber. Few were returned to the golfer after the war. Today there are only 93 courses in France, and the French Golf Federation counts 18,000 golfers who play regularly. There are no municipal courses and few industrial layouts (the course built for the Peugeot automobile workers, near Alsace, is a particularly fine one). The chance of France's becoming a major golf center must be regarded as slim at present, although there has been a sharp upturn in play by French women and this generally is the forerunner of a greater male interest.

The touring golfer is welcome to play everywhere, although most clubs are happier to see him during the week. On weekdays the green fees average from $4 to $6. On weekends, they average from $5 to $10. The highest fees are at Golf Club de Saint-Cloud where they are $15 per round on weekends.

Most courses consist of 18 holes, some offer 27 and 36 holes. Most are interesting and well planned. One of the most illustrious is Golf de Saint-Nom-la-Breteche, which has hosted the Canada Cup (now World Cup) matches. The course lies in an oval-shaped valley several miles from Versailles. Any golfer who enjoys hitting the long ball will find the course's 6,702 yards much to his liking. It's fairly wide open, and a hook or a slice does not always bring disaster; however, there are abundant water hazards and sand traps to test the accuracy of the big hitter. The floral gardens about the clubhouse are among the most gorgeous on display at any golf club anywhere.

Also in the Paris area is Golf Club de Saint-Cloud, another long course, with a magnificent layout. Bring along a full set of woods to play this course. It is not unusual to find a good 200-yard approach shot to one of the par-5 greens. Besides having two outstanding golf courses, Saint-Cloud is an elegant recreational retreat with tennis courts, squash courts, children's playgrounds, table tennis, and—for families with youngsters—a platoon of baby-sitters.

Except on the northern coast and in Normandy, golf is played all year in France. The courses are kept in the finest condition since most of the larger clubs have watering systems and those near the shore receive sufficient rainfall. The fairways are plush and springy and usually a golfer can count on a good lie if his ball is in the fairway.

The design of French courses is very much like that of British courses. Depending on the locale, there is a variety of flat courses as well as very hilly ones in France. The Pau course in the Biarritz area is France's oldest course, and its location on the edge of the Pyrenees makes it a very scenic and interesting layout.

If Monte Carlo is on the itinerary, the golfer should take his clubs along to test his skill on the course at Mont Agel. The course is situated high above Monte Carlo and offers a superb view of the Mediterranean as well as a reasonable chance at coming close to its par of 68. All along the Riviera the traveling golfer has a wide choice of fine courses, as well as the excitement of one of the greatest vacation paradises in the world.

Much has been shown—and said—of France's girl caddies. Don't be misled. Do they look as though they just walked out of the Folies Bergère? No. For the most part, they are roundish women, usually in their fifties. But they are excellent, hard-working caddies who know their way around the course. Once the visiting golfer becomes adjusted to a woman carrying his clubs and suggesting the right club to use, he'll find them very helpful.

Golfers have found the French to be very courteous to visitors and keen students of the game. They are reserved while playing and it is wise to follow their lead and observe the local golf protocol.

SEASON: Year round, depending on location.
HOW TO GET THERE: By Pan Am Jet Clipper, nonstop to Paris, about 7 hours from New York and Boston, about 15 hours

from the U.S. West Coast via jet connection in New York, 11–13 hours from U.S. West Coast cities via polar route. Through Jet Clipper service to Nice on the Riviera via Lisbon and Barcelona, about 10¾ hours from New York. Connections at Lisbon for Paris (2¼ hours). By ship, 5 to 9 days.

GOLF EQUIPMENT: Pro shops and sporting-goods stores carry most American and British equipment in ample supply, but prices are higher than in U.S.

LANGUAGE: With the exposure of two world wars and the boom of American travel abroad, the French speak some English, and sometimes can even understand Americans speaking French.

TIME: Six hours later than U.S. Eastern Standard Time.

Cannes-Antibes-Biot-Golf-Club

LOCATION: Biot, Alpes-Maritimes (3 miles by taxi from Antibes and Juan-les-Pins). COURSE SIZE: 18 holes; 5,538 yards; par 70. AVAILABILITY TO VISITORS: Visitors welcome. GREEN FEES: Per day, $4.05; per week, $24; per month, $70; per year, $132. CADDIE FEES: 9 holes, $2; 18 holes, $3. GOLF CLUB RENTALS: $2 per day. GOLF CART RENTALS: 60¢ per day. MOTORIZED GOLF CART RENTALS: Not available. LESSONS: $3.60 per half hour. CLUBHOUSE FACILITIES: Restaurant and bar available. RECOMMENDED ACCOMMODATIONS: Biot: Le Mas des Orangers. Antibes: Hôtel Royal, Hôtel de la Mer. Juan-les-Pins: Hôtel Eden Roc. Hôtel Côte d'Azur on Nationale 7.

Cannes Country Club

LOCATION: Mougins, Alpes-Maritimes (3 miles from Cannes; 5 miles from Antibes by taxi). COURSE SIZE: 18 holes; 6,150 yards; par 72. AVAILABILITY TO VISITORS: Visitors welcome. GREEN FEES: Daily, $4.05; per week, $16.20; per month, $40.50; season, $81. CADDIE FEES: $1.30 per round. GOLF CLUB RENTALS: Available. GOLF CART RENTALS: Not available. MOTORIZED GOLF CART RENTALS: Not available. LESSONS: $4.05 per half hour. CLUBHOUSE FACILITIES: Restaurant and bar available. RECOMMENDED ACCOMMODATIONS: Cannes: Hôtel Carlton, Hôtel Majestic, Hôtel Martinez, Hôtel Grand.

Cannes Golf Club

LOCATION: Mandelieu-La Napoule, Alpes-Maritimes (4 miles by taxi from Cannes). COURSE SIZE: 18 holes; 6,063 yards; par 73. AVAILABILITY TO VISITORS: Visitors welcome. GREEN FEES: Weekdays, $4; weekends and holidays, $6 per day; per week, $18.25; per month, $60.30; season, $100. CADDIE FEES: $2.80 per 18 holes; 9 holes, $2. GOLF CLUB RENTALS: $2 per round. GOLF CART RENTALS: 65¢ per round. MOTORIZED GOLF CART RENTALS: Not available. LESSONS: $3 per half hour; $5 per hour. CLUBHOUSE FACILITIES: Restaurant and bar available. RECOMMENDED ACCOMMODATIONS: Cannes: Hôtel Carlton, Hôtel Majestic, Hôtel Martinez, Hôtel Grand. La Napoule: Hôtel Ermitage du Riou, La Résidence du Golf, Hôtel Beau Rivage, Hôtel L'Oasis.

Golf and Tennis Club de Valescure

LOCATION: Saint-Raphaël (Var) (½ mile from Valescure; 2½ miles by taxi from Saint-Raphaël; 30 miles west of Cannes). COURSE SIZE: 18 holes; 5,189 yards; par 71. Course reduced to 9 holes in summer. AVAILABILITY TO VISITORS: Visitors welcome. GREEN FEES: Per day, $5; per week, $22; 3 weeks, $50; per month, $60. CADDIE FEES: 9 holes, $1.20; 18 holes, $1.80. GOLF CLUB RENTALS: $2 per day. GOLF CART RENTALS: 60¢ per half day. MOTORIZED GOLF CART RENTALS: Not available. LESSONS: $4 per half hour. CLUBHOUSE FACILITIES: Restaurant and bar available. RECOMMENDED ACCOMMODATIONS: Golf Hôtel (on course) closed in October and November. Agay: Hôtel La Beaumette.

Golf Bordelais

LOCATION: Domaine de Kater, Cauderan, Gironde (2 miles by taxi from Bordeaux). COURSE SIZE: 18 holes; 4,977 yards; par 68. AVAILABILITY TO VISITORS: Visitors welcome. GREEN FEES: Weekdays, $3; Saturdays, $4; Sundays and holidays, $5. CADDIE FEES: $3 per round. GOLF CLUB RENTALS: $1 per day. GOLF CART RENTALS: 60¢ per day. MOTORIZED GOLF CART RENTALS: Not available. LESSONS: $2.10 per half hour; $4.10 per hour, including caddie fee. CLUBHOUSE FACILITIES: Restaurant and bar available. RECOMMENDED ACCOMMODATIONS: Hôtel Splendide, Hôtel Royal Gascogne, Hôtel Normandie.

Golf Club d'Arcachon

LOCATION: La Teste-de-Buch, Gironde (50 miles from Bordeaux on the Atlantic coast). COURSE SIZE: 18 holes; 6,868 yards; par 71. AVAILABILITY TO VISITORS: Visitors welcome. GREEN FEES: July 1-September 30: weekdays, $5.10; weekends, $9 per day; per week, $29. October 1-June 30: weekdays, $3; weekends, $5 per day; per week, $12.15; per month, $30.30; season, $40.20. CADDIE FEES: $2 per 18-hole round. GOLF CLUB RENTALS: Available. Price of rental items depends on the pro who rents them. GOLF CART RENTALS: Available. MOTORIZED GOLF CART RENTALS: Not available. LESSONS: $3.00 per hour, plus 45¢ for the caddie. CLUBHOUSE FACILITIES: Restaurant and bar available. RECOMMENDED ACCOMMODATIONS: Arcachon: Hôtel de France, Hôtel Richelieu, Hôtel Regina. Le Pyla s/mer: Hôtel Haitza, Hôtel la Guitonne.

Golf Club de Chamonix

LOCATION: Les Praz-de-Chamonix, Haute-Savoie (2 miles by taxi from Chamonix). COURSE SIZE: 9 holes; 2,587 yards; par 35. AVAILABILITY TO VISITORS: Visitors welcome. GREEN FEES: Weekdays, $3.50; Saturdays and Sundays, $4 per day. CADDIE FEES: $1 per 18-hole round. GOLF CLUB RENTALS: Not available. GOLF CART RENTALS: 50¢ per day. MOTORIZED GOLF CART RENTALS: Not available. LESSONS: $4.05 per half hour. CLUBHOUSE FACILITIES: Restaurant and bar available. RECOMMENDED ACCOMMODATIONS: Les Praz-de-Chamonix: Hôtel Regina. Chamonix: Hôtel des Alpes, Hôtel Savoy, Hôtel Carlton.

Golf Club de Chantaco

LOCATION: Saint-Jean-de-Luz (6 miles southwest of Biarritz by car). COURSE SIZE: 18 holes; 6,135 yards; par 72. AVAILABILITY TO VISITORS: Visitors welcome. GREEN FEES: Weekdays, $6 (off-season, $3.60); per week, $16.20; per month, $48.60; season, $69. CADDIE FEES: 9 holes, $1; 18 holes, $1.40. GOLF CLUB RENTALS: $3 per round. GOLF CART RENTALS: 40¢ per round. MOTORIZED GOLF CART RENTALS: Not available. LESSONS: $3.60 per half hour. CLUBHOUSE FACILITIES: Restaurant and bar available. RECOMMENDED ACCOMMODATIONS: Biarritz: Hôtel Regina et du Golf, Hôtel de Palais, Hôtel Miramar. Saint-Jean-de-Luz: Hôtel de Chantaco, Hôtel Miramar.

Golf Club de Dinard

LOCATION: Saint-Briac-sur-Mer, on the Golfe de St. Malo (4 miles from Dinard). COURSE SIZE: 18 holes; 5,580 yards; par 70. AVAILABILITY TO VISITORS: Visitors welcome. GREEN FEES: Weekdays, $4.10; 2 days, $7; 3 days, $9; weekends, $4.90 per day; per week, $20; per month, $56. CADDIE FEES: $1.40 per round. GOLF CLUB RENTALS: $1.40 per round. GOLF CART RENTALS: Not available. MOTORIZED GOLF CART RENTALS: Not available. LESSONS: $4 per half hour. CLUBHOUSE FACILITIES: Restaurant and bar available. RECOMMENDED ACCOMMODATIONS: Saint-Briac: Hôtel Britannia. Dinard: Grand Hôtel, Hôtel Roche-Corneille, Hôtel Printania.

Golf Club de Divonne

LOCATION: Divonne-les-Bains, Ain (32 miles from Lausanne, Switzerland, by car). COURSE SIZE: 18 holes; 6,354 yards; par 72. AVAILABILITY TO VISITORS: Visitors welcome. GREEN FEES: Weekdays, $4.10; Saturdays and Sundays, $5 per day (June to September, $6); per week, $22.50; per month, $62.00; per year, $116.50. CADDIE FEES: $1.40 for 9 holes; $2 for 18 holes. GOLF CLUB RENTALS: $2 per day. GOLF CART RENTALS: 80¢ per day. MOTORIZED GOLF CART RENTALS: Not available. LESSONS: $2 per half hour; $3.65 per hour. RECOMMENDED ACCOMMODATIONS: Hôtel du Golf, Hôtel Chicago, Hôtel de Chateau, Hôtel de Parc, Restaurant Marquis.

Golf Club de Marseille-Aix

LOCATION: Domaine de Riquetti-les Milles, Bouches-du-Rhône (5 miles from Aix-en-Provence or 16 miles from Marseilles by taxi). COURSE SIZE: 18 holes; 6,326 yards; par 73. AVAILABILITY TO VISITORS: Visitors welcome at all times and invited to participate in local competition. GREEN FEES: Weekdays, $4.50; Sundays, $5; per week, $12.15; per month, $30.30; per season, $73. CADDIE FEES: 9 holes, $1.20; 18 holes, $3. GOLF CLUB RENTALS: Not available. GOLF CART RENTALS: 30¢ per round. MOTORIZED GOLF CART RENTALS: Not available. LESSONS: $6 per half hour. CLUBHOUSE FACILITIES: Restaurant and bar available. RECOMMENDED ACCOMMODATIONS: Aix-en-Provence: Hôtel Roy René, Hôtel Riviera. Marseilles: Grand Hôtel, Hôtel Splendide.

Golf Club de Pen-guen Saint Cast

LOCATION: Saint Cast, Côtes-du-Nord, on the Golfe de St. Malo. COURSE SIZE: 9 holes; 2,813 yards; par 35. AVAILABILITY TO VISITORS: Visitors permitted limited play; inquire ahead. GREEN FEES: Weekdays, $3.40; weekends, $4 per day; per week, $20; per month, $56. CADDIE FEES: $1 per 18 holes. GOLF CLUB RENTALS: Available. GOLF CART RENTALS: 20¢ per 9-hole round. MOTORIZED GOLF CART RENTALS: Not available. LESSONS: $3 per half hour. CLUBHOUSE FACILITIES: Bar available. RECOMMENDED ACCOMMODATIONS: Saint-Cast Plage: Hôtel Ar-vro, Hôtel Bellevue, Hôtel des Pins, Hôtel de la Mer, Hôtel des Dunes.

Golf Club de Saint-Cloud

LOCATION: Garches, Seine-et-Oise (15 minutes from Place de l'Étoile, Paris). COURSE SIZE: 18 holes; 6,573 yards; par 72. 18 holes; 5,481 yards; par 68. AVAILABILITY TO VISITORS: Visitors permitted limited play; inquire ahead. GREEN FEES: Weekdays, $6; Saturdays and Sundays, $15 per day. Between July 8 and September 10, weekday and weekend fees are reduced to $3 and $6 respectively. CADDIE FEES: $5 per 18-hole round. GOLF CLUB RENTALS: Not available. GOLF CART RENTALS: 20¢ per round. MOTORIZED GOLF CART RENTALS: Not available. LESSONS: $8 per hour. CLUBHOUSE FACILITIES: Restaurant and bar available. RECOMMENDED ACCOMMODATIONS: Hôtel Celtic, Hôtel Windsor-Reynolds, Hôtel Napoléon.

Golf Club des Sables-d'Or-les-Pins

LOCATION: Sables-d'Or-les-Pins, Côtes-du-Nord, on golfe de St. Malo (18 miles from Dinard; 1 mile from Sables-d'Or-les-Pins by taxi). COURSE SIZE: 9 holes (18 tees); 5,609 yards; par 36. AVAILABILITY TO VISITORS: Visitors welcome. GREEN FEES: Weekdays, $3; weekends, $5 per day; per week, $18; per month, $50; season, $80. CADDIE FEES: $1 for 9 holes; $1.60 for 18 holes. GOLF CLUB RENTALS: $1 per day. GOLF CART RENTALS: Not available. MOTORIZED GOLF CART RENTALS: Not available. LESSONS: $2.60 per half hour. CLUBHOUSE FACILITIES: Restaurant and bar available. RECOMMENDED ACCOMMODATIONS: Sables-d'Or: Hôtel des Dunes, Hôtel de Diane, Hôtel des Ajoncs d'Or, Hôtel des Pins, Hôtel au Bon "Accueil," Hôtel à "L'Abri des Flots."

Golf Club d'Hossegor

LOCATION: Hossegor, Landes (12 miles from Biarritz by taxi). COURSE SIZE: 18 holes; 6,407 yards; par 72. AVAILABILITY TO VISITORS: Visitors welcome. GREEN FEES: Weekdays, $3; Saturdays and Sundays, $5 per day; per week, $20.20; per month, $53.50; season (July–September), $75. CADDIE FEES: $1.80 per 9-hole round; $2.40 per 18-hole round. GOLF CLUB RENTALS: Available. GOLF CART RENTALS: 40¢ per day. MOTORIZED GOLF CART RENTALS: Not available. LESSONS: $3.80 per half hour. CLUBHOUSE FACILITIES: Restaurant and bar available. RECOMMENDED ACCOMMODATIONS: Hôtel du Parc, Hôtel Mercedes.

Golf Club d'Ozoir-la-Ferrière

LOCATION: Ozoir-la-Ferrière, Seine-et-Marne (16 miles from Paris by taxi). COURSE SIZE: Course A: 18 holes; 6,130 yards; par 71. Course B: 9 holes; 2,394 yards; par 33. AVAILABILITY TO VISITORS: Visitors welcome. GREEN FEES: Course A: weekdays, $4.05; Saturdays and Sundays per day, $10. Course B: weekdays, $3; Saturdays and Sundays per day, $6. CADDIE FEES: $2 per 18-hole round. GOLF CLUB RENTALS: 50¢ per day. GOLF CART RENTALS: 40¢ per day. MOTORIZED GOLF CART RENTALS: Not available. LESSONS: $4 per half hour. CLUBHOUSE FACILITIES: Restaurant and bar available. RECOMMENDED ACCOMMODATIONS: Ozoir: La Relais, L'Auberge du Parc.

Golf Club du Lac Annecy

LOCATION: Echarvines, Talloires, Haute Savoie (6 miles from Annecy, 20 miles from Aix-les-Bains by taxi). COURSE SIZE: 18 holes; 5,468 yards; par 69. AVAILABILITY TO VISITORS: Visitors welcome. GREEN FEES: Weekdays, $4.40; weekends, $7 per day; per week, $17.20; per month, $46.50; season, $85. CADDIE FEES: 9 holes, $1; 18 holes, $1.60. GOLF CLUB RENTALS: $2 per round. GOLF CART RENTALS: Not available. MOTORIZED GOLF CART RENTALS: Not available. LESSONS: $3 per half hour. CLUBHOUSE FACILITIES: Restaurant and bar available. RECOMMENDED ACCOMMODATIONS: In the surrounding villages of Talloires, Annecy, and Methon-St. Bernard: Hôtel des Dents de Lanfon (on course), Hôtel du Lac, Hôtel Imperial Palace, L'Abbaye Père Bise.

Shell's Wonderful World of Golf

Tee at Mont Agel overlooking the Mediterranean.

The fairways of Saint-Cloud near Paris.

Shell's Wonderful World of Golf

Golf Club du Touquet

LOCATION: Le Touquet, Pas-de-Calais (2 miles from Le Touquet). COURSE SIZE: 18 holes; 6,145 yards; par 74. AVAILABILITY TO VISITORS: Visitors welcome. GREEN FEES: Weekdays, $5.60; weekends, $6 per day; per week, $16.20; per month, $50.65; season, $91. CADDIE FEES: $2.40 per 18-hole round. GOLF CLUB RENTALS: Not available. GOLF CART RENTALS: Available. MOTORIZED GOLF CART RENTALS: Not available. LESSONS: $3 per half hour. CLUBHOUSE FACILITIES: Restaurant and bar available. RECOMMENDED ACCOMMODATIONS: Le Touquet: Manoir Hôtel (on course), Bristol Hôtel, Résidence du Golf, Westminster Hôtel.

Golf de Biarritz

LOCATION: Biarritz, Basses-Pyrénées (just outside the city limits of Biarritz by taxi). COURSE SIZE: 18 holes; 5,840 yards; par 71. AVAILABILITY TO VISITORS: Visitors welcome; closed in February. GREEN FEES: July–September and Easter: per day, $6; per week, $24; per month, $72; season, $102. Off-season: per day, $3.60; per week, $14.40; per month, $43. CADDIE FEES: $3 per 18-hole round. GOLF CLUB RENTALS: $2 per day. GOLF CART RENTALS: 60¢ per day. MOTORIZED GOLF CART RENTALS: Not available. LESSONS: Available, price varies with pro. CLUBHOUSE FACILITIES: Restaurant, bar, and practice range available. RECOMMENDED ACCOMMODATIONS: Hôtel Regina et du Golf, Hôtel Miramar, Hôtel du Palais.

Golf de Chantilly

LOCATION: Vineuil-Saint-Firmin, Oise (1 mile from Chantilly by taxi; 24 miles from Paris). COURSE SIZE: 18 holes; 6,687 yards; par 71. Also 9-hole course: 2,871 yards; par 35. AVAILABILITY TO VISITORS: Visitors welcome. GREEN FEES: Weekdays, $3.05; Saturdays, $7.10; Sundays, $9.10; per week, $20.25; per month, $60.80. CADDIE FEES: $3 per 9-hole round; $4 per 18-hole round. GOLF CLUB RENTALS: Not available. GOLF CART RENTALS: 20¢ per round. MOTORIZED GOLF CART RENTALS: Not available. LESSONS: $8 per hour. CLUBHOUSE FACILITIES: Restaurant and bar available. RECOMMENDED ACCOMMODATIONS: Chantilly: Hôtel du Parc, Hôtel des Terrasses. Senlis: Hôtel du Grand Cerf.

Golf de Chiberta

LOCATION: Anglet, Basses-Pyrénées (2 miles by taxi from Biarritz; 3 miles by taxi from Bayonne). COURSE SIZE: 18 holes; 5,934 yards; par 73. AVAILABILITY TO VISITORS: Visitors welcome. GREEN FEES: November to April: weekdays, $2.85; per week, $11.35. May to October: weekdays, $4; per week, $16.20; per month, $48.60. CADDIE FEES: $2.40 per 18-hole round. GOLF CLUB RENTALS: $1 per day. GOLF CART RENTALS: 40¢ per day. MOTORIZED GOLF CART RENTALS: Not available. LESSONS: $1.25 per half hour. CLUBHOUSE FACILITIES: Restaurant and bar available. RECOMMENDED ACCOMMODATIONS: Hôtel Country Club de Chiberta, Hôtel Regina et du Golf, Hôtel Miramar, Hôtel du Palais.

Golf de Fontainebleau

LOCATION: Fontainebleau, Seine-et-Marne (about 40 miles from Paris). COURSE SIZE: 18 holes; 5,889 yards; par 69. AVAILABILITY TO VISITORS: Visitors welcome; closed Tuesdays. GREEN FEES: Weekdays, $4; Saturdays, $8; Sundays, $10; weekend, $15; per week, $20. CADDIE FEES: $3.20 to $4, depending upon the quality of the caddie. GOLF CLUB RENTALS: Not available. GOLF CART RENTALS: 20¢ per round. MOTORIZED GOLF CART RENTALS: Not available. LESSONS: $2 per half hour. CLUBHOUSE FACILITIES: Restaurant and bar available. RECOMMENDED ACCOMMODATIONS: Hôtel de l'Aigle Noir, Hôtel Legris, Hôtel de Cadran Bleu, Hôtel de Londres.

Golf de Morfontaine

LOCATION: Morfontaine, Oise (about 30 miles from Paris). COURSE SIZE: 18 holes; 6,605 yards; par 72. Also 9-hole course: 2,789 yards; par 36. AVAILABILITY TO VISITORS: Visitors must be accompanied by a member. GREEN FEES: Weekdays, $5; weekends, $6 per day. CADDIE FEES: $4 per 18 holes. GOLF CLUB RENTALS: $2 per day. GOLF CART RENTALS: 20¢ per round. MOTORIZED GOLF CART RENTALS: Not available. LESSONS: $8 per hour. CLUBHOUSE FACILITIES: Restaurant and bar available to guests of members only. RECOMMENDED ACCOMMODATIONS: Chantilly: Hôtel du Parc, Hôtel des Terrasses. Senlis: Hôtel du Grand Cerf.

Golf de Saint-Germain

LOCATION: Saint-Germain, Seine-et-Oise (1½ miles from Saint-Germain; 12 miles from Paris). COURSE SIZE: 18 holes; 6,365 yards; par 72. Also 9-hole course: 1,881 yards; par 31. AVAILABILITY TO VISITORS: Visitors permitted limited play; inquire ahead. Course closed on Mondays. GREEN FEES: Weekdays, $5; Saturdays, Sundays, holidays, $12 a day. Subscription rate available from July 15 through September 15 of $96 per person or $160 per couple. CADDIE FEES: $3 to $3.60 per round. GOLF CLUB RENTALS: $2 per round. GOLF CART RENTALS: 10¢ per hour. MOTORIZED GOLF CART RENTALS: Not available. LESSONS: $3.50 to $4 per half hour. CLUBHOUSE FACILITIES: Restaurant and bar available. RECOMMENDED ACCOMMODATIONS: Saint-Germain: Pavillon Henri IV, Ermitage des Loges, Pavillon d'Estrées.

Golf de Saint-Nom-la-Breteche

LOCATION: Domaine de la Tuilerie, Saint-Nom-la-Breteche, Seine-et-Oise (6 miles from Versailles, 12 miles from Paris by taxi). COURSE SIZE: 18 holes; 6,702 yards; par 74. 18 holes; 6,700 yards; par 73. AVAILABILITY TO VISITORS: Visitors welcome. Course closed Tuesdays. GREEN FEES: Weekdays, $3.40; Saturdays, Sundays, and holidays, $10 per day. CADDIE FEES: $1.60–$2 per 9 holes; $2.40–$3 per 18-hole round. GOLF CLUB RENTALS: Available. GOLF CART RENTALS: 40¢ per round. MOTORIZED GOLF CART RENTALS: $8 per round for two persons. LESSONS: $4 per half hour. CLUBHOUSE FACILITIES: Restaurant and bar available. RECOMMENDED ACCOMMODATIONS: Saint-Germain: Pavillon Henry IV, Pavillon d'Estrées, Ermitage des Loges. Versailles: Hôtel Trianon-Palace. Feucherolles: Hôtel le Clos Saint-Antoine.

Golf d'Evian

LOCATION: Cercle Sportive d'Evian, Evian-les-Baine, Haute-Savoie (on the shores of Lake Geneva, 45 minutes from Geneva by car, 30 minutes from Lausanne by boat). COURSE SIZE: 18 holes; 6,223 yards; par 72. AVAILABILITY TO VISITORS: Visitors welcome. Closed on Tuesdays October to May. GREEN FEES: Weekdays, $4; Saturdays, Sundays, and holidays, $5 per day; per week, $16.20; per month, $44.60; per year, $71. CADDIE FEES: 9 holes, $2; 18 holes, $3. GOLF CLUB RENTALS: $1.20 per day. GOLF CART RENTALS: 30¢ per day. MOTORIZED GOLF CART RENTALS: Not available. LESSONS: $4.80 per hour. CLUB-HOUSE FACILITIES: Restaurant and bar available. RECOMMENDED ACCOMMODATIONS: Grand Hôtel du Parc, Hôtel la Verniaz, Hôtel Royal, Hôtel Splendide, Hôtel du Golf, Hôtel le Lumina.

Golf du Lys

LOCATION: Lamorlaye, Oise (4 miles by taxi from Chantilly; 30 miles from the center of Paris). COURSE SIZE: 18 holes; 6,476 yards; par 73. AVAILABILITY TO VISITORS: Visitors are welcome on the decision of the director. Visitors who are members of golf clubs of the same affiliations as Golf du Lys are invited to play free. GREEN FEES: Weekdays, $4; Saturdays and Sundays, $6 per day; both weekend days, $10. CADDIE FEES: $3.10 per round. GOLF CLUB RENTALS: Not available. GOLF CART RENTALS: 40¢ per round. MOTORIZED GOLF CART RENTALS: Not available. LESSONS: $3–$4 per half hour, according to the professional. CLUBHOUSE FACILITIES: Restaurant and bar available. RECOMMENDED ACCOMMODATIONS: Lys-Chantilly: La Clairière aux Chenes. Chantilly: Hôtel du Parc, Hôtel des Terrasses.

Golf du Racing Club de France

LOCATION: La Boulie, par Versailles, Seine-et-Oise (1 mile from the city limits of Versailles; 9 miles from Paris). COURSE SIZE: 18 holes; 6,720 yards; par 72. Also 9-hole course: 1,651 yards; par 29. Another 18-hole course is being completed at this writing. AVAILABILITY TO VISITORS: Visitors welcome; restricted on weekends only. GREEN FEES: Weekdays, $4.05; Saturdays and Sundays, $10 per day. CADDIE FEES: $3–$4 per 18-hole round, according to caddie. GOLF CLUB RENTALS: $2 per round. GOLF CART RENTALS: 40¢ per round. MOTORIZED GOLF CART RENTALS: Not available. LESSONS: $4 per half hour. CLUBHOUSE FACILITIES: Restaurant and bar available. RECOMMENDED ACCOMMODATIONS: Versailles: Hotel Trianon-Palace. Saint Germain: Pavillon Henry IV, Hermitage des Loges, Pavillon d'Estrées.

Marly Country Club

LOCATION: Port-Marly, Seine-et-Oise (2 miles by taxi from Saint-Germain; 13 miles from Paris by car or train). COURSE SIZE: 18 holes; 4,686 yards; par 65. AVAILABILITY TO VISITORS: Visitors permitted limited play; inquire ahead. GREEN FEES: Weekdays, $2; Saturdays, $3; Sundays, $4; per month, $40.50; 3 months, $100. CADDIE FEES: $2 per round. GOLF CLUB RENTALS: 60¢ per day. GOLF CART RENTALS: 60¢ per day. MOTORIZED GOLF CART RENTALS: Not available. LESSONS: $2.40 per half hour; $4.05 per hour. CLUBHOUSE FACILITIES: Restaurant and bar available. RECOMMENDED ACCOMMODATIONS: Saint-Germain: Pavillon Henri IV, Hermitage des Loges, Pavillon d'Estrées.

Monte Carlo Golf Club

LOCATION: Mont Agel par la Turbie, Alpes-Maritimes (5 miles from La Turbie; 7 miles from Monte Carlo by taxi). COURSE SIZE: 18 holes; 4,939 yards; par 65. AVAILABILITY TO VISITORS: Visitors welcome and invited to play in local competition. GREEN FEES: Weekdays, $4; Saturdays, Sundays, and holidays, $6 per day. CADDIE FEES: $2 per round. GOLF CLUB RENTALS: $2.85 per round. GOLF CART RENTALS: Available. MOTORIZED GOLF CART RENTALS: Not available. LESSONS: $6 per hour. CLUBHOUSE FACILITIES: Restaurant and bar available daily except Mondays. RECOMMENDED ACCOMMODATIONS: Hôtel de Paris, Hôtel Hermitage, Hôtel Metropole, Hôtel Mirabeau.

New Golf Club Deauville

LOCATION: On Canisy Hill overlooking Deauville and Trouville. COURSE SIZE: 18 holes; 6,620 yards; par 72. Also 9-hole course: 2,220 yards; par 34. AVAILABILITY TO VISITORS: Visitors welcome and invited to participate in local competitions. Group rates are available and may be obtained by contacting the manager of the Normandie, Royal, or Golf hotels. GREEN FEES: Weekdays, $5; Saturdays and Sundays, $6.75 per day; all weekend, $11.10; per week, $18.20; per month: June and September, $33; July, $50; August, $61; season, $100. CADDIE FEES: 9 holes, $1.30; 18 holes, $2.40. GOLF CLUB RENTALS: $2 per day. There is also a shop near the course that rents golf shoes. GOLF CART RENTALS: 60¢ per day. MOTORIZED GOLF CART

RENTALS: Not available. LESSONS: $8 per hour. CLUBHOUSE FACILITIES: Bar available. RECOMMENDED ACCOMMODATIONS: Hôtel du Golf (at the course), Hôtel Royal, Hôtel Normandie, Palais Deauville.

Nivelle Golf Club

LOCATION: Saint-Jean-de-Luz (3 miles from Biarritz; 1 mile from Saint-Jean-de-Luz by taxi). COURSE SIZE: 18 holes; 5,796 yards; par 71. AVAILABILITY TO VISITORS: Visitors welcome. GREEN FEES: Daily, $4.05; per week, $16.20; per month, $49; season, $73. CADDIE FEES: 9 holes, $1.40; 18 holes, $2. GOLF CLUB RENTALS: Not available. GOLF CART RENTALS: 40¢ per day. MOTORIZED GOLF CART RENTALS: Not available. LESSONS: $2.40 per half hour. CLUBHOUSE FACILITIES: Restaurant and bar available. RECOMMENDED ACCOMMODATIONS: Saint-Jean-de-Luz: Hôtel de Chantaco, Hôtel Miramar, Hôtel Moderne Madison, Hôtel des Motels. Ciboure: Hôtel di Ciboure.

Sporting Club de Vichy

LOCATION: Vichy, Allier (within the city limits of Vichy). COURSE SIZE: 18 holes; 5,851 yards; par 71. AVAILABILITY TO VISITORS: Visitors welcome. GREEN FEES: Daily, $5, or $8 for any two days; per week, $20.40; 3 weeks, $50; season, $93. CADDIE FEES: 9 holes, $1.60; 18 holes, $2.10. GOLF CLUB RENTALS: According to the pro making the rental. GOLF CART RENTALS: 60¢ per round. MOTORIZED GOLF CART RENTALS: Not available. LESSONS: $4 per half hour. CLUBHOUSE FACILITIES: Restaurant and bar available. RECOMMENDED ACCOMMODATIONS: Hôtel Carleton, Hôtel Thermal Palace, Hôtel Ambassadeurs, Hôtel Elysée-Palace, Hôtel Albert Ier, Pavillon Sévigné.

Germany

Germany is the perfect place for a combination golf-sight-seeing-family vacation. There are fine courses located within a reasonable distance of most tourist centers and large cities, which afford easy opportunity for Dad to slip away for an occasional afternoon round while carrying wife and kids on a cultural tour of the shrines of the Old World.

It is difficult to generalize about the eighty-odd courses in Germany because of the great variety of terrain. Many of the courses, such as the one at Kronberg, are converted or renovated medieval estates with spectacular clubhouses and spacious grounds. Others, such as Berlin's Wansee golf course, appear to be literally clawed from the forest. Fairways are separated by great stands of evergreens, and there is no allowance for errant tee shots; in fact, they probably won't even be found.

The Cologne golf club has fairways like great string beans. It is long, narrow, and frustrating for the less than proficient player. And Hamburg has, among the six clubs in the area, the Grossflottbeker Tennis, Hockey und Golf Club, which has six holes played three times for a total of 4,700 yards, par 69. It's good for the ego. In upper Bavaria, the Berchtesgaden Golf Club near the Austrian border was built for the German ski team. There just isn't a sweet (flat) spot for the ball to land on this course.

Visitors are welcome at most all the courses in Germany; in fact, the National Golf Association encourages visitors to bring their clubs. Rates are reasonable, and most clubs offer attractive restaurant and bar facilities. Whether your interest be festivals, philharmonics, foods, or females, Germany has them all in abundance, with a golf course not far away.

SEASON: All year depending on locality.

HOW TO GET THERE: By Pan Am Jet Clipper, New York to Munich is 10¼ hours; to Düsseldorf, 8¾ hours; Hamburg, 8½ hours;

Frankfurt, 7½ hours; Berlin, 9¾ hours. Frankfurt is 10¼ hours from Chicago and 12½ hours from the U.S. west coast via the polar route. Also through service from Dallas, Houston, Atlanta, Washington (9¾ hours), and New Orleans. Frequent local service via Pan Am between Berlin and Hamburg, Frankfurt, Nuremberg, Stuttgart, Hanover, Cologne, Düsseldorf, Munich. By ship, about 9 days from New York to Hamburg or Bremen.

GOLF EQUIPMENT: Readily available at reasonable prices.

LANGUAGE: English is understood in all the tourist centers, hotels, railway stations, and better shops.

TIME: Six hours later than U.S. Eastern Standard Time.

Berchtesgaden Golf Club

LOCATION: Berchtesgaden (2 miles outside of town; about 20 miles from Salzburg on the Austrian border). COURSE SIZE: 9 holes; 2,822 yards; par 34. AVAILABILITY TO VISITORS: Visitors welcome. GREEN FEES: Weekdays, $2; Saturdays, Sundays, and holidays, $2.50 per day; per week, $13.50; per month, $42.50. CADDIE FEES: 9 holes, 50¢; 18 holes, 90¢. GOLF CLUB RENTALS: 25¢ per day. GOLF CART RENTALS: 35¢ per day. MOTORIZED GOLF CART RENTALS: Not available. LESSONS: Not available. CLUBHOUSE FACILITIES: Restaurant and bar available. RECOMMENDED ACCOMMODATIONS: Berchtesgaden: Hotel Geiger, Hotel Post, Hotel Krone. Ramsa bei Berchtesgaden: Gastehaus Zulehen. Obersalzburg: Hotel zum Turken. Bad Reichenhall: Hotel Luisenbad.

Düsseldorfer Golf Club

LOCATION: Ratingen (north of Düsseldorf; 7½ miles by taxi from the city limits). COURSE SIZE: 18 holes; 6,552 yards; par 72. AVAILABILITY TO VISITORS: Visitors welcome. GREEN FEES: Weekdays, $2.50 per day; weekends and holidays, $3.25 per day. CADDIE FEES: $1.25 per round. GOLF CLUB RENTALS: $1.25 per day. GOLF CART RENTALS: 50¢ per day. MOTORIZED GOLF CART RENTALS: Not available. LESSONS: $4.50 per hour. CLUBHOUSE FACILITIES: Restaurant, bar, and locker rooms available. RECOMMENDED ACCOMMODATIONS: Ratingen: Hotel Haus Kronenthal.

Essener Golf Club

LOCATION: Kettwig a.d. Ruhr, Haus Oefte (6 miles from Essen city limits by taxi). COURSE SIZE: 11 holes (18 tees); 6,452 yards; par 72. AVAILABILITY TO VISITORS: Visitors permitted limited play; inquire ahead. GREEN FEES: Weekdays, $1.90; Saturdays and Sundays, $3.75 per day. CADDIE FEES: 40¢ per hour. GOLF CLUB RENTALS: Not available. GOLF CART RENTALS: Not available. MOTORIZED GOLF CART RENTALS: Not available. LESSONS: $2.50 per hour. CLUBHOUSE FACILITIES: Restaurant and bar available. RECOMMENDED ACCOMMODATIONS: Schloss Hotel Hugenpoet (near course). Essen: Hotel Essener Hof, Hotel Handelshof, Hotel Kaiserhof.

Frankfurter Golf Club

LOCATION: Frankfurt/Main-Niederrad (5 miles from Frankfurt by taxi). COURSE SIZE: 18 holes; 6,398 yards; par 72. AVAILABILITY TO VISITORS: Visitors permitted limited play; inquire ahead. GREEN FEES: Weekdays, $3; Saturdays and Sundays, $5 per day. CADDIE FEES: $1.25 per round. GOLF CLUB RENTALS: Available. GOLF CART RENTALS: 50¢ per day. MOTORIZED GOLF CART RENTALS: Not available. LESSONS: $2.75 per hour or $3.25 per hour, depending on professional. CLUBHOUSE FACILITIES: Restaurant and bar available. RECOMMENDED ACCOMMODATIONS: Waldhotel Unterschweinstiege (near course at Rhein-Main airport). Frankfurt: Hotel Frankfurt Intercontinental, Frankfurter Hof, Hessischer Hof and Park Hotel.

Golf Club am Reichswald

LOCATION: Nuremberg (15–20 minutes by taxi from downtown). COURSE SIZE: 18 holes; 6,562 yards; par 72. AVAILABILITY TO VISITORS: Visitors welcome. GREEN FEES: Weekdays, $2.50; Saturdays, Sundays, and holidays, $3.75 per day. CADDIE FEES: $2.25 per round. GOLF CLUB RENTALS: Not available. GOLF CART RENTALS: Not available. MOTORIZED GOLF CART RENTALS: Not available. LESSONS: $2.75 per ¾ hour. CLUBHOUSE FACILITIES: Restaurant and bar available. RECOMMENDED ACCOMMODATIONS: Nuremberg: Carlton Hotel, Grand Hotel, Deutscher Hof, Hotel Kaiserhof, Hotel Sterntor. Near course: Pension Brendel.

Golf Club Ansbach

LOCATION: Katterbach (about 30 miles from Nuremberg). COURSE SIZE: 9 holes; 3,659 yards; par 36. AVAILABILITY TO VISITORS: Visitors welcome. GREEN FEES: Weekdays, $1.25; Saturdays, Sundays, and holidays, $1.50 per day. CADDIE FEES: No caddies available. GOLF CLUB RENTALS: $1 per day. GOLF CART RENTALS: 25¢ per day. MOTORIZED GOLF CART RENTALS: None available. LESSONS: Not available. CLUB- HOUSE FACILITIES: Light refreshments only. RECOMMENDED ACCOM- MODATIONS: Hotel Deutscher Kaiser, Hotel Stern.

Golf Club Augsburg

LOCATION: 12 miles from Augsburg in Burgwalden. COURSE SIZE: 9 holes; 6,329 yards (for 18); par 72. AVAILABILITY TO VISITORS: Visitors welcome. GREEN FEES: Weekdays, $2; Saturdays, Sundays, and holidays, $3.75 per day; per week, $11.25. CADDIE FEES: 70¢ for 9 holes. GOLF CLUB RENTALS: $1.25. GOLF CART RENTALS: Not avail- able. MOTORIZED GOLF CART RENTALS: Not available. LESSONS: $2.50. CLUBHOUSE FACILITIES: Bar and restaurant only. RECOMMENDED AC- COMMODATIONS: Augsburg: Hotel Drei Mohren.

Golf Club Feldafing

LOCATION: Feldafing (20-mile drive from Munich). COURSE SIZE: 18 holes; 6,200 yards; par 71. AVAILABILITY TO VISITORS: Visitors wel- come. GREEN FEES: Weekdays, $2; Saturdays, Sundays and holidays, $3.75 per day; per week, $12.50. CADDIE FEES: $1.50 per round. GOLF CLUB RENTALS: 75¢ per day. GOLF CART RENTALS: 50¢ per day. MOTORIZED GOLF CART RENTALS: Not available. LESSONS: Pro, $3 per hour; assistant pro, $2.75 per hour. CLUBHOUSE FACILITIES: Restau- rant and bar. RECOMMENDED ACCOMMODATIONS: Feldafing: Hotel Kaiserin Elizabeth.

Golf Club Garmisch-Partenkirchen

LOCATION: Garmisch-Partenkirchen in the German Alps. COURSE SIZE: 9 holes; 3,033 yards; par 36. AVAILABILITY TO VISITORS: Visitors welcome. GREEN FEES: Weekdays, $2; Saturdays, Sundays, and holidays, $3.75 per day; 10-day ticket, $12.50. CADDIE FEES: $1.50 per round. GOLF CLUB RENTALS: Available. GOLF CART RENTALS: 35¢ per day. MOTORIZED GOLF CART RENTALS: Not available. LESSONS: $1.75 per half hour. CLUBHOUSE FACILITIES: Restaurant and bar available. RECOMMENDED ACCOMMODATIONS: Alpenhof, Golf-Hotel Sonnenbichl, Marktplatz, Partenkirchener Hof, Posthotel, Riessersee, Wittelsbach, Hotel Vier Jahrzeiten-am Bahnhof, Hotel Flora.

Golf Club Hamburg Ahrensburg e.V.

LOCATION: Ahrensburg, Am Heidschlag 39 (16 miles north of Hamburg by car or taxi). COURSE SIZE: 18 holes; 6,652 yards; par 71. AVAILABILITY TO VISITORS: Visitors permitted limited play. GREEN FEES: Weekdays, $2; Saturdays and Sundays, $3.75 per day. CADDIE FEES: $1 per round. GOLF CLUB RENTALS: $1.25 per round. GOLF CART RENTALS: 50¢ per day. MOTORIZED GOLF CART RENTALS: Not available. LESSONS: $2.25 per hour. CLUBHOUSE FACILITIES: Restaurant and bar available. RECOMMENDED ACCOMMODATIONS: Ahrensburg: Hotel Hamburger Wald. Tremsbüttel: Schlosshotel Tremsbüttel. Hamburg: Hotel Atlantic, Hotel Vier Jahreszeiten, Hotel Berlin.

Golfclub Hamburg–Walddörfer e.V.

LOCATION: Hoisbuettel near Ahrensburg (14 miles north of Hamburg; by subway to Hoisbuettel, then by car or taxi). COURSE SIZE: 18 holes; 6,380 yards; par 71. AVAILABILITY TO VISITORS: Visitors permitted limited play. GREEN FEES: Weekdays, $2; Saturdays and Sundays, $4 per day. CADDIE FEES: $1.25 per round. GOLF CLUB RENTALS: $1.25. GOLF CART RENTALS: 50¢ per day. MOTORIZED GOLF CART RENTALS: Not available. LESSONS: $2.25 per hour. CLUBHOUSE FACILITIES: Heated indoor swimming pool; restaurant and bar; closed Mondays. RECOMMENDED ACCOMMODATIONS: Hoisbuettel: Hotel Alsterau. Bramfeld: Hotel Windsor. Hamburg: Hotel Atlantic, Hotel Vier Jahreszeiten, Hotel Berlin.

Golf Club Hanau

LOCATION: Hanau (4 miles from town by taxi). COURSE SIZE: 18 holes; 6,808 yards; par 73. AVAILABILITY TO VISITORS: Visitors welcome. GREEN FEES: Weekdays, $2.50; Saturdays, Sundays, and holidays, $3.75 per day. CADDIE FEES: $1.50 per round. GOLF CLUB RENTALS: Not available. GOLF CART RENTALS: Available. MOTORIZED GOLF CART RENTALS: Not available. LESSONS: $3 per hour. CLUBHOUSE FACILITIES: Restaurant and bar available. RECOMMENDED ACCOMMODATIONS: Golf Hotel Hanau/Main, Hotel-Restaurant Golfplatz.

Golf Club Hannover

LOCATION: Garbsen, Hanover (12 miles from the city limits of Hanover by taxi). COURSE SIZE: 18 holes; 6,332 yards; par 71. AVAILABILITY TO VISITORS: Visitors permitted limited play; inquire in advance. GREEN FEES: Weekdays, $2.50; Saturdays, Sundays, and holidays, $3.75 per day. CADDIE FEES: 75¢ per round. GOLF CLUB RENTALS: Not available. GOLF CART RENTALS: Available. MOTORIZED GOLF CART RENTALS: Not available. LESSONS: $1.50 per hour. CLUBHOUSE FACILITIES: Restaurant and bar available. RECOMMENDED ACCOMMODATIONS: Autobahn Resthaus am Blauen See (near course). Hanover: Kastens Hotel Luisenhof, Central Hotel Kaiserhof, Grand Hotel Mussmann.

Golf Club Lindau-Bad Schachen e.V.

LOCATION: Lindau, Kemtener Strasse 125. COURSE SIZE: 9 holes; 6,436 yards; par 73. AVAILABILITY TO VISITORS: Visitors welcome. GREEN FEES: Weekdays, $2.50; Saturdays, Sundays, and holidays, $3.75 per day; per week, $11.25; per month, $30. CADDIE FEES: $1.25 for 18 holes. GOLF CLUB RENTALS: 75¢ per day. GOLF CART RENTALS: 50¢ per day. MOTORIZED GOLF CART RENTALS: None available. LESSONS: $2.50. CLUBHOUSE FACILITIES: Restaurant and bar only. RECOMMENDED ACCOMMODATIONS: Hotel Bad Schachen, Bayerischer Hof, Lindauer Hof, Gästehaus Hof Reutenen.

Golf Club Oberstdorf

LOCATION: Gstad (2½ miles from Oberstdorf). COURSE SIZE: 18 holes; 6,047 yards; par 70. AVAILABILITY TO VISITORS: Visitors welcome. GREEN FEES: Weekdays, $2.50; Saturdays, Sundays, and holidays, $3 per day; per week, $10; per 2 weeks, $15. CADDIE FEES: $1.25 per round. GOLF CLUB RENTALS: 75¢ per round. GOLF CART RENTALS: Available. MOTORIZED GOLF CART RENTALS: Not available.

LESSONS: $1.50 per half hour. CLUBHOUSE FACILITIES: Restaurant and bar available. RECOMMENDED ACCOMMODATIONS: Oberstdorf: Hotel Wittlsbacher Hof (near course), Hotel Filser, Hotel Drei Mohren, Bahnhofshotel, Hotel Sonnenalp, Hotel Bergbach, Stillachhaus, Hotel Weigund, Hotel Garni "Schellenberg."

Golf Club Prien

LOCATION: 2 miles from Prien (near Nuremberg). COURSE SIZE: 18 holes; 5,724 yards; par 68. AVAILABILITY TO VISITORS: Visitors welcome. GREEN FEES: Weekdays, $2; Saturdays, Sundays, and holidays, $3 per day; per week, $12.50. CADDIE FEES: 75¢ for 9 holes. GOLF CLUB RENTALS: $1.25 per round. GOLF CART RENTALS: Not available. MOTORIZED GOLF CART RENTALS: None available. LESSONS: $2.75 for 45 minutes. CLUBHOUSE FACILITIES: Restaurant and bar available. RECOMMENDED ACCOMMODATIONS: Nuremberg: Carlton Hotel, Grand Hotel, Pension Brendel (near course), Deutscher Hof, Hotel Kaiserhof, Hotel Sterntor.

Golf und Land-Club Berlin-Wannsee

LOCATION: Berlin-Wannsee (10 miles from the center of town). COURSE SIZE: 9 holes; 3,019 yards; par 35. AVAILABILITY TO VISITORS: Visitors welcome. GREEN FEES: Weekdays, $2; Saturdays, Sundays, and holidays, $2.50 per day. CADDIE FEES: 40¢ per 9-hole round. GOLF CLUB RENTALS: 75¢ per day. GOLF CART RENTALS: 25¢ per day. MOTORIZED GOLF CART RENTALS: Not available. LESSONS: Two professionals available, $1.75 and $2.25 per hour. CLUBHOUSE FACILITIES: Restaurant and bar available. RECOMMENDED ACCOMMODATIONS: Numerous choices available in Berlin.

Golf und Land-Club Köln

LOCATION: Bensberg-Refrath (9 miles from city limits of Cologne by taxi). COURSE SIZE: 18 holes; 6,720 yards; par 74. AVAILABILITY TO VISITORS: Visitors permitted limited play; inquire ahead. GREEN FEES: Weekdays, $3.10; Saturdays, Sundays, and holidays, $3.75 per day. CADDIE FEES: $1 per round. GOLF CLUB RENTALS: $2.50 per day. GOLF CART RENTALS: Not available. MOTORIZED GOLF CART RENTALS: Not available. LESSONS: $1 per half hour. CLUBHOUSE FACILITIES:

Restaurant and bar available. RECOMMENDED ACCOMMODATIONS: Bensberg-Refrath: Wadhotel Klosterhofshen (near course). Bergisch-Gladbach: Schloss Lerbach. Cologne: Excelsior Hotel Ernst, Dom Hotel.

Golf und Land-Club Kronberg

LOCATION: Schloss Friedrichshof, Kronberg (9 miles from Frankfurt). COURSE SIZE: 18 holes; 5,450 yards; par 69. AVAILABILITY TO VISITORS: Members of foreign clubs and guests of Schloss Hotel Kronberg welcome; others permitted limited play for which advance arrangements should be made. GREEN FEES: Weekdays, $2.50; Saturdays, Sundays, and holidays, $3.75 per day. CADDIE FEES: $1.80 per round. GOLF CLUB RENTALS: $1 per day. GOLF CART RENTALS: 40¢ per day. MOTORIZED GOLF CART RENTALS: Not available. LESSONS: $2.50 per hour. CLUBHOUSE FACILITIES: Restaurant and bar available as well as facilities of Schloss Hotel Kronberg. RECOMMENDED ACCOMMODATIONS: Schloss Hotel Kronberg.

Hamburger Golf Club

LOCATION: Hamburg-Blankenese (9 miles from city limits of Hamburg by taxi). COURSE SIZE: 18 holes; 6,512 yards; par 71. AVAILABILITY TO VISITORS: Only members of other golf clubs permitted unlimited play. GREEN FEES: Weekdays, $2.25; Saturdays, Sundays, and holidays, $4.25 per day; per week, $15; per month, $30; season (six months), $112. CADDIE FEES: $1 per round. GOLF CLUB

Fine grooming and excellent condition of Hamburger Golf Club fairways are typical.

Shell's Wonderful World of Golf

RENTALS: 75¢ per round. GOLF CART RENTALS: 50¢ per round. MOTOR-
IZED GOLF CART RENTALS: Not available. LESSONS: $1.75 per round.
CLUBHOUSE FACILITIES: Restaurant and bar available. RECOMMENDED
ACCOMMODATIONS: Hamburg-Blankenese: Park Hotel Johannesburg,
Hotel Pension Behrmann, Faehrhause Wittenbergen, Pension am
Falkenstein, Wedel Motel Ruland. Hamburg: Hotel Vierjahrzeiten,
Hotel Atlantic, Hotel Reichshof.

Hamburger Land und Golf-Club in der Lueneburger Heide

LOCATION: Post Eddelsen, Hamburg-Harburg (16 miles from the
city limits of Hamburg by taxi). COURSE SIZE: 18 holes; 6,370 yards;
par 74. AVAILABILITY TO VISITORS: Visitors permitted limited play; inquire ahead. GREEN FEES: Weekdays, $2; Saturdays, Sundays, and
holidays, $3.75 per day; per week, $11.25; per month, $30. CADDIE
FEES: $1 per round. GOLF CLUB RENTALS: Not available. GOLF CART
RENTALS: Not available. MOTORIZED GOLF CART RENTALS: Not available. LESSONS: $2 per hour. CLUBHOUSE FACILITIES: Restaurant and
bar available. RECOMMENDED ACCOMMODATIONS: Krowinkel's Hotel
(near course). Bendesdorf bei Hamburg: Hotel Meinsbur. Karoxbos-
tel: Hotel Derboven.

Krefelder Golf Club

LOCATION: Krefeld-Linn (4 miles from Krefeld by taxi). COURSE
SIZE: 18 holes; 6,419 yards; par 73. AVAILABILITY TO VISITORS: Visitors welcome. GREEN FEES: Weekdays, $2; Saturdays, Sundays, and
holidays, $3.75 per day; per week, $10; per month, $30. CADDIE FEES:
$1 per round. GOLF CLUB RENTALS: 90¢ per round. GOLF CART
RENTALS: 40¢ per round. MOTORIZED GOLF CART RENTALS: Not available. LESSONS: $2.50 per hour. CLUBHOUSE FACILITIES: Restaurant
and bar available. RECOMMENDED ACCOMMODATIONS: Hotel Krefelder
Hof, Hotel Haus Schucht, Hotel Romana, Hotel Stadt Geldern, Hotel
Runte, Hotel Gompertz.

Land und Golfclub Düsseldorf

LOCATION: Hubbelrath (about 7-mile drive from Düsseldorf; taxi
is about $3 each way). COURSE SIZE: 18 holes; regulation length; par
73. AVAILABILITY TO VISITORS: Welcome every day. Only on the oc-

casion of matches is the course closed to visitors. Reservations are necessary for weekend play. GREEN FEES: Weekdays, $2.50; weekends and holidays, $3.75 per day. CADDIE FEES: $1.25-$1.50 per round. GOLF CLUB RENTALS: Not available. GOLF CART RENTALS: Not available. MOTORIZED GOLF CART RENTALS: Not available. LESSONS: $2.50 per hour. CLUBHOUSE FACILITIES: Lockers, showers, bar, dining room, outdoor pool. The restaurant is closed Mondays. RECOMMENDED ACCOMMODATIONS: Düsseldorf: Breidenbacherhof, Parkhotel, Gaylord, Savoy, Haus Munch, Atlantik, and Esplanade.

Lubeck-Travemünder Golf Club

LOCATION: Travemünde (1½-hour drive from Hamburg). COURSE SIZE: 9 holes; 3,106 yards; par 36. AVAILABILITY TO VISITORS: Visitors welcome. GREEN FEES: Weekdays, $2.50; Saturdays, Sundays, and holidays, $3.75 per day; per week, $15. CADDIE FEES: $1 per 18-hole round. GOLF CLUB RENTALS: $1 per 18-hole round. GOLF CART RENTALS: 35¢ each 9 holes. MOTORIZED GOLF CART RENTALS: Not available. LESSONS: Two professionals available: $3.50 or $2 for 50 minutes. CLUBHOUSE FACILITIES: Restaurant and bar available. RECOMMENDED ACCOMMODATIONS: Travemünde: Golf Hotel, Ostee-Kurhof, Kurhaus Pension Sonnenklause.

Marienburger Golf Club

LOCATION: Militaerringstrasse, Cologne-Marienburg (3 miles from city limits of Cologne). COURSE SIZE: 9 holes; 3,180 yards; par 37. AVAILABILITY TO VISITORS: Visitors welcome. GREEN FEES: Weekdays, $1.25; Saturdays, Sundays, and holidays, $2.50 per day. CADDIE FEES: 65¢ each 9 holes. GOLF CLUB RENTALS: 25¢ per day. GOLF CART RENTALS: 25¢ per day. MOTORIZED GOLF CART RENTALS: Not available. LESSONS: $1.75 per hour. CLUBHOUSE FACILITIES: Restaurant and bar available. RECOMMENDED ACCOMMODATIONS: Cologne-Marienburg: Hotel Bellevue. Cologne: Excelsior Hotel Ernst, Dom Hotel.

Muenchener Golf Club

LOCATION: Munich 25, Zentrallaendstrasse 40 (9-hole course), and Strasslach, 3 miles from town (18 holes). COURSE SIZE: 9 holes; 2,850 yards; par 35. 18 holes; 6,500 yards; par 74. AVAILABILITY TO

VISITORS: Visitors welcome. GREEN FEES: Weekdays, $2.50; Saturdays, Sundays, and holidays, $3.75 per day. CADDIE FEES: $1.25 for 9 holes; $1.50 for 18 holes. GOLF CLUB RENTALS: 50¢ per day. GOLF CART RENTALS: 25¢ per day. MOTORIZED GOLF CART RENTALS: Not available. LESSONS: Two professionals available: $2.50 per hour. CLUBHOUSE FACILITIES: Restaurant and bar available in each clubhouse. RECOMMENDED ACCOMMODATIONS: Hotel Vier Jahrzeiten, Hotel Bayerischer Hof, Hotel Continental, Hotel Regina Palast.

Niederrheinischer Golf Club

LOCATION: Duisburg-Bucholz (5 miles from the city limits of Duisburg by taxi). COURSE SIZE: 9 holes; 3,285 yards; par 36. AVAILABILITY TO VISITORS: Visitors welcome. GREEN FEES: Weekdays, $1.90; Saturdays, Sundays, and holidays, $3.75 per day. CADDIE FEES: $1.50 per 9-hole round. GOLF CLUB RENTALS: Available. GOLF CART RENTALS: Available. MOTORIZED GOLF CART RENTALS: Not available. LESSONS: Not available. CLUBHOUSE FACILITIES: Restaurant and bar available. RECOMMENDED ACCOMMODATIONS: Duisburg: Hotel Intertouring, Hotel Prince Regent, Hotel Duisburger Hof, Angermund, Hotel Haus Litzbruck.

Tergernseer Golf Club Bad Wiessee

LOCATION: Bad Wiessee (1 mile from town by taxi). COURSE SIZE: 18 holes; 5,653 yards; par 69. AVAILABILITY TO VISITORS: Visitors welcome. GREEN FEES: Weekdays, $2; Saturdays, Sundays, and holidays, $3.75 per day; per week, $17.50. CADDIE FEES: $1.50 per round. GOLF CLUB RENTALS: Not available. GOLF CART RENTALS: 20¢ per round. MOTORIZED GOLF CART RENTALS: Not available. LESSONS: $3 per hour. CLUBHOUSE FACILITIES: Restaurant and bar. RECOMMENDED ACCOMMODATIONS: Bad Wiessee: Werner's Kurhotel Eden. Rottach-Egern: Hotel Bachmair am See.

Wansee Golf Course

LOCATION: Special Services Division, U.S. Forces Europe (10 miles from the center of West Berlin by taxi). COURSE SIZE: 18 holes; 6,940 yards; par 70. AVAILABILITY TO VISITORS: Visitors permitted limited play; inquire ahead. GREEN FEES: Daily, $5; for officers, $1.50

Golf course on the grounds of a private castle near Kronberg.

weekdays, $2.50 per day Saturdays, Sundays, and holidays. CADDIE FEES: Not available. GOLF CLUB RENTALS: 25¢ per day. GOLF CART RENTALS: 25¢ per day. MOTORIZED GOLF CART RENTALS: Not available. LESSONS: $5 per hour; for military, $2 per hour. CLUBHOUSE FACILITIES: Restaurant and bar available. RECOMMENDED ACCOMMODATIONS: Numerous choices in Berlin.

Wiesbadener Golf-Club

LOCATION: Wiesbaden (15 minutes by taxi from the city; bus transportation available from main post office). COURSE SIZE: 9 holes; 2,882 yards; par 35. AVAILABILITY TO VISITORS: Visitors welcome at all times. GREEN FEES: Weekdays, $2; Saturdays, Sundays, and holidays, $3 per day. CADDIE FEES: 75¢ per hour. GOLF CLUB RENTALS: Not available. GOLF CART RENTALS: Not available. MOTORIZED GOLF CART RENTALS: Not available. LESSONS: $2 per 50 minutes. CLUBHOUSE FACILITIES: Restaurant and bar available, closed on Mondays. RECOMMENDED ACCOMMODATIONS: Hotel Rose, Hotel Schwarzer Bock, Hotel Nassauer Hof, Taunushotel, Hotel Blum.

Greece

At Athens' Elliniko Airport, the traveling golfer will be within a good tee shot of the Glyfada Golf Club, the first and only 18-hole course in Greece.

The Glyfada course is excellent by the finest standards. The course is enhanced by fine imported topsoil from which sprout thick green fairways and fertile, contoured greens. The fairways are well defined by a combination of new and old pines, and 17 of the 18 greens have traps at the right front corner, so slicers beware. For a tip on putting, keep in mind that the greens break away from the mountains toward the Aegean Sea—then watch the score improve.

Fifteen miles north of Athens is the Hellenic Golf Club, the only other course in Greece. It is a small 9-hole course that offers a convenient retreat from business or tourist travel and a place for the golfer to sharpen his game. As at Glyfada, visitors are always welcome, and the hospitality is excellent.

SEASON: All year round.

HOW TO GET THERE: By Pan Am Jet Clipper to Rome, then by Olympic Airways only 1¾ hours to Athens; or 2 hours from Beirut via Middle East Airlines. By ship from New York, 12 to 18 days.

GOLF EQUIPMENT: American equipment available at reasonable prices.

LANGUAGE: Greek; English and French are largely understood and spoken.

TIME: Seven hours later than U.S. Eastern Standard Time.

Glyfada Golf Club

LOCATION: Elliniko Airport, Athens (short ride by car, taxi from town). COURSE SIZE: 18 holes; 6,715 yards; par 72. AVAILABILITY TO

54

Typically well-trapped green at Glyfada—17 greens have traps on right front edge.

VISITORS: Visitors welcome. GOLF CART RENTALS: Available. MOTORIZED GOLF CART RENTALS: Not available. CLUBHOUSE FACILITIES: Restaurant and bar available. RECOMMENDED ACCOMMODATIONS: Athens: Grande-Bretagne, Athens Hilton, Amalia, Athénée Palace, King George, and the King's Palace.

Hellenic Golf Club

LOCATION: Athens (about 15 miles north of the city by taxi). COURSE SIZE: 9 holes; 2,888 yards; par 35. AVAILABILITY TO VISITORS: Visitors welcome. GREEN FEES: Per day, $1; per week, $4; two weeks, $7; per month, $10; season, $20. CADDIE FEES: About $1 per 9-hole round. GOLF CLUB RENTALS: $1 per day. GOLF CART RENTALS: $1 per day. MOTORIZED GOLF CART RENTALS: Not available. LESSONS: $1.20 per hour. CLUBHOUSE FACILITIES: Restaurant and bar available. RECOMMENDED ACCOMMODATIONS: See above listing.

Ireland

When a golfer comes to play in Ireland, he had better be ready with his long irons. The courses are really not extraordinarily difficult, but there is a strange phenomenon out here called wind. Strange because, in addition to being strong, it is nearly always in the golfer's face.

The courses themselves are naturally scenic, and there is very little evidence of any tampering by man. In many cases it seems that the flags have been placed at random about the landscape, so well adapted is the design to the terrain. Although the courses are usually waterless, they contain the most formidable hazards ever imagined. A golfer has not truly suffered until forced to hack and stub his way through foot-high roughs, or heather, or gorse.

Many of the golf courses that are available to the traveling golfer are internationally famous. Of course the best known is Portmarnock, which is referred to as the "St. Andrews of Ireland." Playing at this course alone is worth a trip to the Emerald Isle. But there are 200 more to choose from, and they are well distributed about the countryside.

One is never more than a few miles from a starting time, particularly when near the shore. A circle tour along the Irish coast offers at least 20 first-class courses along the way.

And the rates seem to date from the days of the first courses: from 70¢ to no higher than $2.80 per round. Caddies, carts, and clubs are also available at a good price, and if you're staying for any length of time, most clubs offer reduced weekly and monthly rates.

Believe it or not, ladies are welcome to play seven days a week, except at several courses around Dublin. It is wise, however, for gentlemen and ladies alike to inquire of the club secretary before making plans to play. Ireland and its people will certainly welcome a wandering golfer. The courses? Well, good luck.

SEASON: March to November.

HOW TO GET THERE: By Pan American Jet Clipper to Shannon, about 6 hours from New York. Shuttle service from Shannon Airport to Dublin. By ship, about 5 days.

GOLF EQUIPMENT: American equipment available.

LANGUAGE: English.

TIME: When it is noon Eastern Standard Time in New York, it is 5 P.M. in Ireland.

Ballybunion Golf Club

LOCATION: Ballybunion (about 10 miles from the station at Listowel by bus). COURSE SIZE: 18 holes; 7,085 yards; par 75. AVAILABILITY TO VISITORS: Visitors welcome. GREEN FEES: Weekdays, 75¢; weekends, $1.10 per day; per week, $5. CADDIE FEES: Caddies available. GOLF CART RENTALS: Available. MOTORIZED GOLF CART RENTALS: Not available. LESSONS: Available. CLUBHOUSE FACILITIES: Restaurant and bar. RECOMMENDED ACCOMMODATIONS: Hotel Imperial, Marine Hotel, Castle Hotel.

Bundoran Golf Club

LOCATION: Bundoran (County Donegal, on the Atlantic coast). COURSE SIZE: 18 holes; 6,360 yards; par 72. AVAILABILITY TO VISITORS: Visitors welcome. GREEN FEES: Daily, 50¢; per week, $3; two weeks, $4.25. CADDIE FEES: Caddies available. GOLF CART RENTALS: Available. MOTORIZED GOLF CART RENTALS: Not available. LESSONS: Available. CLUBHOUSE FACILITIES: Restaurant and bar. RECOMMENDED ACCOMMODATIONS: Hotel Atlantic, Central Hotel, Hotel G.N.R.

County Louth Golf Club

LOCATION: Baltray, County Louth (4 miles from the Drogheda rail station by bus). COURSE SIZE: 18 holes; 6,605 yards; par 74. AVAILABILITY TO VISITORS: Visitors welcome. GREEN FEES: Weekdays, 70¢; weekends, $1 per day. CADDIE FEES: Caddies available. MOTORIZED GOLF CART RENTALS: Not available. LESSONS: Available. CLUBHOUSE FACILITIES: Restaurant and bar. RECOMMENDED ACCOMMODATIONS: The club offers attractive accommodations, but space is limited; inquire in advance.

County Sligo Golf Club

LOCATION: Rosses Point, County Sligo (5 miles from Sligo railroad station). COURSE SIZE: 18 holes; 6,372 yards; par 72. AVAILABILITY TO VISITORS: Visitors welcome. GREEN FEES: $1.40 per round; per week, $5.60; two weeks, $8.40; per month, $12.60. CADDIE FEES: $1.40 per round, single. GOLF CLUB RENTALS: Limited number available. GOLF CART RENTALS: 20¢ per round. MOTORIZED GOLF CART RENTALS: Not available. LESSONS: Available by appointment, 70¢ per half hour. CLUBHOUSE FACILITIES: Restaurant and bar available to guests. RECOMMENDED ACCOMMODATIONS: Rosses Point (near course): Yeats County Hotel. Sligo: Great Southern Hotel, Imperial Hotel, Grand Hotel.

Killarney Golf and Fishing Club

LOCATION: Mahony's Point, Killarney, County Kerry (3 miles from Killarney; 84 miles from Shannon Airport). COURSE SIZE: 18 holes; 6,353 yards; par 72. AVAILABILITY TO VISITORS: Visitors welcome. GREEN FEES: $1.40 per day if introduced by a member or as a guest of one of the hotels mentioned below; otherwise, $1.60 per day; per week, $7. CADDIE FEES: 80¢ per round. GOLF CLUB RENTALS: 75¢ per round. GOLF CART RENTALS: Available. MOTORIZED GOLF CART RENTALS: Not available. LESSONS: Not available. CLUBHOUSE FACILITIES: Restaurant and bar available to guests. RECOMMENDED ACCOMMODATIONS: The Lake Hotel, Southern Hotel, International Hotel, The Castlerosse, The Muckross Hotel, The Cathernane Hotel, the Europe Hotel, The Arbutus Hotel, the Glebe Hotel.

Lahinch Golf Club

LOCATION: Lahinch, County Clare (25 miles from Shannon Airport). COURSE SIZE: 18 holes; 6,434 yards; par 71. AVAILABILITY TO VISITORS: Visitors welcome. GREEN FEES: Per round, $1.50; per week, $9; season, $18. CADDIE FEES: 75¢ to $1.50 per round, single, depending on caddie. GOLF CLUB RENTALS: 70¢ per round. GOLF CART RENTALS: Available. MOTORIZED GOLF CART RENTALS: Not available. LESSONS: Available by appointment; 75¢ per half hour. CLUBHOUSE FACILITIES: Restaurant and bar available to guests. RECOMMENDED

Bord Failte Photo

Killarney Golf and Fishing Club, County Kerry.

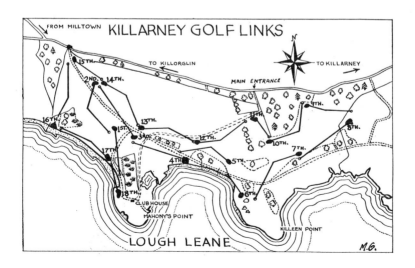

Clubhouse at Portmarnock, County Dublin.

ACCOMMODATIONS: Hotel Aberdeen, Hotel Claremont, Vaughan's Hotel, St. Anthony's Hotel, Santa Maria Hotel, The Dell Hotel, The Falls Hotel.

Portmarnock Golf Club

LOCATION: Portmarnock, County Dublin (9 miles from Dublin). COURSE SIZE: 18 holes; 7,093 yards; par 75. AVAILABILITY TO VISITORS: Visitors welcome; ladies are restricted to weekdays. GREEN FEES: Weekdays, $2.10; Saturdays and Sundays, $4.20 per day; one week, $14. CADDIE FEES: $1.10 per round, single. GOLF CLUB RENTALS: $1.40 per round. GOLF CART RENTALS: 20¢ per round. MOTORIZED GOLF CART RENTALS: Not available. LESSONS: Available by appointment, $1.40 per round. CLUBHOUSE FACILITIES: Restaurant and bar available to guests. RECOMMENDED ACCOMMODATIONS: Portmarnock: Country Club Hotel. Sutton: Marine Hotel. Malahide: Grand Hotel. Dublin: Dublin Inter-Continental, Royal Hibernian, Gresham, Shelbourne, Jury's, and the Russell Hotel.

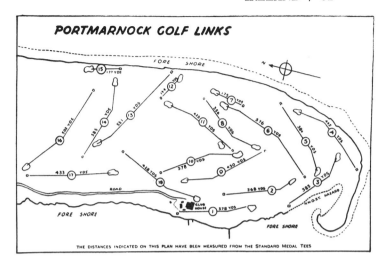

PORTMARNOCK GOLF LINKS

THE DISTANCES INDICATED ON THIS PLAN HAVE BEEN MEASURED FROM THE STANDARD MEDAL TEES

Animal lawn mowers keep the rough in trim at a country club. In the background is one of the inlets to Cork Harbor.

Joe McCarthy

Rosapenna Golf Club

LOCATION: Rosapenna, County Donegal (on the northwest coast). COURSE SIZE: 18 holes; 6,044 yards; par 70. AVAILABILITY TO VISITORS: Visitors welcome. GREEN FEES: Daily, $1.25; per week, $3 if staying at Rosapenna Hotel. CADDIE FEES: $1 per round. GOLF CART RENTALS: 25¢ per day. MOTORIZED GOLF CART RENTALS: Not available. LESSONS: $1 per half hour. CLUBHOUSE FACILITIES: Restaurant and bar available. RECOMMENDED ACCOMMODATIONS: Rosapenna Hotel.

Royal Dublin Golf Club

LOCATION: Dollymount (3 miles from Dublin). COURSE SIZE: 18 holes; 6,657 yards; par 73. AVAILABILITY TO VISITORS: Visitors welcome. GREEN FEES: Weekdays, $2.10; Saturdays, Sundays, and holidays, $4.20 per day. CADDIE FEES: $1.25 per round. GOLF CLUB RENTALS: Not available. GOLF CART RENTALS: 35¢ per round. MOTORIZED GOLF CART RENTALS: Not available. LESSONS: Available by appointment, $3 per half hour. CLUBHOUSE FACILITIES: Restaurant and bar available to guests. RECOMMENDED ACCOMMODATIONS: Within a short distance of all Dublin hotels; see Portmarnock.

Italy

Italians have been so busy producing artists, sculptors, racing drivers, and movie stars that they did not really get around to golf courses until after World War II.

Today, in an effort to capture a greater share of the golfing market, they are developing a number of fine golf resorts as well as remodeling some of the older ones. Most of the thirty-three courses now in operation are north of Rome, and are within reasonable distance of the larger cities and popular tourist centers. Such an arrangement makes it ideal to combine golf with a family vacation or a business trip.

There are no public courses anywhere in Italy, but the touring golfer will find he can play anywhere without red tape. The usual letter of introduction from the golfer's home club will suffice at all stops. If this is not available, check with Pan American's downtown offices in Rome and Milan for assistance.

About thirty minutes north of Rome there is an excellent course at Olgiata that needs no introduction. The 18-hole west course here was the site for the 1964 World Amateur Golf Trophy, aud it has some of the toughest holes in memory: six of the par fours approach the legal limit of 470 yards. The clubhouse is a pleasant blend of modern and historical, and provides all the facilities expected of the top clubs in the U.S. Olgiata is also the focal point of a sophisticated real-estate development in which single lots on the fringe of the course go for an incredible $30,000.

Even closer to Rome, and accessible by streetcar, is the Circolo del Golf di Roma at Acquasanta. The course is immaculately maintained, and the greens can be rated among the best in the world; however, take note that the course has no watering system and becomes quite dry in summer. The best time for play is September through June.

In Venice one can glide to golf in a gondola and play through the ruins of an old fortress overlooking the Adriatic. At Lake Como the Villa d'Este course is picturesque enough to be the subject of a thousand postcards, and is a frequent playground for European royalty. Even on St. Helena island the traveling golfer can play a nine-hole course while his wife sees the relics of Napoleon's exile.

Green fees in Italy are not as low as those in Britain, Portugal, and other bargain areas, but they are substantially below U.S. rates. For weekday play, fees run from $2 to $5, with weekends a dollar or two higher. Caddies are becoming scarce in Italy, as most young boys are now attracted to the higher-paying jobs in the big cities. Fees vary sharply—from 90¢ to about $3—and the bag bearers, like most Italian boys, look for a generous tip. The last time I played in Italy, the caddie tried to cut three holes out of the round, collect for the full 18, and disappear over the hill. And on blind shots, keep the caddie in sight, or the ball may get "lost" in his pocket.

SEASON: All year depending on locality.

HOW TO GET THERE: By Pan American Jet Clipper, 8 hours direct from New York; service also via Paris or Lisbon, Barcelona, and Nice. By ship to Venice, Naples, or Genoa, 8 to 14 days.

GOLF EQUIPMENT: American equipment available at reasonable prices.

LANGUAGE: Italian; English is understood in Rome and other principal cities.

TIME: Six hours later than U.S. Eastern Standard Time.

Barlassina Country Club

LOCATION: Birago di Camnago, Milan (½ hour by car from Milan or Como). COURSE SIZE: 18 holes; 6,652 yards; par 71. AVAILABILITY TO VISITORS: Visitors permitted limited play; inquire ahead. GREEN FEES: Weekdays, $4; Saturdays and Sundays, $6 per day. CADDIE FEES: $2.40 per 9-hole round; $4 per 18-hole round. GOLF CLUB RENTALS: Not available. GOLF CART RENTALS: 80¢ per day. MOTORIZED GOLF CART RENTALS: Not available. LESSONS: $4 per hour. CLUBHOUSE FACILITIES: Bar, restaurant, tennis, swimming pool, and changing rooms. RECOMMENDED ACCOMMODATIONS: Saveso: Hotel Calypso.

Circolo del Golf dell'Ugolino

LOCATION: Grassino, Florence (10 minutes by car from Florence). COURSE SIZE: 18 holes; 5,919 yards; par 72. AVAILABILITY TO VISITORS:

Visitors welcome. GREEN FEES: Weekdays, $3.20; Saturdays and Sundays, $4.80 per day; per month, $48. CADDIE FEES: 9 holes, $2.40; 18 holes, $4. GOLF CLUB RENTALS: Available. GOLF CART RENTALS: Not available. MOTORIZED GOLF CART RENTALS: Not available. LESSONS: $3.20 per hour. CLUBHOUSE FACILITIES: Bar, restaurant, tennis, swimming pool, lockers. RECOMMENDED ACCOMMODATIONS: Florence: Excelsior, Carlton, Villa la Massa, Grand, Villa Medici, Baglioni Palace, Kraft, Anglo-Americano, Astoria, Majestic, Roma, Savoy, or one of the many fine guest houses in the city.

Circolo del Golf di Roma

LOCATION: Acquasanta, Rome (5 miles from the center of Rome by taxi or street car). COURSE SIZE: 18 holes; 6,458 yards; par 71. AVAILABILITY TO VISITORS: Visitors permitted limited play; inquire ahead. Course closed Mondays. GREEN FEES: Weekdays, $3.20; Saturdays and Sundays, $4.80 per day; per month, $40. CADDIE FEES: $3 per 18-hole round. GOLF CLUB RENTALS: $2.50 per day. GOLF CART RENTALS: 50¢ per day. MOTORIZED GOLF CART RENTALS: Not available. LESSONS: $3.25 per hour. CLUBHOUSE FACILITIES: Restaurant, bar, swimming pool, tennis courts, and driving range. RECOMMENDED ACCOMMODATIONS: Hotel de la Ville, Hotel Continentale, Eden Hotel, Hotel Hassler, Palazzo Ambasciatori.

Circolo Golf di Bogliaco

LOCATION: Lago di Garda, Brescia (5 miles from the Gardone Riviera by car, or 26½ miles from Brescia). COURSE SIZE: 9 holes; 2,679 yards; par 37. AVAILABILITY TO VISITORS: Visitors permitted limited play; inquire ahead. GREEN FEES: $2.40 per day. CADDIE FEES: $1.35 per 9-hole round. GOLF CLUB RENTALS: Not available. GOLF CART RENTALS: Not available. MOTORIZED GOLF CART RENTALS: Not available. LESSONS: $2.40 per hour. CLUBHOUSE FACILITIES: Restaurant and bar. RECOMMENDED ACCOMMODATIONS: Gardone Riviera: Grand Hotel Fasano, Savoy Palace Hotel, Astoria Hotel.

Circolo Golf Lido di Venezia

LOCATION: Alberoni, Venice (at the west end of the Lido). COURSE SIZE: 18 holes; 6,080 yards; par 72. AVAILABILITY TO VISITORS:

Visitors welcome. GREEN FEES: Weekdays, $4.80; Sundays, $6.40; per week, $28.80. CADDIE FEES: $1.60 for 9 holes; $2.65 for 18 holes. GOLF CLUB RENTALS: Not available. GOLF CART RENTALS: Available. MOTORIZED GOLF CART RENTALS: Not available. LESSONS: $4.80 per hour. CLUBHOUSE FACILITIES: Restaurant, bar, and bathing establishment (near 14th hole). RECOMMENDED ACCOMMODATIONS: Venice: Gritti Palace, Danielli, Grand, Europa, Regina, Excelsior Palace.

Circolo Golf Olgiata

LOCATION: Rome (11 miles from the city limits by taxi on the Via Cassia). COURSE SIZE: West: 18 holes; 6,247 yards; par 72. East: 9 holes; 3,108 yards; par 36. AVAILABILITY TO VISITORS: Visitors welcome. GREEN FEES: Weekdays, $4; Saturdays and Sundays, $8; two weeks, $42; per month, $64. CADDIE FEES: $1-$1.60 for 9 holes; $2-$2.90 for 18 holes, depending upon caddie. GOLF CLUB RENTALS: Not available. GOLF CART RENTALS: 65¢ per day. MOTORIZED GOLF CART RENTALS: Not available. LESSONS: $3.20 per half hour; $5 per hour. CLUBHOUSE FACILITIES: Restaurant, bar, and swimming pool. RECOMMENDED ACCOMMODATIONS: Bela Motel (on course).

Circolo Golf Sestriere

LOCATION: Sestriere, Torino (located in the center of town). COURSE SIZE: 18 holes; 5,676 yards; par 69. AVAILABILITY TO VISITORS: Visitors welcome. GREEN FEES: Weekdays, $3.75; Saturdays and Sundays, $4 per day; per week, $16; per month, $48. CADDIE FEES: 9 holes, $1.90; 18 holes, $3.20. GOLF CLUB RENTALS: Not available. GOLF CART RENTALS: Not available. MOTORIZED GOLF CART RENTALS: Not available. LESSONS: $4 per hour. CLUBHOUSE FACILITIES: Restaurant, bar, tennis, and swimming pool. RECOMMENDED ACCOMMODATIONS: Hotel Principi di Piemonti, Hotel La Torre.

Courmayeur Golf Club

LOCATION: 2 miles from Courmayeur. COURSE SIZE: 9 holes. AVAILABILITY TO VISITORS: Visitors welcome. GREEN FEES: Weekdays and weekends, $4.80 per day. CADDIE FEES: 9 holes, $1.50. GOLF CLUB RENTALS: Available for rent and purchase; use of equipment free with lessons. Shoes available also. MOTORIZED GOLF CART RENTALS: Not available. LESSONS: $4.80. CLUBHOUSE FACILITIES: Restaurant, bar. RECOMMENDED ACCOMMODATIONS: Hotel Miravalle. All hotels in Courmayeur.

Golf Club Bergamo

LOCATION: Almenno Bartolomeo (8 miles from Bergamo by taxi; 35 miles from Milan). COURSE SIZE: 18 holes; 6,600 yards; par 72. AVAILABILITY TO VISITORS: Visitors welcome. GREEN FEES: Weekdays, $3.20; Saturdays, $4.80; Sundays, $6.40. CADDIE FEES: $4.80 per round. GOLF CLUB RENTALS: Not available. GOLF CART RENTALS: 50¢ per round. MOTORIZED GOLF CART RENTALS: Not available. LESSONS: Per ½ hour, $2.40; per hour, $4. CLUBHOUSE FACILITIES: Restaurant and bar. RECOMMENDED ACCOMMODATIONS: Bergamo: Hotel San Marco, Viale Vittorio Emanuele, Grand Hotel Moderno.

Golf Club Biella "Le Betuelle"

LOCATION: Magnago Biellese (Biella, Vercelli; about 30 miles north of Torino by car). COURSE SIZE: 18 holes; 6,463 yards; par 72. AVAILABILITY TO VISITORS: Members of other clubs only; make arrangements in advance. GREEN FEES: Weekdays, $3.20; Saturdays and Sundays, $6.40 per day; monthly tickets, $64. CADDIE FEES: 9 holes, $1.60; 18 holes, $3.20. GOLF CLUB RENTALS: Not available. GOLF CART RENTALS: 35¢ per day. MOTORIZED GOLF CART RENTALS: Not available. LESSONS: Three professionals available: $3.20 per hour. CLUBHOUSE FACILITIES: Restaurant, bar, and living accommodations. RECOMMENDED ACCOMMODATIONS: Dormy House at course. Biella: Hotel Astoria.

Golf Club Bologna

LOCATION: Bologna (10 minutes by car from town). COURSE SIZE: 18 holes; 6,067 yards; par 70. AVAILABILITY TO VISITORS: Visitors welcome. GREEN FEES: Weekdays, $6.40; Saturdays and Sundays, $8 per day. CADDIE FEES: 9 holes, $1.50; 18 holes, $2.70. GOLF CLUB RENTALS: Available; also shoes. GOLF CART RENTALS: Available. MOTORIZED GOLF CART RENTALS: Not available. LESSONS: $5.60 per hour. CLUBHOUSE FACILITIES: Restaurant, bar, and swimming pool. RECOMMENDED ACCOMMODATIONS: Bazzano: Albergo la Rocca (near course).

Golf Club Compo Carlo Magno

LOCATION: Madonna di Campiglio (55 miles from Trento). COURSE SIZE: 9 holes; 2,775 yards; par 34. AVAILABILITY TO VISITORS: Visitors welcome. GREEN FEES: As hotel guests, $2.40; others, $4.80. CADDIE FEES: 9 holes, $1.20. GOLF CLUB RENTALS: Not available. GOLF CART RENTALS: 90¢. MOTORIZED GOLF CART RENTALS: Not available. LESSONS: $5.20 per hour, but only after July 15. CLUBHOUSE FACILITIES: The Golf Hotel Madonna di Campiglio houses all the facilities.

Golf Club Carezza al Lago (completing renovation at this writing)

LOCATION: Lago Carezza (17 miles from Balzano by car). COURSE SIZE: 18 holes; 5,043 yards; par 69. AVAILABILITY TO VISITORS: Visitors welcome. GREEN FEES: Per day, $2.40; per week, $11.20; two weeks, $19.20; season, $32. CADDIE FEES: 9 holes, 80¢; 18 holes, $1.30. GOLF CLUB RENTALS: Not available. GOLF CART RENTALS: Not available. MOTORIZED GOLF CART RENTALS: Not available. LESSONS: $2.40 per half hour; $4 per hour. CLUBHOUSE FACILITIES: Restaurant and bar available. RECOMMENDED ACCOMMODATIONS: Golf Hotel Carezza al Lago.

Golf Club Carimate Parco

LOCATION: Carimate (10 miles from Como). COURSE SIZE: 18 holes; 5,940 yards; par 70. AVAILABILITY TO VISITORS: Visitors welcome. GREEN FEES: Weekdays, $4.80; weekends, $9.60 per day. CADDIE FEES: 9 holes, $1.28; 18 holes, $2.40. GOLF CLUB RENTALS: Not available. GOLF CART RENTALS: 80¢. MOTORIZED GOLF CART RENTALS: Not available. LESSONS: $4 per hour. CLUBHOUSE FACILITIES: Restaurant, bar, swimming pool, tennis, and horseback riding. RECOMMENDED ACCOMMODATIONS: Como: Barchetta Excelsior, Metropole & Suisse, Villa Flori.

Golf Club Cervinia

LOCATION: Valle d'Aosta (5 minutes by taxi from Cervinia). COURSE SIZE: 9 holes; 2,869 yards; par 35. AVAILABILITY TO VISITORS:

Visitors welcome. GREEN FEES: Per day, $4.80; per week, $20. CADDIE FEES: $2.50 per 9-hole round; $4 per 18-hole round. GOLF CLUB RENTALS: Not available. GOLF CART RENTALS: Not available. MOTORIZED GOLF CART RENTALS: Not available. LESSONS: $4 per hour. CLUBHOUSE FACILITIES: Bar only. RECOMMENDED ACCOMMODATIONS: Grand Hotel Cervinia.

Golf Club Consiglio

LOCATION: Vittorio Veneto (50 miles from Venice; 13 miles from Vittorio Veneto by car). COURSE SIZE: 9 holes; 2,729 yards; par 35. AVAILABILITY TO VISITORS: Visitors welcome. GREEN FEES: Weekdays, $2.40; Saturdays and Sundays, $4 per day. CADDIE FEES: $1.80 for 18 holes. GOLF CLUB RENTALS: Not available. GOLF CART RENTALS: 50¢ per day. MOTORIZED GOLF CART RENTALS: Not available. LESSONS: $1.30 per half hour; $1.90 per hour. CLUBHOUSE FACILITIES: Restaurant and bar available.

Golf Club di Villa Condulmer

LOCATION: Zerman di Mogliano Veneto (9 miles from Venice; 8 miles from Treviso by taxi). COURSE SIZE: 9 holes; 2,822 yards; par 35. AVAILABILITY TO VISITORS: Visitors welcome. GREEN FEES: Weekdays, $2.40; Saturdays and Sundays, $3.20 per day; per week, $14. CADDIE FEES: 9 holes, $1.30; 18 holes, $2.10. GOLF CLUB RENTALS: Available. GOLF CART RENTALS: 50¢ per day. MOTORIZED GOLF CART RENTALS: Not available. LESSONS: $2.40 per half hour. CLUBHOUSE FACILITIES: Restaurant, bar, and driving range. RECOMMENDED ACCOMMODATIONS: Mogliano: Hotel Villa Condulmer (with swimming pool).

Golf Club Euganeo

LOCATION: Galzignano (12 miles from Padua). COURSE SIZE: 18 holes; par 72. AVAILABILITY TO VISITORS: Visitors welcome. GREEN FEES: Weekdays, $4.50; weekends, $6 per day. CADDIE FEES: 18 holes, $1.60; 9 holes, 90¢. GOLF CLUB RENTALS: Available; also shoes. GOLF CART RENTALS: Available. MOTORIZED GOLF CART RENTALS: Not available. LESSONS: $4.50. CLUBHOUSE FACILITIES: Bar, restaurant, tennis, swimming pool. RECOMMENDED ACCOMMODATIONS: Royal Orologio Hotel, Hotel Bristo Buyatrieste (both in Albano Tereme, 3 miles from the club).

Golf Club Fiuggi

LOCATION: Fiuggi Fonte, Frosinone (50 miles south of Rome). COURSE SIZE: 9 holes; 3,226 yards; par 35. AVAILABILITY TO VISITORS: Visitors welcome. GREEN FEES: Weekdays, $2.40; Saturdays and Sundays, $3.20 per day. CADDIE FEES: 9-hole round, $1.60; 18-hole round, $2.40. GOLF CLUB RENTALS: Available; also shoes. GOLF CART RENTALS: Available. MOTORIZED GOLF CART RENTALS: Not available. LESSONS: $2 per half hour. CLUBHOUSE FACILITIES: Restaurant and bar.

Golf Club Garlenda

LOCATION: Albenga (10 miles from Alassio and 25 miles from Savona). COURSE SIZE: 18 holes; 6,600 yards; par 71. AVAILABILITY TO VISITORS: Visitors welcome. GREEN FEES: Weekdays, $3.20; weekends, $4.80 per day. CADDIE FEES: $1.28 for 9 holes; $2.40 for 18 holes. GOLF CLUB RENTALS: Available; also shoes. GOLF CART RENTALS: 80¢. MOTORIZED GOLF CART RENTALS: Not available. LESSONS: $3.20 per hour. CLUBHOUSE FACILITIES: Restaurant, bar, and sleeping lodge. RECOMMENDED ACCOMMODATIONS: Hotel Diana, Hotel Mediterranée, Hotel Spiaggia.

Golf Club Milano

LOCATION: Parco di Monza (4 miles from Monza; 11 miles from Milan by taxi). COURSE SIZE: 18 holes; 6,900 yards; par 72. Also 9-hole course. AVAILABILITY TO VISITORS: Visitors permitted limited play. GREEN FEES: Weekdays, $4.80; Saturdays and Sundays, $6.40 per day. CADDIE FEES: $2.40 and $3.20 per 9-hole round; $3.20 and $4 per 18-hole round. Price depends on caddie. GOLF CLUB RENTALS: Available; shoes also available. GOLF CART RENTALS: Free. MOTORIZED GOLF CART RENTALS: 9 holes, $4.80; 18 holes, $8. LESSONS: $4 per hour. CLUBHOUSE FACILITIES: Restaurant, bar, sauna bath, swimming pool. RECOMMENDED ACCOMMODATIONS: Monza: Hotel de la Ville (on course). Milan: Excelsior Hotel Gallia, Hotel Francia-Europa, Palace, Duomo, Continental, Cavalieri, Principe Savoia.

Golf Club Miramonti

LOCATION: Cortina d'Ampezzo (1 mile from the center of town). COURSE SIZE: 9 holes; 2,297 yards; par 31. AVAILABILITY TO VISITORS: Visitors welcome. GREEN FEES: Per day, $3.20; per week, $19.20; per month, $48.00; season, $60. CADDIE FEES: 9 holes, 80¢; 18 holes, $1.60. GOLF CLUB RENTALS: Available; also shoes. GOLF CART RENTALS: Not available. MOTORIZED GOLF CART RENTALS: Not available. LESSONS: $4 per hour. CLUBHOUSE FACILITIES: Restaurant, bar, and tennis facilities. RECOMMENDED ACCOMMODATIONS: Miramonti, Majestic Hotel, Hotel de la Poste.

Golf Club Piandisole

LOCATION: Premeno-Verbania (2 miles from Lake Maggiore). COURSE SIZE: 9 holes; par 3. AVAILABILITY TO VISITORS: Visitors welcome. GREEN FEES: Weekdays, $3; weekends, $4 per day. CADDIE FEES: $1.30. GOLF CLUB RENTALS: Available; also shoes. GOLF CART RENTALS: 80¢. MOTORIZED GOLF CART RENTALS: Not available. LESSONS: $3.20 per hour. CLUBHOUSE FACILITIES: Bar and restaurant. RECOMMENDED ACCOMMODATIONS: Hotel Majestic, Hotel Montezeda.

Golf Club Punta Ala

LOCATION: Punta Ala (Grosseto; situated 100 yards from the sea). COURSE SIZE: 18 holes; 6,750 yards; par 72. AVAILABILITY TO VISITORS: Visitors welcome. GREEN FEES: $4.50. CADDIE FEES: 18 holes, $3.50; 9 holes, $2.90. GOLF CLUB RENTALS: Available; also shoes. GOLF CART RENTALS: Free. MOTORIZED GOLF CART RENTALS: Available. LESSONS: $3.75. CLUBHOUSE FACILITIES: Bar, restaurant. RECOMMENDED ACCOMMODATIONS: Gallia Palace Hotel, Golf Hotel, Hotel Alleluia.

Golf Club Torino "La Mandria"

LOCATION: Fiano Torinese, Torino. COURSE SIZE: 18 holes; 6,655 yards; par 73. Also additional 9-hole course. AVAILABILITY TO VISITORS:

Visitors permitted limited play; inquire ahead. GREEN FEES: Weekdays, $3.20; Saturdays and Sundays, $4.80 per day. CADDIE FEES: 9 holes, $1.80; 18 holes, $2.90. GOLF CLUB RENTALS: Available; also shoes. GOLF CART RENTALS: Available. MOTORIZED GOLF CART RENTALS: Not available. LESSONS: $4 per hour. CLUBHOUSE FACILITIES: Restaurant, bar, tennis, and swimming pool. RECOMMENDED ACCOMMODATIONS: Albergo Piemonte di Lanzo, Corona, Grossa di Cirie, Hotel Turin, Hotel Ligure, Grand Hotel Ambasciatori, Albergo Principi di Piemonte.

Golf Club Trieste

LOCATION: Trieste (4 miles from the center of town by taxi). COURSE SIZE: 9 holes; 2,887 yards; par 35. AVAILABILITY TO VISITORS: Visitors welcome. GREEN FEES: $4 per day. CADDIE FEES: $2.40 for 18 holes. GOLF CLUB RENTALS: Not available. GOLF CART RENTALS: Not available. MOTORIZED GOLF CART RENTALS: Not available. LESSONS: $2.40 per hour. CLUBHOUSE FACILITIES: Restaurant and bar available. RECOMMENDED ACCOMMODATIONS: Hotel Excelsior Savoia, Grand Hotel de la Villa, Jolly Hotel, Hotel Regina.

Golf Club Varese

LOCATION: Monastero di Luvinate, Varese (38 miles from Milan; 28 miles from Como; 3 miles from the center of Varese by taxi). COURSE SIZE: 18 holes; 6,644 yards; par 72. AVAILABILITY TO VISITORS: Visitors welcome. GREEN FEES: Weekdays, $3.20; Saturdays and Sundays, $6.40 per day. CADDIE FEES: Weekdays, $2.40 per round; Saturdays and Sundays, $3.20 per round. GOLF CLUB RENTALS: Not available. GOLF CART RENTALS: Available. MOTORIZED GOLF CART RENTALS: Not available. LESSONS: $4.80 per hour. CLUBHOUSE FACILITIES: Restaurant and bar available. RECOMMENDED ACCOMMODATIONS: Varese: Palace Hotel, Albergo Hermitage, Pension Moderna, Du Parc Hotel.

Golf Country Club

LOCATION: 5 miles from Verona. COURSE SIZE: 9 holes; par 36. AVAILABILITY TO VISITORS: Visitors welcome. GREEN FEES: Weekdays,

$3.50; weekends, $4.40 per day. CADDIE FEES: 9 holes, 90¢. GOLF CLUB RENTALS: Not available. GOLF CART RENTALS: Available. MOTORIZED GOLF CART RENTALS: Not available.LESSONS: $3.50 per hour. CLUBHOUSE FACILITIES: Restaurant, bar, swimming pool. RECOMMENDED ACCOMMODATIONS: Verona: Grand Hotel, Hotel Due Torri.

Golf di Stresa

LOCATION: Vezzo Sopra Stresa, Novara (5 miles from Stresa by taxi). COURSE SIZE: 9 holes; 2,822 yards; par 35. AVAILABILITY TO VISITORS: Visitors permitted limited play; inquire ahead. GREEN FEES: Weekdays, $4.80; Saturdays and Sundays, $6.40 per day; per week, $32; per month, $96. CADDIE FEES: $2.40 for 18 holes. GOLF CLUB RENTALS: Not available. GOLF CART RENTALS: Available. MOTORIZED GOLF CART RENTALS: Not available. LESSONS: $3.20 per hour. CLUBHOUSE FACILITIES: Restaurant and bar available. RECOMMENDED ACCOMMODATIONS: Alpino: Grand Hotel Alpino, Albergo Panorama Vezzo, Albergo Fioravanti. Stresa: Hotel Regina Palace, Hotel et des Iles Borromees.

Menaggio Cadenabbia Golf Club

LOCATION: Grandola ed Uniti, Como (3 miles from Managgio; 10 miles from Lugano by taxi). COURSE SIZE: 18 holes; 4,461 yards; par 65. AVAILABILITY TO VISITORS: Visitors welcome. GREEN FEES: Weekdays, $2.90; Saturdays and Sundays, $4.20 per day; per week, $16.70; two weeks, $33.40; per month, $42. CADDIE FEES: $1.60 per 9-hole round; $2.90 per 18-hole round. GOLF CLUB RENTALS: Available. GOLF CART RENTALS: Available. MOTORIZED GOLF CART RENTALS: Not available. LESSONS: $4 per hour. CLUBHOUSE FACILITIES: Restaurant and bar available. RECOMMENDED ACCOMMODATIONS: Menaggio: Grand Hotel Victoria-au-Lac, Grand Hotel Menaggio, Hotel Bellavista, Hotel Loveno, Pension Castello, Pension Adler.

Rapallo Golf Club

LOCATION: Rapallo, Genoa (within city limits of Rapallo). COURSE SIZE: 9 holes; 2,475 yards; par 33. AVAILABILITY TO VISITORS: Visitors welcome. GREEN FEES: Per day, $3.20. CADDIE FEES: 9 holes, $2.40;

Phil Rogers misses one on the narrow fairways at Villa d'Este.

18 holes, $3.20. **GOLF CLUB RENTALS:** Available. **GOLF CART RENTALS:** 50¢ per day. **MOTORIZED GOLF CART RENTALS:** Not available. **LESSONS:** $3.70 per hour. **CLUBHOUSE FACILITIES:** Restaurant, bar, and tennis. **RECOMMENDED ACCOMMODATIONS:** Rapallo: Grand Hotel Bristol,

Clubhouse and 18th green, Villa d'Este.

Grand Hotel Excelsior, Grand Hotel Savoia. Portofino: Hotel Splendido. S. Margherita Ligure: Parc Hotel Suisse, Hotel Miramare.

Villa d'Este Golf Club

LOCATION: Cernobbio-Lago di Como (5 miles from the center of Como by taxi). COURSE SIZE: 18 holes; 6,554 yards; par 70. AVAILABILITY TO VISITORS: Visitors welcome. GREEN FEES: Weekdays, $4.80; Saturdays and Sundays, $8 per day. CADDIE FEES: 9 holes, $2.40; 18 holes, $4. GOLF CLUB RENTALS: Available; also shoes. GOLF CART RENTALS: Available. MOTORIZED GOLF CART RENTALS: Not available. LESSONS: $4 per hour. CLUBHOUSE FACILITIES: Restaurant, bar, swimming pool, tennis courts, and the lake. RECOMMENDED ACCOMMODATIONS: Cernobbio: Grand Hotel Villa d'Este. Como: Hotel Metropole and Suisse, Hotel Bârchetta, Hotel Firenze.

The Netherlands

Any Dutchman will tell you that golf was invented in Holland more than 600 years ago. The Dutch played the game with great wooden cudgels and leather-wrapped wooden balls in churchyards or on frozen lakes, depending on the season. If the weather turned inclement, they would simply move indoors and play in the church nave, a practice somewhat frowned upon today.

Golf facilities in the Netherlands are few but excellent. The size of the country sets a definite limitation on space. Today there are only twenty courses in the country, but the Netherlands Golf Association and the Dutch PGA have been discussing the possibilities of building new courses around airports where there is still some room left.

Most of the courses are flat and not too long; only one 18-hole golf course exceeds 6,500 yards. Most of the others, due to cramped quarters, are under 6,000 yards. But, for the golfer who can belt the long ball, several of the 9-hole courses are long and can provide an interesting round when played twice.

On the courses by the sea, the golfer will find sand dunes dotting many of the fairways. Often these dunes are vast beaches which can require several shots to overcome, or several hundred depending on your temper. At certain times of the year the ball can be buried so deep that it must be declared an unplayable lie. Wind also will affect the player's game considerably on the seaside golf courses, so it is advisable for him to have his caddie choose his club for him, at least at first.

Inland courses in Holland are slightly different from the ones at the seaside. On most of these courses trees serve as obstacles and fairway borders. Greens are small and the rough is cut tight to the putting surface. Screened greens are common, and a golfer can get in trouble with just a slight fade or draw on his ball. Even good golfers agree that an off-line tee shot here insures bogey.

Most of the courses in Holland are located near major cities, so golf can easily be combined with other tourist attractions. Clubs are not usually crowded, and foreign visitors are welcome. There are only 6,000 golfers in the Netherlands, leaving plenty of room for the visiting player.

SEASON: April to October.

HOW TO GET THERE: By Pan Am Jet Clipper, nonstop flights to Amsterdam from New York, 8¾ hours; 1 hour from London. By boat from New York, 7 to 11 days.

GOLF EQUIPMENT: American equipment available at reasonable prices.

LANGUAGE: English is understood and spoken everywhere.

TIME: Six hours later than U.S. Eastern Standard Time.

Amsterdamsche Golf Club

LOCATION: Amsterdam (about 15 minutes by taxi from Amsterdam). COURSE SIZE: 18 holes; 5,678 yards; par 72. AVAILABILITY TO VISITORS: Visitors welcome. GREEN FEES: Weekdays, $2.25; Saturdays and Sundays, $3.00 per day. CADDIE FEES: About $2 per round. MOTORIZED GOLF CARTS: Not available. CLUBHOUSE FACILITIES: Restaurant and bar. RECOMMENDED ACCOMMODATIONS: Amstel Hotel, Amsterdam Hilton, Apollo Hotel.

Domburgsche Golf Club

LOCATION: Domburg (10 miles from Middleburg). COURSE SIZE: 9 holes; 2,551 yards; par 35. AVAILABILITY TO VISITORS: Visitors welcome. GREEN FEES: Weekdays, $1.10; Saturdays and Sundays, $1.40 per day; per week, $5.50; per month, $16.20. CADDIE FEES: 70¢ per 9 holes. MOTORIZED GOLF CARTS: Not available. LESSONS: $1.35 per hour. CLUBHOUSE FACILITIES: Restaurant and bar. RECOMMENDED ACCOMMODATIONS: Badhotel, Hotel Britannia.

Eindhovensche Golf Club

LOCATION: Eindhoven (5 miles from center of Eindhoven). COURSE SIZE: 18 holes; 6,567 yards; par 74. AVAILABILITY TO VISITORS: Visitors welcome on weekdays. GREEN FEES: Weekdays, $2; Saturdays and Sundays, $4 per day; per week, $12. CADDIE FEES: About 80¢ per round. MOTORIZED GOLF CARTS: Not available. LESSONS: $2 per hour. CLUBHOUSE FACILITIES: Restaurant and bar. RECOMMENDED ACCOMMODATIONS: Eindhoven: Hotel Parkzicht, Motel Jagerhorst Leende.

Golf Club de Dommel

LOCATION: s'Hertogenbosch (about 6 miles from town). COURSE SIZE: 9 holes; 3,075 yards; par 36. AVAILABILITY TO VISITORS: Visitors welcome. GREEN FEES: Weekdays, $1; Saturdays and Sundays, $1.20 per day; per week, $4; per month, $12. CADDIE FEES: 45¢ per 9 holes. MOTORIZED GOLF CARTS: Not available. LESSONS: $2 per hour. CLUBHOUSE FACILITIES: Restaurant and bar. RECOMMENDED ACCOMMODATIONS: Orange Hotel, Hotel Royal.

Golf en Country Club Wittem

LOCATION: Wittem (near Maastricht on the German border). COURSE SIZE: 9 holes; 3,255 yards; par 37. AVAILABILITY TO VISITORS: Visitors welcome. GREEN FEES: Weekdays, $1.35; Saturdays and Sundays, $2.30 per day; per week, $5.50; per month, $16. CADDIE FEES: 50¢ per 9 holes. MOTORIZED GOLF CARTS: Not available. LESSONS: $1.60 per lesson. CLUBHOUSE FACILITIES: Restaurant and bar. RECOMMENDED ACCOMMODATIONS: Hotel Prinses Juliana Valkenburg, Hotel Kasteel Neubourg Gulpen, Hotel du Casque, Hotel Kasteel Wittem.

Haagsche Golf en Country Club

LOCATION: Wassemaar (4 miles from Den Haag). COURSE SIZE: 18 holes; 6,014 yards; par 73. AVAILABILITY TO VISITORS: Visitors welcome. GREEN FEES: Weekdays, $2.80; Saturdays and Sundays, $5.60 per day; weekends, $8.25. CADDIE FEES: $1.25 per round. GOLF CLUB RENTALS: Available. GOLF CART RENTALS: 50¢ per round. MOTORIZED GOLF CARTS: Not available. LESSONS: $2.20 per half hour. CLUBHOUSE FACILITIES: Restaurant and bar. RECOMMENDED ACCOMMODATIONS: Kasteek Wassenaar and Hotel Des Indes.

Haagsche Golf en Country Club.

Hattemse Golf and Country Club

LOCATION: Hattem (about 60 miles from Amsterdam). COURSE SIZE: 9 holes; 2,766 yards; par 36. AVAILABILITY TO VISITORS: Visitors welcome. GREEN FEES: Weekdays, 80¢; Saturdays and Sundays, $1.10 per day; per week, $4. CADDIE FEES: Caddies not available. GOLF CLUB RENTALS: Not available. GOLF CART RENTALS: Not available. MOTORIZED GOLF CARTS: Not available. CLUBHOUSE FACILITIES: Restaurant and bar. RECOMMENDED ACCOMMODATIONS: Hattem: Blommenstein, Veldig. Zwolle: Hotel Wientjes.

Hilversumsche Golf Club

LOCATION: Hilversum (2 miles from Hilversum; 20 miles from Amsterdam). COURSE SIZE: 18 holes; 6,246 yards; par 74. AVAILABILITY TO VISITORS: Visitors welcome. GREEN FEES: Weekdays, $2.25; Saturdays and Sundays, $4.25 per day; weekends, $7. CADDIE FEES: Very few caddies available. GOLF CART RENTALS: Available. MOTORIZED GOLF CARTS: Not available. LESSONS: $1.90 per hour. CLUBHOUSE FACILITIES: Restaurant and bar. RECOMMENDED ACCOMMODATIONS:

Hotel Heidepark, Hotel Gooiland, Hotel Groot Kievitsdal, Kasteel de Hooge Vuursche.

Kennemer Golf and Country Club

LOCATION: Zandvoort (4 miles from city of Haarlem). COURSE SIZE: 18 holes; 6,223 yards; par 74. AVAILABILITY TO VISITORS: Play is restricted; inquire ahead. GREEN FEES: Weekdays, $2.70; Saturdays and Sundays, $4 per day; per week, $9.50. CADDIE FEES: $1 per round. MOTORIZED GOLF CARTS: Not available. LESSONS: $2 per lesson. CLUBHOUSE FACILITIES: Restaurant and bar. RECOMMENDED ACCOMMODATIONS: Hotel Bouwes.

Keppelse Golf Club

LOCATION: Laag-Keppel (less than a mile from Laag-Keppel). COURSE SIZE: 9 holes; 2,075 yards; par 31. AVAILABILITY TO VISITORS: Visitors welcome. GREEN FEES: Weekdays, 55¢; Saturdays and Sundays, $1.10 per day; per week, $2.70. MOTORIZED GOLF CARTS: Not available. CLUBHOUSE FACILITIES: Not available. RECOMMENDED ACCOMMODATIONS: De Gouden Leeuw, De Gouden Karper.

Noord Nederlands Golf and Country Club de Poll

LOCATION: Groningen (5 miles from Groningen). COURSE SIZE: 9 holes; 2,717 yards; par 36. AVAILABILITY TO VISITORS: Visitors welcome. GREEN FEES: Weekdays, $1.90; Saturdays and Sundays, $2.70 per day; per week, $13.50; per month, $47. CADDIE FEES: 70¢ per 9 holes. MOTORIZED GOLF CARTS: Not available. CLUBHOUSE FACILITIES: Restaurant and bar. RECOMMENDED ACCOMMODATIONS: Familiehotel; limited accommodations for guests in clubhouse.

Noordwijksche Golf Club

LOCATION: Noordwijk (about 17 miles from Amsterdam by car; 25 miles from Rotterdam). COURSE SIZE: 9 holes with 18 tees;. 6,144 yards; par 70. AVAILABILITY TO VISITORS: Visitors welcome. GREEN FEES: Weekdays, $2.20; Saturdays or Sundays, $3.35; weekends, $5;

per week, $13.60; two weeks, $22.25. CADDIE FEES: $1.50 per round. GOLF CLUB RENTALS: 30¢ per round. GOLF CART RENTALS: 30¢ per round. MOTORIZED GOLF CARTS: Not available. LESSONS: $2.20 per hour. CLUBHOUSE FACILITIES: Restaurant and bar. RECOMMENDED ACCOMMODATIONS: Ample accommodations in Amsterdam and Rotterdam.

Rosendaelsche Golf Club

LOCATION: Arnhem (about 3 miles from Arnhem). COURSE SIZE: 9 holes; 2,850 yards; par 36. AVAILABILITY TO VISITORS: Visitors welcome. GREEN FEES: Weekdays, $2; Saturdays and Sundays, $3.15 per day; per week, $10; two weeks, $15; per month, $20. CADDIE FEES: About 75¢ per round. MOTORIZED GOLF CARTS: Not available. LESSONS: $1.60 per lesson. CLUBHOUSE FACILITIES: Restaurant and bar. RECOMMENDED ACCOMMODATIONS: Arnhem: Hotel Haarhuis, Rijnhotel, Hotel Groot Warnsborn, Hotel Bellevue Sonsbeek, Hotel Bosch. Rozendaal: Hotel Rozendaal.

Rotterdamsche Golf Club

LOCATION: Rotterdam (6 miles from Rotterdam). COURSE SIZE: 9 holes; 2,781 yards; par 36. AVAILABILITY TO VISITORS: Visitors welcome. GREEN FEES: Weekdays, $2.25; Saturdays and Sundays, $3.50 per day. CADDIE FEES: $1 per 18 holes. Very few caddies available. GOLF CART RENTALS: 60¢ per 18 holes. MOTORIZED GOLF CARTS: Not available. LESSONS: $1.20 per lesson. CLUBHOUSE FACILITIES: Restaurant and bar. RECOMMENDED ACCOMMODATIONS: Several hotels in the immediate vicinity of the course, as well as accommodations in Rotterdam.

Sallandsche Golf Club de Hoek

LOCATION: Diepenveen (4 miles from Deventer). COURSE SIZE: 9 holes; 3,051 yards; par 36. AVAILABILITY TO VISITORS: Visitors welcome. GREEN FEES: Weekdays, $1.40; Saturdays and Sundays, $2.10 per day; per week, $7; per month, $21. CADDIE FEES: 50¢ per round. GOLF CLUB RENTALS: Not available. GOLF CART RENTALS: Not available. LESSONS: $1.60 per lesson. CLUBHOUSE FACILITIES: Restaurant and bar. RECOMMENDED ACCOMMODATIONS: Deventer: Hotel de Keizerskroon.

Toxandria Golf Club

LOCATION: Breda (5 miles from Breda by car). COURSE SIZE: 18 holes; 5,993 yards; par 74. AVAILABILITY TO VISITORS: Visitors welcome. GREEN FEES: Weekdays, $2; Saturdays and Sundays, $4 per day; per week, $11; per month, $13.50. CADDIE FEES: $1 per round. MOTORIZED GOLF CARTS: Not available. LESSONS: $2 per hour. CLUBHOUSE FACILITIES: Restaurant and bar. RECOMMENDED ACCOMMODATIONS: A few accommodations available in clubhouse. Breda: Motel Mastbosch.

Twentsche Golf Club

LOCATION: Hengelo (2 miles from Hengelo). COURSE SIZE: 9 holes; 3,024 yards; par 36. AVAILABILITY TO VISITORS: Visitors welcome. GREEN FEES: Weekdays, $2; Saturdays and Sundays, $3 per day; per week, $7; per month, $12.50. CADDIE FEES: No caddies available. MOTORIZED GOLF CARTS: Not available. LESSONS: $1.60 per lesson. CLUBHOUSE FACILITIES: Restaurant and bar. RECOMMENDED ACCOMMODATIONS: Delden: Hotel Carelshaven. Hengelo: Amstel Hotel, Hotel Lansink. Enschede: Memphis Hotel.

Utrechtsche Golf Club de Pan

LOCATION: Utrecht (about 4 miles from Utrecht). COURSE SIZE: 18 holes; 6,227 yards; par 73. AVAILABILITY TO VISITORS: Visitors welcome; for weekend play, must be accompanied by a member. GREEN FEES: Weekdays, $2.50; weekends, $4 per day; per week, $5.50; per month, $14.50. CADDIE FEES: Caddies not available. GOLF CART RENTALS: 30¢ per day. MOTORIZED GOLF CARTS: Not available. LESSONS: $2 per lesson. CLUBHOUSE FACILITIES: Restaurant and bar. RECOMMENDED ACCOMMODATIONS: Utrecht: Pays Bas. Zeist: 'tKerkebosh.

Portugal

The traveling golfer who wants to get the most for his money will find Portugal one of the most attractive stopovers in Europe.

Golf is making substantial progress in Portugal; the number of courses operating has nearly doubled—from five to nine—in the last few years. There is a new 9-hole course at Vimiero, and there will be three championship courses in the Algarve, at Penina, Vilamoura, and Vale do Lobo.

The best known course in Portugal is the attractive Estoril Golf Club. Located in the heart of the resort area on Portugal's famous Sun Coast, Estoril is one of the five 18-hole courses in the country. Its par 69 and 5,590 yards are very deceptive, for the course runs through hills, and entire fairways can be inclined in almost any direction. The rough would be a good substitute for a neglected cow pasture. A No. 3 wood or an iron off the tees will save a lot of strokes and a lot of balls.

Estoril gives the golfer little chance to warm up. The fairway of the very first hole—a par 4, 385-yarder—is threaded between stands of menacing pine trees. Only the exceptionally confident—or the foolhardy—ever consider a drive on this one. But the first hole is a duffer's delight compared to the thirteenth, which is probably the toughest on the course. Before a breathtaking view of the sea, the player hits from an elevated tee to a fairway that is barely 50 yards wide. Heavy growth continues to narrow the approach to the green, and constantly shifting winds blowing in from the sea increase the already good chances for disaster.

Although Estoril is more expensive than the other course in the Lisbon area, the Lisbon Sports Club, the visiting golfer will find that he can play this fine course on a weekday, have the services of a well-trained caddie, enjoy a delicious lunch, and still spend less than $5.

Traveling northwest in Portugal, be sure to stop at Espinho to

83

play at the Oporto Golf Club, which is one of the oldest courses in Europe. It has fine facilities and an excellent view of the sea.

Traveling south, to the Algarve, there are three magnificent new championship courses. One—Penina—is already open. This course was used in 1967 on the Shell Wonderful World of Golf series, as the site for the European Ladies Team Championship, the "Port Wine Open," and the International Portuguese Open Championship. In addition to a brand new luxury hotel, the club offers tennis courts, an Olympic-size pool, driving range, putting green, a marvelous view of the ocean, and complete dining and bar facilities. The other two new courses—Vilamoura and Vale do Lobo—are due to be opened during 1968 and promise accommodations of the same caliber as Penina.

SEASON: Year round.

HOW TO GET THERE: By Pan Am Jet Clipper, only 6½ hours (non-stop) from New York to Lisbon, 10¼ hours from Miami, 2¼ hours from Paris, 1 hour from Madrid. By ship, from 6 to 9 days.

GOLF EQUIPMENT: American equipment available at reasonable prices.

LANGUAGE: The official language is Portuguese. In the large cities and tourist areas it is not difficult to find someone who speaks English.

TIME: Six hours later than U.S. Eastern Standard Time.

Club de Golf de Vidago

LOCATION: Vidago (1½ miles from Vidago railroad station; 2 hours by car from Oporto). COURSE SIZE: 9 holes; 2,789 yards; par 33. AVAILABILITY TO VISITORS: Visitors welcome. GREEN FEES: 70¢ per round. CADDIE FEES: 35¢ per round, single. GOLF CLUB RENTALS: Not available. GOLF CART RENTALS: Not available. MOTORIZED GOLF CART RENTALS: Not available. LESSONS: Available. CLUBHOUSE FACILITIES: None. RECOMMENDED ACCOMMODATIONS: Vidago: Hotel Palace, Hotel do Golf, Grande Hotel, Hotel Avelames, Hotel Parque.

Estoril Golf Club

LOCATION: Estoril (2 miles outside of town; 17 miles west of Lisbon by car or electric train plus short taxi ride). COURSE SIZE: 18 holes; 5,590 yards; par 69. AVAILABILITY TO VISITORS: Visitors wel-

Shell's Wonderful World of Golf

The 9th at Estoril: an 8-iron through traffic.

come during the week and according to course availability on week-
ends. GREEN FEES: Weekdays, $2.60; weekends and holidays, $5.25
per day; per week, $14; two weeks, $21; per month, $26; 3 months,
$35; 6 months, $52. CADDIE FEES: $1 per round, single. GOLF CLUB
RENTALS: First class set, $1; limited set, 70¢. GOLF CART RENTALS:
Not available. MOTORIZED GOLF CART RENTALS: Not available. LESSONS:
Available by appointment, $2.50 per half hour. CLUBHOUSE FACILITIES:
Locker room, showers, restaurant, bar, driving range, putting green.
RECOMMENDED ACCOMMODATIONS: Lisbon: Hotel Ritz, Hotel Avenida
Palace, Hotel Fenix, Hotel Eduardo VII, Hotel Embaixador, Hotel

Mundial, Hotel Florida, Hotel Presidente, Hotel Don Carlos and others. Estoril: Estoril Sol, Palacio, Cibra, Atlantico.

Golf do Vimeiro

LOCATION: Vimeiro Spa, Torres Vedras (an hour driving from Lisbon; bus and train service also available). COURSE SIZE: 9 holes; 2,550 yards; par 34. AVAILABILITY TO VISITORS: Visitors welcome. GREEN FEES: $1.75 per day. CADDIE FEES: 35¢ per round. GOLF CLUB RENTALS: 70¢ per round. GOLF CART RENTALS: Not available. MOTORIZED GOLF CART RENTALS: Not available. LESSONS: $1.20 per hour. CLUBHOUSE FACILITIES: Hotel Golf Mar serves as clubhouse and has complete facilities, as well as hunting, fishing, ocean and pool swimming, and a mineral water spa. RECOMMENDED ACCOMMODATIONS: Hotel Golf Mar (provides transfers from Lisbon airport), Hotel das Termas do Vimiero.

Lisbon Sports Club

LOCATION: Carregueira, Belas (10 miles northwest of Lisbon). COURSE SIZE: 9 holes; 2,955 yards; par 35. AVAILABILITY TO VISITORS: Visitors welcome; however, prior arrangements are necessary. GREEN FEES: $1.40 per day. CADDIE FEES: 50¢ per 18-hole round. GOLF CLUB RENTALS: Not available. GOLF CART RENTALS: Not available. MOTORIZED GOLF CART RENTALS: Not available. LESSONS: Not available. CLUBHOUSE FACILITIES: Bar, dining room, children's park, 3 tennis courts, swimming pool. RECOMMENDED ACCOMMODATIONS: See Estoril listing.

Miramar Golf Club

LOCATION: On the outskirts of Miramar, 10 miles south of Oporto. COURSE SIZE: 9 holes; 2,720 yards; par 34. AVAILABILITY TO VISITORS: Visitors welcome. GREEN FEES: Weekdays, $1.05; weekends, $1.75 per day; per week, $8.75. CADDIE FEES: 65¢ per 18-hole round. GOLF CLUB RENTALS: Not available. GOLF CART RENTALS: Not available. MOTORIZED GOLF CART RENTALS: Not available. LESSONS: Available by appointment. CLUBHOUSE FACILITIES: Locker room, showers, restaurant, and bar. RECOMMENDED ACCOMMODATIONS: Praia de Miramar, Hotel Infante de Sages. Oporto: Imperio, Batalha, Albergaria S. João.

Oporto Golf Club

LOCATION: Silvalde, Espinho (on the outskirts of Espinho; 15 miles south of Oporto). COURSE SIZE: 18 holes; 5,323 yards; par 70. AVAILABILITY TO VISITORS: Visitors welcome. GREEN FEES: Weekdays, $1.40; weekends, $2.50 per day; per week, $7; two weeks, $10.50; per month, $13.90; three months, $17.40. Minors, 35¢ per round. CADDIE FEES: 50¢-70¢ per round. GOLF CLUB RENTALS: Not available. GOLF CART RENTALS: Not available. MOTORIZED GOLF CART RENTALS: Not available. LESSONS: Available by appointment. CLUBHOUSE FACILITIES: Locker room, showers, bar, restaurant, and driving range. RECOMMENDED ACCOMMODATIONS: Espino: Hotel de Espinho, Hotel de Granja, Praia de Granja, Hotel de Miramar, Praia de Miramar. Oporto: see above listing.

Penina Golf Course

LOCATION: Montes de Alvor, Algarve (150 miles by air to Faro, they by car 35 miles to the Penina Golf Hotel). COURSE SIZE: 18 holes; 6,889 yards; par 73. AVAILABILITY TO VISITORS: Visitors welcome, but priority of starting time given to guests of the Penina Golf Hotel. GREEN FEES: Hotel guests: per day, $1.75; 8 days, $10.50; 15 days, $17.50; monthly, $26. Visitors: weekdays, $3.50; Sundays and holidays, $5.25 per day; 8 days, $21; 15 days, $34.75; monthly, $55.75. CADDIE FEES: 9 holes, 90¢; 18 holes, $1.40. GOLF CLUB RENTALS: $1 per 9-hole round; $2.75 all day. GOLF CART RENTALS: $1 per round. MOTORIZED GOLF CART RENTALS: Not available. LESSONS: 80¢ per half hour. Group lessons by arrangement. CLUBHOUSE FACILITIES: Restaurant, bar, lockers, sauna baths, hairdressing, table tennis, billiards, lawn bowling, tennis, and swimming pool. RECOMMENDED ACCOMMODATIONS: Penina Golf Hotel, 210 rooms, right on course, open all year.

Scotland

This is where it all began more than four hundred years ago. When a Scottish clansman picked up a stick and swatted a ball with it, little did he know that he had started a sport that eventually would become a favorite of millions of people throughout the world.

To the Scots, golf is more than a game. It is a way of life shared by almost all of the country's population. For the traveling golfer, Scotland offers the ideal second home. Here is a country that understands him and is ready to accept him with open arms.

The Scottish golf courses themselves are not nearly so hospitable. Many of the four hundred or so courses literally dominating the country have been responsible for taking a golfer's game apart hole by hole. Many courses have for hundreds of years challenged the world's best golfers. But win, lose, or draw, the experience is one to be remembered.

To score well on Scotland's finest courses, three basic principles should be followed: Be constantly aware of the effect the blowing winds will have on the ball; stay on the fairway at all times; and stay out of sand dunes and traps. By following these three rules, the visiting golfer can walk away from any Scottish course with his head held high and his score low. But he should not expect to keep the promises he makes to himself all the time . . . no one has yet.

In a country where almost every course has a famous history and tradition, several still stand out from the rest. Easily the most famous is the Royal and Ancient Golf Club, better known as St. Andrews. Often referred to as the actual home of golf, St. Andrews is a golf course in its most natural state. It is not manicured and has very few man-made hazards, but it has truly tested the greatest golfers down through the history of golf.

St. Andrews is far from being a typical Scottish golf course. Except for two holes on the Old Course, all of the holes share double-greens. It is not unusual for a golfer to face an 85-foot putt. In addition to the vast putting surfaces, St. Andrews has a wide assortment of bunkers. Their sizes vary from large excavations to groups of little "gopher holes," such as those on the twelfth fairway. A golfer can get out of them if he knows how to handle a sand wedge well, but he shouldn't count on achieving distance.

Another great and historic golf club is the Honourable Company of Edinburgh Golfers at Muirfield. This is recognized as the world's oldest golf club. The course is considered by many experts to be the toughest in Scotland and possibly in the world. Fairways are narrow and hazards are readily visible. But, to the player, it seems as though the course knows every move he is going to make and is ready to defend itself against him. Its treacherous bunkers and roughs combine with heavy gusts of wind blowing in from the sea to test to the limit the skills of the best golfers.

Troon, Carnoustie, Royal Aberdeen, Prestwick—the list goes on and on. As the visiting golfer travels around Scotland, he will find one golf course after another refreshing, challenging, and a toast to his favorite sport. But it probably won't be until he returns home again that he will realize for the first time what his holiday has done for his golf game. Few forget the challenges of Scottish golf courses and many play a better game because they have played there.

SEASON: May to October.

HOW TO GET THERE: By Pan Am Jet Clipper, New York to Glasgow, 6¼ hours. By ship, 5 days.

GOLF EQUIPMENT: American equipment available.

LANGUAGE: English.

TIME: Six hours later than U.S. Eastern Standard Time.

Blairgowrie Golf Club

LOCATION: Rosemont, Blairgowrie, Pertshire (15 miles by bus from Perth and Dundee). COURSE SIZE: 18 holes; 6,490 yards; par 72. AVAILABILITY TO VISITORS: Visitors permitted to play unlimited, except Wednesdays, Saturdays, and Sundays between 1 and 3 P.M. GREEN FEES: Weekdays (except Wednesday), $2.80; Wednesday and weekends, $4.20 a day; per week, $8.40; two weeks, $11.20; per month, $14. CADDIE FEES: $1.50 per round, single. GOLF CLUB RENTALS: $3.50 per day. GOLF CART RENTALS: 20¢ per round. MOTORIZED GOLF CART RENTALS: Not available. LESSONS: Available by appointment, $1.50 per half hour. CLUBHOUSE FACILITIES: Restaurant and bar. RECOMMENDED ACCOMMODATIONS: Blairgowrie: Angus Hotel, Wellmeadow (near course), Queens Hotel, Royal Hotel, Glen Ericht

Hotel, Kinloch House Hotel. Coupar Angus: Red House Hotel (near course), Moorfield Hotel.

Carnoustie Golf Club

LOCATION: Carnoustie, Angus (short walk from Carnoustie railroad station). COURSE SIZE: Championship Course: 18 holes; 7,103 yards; par 74. Burnside Course: 18 holes; 6,398 yards; par 74. AVAILABILITY TO VISITORS: Visitors welcome. GREEN FEES: Championship Course: Weekdays, 85¢; weekends, $3.65 per day; per week, $5.20; fortnight, $8.40. Burnside Course: Weekdays, 35¢; weekends, $1.40 per day; per week, $2.45; per month, $4.20. Also 18-hole putting course available: weekdays, 5¢; weekends, 7¢. CADDIE FEES: By special arrangement. GOLF CLUB RENTALS: $3 per day. GOLF CART RENTALS: 20¢ per round. MOTORIZED GOLF CART RENTALS: Not available. LESSONS: Available by appointment. CLUBHOUSE FACILITIES: Restaurant and bar available. RECOMMENDED ACCOMMODATIONS: Carnoustie: Glencoe Hotel, Bruce Hotel.

Gleneagles Hotel Golf Courses

LOCATION: Gleneagles, Perthshire (1 mile from Gleneagles railroad station). COURSE SIZE: King's Course: 18 holes; 6,597 yards; par 71. Queen's Course: 18 holes; 6,012 yards; par 69. Wee Course: 9 holes; 2,625 yards; par 35. AVAILABILITY TO VISITORS: Visitors welcome. GREEN FEES: Weekdays, $2.45; weekends, $4.20 per day. (Guests of Gleneagles Hotel receive reduced rates.) CADDIE FEES: By arrangement. GOLF CLUB RENTALS: $3 per day. GOLF CART RENTALS: 35¢ per round. MOTORIZED GOLF CART RENTALS: Not available. LESSONS: Available by appointment. CLUBHOUSE FACILITIES: Restaurant and bar at Gleneagles Hotel. RECOMMENDED ACCOMMODATIONS: Gleneagles Hotel.

Gullane Golf Club

LOCATION: Gullane, East Lothian (5 miles from North Berwick railroad station; 18 miles from Edinburgh). COURSE SIZE: Course No. 1: 18 holes; 6,461 yards; par 72. Course No. 2: 18 holes; 5,952 yards; par 70. Course No. 3: 18 holes; 5,008 yards; par 68. AVAILABILITY TO

VISITORS: Visitors welcome. GREEN FEES: Course No. 1: Weekdays, $1.40; weekends, $3.50 per day; per week, $5.90; two weeks, $11.20. Course No. 2: Weekdays, $1.05; weekends, $1.40 per day; per week, $4.20; two weeks, $7. Course No. 3: Weekdays, 70¢; weekends, $1.05 per day; per week, $2.80; two weeks, $4.20. CADDIE FEES: $1.75 per round, single. GOLF CLUB RENTALS: 70¢ per round. GOLF CART RENTALS: 20¢ per round. MOTORIZED GOLF CART RENTALS: Not available. LESSONS: Available by appointment, $1.05 per half hour. CLUBHOUSE FACILITIES: Restaurant and bar. RECOMMENDED ACCOMMODATIONS: Greywalls Hotel, Queens Hotel (both near course).

Honourable Company of Edinburgh Golfers

LOCATION: Muirfield, East Lothian (4 miles from Drem railroad station). COURSE SIZE: 18 holes; 6,806 yards; par 74. AVAILABILITY TO VISITORS: Visitor with letter from own club permitted to play when course is not reserved. GREEN FEES: Contact secretary of the club. CADDIE FEES: Caddies available by arrangement. GOLF CLUB RENTALS: Not available. GOLF CART RENTALS: Available. MOTORIZED GOLF CART RENTALS: Not available. LESSONS: Available by appointment. CLUBHOUSE FACILITIES: Restaurant and bar. RECOMMENDED ACCOMMODATIONS: Gullane: Greywalls Hotel, Queens Hotel.

Nairn Golf Club

LOCATION: Nairn, Nairnshire (1 mile from Nairn railroad station). COURSE SIZE: 18 holes; 6,342 yards; par 71. AVAILABILITY TO VISITORS: Visitors welcome. GREEN FEES: Weekdays, $1.75; weekends, $1.75 per day; per week, $5.60; two weeks, $8.40; per month, $11.20; season, $23.52. CADDIE FEES: $1.40 per round, single. GOLF CLUB RENTALS: Available. GOLF CART RENTALS: 35¢ per round. MOTORIZED GOLF CART RENTALS: Not available. LESSONS: Available by appointment, $2.10 per half hour. CLUBHOUSE FACILITIES: Restaurant and bar. RECOMMENDED ACCOMMODATIONS: Nairn: Alton Burn Hotel, Golf View Hotel, Newton Hotel, Windsor Hotel, Marine Hotel, Invernairne Hotel (all near course).

North Berwick Golf Club

LOCATION: North Berwick, East Lothian (½ mile from North Berwick railroad station; 24 miles from Edinburgh). COURSE SIZE: 18

The 1st green at King's Course at Gleneagles Hotel.

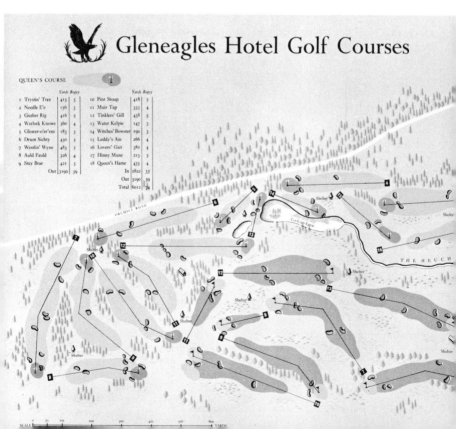

Gleneagles Hotel Golf Courses

QUEEN'S COURSE

	Yards	Bogey			Yards	Bogey
1 Trystin' Tree	415	5	10 Pint Stoup		418	5
2 Needle E'e	156	3	11 Muir Tap		333	4
3 Gushet Rig	416	5	12 Tinklers' Gill		438	5
4 Warlock Knowe	360	4	13 Water Kelpie		147	3
5 Glower-o'er'em	183	3	14 Witches' Bowster		190	3
6 Drum Sichty	430	5	15 Leddy's Ain		266	4
7 Westlin' Wyne	483	5	16 Lovers' Gait		382	4
8 Auld Fauld	326	4	17 Hinny Mune		213	3
9 Stey Brae	421	5	18 Queen's Hame		435	4
Out	3190	39	In		2822	35
			Out		3190	39
			Total		6012	74

ORCHILL ROAD

Loch-an-Eagle

THE HEUCH

Shelter

SCALE   YARDS

Associated Newspapers, Ltd.

The 10th green, King's Course, and 10th green, Queen's Course, during Scottish Daily Mail Foursomes, 1955.

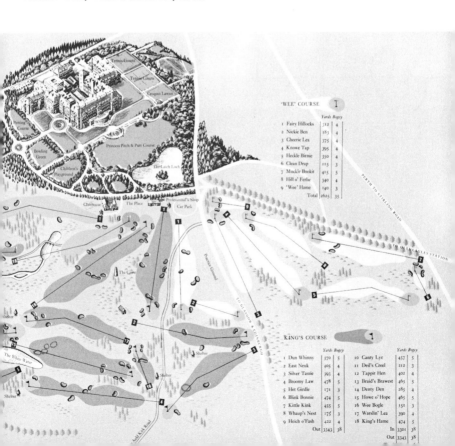

'WEE' COURSE

		Yards	Bogey
1	Fairy Hillocks	312	4
2	Nickie Ben	183	4
3	Cheerie Lea	375	4
4	Knowe Tap	395	4
5	Heckle Birnie	350	4
6	Clean Drap	115	3
7	Muckle Bookit	415	5
8	Hill o' Ferlie	340	4
9	'Wee' Hame	140	3
	Total	2625	35

KING'S COURSE

		Yards	Bogey			Yards	Bogey
1	Dun Whinny	370	5	10	Canty Lye	457	5
2	East Neuk	405	4	11	Deil's Creel	212	3
3	Silver Tassie	393	4	12	Tappit Hen	402	4
4	Broomy Law	478	5	13	Braid's Brawest	465	5
5	Het Girdle	171	3	14	Denty Den	285	4
6	Blink Bonnie	474	5	15	Howe o' Hope	465	5
7	Kittle Kink	455	5	16	Wee Bogle	151	3
8	Whaup's Nest	175	3	17	Warslin' Lea	390	4
9	Heich o' Fash	422	4	18	King's Hame	474	5
	Out	3343	38		In	3301	38
					Out	3343	38

The beauty of Gleneagles is deceiving—there is little room for error.

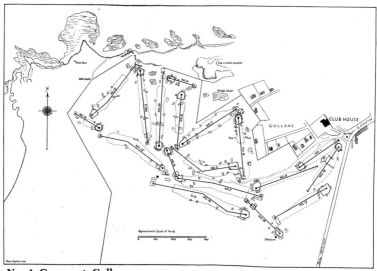

No. 1 Course at Gullane.

holes; 6,321 yards; par 71. AVAILABILITY TO VISITORS: Visitors welcome. GREEN FEES: April-September: weekdays, $1.05; weekends, $1.40 per day; per month, $9.10. October-May: weekdays, 84¢; weekends, 98¢ per day; per month, $7. CADDIE FEES: $1.75 per round, single. GOLF CLUB RENTALS: $3 per day. GOLF CART RENTALS: 35¢ per round. MOTORIZED GOLF CART RENTALS: Not available. LESSONS: Available by appointment. CLUBHOUSE FACILITIES: Restaurant and bar. RECOMMENDED ACCOMMODATIONS: North Berwick: Marine Hotel, Royal Hotel, Point Garry Hotel, Nether Abbey Hotel.

Pitlochry Golf Club

LOCATION: Pitlochry, Pertshire (½ mile from Pitlochry railroad station). COURSE SIZE: 18 holes; 5,687 yards; par 69. AVAILABILITY TO VISITORS: Visitors welcome. GREEN FEES: Weekdays, 85¢; weekends, $1.40 per day; per week, $2.80; two weeks, $4.90; per month, $7; season, $11.75. CADDIE FEES: 85¢ per round, single. GOLF CLUB RENTALS: 35¢ per round. GOLF CART RENTALS: 30¢ per round. MOTORIZED GOLF CART RENTALS: Not available. LESSONS: Available by appointment, $1.05 per half hour. CLUBHOUSE FACILITIES: Restaurant and bar. RECOMMENDED ACCOMMODATIONS: Pitlochry: Hydro Hotel, Airdaniar Hotel, Burnside Hotel, Wellwood Hotel, Moulin Hotel (all near course).

Prestwick Golf Club

LOCATION: Prestwick, Ayrshire (near Prestwick railroad station; 30 miles from Glasgow). COURSE SIZE: 18 holes; 6,571 yards; par 72. AVAILABILITY TO VISITORS: Visitors permitted limited play when introduced by member or by letter from own club. GREEN FEES: Weekdays, $2.10; Sundays, $2.80. CADDIE FEES: $1.75 per round, single. GOLF CLUB RENTALS: $3 per day. GOLF CART RENTALS: 35¢ per round. MOTORIZED GOLF CART RENTALS: Not available. LESSONS: Not available. CLUBHOUSE FACILITIES: Restaurant and bar. RECOMMENDED ACCOMMODATIONS: Prestwick: Queens Hotel, Links Hotel; Ayr: Station Hotel. Troon: Craiglea Hotel, Marine Hotel, Sun Court Hotel, Hotel Welbeck, South Beach Hotel.

Royal Aberdeen Golf Club

LOCATION: Aberdeen, Aberdeenshire (2 miles from Aberdeen railroad station). COURSE SIZE: Balgownie Course: 18 holes; 6,384 yards; par 72. Relief 9-hole course: 5,500 yards; par 64 (18-hole round). AVAILABILITY TO VISITORS: Visitors welcome when introduced by member or by letter from own club. GREEN FEES: 18-hole course: $1.40. 9-hole course: per day, 50¢; per week, $2.10. CADDIE FEES: By special arrangement. GOLF CLUB RENTALS: Not available. GOLF CART RENTALS: Available. MOTORIZED GOLF CART RENTALS: Not available. LESSONS: Available by appointment. CLUBHOUSE FACILITIES: Restaurant and bar. RECOMMENDED ACCOMMODATIONS: Aberdeen: Woodside House Hotel, Northern Hotel.

Royal and Ancient Golf Club of St. Andrews

LOCATION: St. Andrews, Fife (at the St. Andrews railroad station; 76 miles from Glasgow). COURSE SIZE: Old Course: 18 holes; 6,936 yards; par 73. New Course: 18 holes; 6,612 yards; par 73. AVAILABILITY TO VISITORS: Visitors welcome. GREEN FEES: Old Course: week-

Crowds watch Eric Brown leave the course at St. Andrews.

United Press International Photo

The old master coming home at St. Andrews.

days, $1.05; no play on Sunday. New Course: weekdays, 49¢; Sundays, 70¢; per week, $2.80; two weeks, $4.90. CADDIE FEES: $2.10 per round, single. GOLF CLUB RENTALS: $2.80 per round or $3.50 per day (includes cart). GOLF CART RENTALS: 20¢ per round. MOTORIZED GOLF CART RENTALS: Not available. LESSONS: Available by appointment. CLUBHOUSE FACILITIES: Restaurant and bar. Available to members only. RECOMMENDED ACCOMMODATIONS: St. Andrews: Russacks Hotel, Royal Hotel, Scores Hotel, Rufflets Hotel, Station and Windsor Hotel, Imperial Hotel, Atholl Hotel.

Royal Dornoch Golf Club

LOCATION: Dornoch, Sutherland (14 miles from Bonar Bridge railroad station). COURSE SIZE: 18 holes; 6,505 yards; par 72. AVAILABILITY TO VISITORS: Visitors welcome. GREEN FEES: Weekdays, 85¢; no play on Sunday; per week, $4.20. CADDIE FEES: By arrangement, 75¢ to $1.05 per round, single. GOLF CLUB RENTALS: Available by special arrangement only. GOLF CART RENTALS: 30¢ per round; 45¢ per day. MOTORIZED GOLF CART RENTALS: Not available. LESSONS: Available by appointment, 85¢ per half hour. CLUBHOUSE FACILITIES: Restaurant and bar. RECOMMENDED ACCOMMODATIONS: Dornoch: Dornoch Hotel (near course), Royal Golf Hotel, Dornoch Castle Hotel, Burghfield House Hotel.

Troon Golf Club

LOCATION: Troon, Ayrshire (1 mile from Troon railroad station; 30 miles from Glasgow). COURSE SIZE: Old Course: 18 holes; 6,533 yards; par 72. Portland Course: 18 holes; 6,113 yards; par 72. AVAILABILITY TO VISITORS: Visitors permitted limited play when introduced by member or by letter from own club. GREEN FEES: Old Course: weekdays, $2.10; Sundays, $5.60; per week, $7. Portland Course: weekdays, $1.40; Sundays, $2.80; per week, $5.60. CADDIE FEES: $1.75 per round, single. GOLF CLUB RENTALS: $3 per day. GOLF CART

Course chart of Troon Golf Club Old Course.

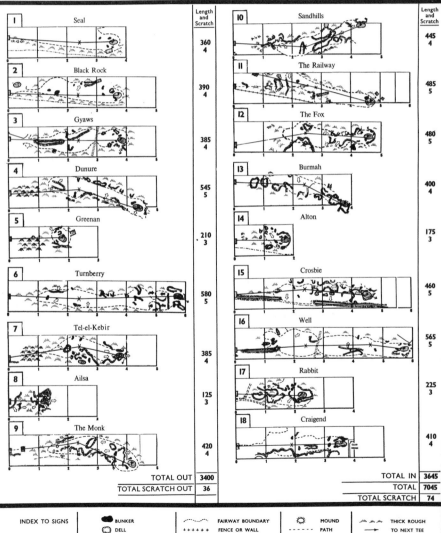

	Length and Scratch
1 — Seal	360 / 4
2 — Black Rock	390 / 4
3 — Gyaws	385 / 4
4 — Dunure	545 / 5
5 — Greenan	210 / 3
6 — Turnberry	580 / 5
7 — Tel-el-Kebir	385 / 4
8 — Ailsa	125 / 3
9 — The Monk	420 / 4
10 — Sandhills	445 / 4
11 — The Railway	485 / 5
12 — The Fox	480 / 5
13 — Burmah	400 / 4
14 — Alton	175 / 3
15 — Crosbie	460 / 5
16 — Well	565 / 5
17 — Rabbit	225 / 3
18 — Craigend	410 / 4
TOTAL OUT	3400
TOTAL SCRATCH OUT	36
TOTAL IN	3645
TOTAL	7045
TOTAL SCRATCH	74

INDEX TO SIGNS

BUNKER · DELL · DOWNWARD SLOPE · STEEP SLOPE · FAIRWAY BOUNDARY · FENCE OR WALL · LAKE OR POND · LINE OF PLAY · MOUND · PATH · ROUGH · ROAD · THICK ROUGH · TO NEXT TEE · TREES & BUSHES · WATER DITCH

The 6th green Ailsa Course at Turnberry Hotel in Ayrshire.

Turnberry Hotel from the golf course.

RENTALS: 30¢ per day. MOTORIZED GOLF CART RENTALS: Not available. LESSONS: Available by appointment, $1.40 per half hour. CLUBHOUSE FACILITIES: Restaurant and bar. RECOMMENDED ACCOMMODATIONS: Troon: Craiglea Hotel, Marine Hotel, Sun Court Hotel, Hotel Welbeck, South Beach Hotel.

Turnberry Hotel Golf Courses

LOCATION: Turnberry, Ayrshire (5 miles from Girvan railroad station). COURSE SIZE: Ailsa Course: 18 holes; 7,025 yards; par 71. Arran Course: 18 holes; 6,653 yards; par 73. AVAILABILITY TO VISITORS: Visitors welcome. GREEN FEES: Weekdays, $1.75; weekends, $3.15 per day. (Guests of Turnberry Hotel play at reduced green fees.) CADDIE FEES: $2.10 per round, single. GOLF CLUB RENTALS: $3 per day. GOLF CART RENTALS: 35¢ per round; 70¢ per day. MOTORIZED GOLF CART RENTALS: Not available. LESSONS: Available by appointment, $1.75 per half hour. CLUBHOUSE FACILITIES: Restaurant and bar at Turnberry Hotel. RECOMMENDED ACCOMMODATIONS: Turnberry Hotel.

Spain

Although the language is different and the scenery unfamiliar, golf in Spain is very much like golf in many parts of the United States.

Generally, Spanish golf courses are very well groomed and have the sleek appearance of the well-appointed country club. Most of the courses are only 9 holes, but when doubled for a complete round, they are tough and long.

As is the case in many European countries, courses in Spain offer an abundance of elevated tees. Therefore, expect to find tee shots booming farther over the horizon than usual. This is a great boost for the spirit, save that there is usually a cluster of cavernous traps and assorted other hazards in the landing area. Because of the fine grooming and the normally excellent weather, however, scores should be satisfying.

There are two outstanding features of Spanish golf that the visiting player will immediately discover: there is absolutely no waiting, and the cost of playing is not a pain on the pocketbook. The sport is in its infancy here, and has not reached the mass popularity it has found in the United States, Great Britain, Japan, and other countries. It is not unusual for a visitor to call for a reservation at a Spanish club and find when he gets there that he is playing with the local pro.

As far as costs are concerned, it is common to be able to play a round with a caddie for less than $3 total. The most luxurious courses charge higher green fees, but $5 per round usually is tops, even on weekends.

Spring and fall are the best seasons for golf in Spain. During the summer the midday sun is a bit warm for anything but siesta, and in winter the grass is not very good. The grass problem may soon be overcome with the advent of automatic watering systems and sophisticated soil-nutrition programs. None of this is to say that golf is not available at these times, it simply is not at its best.

101

Two of the Canary Islands have interesting courses. On the island of Tenerife is the Club de Golf de Tenerife, which, with a great deal of imagination, has been cut out of a mountainside. Misjudgment in club selection is common, since most shots involve an incline in some direction and most tees are elevated. On the island of Gran Canaria is the Club de Golf de las Palmas, which is also scratched out of the hills. Novel hazards here are the volcanic craters: ever try blasting a wedge shot out of volcanic ash?

On the mainland, fine courses can be found about Madrid, Barcelona, the Costa del Sol, and the northwest coast. In the Madrid region, Club de Campo and La Puerta de Hierro are considered the two best clubs in the country. Campo has five pros on duty and La Puerta de Hierro eight—service doesn't come any better than that anywhere.

On the Costa del Sol, there are two new super resort hotels, Sotogrande and Atalaya Park, which offer everything but money—that you have to bring. In addition to championship-caliber courses, they offer horses, tennis, private beaches, bungalows, beauty shops, and not far away, gambling. According to the managers at Sotogrande, these facilities are just the beginning of a complex that will encompass a wealthy real estate development, yacht basin, bull ring, private airport. If anyone is interested, sites are still available.

In Barcelona, be sure to tee off at the Real Club de Golf El Prat, which measures about 6,500 yards and offers an exciting round.

Visiting players should have no difficulty with access to Spanish courses. Although most courses are private, except those directly connected with resorts, visitors are usually welcome. However, it is necessary to observe the formality of contacting the club secretary or manager in advance to arrange for play. An introductory letter from the golfer's home club will be very useful.

SEASON: Year round.

HOW TO GET THERE: By Pan Am Jet Clipper, about 9 hours to Barcelona; Madrid is about 1 hour by air from Lisbon, 2 hours from Rome, and 1½ hours from Barcelona. By ship, about 7 days to Lisbon, 6 to 8 days to Gibraltar.

GOLF EQUIPMENT: American equipment available at reasonable prices.

LANGUAGE: Spanish; in Barcelona, Catalan; other areas have other dialects. English is understood in large cities and tourist centers only.

TIME: Six hours later than U.S. Eastern Standard Time.

Atalaya Park Hotel Golf and Country Club

LOCATION: Estepona-Marbella (40 miles from Gibraltar and Malaga). COURSE SIZE: 18 holes; 6,800 yards; par 72. AVAILABILITY TO VISITORS: Visitors welcome. GREEN FEES: $2.50 daily; hotel guests free. CADDIE FEES: $1 per round. GOLF CLUB RENTALS: Available. GOLF CART RENTALS: Not available. MOTORIZED GOLF CART RENTALS: Not available. LESSONS: Available. CLUBHOUSE FACILITIES: Putting green, pitching green, driving range, restaurant, and bar. Horseback riding, tennis, swimming pool, and private beach also available at the hotel. RECOMMENDED ACCOMMODATIONS: Atalaya Park Hotel.

Club de Golf Costa de Azahar

LOCATION: Costa de Azahar, Grao de Castellon (on outskirts of El Grao; by car, 40 miles south of Valencia). COURSE SIZE: 9 holes; 3,391 yards; par 37. AVAILABILITY TO VISITORS: Visitors welcome. GREEN FEES: Guests of Hotel del Golf: per day, 80¢; per week, $4.10; 15 days, $5.20; per month, $9. Nonguests: per day, $1.65; per week, $5.80; 15 days, $9; per month, $16.50. CADDIE FEES: 30¢ per 9 holes, single. GOLF CLUB RENTALS: 80¢ per day. GOLF CART RENTALS: 25¢ per round. MOTORIZED GOLF CART RENTALS: Not available. LESSONS: Available by appointment, 70¢ per half hour. CLUBHOUSE FACILITIES: Small clubhouse, restaurant, bar, and rooms for changing. RECOMMENDED ACCOMMODATIONS: Course is part of Hotel del Golf. No other hotel in area.

Club de Golf de Las Palmas

LOCATION: Bandama, Gran Canaria (9 miles from Las Palmas by car). COURSE SIZE: 18 holes; 6,250 yards; par 71. AVAILABILITY TO VISITORS: Visitors welcome. GREEN FEES: Weekdays, $1; weekends, $1.65 per day; per week, $5.80; two weeks, $11.55; per month, $16.50. CADDIE FEES: 50¢ per round, single. GOLF CLUB RENTALS: 80¢ per round. GOLF CART RENTALS: Not available. MOTORIZED GOLF CART RENTALS: Not available. LESSONS: Available by appointment, 80¢ per hour. CLUBHOUSE FACILITIES: Restaurant and bar. RECOMMENDED ACCOMMODATIONS: Las Palmas de Gran Canaria: Hotel Santa Brigida, Hotel Bandama, Hotel Lentiscal, Hotel Los Frailes, Hotel Santa

Catalina, Hotel Gran Canaria, Hotel Parque, Hotel Metropol, Hotel Piño de Oro, Hotel Las Vegas.

Club de Golf de San Cugat

LOCATION: San Cugat del Valles (10 miles west of Barcelona by car). COURSE SIZE: 18 holes; 5,665 yards; par 68. AVAILABILITY TO VISITORS: Visitors welcome. GREEN FEES: Weekdays, $1.65; weekends, $3.30 per day. CADDIE FEES: 50¢ per 9 holes, single; 90¢ per 18 holes, single. GOLF CLUB RENTALS: $1.25 per day. GOLF CART RENTALS: Not available. MOTORIZED GOLF CART RENTALS: Not available. LESSONS: Available by appointment, 50¢ per half hour. CLUBHOUSE FACILITIES: Restaurant, bar, locker rooms, and pool. RECOMMENDED ACCOMMODATIONS: San Cugat: Fonda Casa Tadeo, Hotel Rusinol (near course). Barcelona: Hotel Avenida Palace, Hotel Ritz, Hotel Colon, Hotel Arycasa, Manila Hotel.

Club de Golf de Tenerife El Penon

LOCATION: Tenerife, Canary Islands (1 mile from airport; 10 miles from Santa Cruz de Tenerife by car). COURSE SIZE: 18 holes; 5,559 yards; par 72. AVAILABILITY TO VISITORS: Visitors welcome. GREEN FEES: Per day, $1.65; per week, $8.25; two weeks, $9.90; per month, $18.15. CADDIE FEES: 50¢ per round, single. GOLF CLUB RENTALS: $1.65 per day. GOLF CART RENTALS: Available. MOTORIZED GOLF CART RENTALS: Not available. LESSONS: Available by appointment, 60¢ per hour. CLUBHOUSE FACILITIES: Restaurant and bar. RECOMMENDED ACCOMMODATIONS: Santa Cruz de Tenerife: Hotel Mencey, Hotel Residencia Principe, Hotel Orotava, Hotel Anaga. Puerto de la Cruz: Hotel Taora, Hotel Las Vegas, Hotel Oro Negro, Hotel Vallemar.

Club de Golf Reina Cristina

LOCATION: Algeciras (10 miles west of Gibraltar by car). COURSE SIZE: 9 holes; 2,485 yards; par 36. AVAILABILITY TO VISITORS: Visitors welcome. GREEN FEES: Per day, 85¢; per week, $3.30; per month, $8.40; per year, $25. CADDIE FEES: 35¢ per 18 holes, single. GOLF CLUB RENTALS: 60¢ per round. GOLF CART RENTALS: Not available. MOTORIZED GOLF CART RENTALS: Not available. LESSONS: Not available. CLUBHOUSE FACILITIES: Restaurant, bar, and pool available to guests at hotel. Bar and changing rooms at the course. RECOMMENDED ACCOMMODATIONS: Course is part of Reina Cristina Hotel.

Club de Golf Sotogrande

LOCATION: Costa del Sol (30 miles by car from Gibraltar). COURSE SIZE: Championship course: 18 holes; 6,967 yards; par 72. Smaller course: 9 holes; 1,431 yards; par 29. AVAILABILITY TO VISITORS: Visitors welcome to courses; facilities available to members of recognized golf clubs. GREEN FEES: Weekdays, $1.65; weekends and holidays, $2.50 per day. CADDIE FEES: $1 per day. GOLF CLUB RENTALS: $1.65 per day. GOLF CART RENTALS: Not available. LESSONS: Francisco "Mike" Lopez, pro. CLUBHOUSE FACILITIES: Restaurant, swimming pool, dressing rooms, players' grill, poolside snack bar, pro shop, women's boutique. RECOMMENDED ACCOMMODATIONS: Twelve guest villas are available to members and temporary members of the club. Also available Hostal del Leon.

Club de Golf Terramar

LOCATION: Sitges (24 miles from Barcelona by car). COURSE SIZE: 9 holes; 2,941 yards; par 35. AVAILABILITY TO VISITORS: Visitors welcome. GREEN FEES: Weekdays, $3.30; weekends, $4.95 per day; per week, $25; two weeks, $36.75; per month, $58.35. CADDIE FEES: 50¢ per 9 holes, single. GOLF CLUB RENTALS: 85¢ per day. GOLF CART RENTALS: 45¢ per day. MOTORIZED GOLF CART RENTALS: Not available. LESSONS: Available by appointment, 80¢ per half hour. CLUBHOUSE FACILITIES: Bar. RECOMMENDED ACCOMMODATIONS: Sitges: Hotel Calipolis, Park Hotel, Hotel Subur, Hotel Miramar, Hotel Mariangel, Hotel La Sonrisa, Hotel Astor, Hotel Arcadia, Hotel Platjador, Hotel Las Moreras, Hotel La Cala.

Club Pineda de Sevilla

LOCATION: Sevilla (2 miles outside of town). COURES SIZE: 9 holes; 5,256 yards for 18 holes; par 70. AVAILABILITY TO VISITORS: Visitors permitted limited play. GREEN FEES: $1.65 per day. CADDIE FEES: 40¢ per 9 holes, single. GOLF CLUB RENTALS: Not available. GOLF CART RENTALS: Not available. MOTORIZED GOLF CART RENTALS: Not

Bunkers at Sotogrande are filled with a pulverized white marble instead of the usual sand. Aside from adding to the attractiveness of the course, this substance is superior to sand from the standpoint of drainage and texture, according to architect Robert Trent Jones.

available. LESSONS: Available by appointment, $1 per hour. CLUB-HOUSE FACILITIES: Restaurant and bar. RECOMMENDED ACCOMMODA-TIONS: Sevilla: Hotel Andalucia, Hotel Inglaterra, Hotel Christina.

Golf Club Guadalmina

LOCATION: San Pedro de Alcantara (6½ miles from Marbella; 52 miles north of Gibraltar by car). COURSE SIZE: 18 holes; 6,849 yards; par 74. AVAILABILITY TO VISITORS: Visitors welcome. GREEN FEES: Guests of Hotel Guadalmina, $1.70 per day; nonguests, $6.75 per day. CADDIE FEES: 65¢ per 9 holes, single; $1 per 18 holes, single. GOLF CLUB RENTALS: $1.25 per day. GOLF CART RENTALS: Not available. MOTORIZED GOLF CART RENTALS: Not available. LESSONS: Available by appointment, $2 per hour. CLUBHOUSE FACILITIES: Restaurant, 3 bars, 3 pools, and tennis (sandy beach adjoins golf course). RECOMMENDED ACCOMMODATIONS: Course is part of Golf Hotel Guadalmina. Others available: Hotel Atalaya Park, Hotel Cortiho Blanco, Hotel Marbella-Club, Hotel Don Pepe, Hotel Skol, Hotel Los Monteros, Hotel Santa Marta.

Real Club de Golf El Prat

LOCATION: Prat de Llobregat (1½ miles from Prat de Llobregat Airport; 7 miles from Barcelona by car). COURSE SIZE: 18 holes; 6,509

The 7th green at the Club de Golf, Sotogrande.

yards; par 72. AVAILABILITY TO VISITORS: Visitors welcome. Membership fee: 80¢. GREEN FEES: Weekdays, $1.65; weekends, $4.10 per day; per week, $16.40; 15 days, $24.60; per month, $41. CADDIE FEES: 50¢ per 9 holes, single; 80¢ per 18 holes, single. GOLF CLUB RENTALS: 80¢ per day. GOLF CART RENTALS: 15¢ per day. MOTORIZED GOLF CART RENTALS: Not available. LESSONS: Available by appointment, $1 per half hour. CLUBHOUSE FACILITIES: Restaurant, bar, locker rooms, and pool (May–September). RECOMMENDED ACCOMMODATIONS: Castelldefels: Hotel Playafels (near course), Hotel Neptune (near course). Barcelona: Manila Hotel, Hotel Avenida Palace, Hotel Ritz, Hotel Colon, Hotel Arycasa.

Real Club de la Puerta de Hierro

LOCATION: Madrid (3 miles west of town by car). COURSE SIZE: 18 holes; 5,960 yards; par 72 (also a newly constructed 9-hole course available). AVAILABILITY TO VISITORS: Visitors welcome. GREEN FEES: Weekdays, $2.50; weekends, $3.30 per day; 15 days, $16.50; per month, $24.75. CADDIE FEES: 60¢ per 9 holes, single; 75¢ per 18 holes, single. GOLF CLUB RENTALS: Available; brand of clubs determines fee. GOLF CART RENTALS: Not available. MOTORIZED GOLF CART RENTALS: Not available. LESSONS: Available by appointment, 80¢ per hour. CLUBHOUSE FACILITIES: Restaurant, bar, locker rooms, and pool (June–September). RECOMMENDED ACCOMMODATIONS: Madrid: Castellana Hilton, Hotel Plaza, Hotel Carlton, Hotel Palace, Hotel Ritz.

Real Golf de Pedrena

LOCATION: On peninsula in Bay of Biscay, 14 miles from Santander; club provides motorboat from Santander to the course. COURSE SIZE: 18 holes; 6,258 yards; par 70. AVAILABILITY TO VISITORS: Visitors welcome. GREEN FEES: Per day, $3; per week, $14.85; two weeks, $24.75; per month, $33. CADDIE FEES: 60¢ per round, single. GOLF CLUB RENTALS: Not available. GOLF CART RENTALS: Not available. MOTORIZED GOLF CART RENTALS: Not available. LESSONS: Not available. CLUBHOUSE FACILITIES: Restaurant and bar. RECOMMENDED ACCOMMODATIONS: Hotel Bahia, Hotel Real, Hotel Rex.

Real Sociedad Hipica Española Club de Campo

LOCATION: Carretera de la Coruna (2½ miles by car from Madrid). COURSE SIZE: 18 holes; 6,735 yards; par 74. AVAILABILITY TO VISITORS: Visitors permitted limited play; inquire in advance. GREEN FEES: Weekdays, 80¢; weekends, $1.65 per day. CADDIE FEES: 70¢ per 9 holes, single; 90¢ per 18 holes, single. GOLF CLUB RENTALS: Available; brand of clubs determines fee. GOLF CART RENTALS: Not available. MOTORIZED GOLF CART RENTALS: Not available. LESSONS: Available by appointment, 60¢ per half hour. CLUBHOUSE FACILITIES: Restaurant, bar, locker rooms, and pool. RECOMMENDED ACCOMMODATIONS: Madrid: Castellana Hilton, Hotel Plaza, Hotel Carlton, Hotel Palace, Hotel Ritz.

Sociedad de Golf de Neguri La Galea

LOCATION: Guecho, Vizcaya (12 miles from Bilbao by car). COURSE SIZE: 18 holes; 6,721 yards; par 72. AVAILABILITY TO VISITORS: Visitors welcome. GREEN FEES: Per day, $3.30; per week, $10.75; two weeks, $21.50; per month, $43. CADDIE FEES: $1 per round, single. GOLF CLUB RENTALS: Not available. GOLF CART RENTALS: Not available. MOTORIZED GOLF CART RENTALS: Not available. LESSONS: Available by appointment, 65¢ per half hour. CLUBHOUSE FACILITIES: Restaurant and bar. RECOMMENDED ACCOMMODATIONS: Guecho: Los Tamarises (near course). Bilbao: Hotel Carlton, Hotel Torrontegui, Hotel Almirante, Hotel Excelsior.

Switzerland

Switzerland, the capital of the winter-sports world, also enjoys a bustling traffic of golf bag-toting tourists during the summer. There are few places in the world that can match its beauty; few places that hold the promise of a more memorable golfing holiday.

This doesn't mean that Switzerland has the best golf courses in the world. Not at all. It has 24 layouts, some presenting championship tests. Others are something less than a stiff challenge. But all exist in a setting so magnificent that the visiting golfer may find it difficult to concentrate on his game.

Swiss courses are well conditioned—something to be expected in a nation that is famous for quality and expert workmanship. Fairways are generally rolling or hilly, and the sturdy Alpine grass provides a good lie. A temperate climate (similar to New York and Chicago) and an abundance of water enable the courses to flourish during the relatively short season. Water holes are commonplace, and towering pines —which seem to grow everywhere—reduce many fairways to narrow, exacting tests from the tee.

Since Swiss golf usually is high-altitude golf, it is wise to heed carefully the clubbing advice of the caddie. The thin mountain air results in a much longer carry on the drives, and the uninitiated will be in for an afternoon of trouble unless they receive some expert help from the natives.

The golf season generally runs from April through September, except in the southern part of Switzerland, where it starts a month earlier and lasts through Otcober. While the climate generally is delightful during the season, the mountainous areas often experience surprising shifts in the weather. Take along rain gear and an extra sweater just to be sure.

While Switzerland is regarded as one of Europe's more expensive stops on the tourist circuit, golf does not come high. In many places, green fees are less than $2 during the week and below $3 on weekends. Caddie fees vary from area to area, but generally are less than $1.50 for an 18-hole round. The Swiss are not as tip-conscious as some of their neighbors (the Italians and French, for instance). A 25-cent tip will please the caddie.

Several Swiss courses are in resort areas that combine skiing and golf. One of these is the Crans Golf Club, Switzerland's best and biggest layout and the first organized golf club on the Continent. Located in the Valais, one of the most magnificent areas in the Alps, Crans has a 27-hole spread and its championship 18-hole course is one of the finest anywhere. Local farmers, who own most of the course, are permitted to cut the Crans rough for their hay. Since they do this infrequently, a golfer can drop a ball from his pocket and not be able to find it in the rough. But when cutting season comes, the farmers scoop up enough balls to stock several driving ranges. They probably make more on the resale of balls than they do on the hay.

Almost as famous as Crans is the Engadine Golf Club in Samedan. This championship course is one of the finest in the country. It is here that the Swiss Open and many major international golf matches are held. Being very close to St. Moritz, Engadine usually caters to the cream of European aristocracy.

Near the German border in Basel, try the 9-hole Basel golf club. Don't be misled by its short yardage. It is disastrous on hookers and slicers. Water, thick rough, woods, and other assorted hazards have been strategically positioned to give even scratch golfers a great deal of trouble.

Switzerland is not much larger than the state of New Jersey. Travel throughout the land is excellent. The Swiss are cordial and courteous—although somewhat more reserved than most Europeans—and the vacationing golfer will be welcomed everywhere.

SEASON: All year, depending on locality.

HOW TO GET THERE: By Jet Clipper from New York to London, Paris, or Frankfurt with connections to Zurich, 10 hours. Or from the U.S. west coast about 10½ hours to London via Pan Am's polar route, then to Zurich. Zurich is 1½ hours from Rome by air. Geneva is a 1½ hour's flight from London. By ship 5 to 9 days to western Atlantic or Mediterranean ports and then overnight by train. Switzerland is the crossroads of the European railway network; from London and Paris the Simplon Express passes through Lausanne to Italy, and the Arlburg Express passes through Basel with connections to Klosters, Davos, Arosa, and St. Moritz, on the way to Vienna. "Europabus" from Amsterdam goes to Basel, Lucerne, Interlaken, and Montreux, with connections to Milan and Nice. You can even go by Rhine boat from Rotterdam to Basel in summer.

GOLF EQUIPMENT: American equipment readily available at reasonable prices.

LANGUAGE: French, German, and Italian are recognized official languages; English is understood in most places.

TIME: Six hours later than U.S. Eastern Standard Time.

Crans Golf Club

LOCATION: Crans-sur-Sierre, Valais (within city limits). COURSE SIZE: 18 holes; 7,135 yards; par 73. 9 holes; 2,849 yards; par 34.

Crans Golf Club—one of the very best.

Shell's Wonderful World of Golf

AVAILABILITY TO VISITORS: Visitors welcome. GREEN FEES: Weekdays, $4.70; per week, $26; per season, $128. CADDIE FEES: 80¢ per 9-hole round; $1.50 per 18-hole round. GOLF CLUB RENTALS: Not available. GOLF CART RENTALS: Not available. MOTORIZED GOLF CART RENTALS: Not available. LESSONS: $4 to $8 per lesson. CLUBHOUSE FACILITIES: Restaurant and bar available. RECOMMENDED ACCOMMODATIONS: Contact Tourist Office in Crans-sur-Sierre.

Dolder Golf Club

LOCATION: Zurich (2 miles from town by taxi). COURSE SIZE: 9 holes; 1,832 yards; par 30. AVAILABILITY TO VISITORS: Visitors welcome. GREEN FEES: Weekdays, $2.10; Saturdays and Sundays, $4 per day; per week, $8; per month, $17.15. CADDIE FEES: $1.40 per 18-hole round. GOLF CLUB RENTALS: $1.85 per day. MOTORIZED GOLF CART RENTALS: Not available. LESSONS: $2.50 per half hour; $4.60 per hour. CLUBHOUSE FACILITIES: Restaurant and bar available. RECOMMENDED ACCOMMODATIONS: Dolder Grand Hotel, Hotel Waldhaus Dolder, Hotel Sonnenberg.

Engadine Golf Club

LOCATION: Samedan-St. Moritz (2 miles from St. Moritz). COURSE SIZE: 18 holes; 6,289 yards; par 70. AVAILABILITY TO VISITORS: Visitors welcome (entrance fee for nonmembers $1). GREEN FEES: Weekdays, $6; Saturdays and Sundays, $7 per day; per week, $32; two weeks, $56; per month, $80; season, $120. CADDIE FEES: $1 per 18-hole round. GOLF CLUB RENTALS: Available. GOLF SHOES RENTAL: Not available. GOLF CART RENTALS: Available. MOTORIZED GOLF CART RENTALS: Not available. LESSONS: Three professionals available: $5.25 and $8.50 per half hour. CLUBHOUSE FACILITIES: Restaurant and bar available. RECOMMENDED ACCOMMODATIONS: St. Moritz: Kulm Hotel, Carlton Hotel, Palace Hotel, Hotel Suvretta.

Golf and Country Club Blumisberg

LOCATION: Blumisberg-Wuennewil/Frib (10 miles from Bern; 8 miles from Fribourg). COURSE SIZE: 18 holes; 6,649 yards; par 73. AVAILABILITY TO VISITORS: Visitors welcome. GREEN FEES: Weekdays, $3.50; Saturdays and Sundays, $4.65 per day; per week, $14; per month, $35. CADDIE FEES: 95¢ per 9-hole round; $1.90 per 18-hole round. GOLF CLUB RENTALS: $1 per day. GOLF CART RENTALS: 50¢ per day. MOTORIZED GOLF CART RENTALS: Not available. LESSONS: $1.80 per half hour; $3.50 per hour. CLUBHOUSE FACILITIES: Restaurant and bar available. RECOMMENDED ACCOMMODATIONS: Bern: Hotel Schweizerhof, Bellevue Palace Hotel, Hotel Bären, City Hotel.

Golf and Country Club Zumikon

LOCATION: Zurich-Zumikon (6 miles from center of Zurich). COURSE SIZE: 18 holes; 6,315 yards; par 72. AVAILABILITY TO VISITORS: Visitors welcome weekdays only. GREEN FEES: Weekdays, $5. CADDIE FEES: $1.50 per 9-hole round; $2.25 per 18-hole round. GOLF CLUB RENTALS: $1.50. GOLF CART RENTALS: 75¢. MOTORIZED GOLF CART RENTALS: Not available. LESSONS: $2.50 per half hour; $4.50 per hour. CLUBHOUSE FACILITIES: Restaurant and bar available. RECOMMENDED ACCOMMODATIONS: Zumikon-Zurich: Gashof Rössli (near course). Zurich: Dolder Grand Hotel, Hotel Eden au Lac, St. Gotthard.

Golf Club Arosa

LOCATION: Arosa (½ mile from Arosa). COURSE SIZE: 9 holes; 2,675 yards; par 33. AVAILABILITY TO VISITORS: Visitors welcome. GREEN FEES: Per day, $2; per week, $10; per month, $25; season, $30. CADDIE FEES: 50¢ per 9-hole round. GOLF CLUB RENTALS: $1.14 per day. GOLF CART RENTALS: Not available. MOTORIZED GOLF CART RENTALS: Not available. LESSONS: $4 per hour. CLUBHOUSE FACILITIES: Restaurant and bar available. RECOMMENDED ACCOMMODATIONS: Arosa: Hotel Hof Maran (near golf course), Hotel Valsana, Hotel Post, Alexander Golf Hotel, Hotel Ratia, Hotel Seehof, Waldhotel-National.

Golf Club Bad Ragaz

LOCATION: Bad Ragaz, St. Gallen (within city limits). COURSE SIZE: 18 holes; 6,408 yards; par 71. AVAILABILITY TO VISITORS: Visitors welcome. GREEN FEES: Weekdays, $2.80; Saturdays and Sundays, $4.20 per day; per week, $16.50; per month, $35. CADDIE FEES: $1.40 per round. GOLF CLUB RENTALS: Available. GOLF CART RENTALS: Available. MOTORIZED GOLF CART RENTALS: Not available. LESSONS: Available. CLUBHOUSE FACILITIES: Restaurant and bar available. RECOMMENDED ACCOMMODATIONS: Hotel Quellenhof, Grand Hotel Hof Ragaz (near the clubhouse), Hotel Lattman, Hotel Wartenstein.

Golf Club Basel

LOCATION: Basel (4 miles from city limits). COURSE SIZE: 9 holes; 2,430 yards; par 33. AVAILABILITY TO VISITORS: Visitors welcome. GREEN FEES: Weekdays, $1.80; Saturdays and Sundays, $2.75 per day; per week, $11.50; per month, $34; season, $80. CADDIE FEES: 50¢ per 9-hole round. GOLF CLUB RENTALS: Not available. GOLF CART RENTALS: Available. MOTORIZED GOLF CART RENTALS: Not available. LESSONS: $1.80 per half hour; $3.50 per hour. CLUBHOUSE FACILITIES: Restaurant and bar available. RECOMMENDED ACCOMMODATIONS: Hotel Landgasthof Schluessel (near course). Basel: Hotel Drei Koenige, Hotel Euler, Hotel Schweizerhof, Hotel City, Hotel Drachen, Hotel International, Hotel Victoria-National, Hotel Excelsior.

Golf Club Burgenstock

LOCATION: Burgenstock, Nidwalden (10 miles from Lucerne). COURSE SIZE: 9 holes; 2,300 yards; par 36. AVAILABILITY TO VISITORS: Visitors welcome. GREEN FEES: Per day, $2. CADDIE FEES: 90¢ per 18-hole round. GOLF CLUB RENTALS: 75¢ per day. GOLF CART RENTALS: Not available. MOTORIZED GOLF CART RENTALS: Not available. LESSONS: $3.75 per hour. CLUBHOUSE FACILITIES: Restaurant and bar available. RECOMMENDED ACCOMMODATIONS: Burgenstock: Grand-Hotel, Palace Hotel, Park Hotel.

Golf Club Davos

LOCATION: Davos (5 minutes from town). COURSE SIZE: 9 holes; 2,875 yards; par 36. AVAILABILITY TO VISITORS: Visitors welcome. GREEN FEES: Per day, $1.80; per week, $8; per month, $18. CADDIE FEES: 90¢ per 18-hole round. GOLF CLUB RENTALS: Not available. GOLF CART RENTALS: Available. MOTORIZED GOLF CART RENTALS: Not available. LESSONS: $3.20 per hour. CLUBHOUSE FACILITIES: Restaurant and bar available. RECOMMENDED ACCOMMODATIONS: Davos: Central Sporthotel, Sporthotel Meierhof, Hotel Europe, Hotel Schweizerhof, Hotel Angleterre, Hotel Terminus, Hotel Morosani's Post.

Golf Club de Genève

LOCATION: Onex-Genève (3 miles from Geneva). COURSE SIZE: 18 holes; 6,326 yards; par 73. AVAILABILITY TO VISITORS: Visitors welcome. GREEN FEES: Weekdays, $3.40; Saturdays and Sundays, $4.50; per week, $17.15; per month, $40; season, $171. CADDIE FEES: $1.40 per round. GOLF CLUB RENTALS: $1.10 per day. GOLF CART RENTALS: 60¢ per day. MOTORIZED GOLF CART RENTALS: Not available. LESSONS: $1.60 per half hour; $2.75 per hour. CLUBHOUSE FACILITIES: Restaurant and bar available. RECOMMENDED ACCOMMODATIONS: Geneva: Hotel Bristol, Hotel Rivage, Hotel de la Paix, Hotel Montana, Hotel Astoria, Hotel Angleterre, Hotel du Rhône, Hotel Richmond, Hotel des Bergues.

Golf Club de Neuchâtel

LOCATION: Pierre à Bots/Neuchâtel (2 miles from Neuchâtel). COURSE SIZE: 9 holes; 2,486 yards; par 35. AVAILABILITY TO VISITORS: Visitors welcome. GREEN FEES: Weekdays, $1.15; Saturdays and Sundays, $2.25 per day; per week, $5.75; per month, $11.50; season, $34. CADDIE FEES: 50¢ per 9-hole round. GOLF CLUB RENTALS: 50¢ per day. GOLF CART RENTALS: 50¢ per 18-hole round. MOTORIZED GOLF CART RENTALS: Not available. LESSONS: Available. CLUBHOUSE FACILITIES: Restaurant and bar. RECOMMENDED ACCOMMODATIONS: Chaumont et Golf Hotel (near course). Neuchâtel: Hotel Beau Lac, Hotel Touring.

Golf Club Lausanne

LOCATION: Chalet à Gobert-Vaud (4 miles from Lausanne). COURSE SIZE: 18 holes; 6,742 yards; par 72. AVAILABILITY TO VISITORS: Visitors welcome. GREEN FEES: Weekdays, $3.50; Saturdays and Sundays, $4.50 per day; per month, $45. CADDIE FEES: $1.50 per round. GOLF CLUB RENTALS: $1.10 to $2 per day. GOLF CART RENTALS: 50¢ per day. MOTORIZED GOLF CART RENTALS: Not available. LESSONS: $2 per half hour; $3.50 per hour. CLUBHOUSE FACILITIES: Restaurant and bar available. RECOMMENDED ACCOMMODATIONS: Hotel du Golf et Forêt (near course), Motel Vert-Bois (near course). Lausanne: Hotel Lausanne Palace, Hotel Beau Rivage, Hotel Royal, Hotel de la Paix, Hotel Carlton, Hotel Alexandria, Hotel Mirabeau.

Golf Club Lenzerheide-Valbella

LOCATION: Lenzerheide, Graubünden (½ mile from Lenzerheide). COURSE SIZE: 18 holes; 5,745 yards; par 70. AVAILABILITY TO VISITORS: Visitors welcome. GREEN FEES: Weekdays, $2.50; Saturdays, $3.20; Sundays, $3.75; per week, $11.50; per month, $33; season, $57.17. CADDIE FEES: 35¢ per 9-hole round; $1 per 18-hole round. GOLF CLUB RENTALS: Available. GOLF CART RENTALS: Available. MOTORIZED GOLF CART RENTALS: Not available. LESSONS: Two professionals available: $2 and $2.75 per half hour; $3.20 and $4.50 per hour. CLUBHOUSE FACILITIES: Restaurant and bar available. RECOMMENDED ACCOMMODATIONS: Grand Hotel Kurhaus, Grand Hotel Schweizerhof, Hotel Lenzerhorn, Park Hotel.

Golf Club Lugano Magliaso

LOCATION: Magliaso/Ticino (5 miles from Lugano). COURSE SIZE: 9 holes and 18 tees; 5,992 yards; par 72. AVAILABILITY TO VISITORS: Visitors welcome. GREEN FEES: Weekdays, $2; Saturdays and Sundays, $3.20 per day; per week, $11.50; per month, $27.50; season, $57. CADDIE FEES: $1.50 per 18-hole round. GOLF CLUB RENTALS: 90¢ per day. GOLF CART RENTALS: 25¢ per 18-hole round. MOTORIZED GOLF CART RENTALS: Not available. LESSONS: $2.75 per hour. CLUBHOUSE FACILITIES: Restaurant and bar available. RECOMMENDED ACCOMMODATIONS: Lugano-Magliaso: Villa Magliasina. Lugano: Hotel Paladina, Hotel Bellevue, Hotel Royal Splendide, Grand Palace Hotel.

Golf Club Patriziale

LOCATION: Ascona/TI (½ mile from Ascona; 2½ miles from Locarno). COURSE SIZE: 18 holes; 6,376 yards; par 72. AVAILABILITY TO VISITORS: Visitors welcome. GREEN FEES: Weekdays, $3; Saturdays and Sundays, $3.75 per day; per week, $17.50; per month, $45. CADDIE FEES: $1.40 per round. GOLF CLUB RENTALS: 50¢ per round. GOLF CART RENTALS: 50¢ per round. MOTORIZED GOLF CART RENTALS: Not available. LESSONS: $4.20 per hour. CLUBHOUSE FACILITIES: Restaurant and bar available. RECOMMENDED ACCOMMODATIONS: Ascona: Hotel Delta, Castelle del Sole, Hotel Europe au Lac, Hotel Monte Verità, Hotel Schweizerhof, Hotel Ascona, Hotel al Porto.

Shell's Wonderful World of Golf

Gene Sarazen tees off in the Swiss Alps.

Golf Club Saanenland

LOCATION: Gstaad (15 minutes from Gstaad; 10 minutes from Schönried; 5 minutes from Saanenmöser). COURSE SIZE: 9 holes; 3,095 yards; par 36. AVAILABILITY TO VISITORS: Visitors welcome. GREEN FEES: Weekdays, $2.25; Saturdays and Sundays, $3.50 per day; per week, $10; per month, $23. CADDIE FEES: $1.60 per 18-hole round. GOLF CLUB RENTALS: Available. GOLF CART RENTALS: 50¢ per day. MOTORIZED GOLF CART RENTALS: Not available. LESSONS: $4.10 per hour. CLUBHOUSE FACILITIES: Restaurant and bar available. RECOMMENDED ACCOMMODATIONS: Gstaad: Palace Hotel, Grand Hotel Alpina, Grand Hotel Bellevue, Bernerhof, Park Hotel, National, Meurice, Olden, Neueret, Rössli, Victoria, Christiana-Garni. Saanenmöser: Golf-and-Sport Hotel, Pension Hornberg. Schönried: Hotel Ermitage and Golf. Saanen: Saanenhof.

Golf Club Vulpera

LOCATION: Vulpera (in center of town). COURSE SIZE: 9 holes; 4,044 yards; par 33. AVAILABILITY TO VISITORS: Visitors permitted limited play, inquire ahead. GREEN FEES: Per day, $2; per week, $9.15; season, $20.50. CADDIE FEES: 60¢ per 9-hole round. GOLF CLUB RENTALS: $1.25 per round; $1.60 per day. GOLF CART RENTALS: $1.25 to $1.60 per day. MOTORIZED GOLF CART RENTALS: Not available. LESSONS: $2 per half hour; $3.50 per hour. CLUBHOUSE FACILITIES: Restaurant and bar available. RECOMMENDED ACCOMMODATIONS: Hotel Schweizerhof, Hotel Villa Silvana, Hotel Villa Maria, Waldhaur Vulpura (all near course).

Golf d'Evian

On the shores of Lake Geneva. See listing under France.

Kulm Golf and Country Club

LOCATION: St. Moritz (in St. Moritz). COURSE SIZE: 9 holes; 3,100 yards; par 34. AVAILABILITY TO VISITORS: Visitors welcome. GREEN FEES: Per day, $1.60; per week, $7.25; per month, $18. CADDIE FEES:

50¢ per 9-hole round; 80¢ per 18-hole round. GOLF CLUB RENTALS: $1.50 per 18-hole round. GOLF CART RENTALS: Not available. MOTORIZED GOLF CART RENTALS: Not available. LESSONS: $2 per half hour; $3.50 per hour. CLUBHOUSE FACILITIES: Restaurant and bar available. RECOMMENDED ACCOMMODATIONS: St. Moritz: Kulm Hotel, Carlton Hotel, Palace Hotel, Crystal Hotel, Villa Suvretta.

Lucerne Golf Club

LOCATION: Dietschiberg, Lucerne (1 mile from Lucerne). COURSE SIZE: 18 holes; 5,480 yards; par 70. AVAILABILITY TO VISITORS: Visitors welcome. GREEN FEES: Weekdays: half day, $2.80; full day, $3.70; Sundays, $4.65; per week, $17.40; two weeks, $27.90; per month, $46.50; season, $186. CADDIE FEES: $1.40 per round. GOLF CLUB RENTALS: $1.90 per day. GOLF CART RENTALS: 75¢ per day. MOTORIZED GOLF CART RENTALS: Not available. LESSONS: $2.50 per half hour; $4.40 per hour. CLUBHOUSE FACILITIES: Restaurant and bar available. RECOMMENDED ACCOMMODATIONS: Lucerne: Hotel Schweizerhof, Palace Hotel, Hotel Carlton Tivoli, Hotel Eden, Hotel Wilden Mann, Hotel Astoria, Hotel National, Hotel Europe, Hotel Chateau Gutsch.

Montreux Golf Club

LOCATION: Aigle-Montreux (9 miles from Montreux). COURSE SIZE: 18 holes; 5,848 yards; par 70 (18 holes under construction). AVAILABILITY TO VISITORS: Visitors welcome. GREEN FEES: Weekdays, $2.50; Saturdays and Sundays, $2.75 per day; per week, $11.50; per month, $27.50; season, $45. CADDIE FEES: 80¢ per 9-hole round; $1.50 per 18-hole round. GOLF CLUB RENTALS: Available. GOLF CART RENTALS: Available. MOTORIZED GOLF CART RENTALS: Not available. LESSONS: $1.60 per half hour; $2.75 per hour. CLUBHOUSE FACILITIES: Restaurant and bar available. RECOMMENDED ACCOMMODATIONS: Montreux: Montreux Palace Hotel, Hotel Excelsior, Hotel Belmont.

Ostschweizerischer Golf Club

LOCATION: St. Gallen (12 miles from St. Gallen). COURSE SIZE: 18 holes; 6,444 yards; par 72. AVAILABILITY TO VISITORS: Visitors welcome. GREEN FEES: Weekdays, $2.25; Saturdays and Sundays, $3.50;

per week, $11.50; per month, $18. CADDIE FEES: 90¢ per 18-hole round. GOLF CLUB RENTALS: Not available. GOLF CART RENTALS: Not available. MOTORIZED GOLF CART RENTALS: Not available. LESSONS: $3.20 per hour. CLUBHOUSE FACILITIES: Restaurant and bar available. RECOMMENDED ACCOMMODATIONS: St. Gallen: Hotel Metropole. Wil: Hotel Derby. Uzwil: Hotel Uzwil. Flawil: Hotel Rössli.

Villars Golf Club

LOCATION: Villars Palace, Villars-sur-Ollon (2 miles from center of town). COURSE SIZE: 9 holes; 3,600 yards; par 31. AVAILABILITY TO VISITORS: Visitors welcome. GREEN FEES: Per day, $2; per week, $8; per month, $23; season, $34. CADDIE FEES: 60¢ per 9-hole round; 90¢ per 18-hole round. GOLF CLUB RENTALS: $1.10 and $2.25 per day. GOLF CART RENTALS: 75¢ per day. MOTORIZED GOLF CART RENTALS: Not available. LESSONS: $4.50 per hour. CLUBHOUSE FACILITIES: Restaurant and bar available. RECOMMENDED ACCOMMODATIONS: Villars: Hotel Villars Palace, Hotel du Parc, Hotel de la Renadière.

SCANDINAVIA

Golf found its way to Scandinavia in 1888 when an Englishman designed a private 9-hole course for a Swedish landowner. The game caught on rapidly in Sweden, but the rest of Scandinavia was slow in taking up the sport. Full-scale development did not begin until after World War II.

Sweden is the Mecca of Scandinavian golf. It has 94 courses, 31 of which are 18-hole layouts. And it boasts the northernmost golf course in the world at Boden, just south of the Arctic Circle. At this course one can play all night during June and July; the midnight sun takes care of the lighting. In the rest of Sweden it is possible to play between 3 A.M. and 10 P.M. throughout the summer.

International golf weeks at many clubs along the sunny southwest coast offer a series of tournaments open to the visiting golfer, and make Sweden especially popular for the summer sportsman. The vast coniferous forests and rich vegetation common to all of Sweden make golf here a memorable and refreshing experience.

Denmark is a greenkeeper's delight. Although it sits in the northern tier of the Continent, there are no extremes of heat or cold, and the entire countryside is constantly carpeted in lush green.

Golf was introduced in Denmark in 1898, but it was not until around 1930 that the game began to catch on. In recent years it has taken on a new popularity and considerable new course construction has taken place. The Danes now have 19 golf courses, up from 13 two years ago. British architects are principally responsible for the course design and have done an imaginative job of blending their work with the heavily wooded, hilly countryside. Surrounded by castles, quaint villages, and historic fortresses, many clubs are like a bit of fairyland come to life. The Copenhagen and Rungsted courses are among the best examples, although most tourists will also want to visit the sporty layout at Helsingør near Kronborg Castle. Kronborg, of course, is famous as the setting of *Hamlet*.

The golf season in Denmark runs from March through November, although there are many days of good golfing weather in the three winter months. During the summer, daylight hours are long and it is even possible to get in a few holes after dinner.

121

Norway has only six courses, but interest is increasing, and new ones are on the way. During the summer the player can golf around the clock. In fact, midnight cup tournaments take place in Trondheim. Tee-off time is 10 P.M. and all participants receive a Midnight Sun Golf Certificate to display at their home club (cost, $2).

Finland is a do-it-yourself paradise for the budget-minded golfer. There are only seven courses, but five others are near completion. The traveling golfer must take his own clubs because he won't be able to rent any there. Don't worry about caddie fees because there probably won't be any caddies. Visitors are often exempt from green fees, too. Be prepared to take all balls, tees, scorecards, and other accessory equipment, as there is a good chance they will not be there either. It sort of leaves one feeling like the Marco Polo of the golf world, but it's fun.

Denmark

SEASON: March through November.

HOW TO GET THERE: By Pan American Jet Clipper, about 9¼ hours (elapsed time) from New York via London; or fly Pan Am nonstop to Oslo in 7 hours, then to Copenhagen in about 1½ hours. By ship, about 10 days.

GOLF EQUIPMENT: American equipment is readily available.

LANGUAGE: Danish; English is understood everywhere by the man in the street.

TIME: Six hours later than U.S. Eastern Standard Time. Denmark uses the 24-hour clock (12:01 to 24 is P.M.).

Aalborg Golf Club

LOCATION: Sohngaardsholm (about 2½ miles from Aalborg). COURSE SIZE: 9 holes; 6,385 yards when played as 18 holes from different tees. AVAILABILITY TO VISITORS: Visitors welcome. GREEN FEES: Weekdays, $2.15; Saturdays and Sundays, $2.85 daily; weekend, $5; per week, $8.60. CADDIE FEES: Caddies not available. GOLF CLUB RENTALS: Not available. GOLF CART RENTALS: Not available. MOTORIZED GOLF CART RENTALS: Not available. LESSONS: $4 per hour. CLUBHOUSE FACILITIES: Restaurant and bar available. RECOMMENDED ACCOMMODATIONS: Hotel Aalborg (with a beautiful view of the course), Hotel Phoenix.

Asserbo Golf Club

LOCATION: Bodkergarden, Frederiksvaerk, Sjelland (2 miles by taxi from Frederiksvaerk). COURSE SIZE: 9 holes; 2,680 yards; par 34. AVAILABILITY TO VISITORS: Visitors welcome. GREEN FEES: Weekdays, $2.15; Saturdays, $2.85; Sundays, $3.60. CADDIE FEES: $1 per 9-hole round. GOLF CLUB RENTALS: Not available. GOLF CART RENTALS: Not available. LESSONS: $2.40 per half hour. CLUBHOUSE FACILITIES: Restaurant and bar available. RECOMMENDED ACCOMMODATIONS: Asserbo clubhouse. Liselje: Several good hotels and pensions. Asserbo: Hotel Sandkroen. Frederiksvaerk: Hotel Frederiksvaerk.

Copenhagen Golf Club

LOCATION: Springforbi (8 miles north of Copenhagen by taxi). COURSE SIZE: 18 holes; 6,328 yards; par 71. AVAILABILITY TO VISITORS: Visitors welcome. GREEN FEES: Weekdays, $3.60; Saturday or Sunday, $5; all weekend, $7.25; per week, $14.50; per two weeks, $21.50; per month, $35.75. CADDIE FEES: $1 per 9-hole round; $1.50 per 18-hole round. GOLF CLUB RENTALS: $2 per day. GOLF CART RENTALS: 75¢ per day. LESSONS: $3 per half hour. CLUBHOUSE FACILITIES: Restaurant and bar available. RECOMMENDED ACCOMMODATIONS: Springforbi: Hotel Beaulieu (near course). Klampenborg: Hotel Bellevue, Pension Patricia. Copenhagen: Hotel D'Angleterre, Palace Hotel, Royal Hotel.

Esbjerg Golf Club

LOCATION: Gjesing Copse (about 3 miles north of Esbjerg). COURSE SIZE: 9 holes; 3,025 yards. AVAILABILITY TO VISITORS: Visitors welcome. GREEN FEES: $2.15 per day. CADDIE FEES: 50¢ for 9 holes. GOLF CLUB RENTALS: Not available. GOLF CART RENTALS: Not available. MOTORIZED GOLF CART RENTALS: Not available. LESSONS: $1.80 per half hour. CLUBHOUSE FACILITIES: Restaurant.

Fanø Golf Club

LOCATION: Fanø Vesterhaysdad (on the island of Fanø, by railroad from Esbjerg). COURSE SIZE: 18 holes; 4,800 yards; par 67. AVAILABILITY TO VISITORS: Visitors welcome. GREEN FEES: Per day, $2.85; per week, $6.50; per two weeks, $25. CADDIE FEES: 45¢ per round. GOLF CLUB RENTALS: Not available. GOLF CART RENTALS: Not available. LESSONS: Available from July–August 10; $2.15 per half hour. CLUBHOUSE FACILITIES: Restaurant and bar available. RECOMMENDED ACCOMMODATIONS: Fanø: Hotel Atlantic, Hotel Kongen af Denmark, Golf Villa, Strandhotellet.

Helsingør Golf Club

LOCATION: Lille Godthaab, Gl. Hellebaekvej, Helsingør (1 mile from Helsingør). COURSE SIZE: 18 holes; 6,300 yards; par 69. AVAILABILITY TO VISITORS: Visitors welcome. GREEN FEES: Weekdays, $2.15; Saturdays, $2.85; Sundays, $3.60; per week, $7.25; per month, $14.50; season, $36.20. CADDIE FEES: $1.50 per round. GOLF CLUB RENTALS: Available. GOLF CART RENTALS: Available. LESSONS: $2.45 per half hour. CLUBHOUSE FACILITIES: Restaurant is not available. RECOMMENDED ACCOMMODATIONS: Helsingør: Hotel Marienlyst, Hotel Prins Hamlet. Hellebaek: Hotel Hellebaek Kyst. Snekkersten: Kystens Perle.

Holbaek Golf Club

LOCATION: On an island about 3 miles from the Holbaek ferry at Drogerup. COURSE SIZE: 9 holes; 2,900 yards; par 35. AVAILABILITY TO VISITORS: Visitors welcome. GREEN FEES: Weekdays, $2.15; Saturdays, $2.85; Sundays, $3.60. CADDIE FEES: No caddies available. GOLF CLUB RENTALS: 75¢ per day. GOLF CART RENTALS: 45¢ per day. MOTORIZED GOLF CART RENTALS: Not available. LESSONS: $2.15 per half hour. CLUBHOUSE FACILITIES: Restaurant, driving range. RECOMMENDED ACCOMMODATIONS: Holbaek: Hotel Strandparken.

Kolding Golf Club

LOCATION: Emerholtsvej, Kolding-Jutland (1 mile from Kolding). COURSE SIZE: 18 holes. AVAILABILITY TO VISITORS: Visitors welcome. GREEN FEES: Weekdays, $1.45; Saturdays and Sundays, $2.15 per day. CADDIE FEES: Caddies are not available. GOLF CLUB RENTALS: $1 per day. GOLF CART RENTALS: 50¢ per day. LESSONS: Available one week per month: $1.20 per half hour; $2.20 per hour. CLUBHOUSE FACILITIES: Restaurant is not available. RECOMMENDED ACCOMMODATIONS: Kolding: Hotel Saxildhus, Hotel Kolding.

Nyborg GolfKlub

LOCATION: At Nyborg on the coast of the Store Baelt (approximately 25-mile drive from Odense). COURSE SIZE: 18 holes. AVAILABIL-

ITY TO VISITORS: Visitors welcome. GREEN FEES: Weekdays, $2.85; Saturdays, $4.35; Sundays, $5; weekend, $8.60; per week, $14.30. CADDIE FEES: $1.45 per round. GOLF CLUB RENTALS: Available at reasonable rates. GOLF CART RENTALS: Available. MOTORIZED GOLF CART RENTALS: Not available. LESSONS: $2.85 per hour. CLUBHOUSE FACILITIES: Big, modern clubhouse with bar, dining room, attractive fireplace, and full locker facilities. RECOMMENDED ACCOMMODATIONS: Nyborg: Hotel Nyborg Strand, Hotel Nyborg, Hotel Hesselet.

Randers Golf Club

LOCATION: 4 miles west of Randers. COURSE SIZE: 9 holes; 2,780 yards. AVAILABILITY TO VISITORS: Visitors welcome. GREEN FEES: Weekdays, $2.15; Saturdays and Sundays, $2.85 daily; weekend, $5; per week, $9.30. CADDIE FEES: Caddies not available. GOLF CLUB RENTALS: Not available. GOLF CART RENTALS: Not available. MOTORIZED GOLF CART RENTALS: Not available. LESSONS: $2.25 per hour. CLUBHOUSE FACILITIES: Restaurant. RECOMMENDED ACCOMMODATIONS: Randers Hotel.

Rungsted Golf Club

LOCATION: Rungsted Kyst (city limits of Rungsted; 35 minutes by car from Copenhagen). COURSE SIZE: 18 holes; 6,640 yards; par 72. AVAILABILITY TO VISITORS: Visitors welcome. GREEN FEES: Weekdays, $4.30; Saturdays, $5.75; Sundays, $7.15; weekends, $11.50; per week, $21.50. CADDIE FEES: $2.15 per 18-hole round. GOLF CLUB RENTALS: $1.45 per day. GOLF CART RENTALS: 30¢ per day. LESSONS: One professional available: $2.90 per half hour; two assistants: $2.50 per half hour. CLUBHOUSE FACILITIES: Restaurant and bar available. RECOMMENDED ACCOMMODATIONS: Klampenborg: Bellevue Strandhotel. Fredensborg: Hotel Storekro. Horsholm: Horsholm Hotel. Rungsted Kyst: "Birkehuset" (near course).

St. Knud Golf Club

LOCATION: Slipshavnsvej, Nyborg (17 miles from Odense; 1½ miles from center of Nyborg). COURSE SIZE: 18 holes; 6,562 yards; par 71. AVAILABILITY TO VISITORS: Visitors welcome. GREEN FEES: Weekdays, $2.20; weekend, $4.35, or $2.90 per day; per week, $9.50.

Tony Lema approaches gigantic green at Rungsted, Copenhagen.

CADDIE FEES: 75¢ per round. GOLF CLUB RENTALS: Not available. GOLF CART RENTALS: 45¢ per round; 75¢ per day. LESSONS: $2.20 per hour. CLUBHOUSE FACILITIES: Restaurant and bar available. RECOMMENDED ACCOMMODATIONS: Nyborg: Hotel Nyborg Strand, Christianslund Badehotel. Odense: Grand Hotel, Motel Odense.

Silkeborg Golf Klub

LOCATION: Resenbro near Silkeborg in the lake area. COURSE SIZE: 18 holes; 6,250 yards. AVAILABILITY TO VISITORS: Welcome. GREEN FEES: Weekdays, $2.15; Saturdays, $2.85; Sundays, $3.60. CADDIE FEES: No caddies available. GOLF CLUB RENTALS: Not available. GOLF CART RENTALS: Not available. MOTORIZED GOLF CART RENTALS: Not available. LESSONS: $1.75 per half hour when pro is available. CLUBHOUSE FACILITIES: Clubhouse offers basic facilities but no restaurant; bar is self-service. RECOMMENDED ACCOMMODATIONS: Silkeborg: Dania, Silkeborg Bad, Gl. Skovriddergaard. Kongensbro: Kongensbro Kro.

Finland

SEASON: April through October.

HOW TO GET THERE: By Pan Am Jet Clipper from New York to Helsinki, about 10½ hours (elapsed time) via Oslo and Stockholm. Or fly by Pan Am Jet to London, Paris, Amsterdam, Frankfurt, or Copenhagen and make connections for Helsinki. Helsinki is only 1 hour's flying time from Stockholm. By ship, about 10 days from New York to Helsinki.

GOLF EQUIPMENT: American equipment available.

LANGUAGE: Finland is a bilingual country where approximately 90 per cent of the population speaks Finnish, the rest Swedish. English is spoken in Helsinki and other large cities.

TIME: Six hours later than U.S. Eastern Standard Time.

Aulangon Golfklubi

LOCATION: Hameenlinna (2 miles from Hameenlinna by car). COURSE SIZE: 9 holes, 2,623 yards; par 35. AVAILABILITY TO VISITORS: Visitors welcome. GREEN FEES: Per day, $2.80. CADDIE FEES: 65¢ per round. GOLF CLUB RENTALS: 95¢ per day. GOLF CART RENTALS: 65¢ per day. LESSONS: Not available. CLUBHOUSE FACILITIES: Restaurant and bar available. RECOMMENDED ACCOMMODATIONS: Hotel Aulanko.

Helsingin Golfklubi

LOCATION: Helsinki (4 miles from Helsinki by car). COURSE SIZE: 18 holes; 6,535 yards; par 70. AVAILABILITY TO VISITORS: Visitors welcome. GREEN FEES: Weekdays, $3.10; Saturdays and Sundays, $4.65 per day. CADDIE FEES: About $1.55 per round. GOLF CLUB RENTALS: $1.25 per day. GOLF CART RENTALS: 50¢ per round. LESSONS: Available. CLUBHOUSE FACILITIES: Restaurant and bar, showers, and sauna bath. RECOMMENDED ACCOMMODATIONS: Helsinki: Vaakuna Hotelli, Palace Hotel, Hotel Torni, Hotel Marski, Hotel Helsinki.

Kokkola-Gamalarkarleby Golf R.F.

LOCATION: Kokkola (1 mile from Kokkola-Gamalakarleby by car). COURSE SIZE: 9 holes; 2,272 yards; par 30. AVAILABILITY TO VISITORS: Visitors welcome. GREEN FEES: None required by guests. CADDIE FEES: Caddies are not available. GOLF CLUB RENTALS: Not available. GOLF CART RENTALS: Not available. MOTORIZED GOLF CART RENTALS: Not available. LESSONS: Not available. CLUBHOUSE FACILITIES: Not available. RECOMMENDED ACCOMMODATIONS: Kokkola-Gamalakarleby: Hotel Grand.

Lahden Golf R.Y.

LOCATION: Lahti (15 minutes by car from the city limits). COURSE SIZE: 9 holes; 3,770 yards; par 30. AVAILABILITY TO VISITORS: Visitors welcome. CADDIE FEES: Caddies are not available. GOLF CART RENTALS: Not available. MOTORIZED GOLF CART RENTALS: Not available. LESSONS: Not available. CLUBHOUSE FACILITIES: Not available.

Viipurin Golf R.Y.

LOCATION: Lappeenranta (less than a mile from the city by car). COURSE SIZE: 9 holes; 2,257 yards; par 35. AVAILABILITY TO VISITORS: Visitors welcome. GREEN FEES: Guests are not required to pay green fees. CADDIE FEES: Caddies are not available. GOLF CART RENTALS: Not available. MOTORIZED GOLF CART RENTALS: Not available. CLUBHOUSE FACILITIES: Not available. RECOMMENDED ACCOMMODATIONS: Lappeenranta: Hotel Patria, Hotel Hospitz.

Norway

SEASON: May to September.

HOW TO GET THERE: Through plane service by Pan Am Jet Clipper to Oslo, 7 hours from New York (or connect from Jet Clipper to Copenhagen). By sea, 7 to 8 days.

GOLF EQUIPMENT: American equipment available.

LANGUAGE: English is spoken everywhere.

TIME: Six hours later than U.S. Eastern Standard Time.

Bergen Golfklubb

LOCATION: Bergen (15 minutes by car from town). COURSE SIZE: 9 holes; 2,275 yards; par 67 (double tees). AVAILABILITY TO VISITORS: Visitors welcome. GREEN FEES: Weekdays, $2.10; per week, $10.50. CADDIE FEES: 70¢ per 9-hole round. MOTORIZED GOLF CART RENTALS: Not available. LESSONS: Bill Tomlinson, $2.80 per lesson. CLUBHOUSE FACILITIES: Restaurant not available. RECOMMENDED ACCOMMODATIONS: Bergen: Hotel Norge, Hotel Bristol, Hotel Orion, Hotel Teminus, Hotel Alrek, Hotel Neptun.

Borregaard Golf Club (Sarpsborg)

LOCATION: Borregaard (2 miles from town). COURSE SIZE: 9 holes; 2,515 yards; par 33. AVAILABILITY TO VISITORS: Visitors welcome. RECOMMENDED ACCOMMODATIONS: St. Olafś Hotel.

Oslo Golfklubb

LOCATION: Oslo (5 miles from city limits). COURSE SIZE: 18 holes; 6,586 yards; par 71. AVAILABILITY TO VISITORS: Members of recognized golf clubs welcome; beginners not permitted to play. GREEN FEES: Weekdays, $2.80; Saturdays and Sundays, $4.90 per day; weekends, $5.60; per week, $8.60; season, temporary membership, $98. CADDIE FEES: $1.20 per 9-hole round; $1.60 per 18-hole round. GOLF

CLUB RENTALS: $1.50 per round. GOLF CART RENTALS: 56¢ per day. MOTORIZED GOLF CART RENTALS: Not available. LESSONS: $1 per 25 minutes. CLUBHOUSE FACILITIES: Restaurant and bar available. RECOMMENDED ACCOMMODATIONS: Holmenkollen Turisthotell, KNA Hotellet, Hotell Continental, Bristol Hotel, Grand, and many more down town.

Stavanger Golfklubb

LOCATION: Stavanger (3 miles from center of town, 10 minutes by car). COURSE SIZE: 18 holes; 5,653 yards; par 68. AVAILABILITY TO VISITORS: Visitors welcome. GREEN FEES: Weekdays, $2.10; Saturdays and Sundays, $2.80 per day; per weekend, $4.92; per week, $10.50. CADDIE FEES: $1.05 per round. MOTORIZED GOLF CART RENTALS: Not available. LESSONS: $2.10 per lesson. CLUBHOUSE FACILITIES: Restaurant and bar available. RECOMMENDED ACCOMMODATIONS: A/S Hotel Atlantic, Royal Norwegian Automobile Club's Hotel, Hotel Victoria, Hotel Alstor.

Trondheim Golfklubb

LOCATION: Trondheim (a few minutes from center of town). COURSE SIZE: 9 holes; 5,300 yards; par 70 (for 18 holes). AVAILABILITY TO VISITORS: Visitors welcome. GREEN FEES: $2.10 daily. CADDIE FEES: $1 per 18-hole round. GOLF CLUB RENTALS: Available. GOLF CART RENTALS: Available. MOTORIZED GOLF CART RENTALS: Not available. LESSONS: $1.50 per half hour. CLUBHOUSE FACILITIES: Restaurant and bar available. RECOMMENDED ACCOMMODATIONS: Hotel Britannia, Hotel Prinsen, Astoria Hotel.

Vestfold Golfklubb

LOCATION: Tonsberg (5 miles from Tonsberg—10 minutes by car; 14 miles from Sandeford—20 minutes by car; 22 miles from Sarvik; 66 miles from Oslo—1½ hours by car). COURSE SIZE: 18 holes; 6,500 yards; par 72. AVAILABILITY TO VISITORS: Members of recognized golf clubs welcome. GREEN FEES: Weekdays, $1.50; Saturdays or Sundays, $2.10; weekends, $3.50; per week, $7; per month, $14. CADDIE FEES: Caddies are not available. GOLF CLUB RENTALS: 70¢ per day. MOTORIZED GOLF CART RENTALS: Not available. LESSONS: $1.75 per half hour. CLUBHOUSE FACILITIES: Restaurant and bar available (only soft drinks). RECOMMENDED ACCOMMODATIONS: Hotel Klubben, Grand Hotel, Park Hotel, Hotel Kong Karl, Hotel Atlantic.

Sweden

SEASON: May through September.

HOW TO GET THERE: By Pan Am's through-plane Jet Clipper service from New York, about 8¾ hours to Stockholm via Oslo, or connect from transatlantic Jet Clippers to London (6½ hours) or Copenhagen (9 hours). By ship, 8 to 10 days from New York to Göteborg.

GOLF EQUIPMENT: American equipment available.

LANGUAGE: English is spoken and understood by most people.

TIME: Six hours later than U.S. Eastern Standard Time.

Åtvidabergs Golfklubb

LOCATION: Åtvidaberg (one mile by taxi west of Åtvidaberg; 23 miles southeast of Linköping). COURSE SIZE: 18 holes; 6,200 yards; par 72. AVAILABILITY TO VISITORS: Visitors welcome. GREEN FEES: Weekdays, $2; Saturdays or Sundays, $4; weekends, $6; per week, $10; per month, $30. CADDIE FEES: Not available. GOLF CLUB RENTALS: 60¢ per day. GOLF CART RENTALS: 60¢ per round. MOTORIZED GOLF CART RENTALS: Not available. LESSONS: $1.40 per lesson. CLUBHOUSE FACILITIES: Restaurant and bar available. RECOMMENDED ACCOMMODATIONS: Tragårdshotellet (by the first tee). Åtvidaberg: Hotel Stallet.

Båstads Golfklubb

LOCATION: Haljarp (4 miles southwest of Båstad). COURSE SIZE: 18 holes; 6,065 yards; par 71. AVAILABILITY TO VISITORS: Visitors welcome. GREEN FEES: June 15–August 15: per day, $4; per week, $20; per month, $40. Other times: per day, $3; per week, $17. CADDIE FEES: $1.50. GOLF CLUB RENTALS: $1 per day. GOLF CART RENTALS:

40¢ per day. MOTORIZED GOLF CART RENTALS: Not available. LESSONS: $1.80 per lesson. CLUBHOUSE FACILITIES: Restaurant and bar available. RECOMMENDED ACCOMMODATIONS: Båstad: Hotel Skanegarden, Hotel Båstad, Hotel Borgen.

Boden Golf Club

LOCATION: 10 miles north of Boden; the world's northernmost golf course. COURSE SIZE: 9 holes; 5,580 yards; par 34. AVAILABILITY TO VISITORS: Visitors welcome. GREEN FEES: Per day, $2; per week, $5. CADDIE FEES: Caddies not available. GOLF CLUB RENTALS: Not available. GOLF CART RENTALS: Not available. MOTORIZED GOLF CART RENTALS: Not available. LESSONS: No professional. CLUBHOUSE FACILITIES: Refreshments, golf shop. RECOMMENDED ACCOMMODATIONS: Boden: Hotel Hercules.

Borås Golfklubb

LOCATION: Ostra Vik (4 miles south of Borås). COURSE SIZE: 18 holes; 5,850 yards; par 70. AVAILABILITY TO VISITORS: Visitors welcome. GREEN FEES: $2 per day. CADDIE FEES: Not available. MOTORIZED GOLF CART RENTALS: Not available. LESSONS: $2.40 per hour. CLUBHOUSE FACILITIES: Restaurant available. RECOMMENDED ACCOMMODATIONS: Hotel de Nord, Park Hotel, Hotel City, Stadshotellet.

Delsjö Golfklubb

LOCATION: Kallebäck, Göteborg. COURSE SIZE: 18 holes; 6,310 yards; par 72. AVAILABILITY TO VISITORS: Visitors welcome. GREEN FEES: Weekdays, $3.50; Saturdays and Sundays, $5 per day. CADDIE FEES: Caddies not available. GOLF CLUB RENTALS: $1 per day. GOLF CART RENTALS: $1 per day. MOTORIZED GOLF CART RENTALS: Not available. LESSONS: $2.40 for 25 minutes. CLUBHOUSE FACILITIES: Restaurant and pro shop. RECOMMENDED ACCOMMODATIONS: See Göteborgs Golfklubb listing.

Djursholms Golfklubb

LOCATION: Djursholm (5 miles north of Stockholm; by electric tramway to Eddavagen). COURSE SIZE: 18 holes; 5,740 yards; par 72. Plus 9-hole course. AVAILABILITY TO VISITORS: Visitors welcome.

GREEN FEES: Weekdays, $2; Saturdays or Sundays, $4; weekends, $8; per week, $10; per month, $30. CADDIE FEES: Not available. GOLF CLUB RENTALS: $1 per day. GOLF CART RENTALS: 50¢ per day. MOTORIZED GOLF CART RENTALS: Not available. LESSONS: $3 per lesson. CLUBHOUSE FACILITIES: Restaurant and bar available. RECOMMENDED ACCOMMODATIONS: Carlton Hotel, Continental Hotel, Flamingo Hotel, Foresta Hotel, Gillet Hotel, Grand Hotel Royal, Hotel Grand-Esplanade, Hotel Plaza, Hotel Stockholm, Hotel Strand, Hotel Reisen, Hotel Apollonia, Hotel Malmen, Place Hotel, Strandvagshotellet.

Drottningholms Golfklubb

LOCATION: Stockholm (near the Royal Castle of Drottningholm, 4 miles northwest of Stockholm). COURSE SIZE: 18 holes; 6,450 yards; par 71. AVAILABILITY TO VISITORS: Visitors welcome. GREEN FEES: Weekdays, $2; Saturdays and Sundays, $4 per day. CADDIE FEES: Not available. GOLF CLUB RENTALS: $2 per day, includes cart rental. MOTORIZED GOLF CART RENTALS: Not available. LESSONS: $2 per lesson. CLUBHOUSE FACILITIES: Restaurant and bar available. RECOMMENDED ACCOMMODATIONS: Carlton Hotel, Continental Hotel, Flamingo Hotel, Foresta Hotel, Gillet Hotel, Grand Hotel Royal, Hotel Grand-Esplanade, Hotel Plaza, Hotel Stockholm, Hotel Strand, Hotel Reisen, Hotel Apollonia, Hotel Malmen, Palace Hotel, Strandvagshotellet.

Falsterbo Golfklubb

LOCATION: Falsterbo (20 miles south of Malmö by car). COURSE SIZE: 18 holes; 6,365 yards; par 71. AVAILABILITY TO VISITORS: Visitors welcome. GREEN FEES: Weekdays, $3; Saturdays and Sundays, $5 per day; per month, $20 (July, $30). CADDIE FEES: $1.40 per round. GOLF CLUB RENTALS: Available. GOLF CART RENTALS: Available. LESSONS: $2 per half hour. CLUBHOUSE FACILITIES: Restaurant and bar available June through August. RECOMMENDED ACCOMMODATIONS: Falsterbo: Falsterbohus, Strandhotellet. Malmö: Arkaden, Grand Hotel, Hotel Kramer, Hotel Savoy, Hotel St. Jorgen, Hotel Tunneln.

Flommens Golfklubb

LOCATION: Falsterbo (20 miles south of Malmö by car). COURSE SIZE: 18 holes; 6,235 yards; par 73. AVAILABILITY TO VISITORS: Visitors welcome. GREEN FEES: Weekdays, $3; Saturdays and Sundays, $5 per day. CADDIE FEES: Not available. GOLF CLUB RENTALS: Not available. GOLF CART RENTALS: Not available. MOTORIZED GOLF CART RENTALS: Not available. LESSONS: $2.40 per half hour. CLUBHOUSE FACILITIES: Restaurant, pro shop. RECOMMENDED ACCOMMODATIONS: See Falsterbo Golfklubb listing.

Göteborgs Golfklubb

LOCATION: Hovas (7 miles south of Göteborg by car). COURSE SIZE: 18 holes; 5,525 yards; par 70. AVAILABILITY TO VISITORS: Visitors welcome. GREEN FEES: Weekdays, $4; weekends, $5 per day; per week, $15; per month, $30. CADDIE FEES: $1.50 per round. GOLF CLUB RENTALS: $1.40 per day. GOLF CART RENTALS: 70¢ per round. MOTORIZED GOLF CART RENTALS: Not available. LESSONS: $3 per hour. CLUBHOUSE FACILITIES: Restaurant available. RECOMMENDED ACCOMMODATIONS: Park Avenue, Grand Palace Hotel, Eggers, Opalen, Kung Karl.

Halmstad Golfklubb

LOCATION: Tylösand (6 miles northwest of Halmstad by car). COURSE SIZE: 18 holes; 6,480 yards; par 72. Plus 9-hole course. AVAILABILITY TO VISITORS: Visitors welcome. GREEN FEES: June 15 to October 15; per day, $5; per week, $30; per month, $60. Other times: per day, $3; weekends, $4 per day; per week, $20; per month, $40. CADDIE FEES: $1.40 per round. GOLF CLUB RENTALS: $3 per day. GOLF CART RENTALS: $1 per day. MOTORIZED GOLF CART RENTALS: Not available. LESSONS: $3 per hour. CLUBHOUSE FACILITIES: Restaurant and bar available. RECOMMENDED ACCOMMODATIONS: Halmsted Golfklubb Hotel and Restaurant, Hotel Tylogarden, Tylosands Havsbad, Villa Gotthem, Hotel Martensson, Hotel Svea-Gillet, Grand Hotel (Halmstad).

Shell's Wonderful World of Golf

Typically narrow, wooded fairway at Halmsted Golfklubb.

Jönköping-Huskvarna Golfklubb

LOCATION: Jönköping (2 miles south of town). COURSE SIZE: 18 holes; 6,065 yards; par 72. AVAILABILITY TO VISITORS: Visitors welcome. GREEN FEES: Weekdays, $3; Saturdays and Sundays, $4 per day. CADDIE FEES: $1.20 per round. GOLF CLUB RENTALS: $1 per round. GOLF CART RENTALS: 40¢ per day. MOTORIZED GOLF CART RENTALS: Not available. LESSONS: $1.60 per hour. CLUBHOUSE FACILITIES: Restaurant available. RECOMMENDED ACCOMMODATIONS: Jönköping: Stora Hotellet, Opalen, Hotel Savoy.

Kalmar Golf Club

LOCATION: Kalmar (6 miles north of Kalmar). COURSE SIZE: 18 holes; 6,500 yards; par 72. AVAILABILITY TO VISITORS: Visitors welcome. GREEN FEES: Per day, $2. CADDIE FEES: Not available. MOTORIZED GOLF CART RENTALS: Not available. LESSONS: $1.40 per half hour. CLUBHOUSE FACILITIES: Restaurant available. RECOMMENDED ACCOMMODATIONS: Kalmar: Stadshotellet.

Lidingö Golfklubb

LOCATION: Sticklinge (4 miles east of Stockholm). COURSE SIZE: 18 holes; 6,700 yards; par 72. AVAILABILITY TO VISITORS: Visitors welcome. GREEN FEES: Weekdays, $2; Saturdays and Sundays, $4 per day; per week, $12; per month, $30. CADDIE FEES: $1.40 per round. GOLF CLUB RENTALS: $2 per day. GOLF CART RENTALS: $1 per day. LESSONS: $3 for 50 minutes. CLUBHOUSE FACILITIES: Restaurant available. RECOMMENDED ACCOMMODATIONS: Stockholm Golfklubb.

Linköpings Golfklubb

LOCATION: Linköping (2 miles west of town). COURSE SIZE: 18 holes; 6,200 yards; par 72. AVAILABILITY TO VISITORS: Visitors welcome. GREEN FEES: Weekdays, $2; Saturdays or Sundays, $3; weekends, $5; per week, $10; per month, $25. CADDIE FEES: Not available. MOTORIZED GOLF CART RENTALS: Not available. LESSONS: Available. CLUBHOUSE FACILITIES: Restaurant available. RECOMMENDED ACCOMMODATIONS: Frimurarehotellet, Hotel Rally.

Ljunghusens Golfklubb

LOCATION: Malmö (17 miles south of Malmö). COURSE SIZE: 18 holes; 6,500 yards; par 72. Plus 9-hole course. AVAILABILITY TO VISITORS: Visitors welcome. GREEN FEES: Weekdays, $3; Saturdays and Sundays, $4 per day. CADDIE FEES: $1.50 per round. MOTORIZED GOLF CART RENTALS: Not available. LESSONS: $1.60 per hour. CLUBHOUSE FACILITIES: Restaurant available. RECOMMENDED ACCOMMODATIONS: Falsterbo: Falsterbohus.

Lunds Akademiska Golfklubb

LOCATION: Lund (4 miles east of town). COURSE SIZE: 18 holes; 6,000 yards; par 72. AVAILABILITY TO VISITORS: Visitors welcome. GREEN FEES: Weekdays, $2; Saturdays and Sundays, $4 per day. CADDIE FEES: Not available. GOLF CLUB RENTALS: $1 per day. GOLF CART RENTALS: $1 per day. MOTORIZED GOLF CART RENTALS: Not available. LESSONS: $3.60 per hour. CLUBHOUSE FACILITIES: Restaurant available. RECOMMENDED ACCOMMODATIONS: Grand Hotel and La Strada in Lund.

Mölle Golfklubb

LOCATION: Helsingborg (in the national park of Kullen, about 2 miles by car northwest of Mölle). COURSE SIZE: 18 holes; 5,600 yards; par 70. AVAILABILITY TO VISITORS: Visitors welcome. GREEN FEES: Weekdays, $3; Saturdays and Sundays, $4 per day; per week, $15. CADDIE FEES: $1.80 per round. GOLF CLUB RENTALS: $1 per day. GOLF CART RENTALS: $1 per day. MOTORIZED GOLF CART RENTALS: Not available. LESSONS: $2.80 per hour. CLUBHOUSE FACILITIES: Restaurant available. RECOMMENDED ACCOMMODATIONS: Mölle: Hotel Kullagarden (clubhouse), Grand Hotel, Hotel Kullaberg, Turisthotellet.

Örebro Golfklubb

LOCATION: Örebro (12 miles west of Örebro; 30 minutes by bus from Örebro). COURSE SIZE: 18 holes; 6,250 yards; par 71. AVAILABILITY TO VISITORS: Visitors welcome. GREEN FEES: Weekdays, $2; Satur-

Shell's Wonderful World of Golf

Sarazen in Sweden. Note thick rough and trees.

days and Sundays, $3 per day; per week, $12. CADDIE FEES: Not available. GOLF CLUB RENTALS: $1 per day. GOLF CART RENTALS: 40¢ per day. MOTORIZED GOLF CART RENTALS: Not available. LESSONS: $1 per half hour. CLUBHOUSE FACILITIES: Restaurant and bar available. RECOMMENDED ACCOMMODATIONS: Örebro: Stora Hotellet, Hotell Grey Rosen, Hotel Bergsmannen. Kumla: Stadshotellet.

Östersund-Frösö Golfklubb

LOCATION: Östersund (on the island of Frösön, 6 miles west of Östersund; midnight golf can be played in June and July). COURSE SIZE: 9 holes (18 tees); 5,630 yards; par 69. AVAILABILITY TO VISITORS: Visitors welcome. GREEN FEES: Weekdays, $1.50; Saturdays and Sundays, $2 per day; per week, $7; per month, $20. CADDIE FEES: Not available. GOLF CLUB RENTALS: Not available. GOLF CART RENTALS: Not available. MOTORIZED GOLF CART RENTALS: Not available. LESSONS: Not available. CLUBHOUSE FACILITIES: Restaurant and bar available. RECOMMENDED ACCOMMODATIONS: Frösön: Ostbergsgarden. Östersund: Hotel Standard, Hotel Östersund, Hotel Zata, Hotel Linden, Hotel Algen.

Rättviks Golfklubb

LOCATION: Rättvik, Dalecarlia. COURSE SIZE: 9 holes (18 tees); 6,000 yards; par 71. AVAILABILITY TO VISITORS: Visitors welcome. GREEN FEES: Weekdays, $2.40; Saturdays and Sundays, $2.40 per day; per week, $6. CADDIE FEES: Caddies not available. GOLF CLUB RENTALS: $1 per day. GOLF CART RENTALS: Not available. MOTORIZED GOLF CART RENTALS: Not available. LESSONS: Not available. CLUBHOUSE FACILITIES: Snack bar, golf shop. RECOMMENDED ACCOMMODATIONS: Hotel Lerdalshöjden, Hotel Persborg, Hotel Touristhemmet, Motel Tre Hästar.

Rya Golfklubb

LOCATION: Rya (6 miles south of Helsingborg). COURSE SIZE: 18 holes; 6,200 yards; par 71. AVAILABILITY TO VISITORS: Visitors welcome. GREEN FEES: Weekdays, $3; Saturdays and Sundays, $4 per day; per week, $18; per month, $50. CADDIE FEES: $1.40 per round. GOLF CLUB RENTALS: $1.50 per day. GOLF CART RENTALS: 70¢ per day. MOTORIZED GOLF CART RENTALS: Not available. LESSONS: $2.80 per lesson. CLUBHOUSE FACILITIES: Restaurant and bar available. RECOMMENDED ACCOMMODATIONS: Helsingborg: Hotel Mollberg, Grand Hotel.

Stockholms Golfklubb

LOCATION: Danderyd (4 miles north of Stockholm). COURSE SIZE: 18 holes; 5,810 yards; par 70. AVAILABILITY TO VISITORS: Visitors welcome. GREEN FEES: Weekdays, $2; Saturdays and Sundays, $4 per day; per week, $10; per month, $30. CADDIE FEES: $1.40 per round. GOLF CLUB RENTALS: $1-$2 per day. GOLF CART RENTALS: 60¢ per day. MOTORIZED GOLF CART RENTALS: Not available. LESSONS: $3 per lesson. CLUBHOUSE FACILITIES: Restaurant and bar available. RECOMMENDED ACCOMMODATIONS: Carlton Hotel, Continental Hotel, Flamingo Hotel, Foresta Hotel, Gillet Hotel, Grand Hotel Royal, Hotel Grand-Esplanade, Hotel Plaza, Hotel Stockholm, Hotel Strand, Hotel Reisen, Hotel Apollonia, Hotel Malmen, Palace Hotel, Strandvagshotellet.

Sundsvall Golfklubb

LOCATION: Kvissleby (10 miles south of Sundsvall). COURSE SIZE: 18 holes; 6,175 yards; par 72. AVAILABILITY TO VISITORS: Visitors welcome. GREEN FEES: Weekdays, $1.50; Saturdays and Sundays, $2 per day; per week, $8. GOLF CLUB RENTALS: No charge. GOLF CART RENTALS: No charge. MOTORIZED GOLF CART RENTALS: Not available. LESSONS: $1.50 per lesson. CLUBHOUSE FACILITIES: Restaurant and bar available. RECOMMENDED ACCOMMODATIONS: Liz Motel, 5 miles south of Sundsvall; Hotel Knaust in Sundsvall.

Visby Golfklubb

LOCATION: On the island of Gotland, 17 miles from Visby. COURSE SIZE: 18 holes; 6,330 yards; par 72. AVAILABILITY TO VISITORS: Visitors welcome. GREEN FEES: Weekdays, $2.40; Saturdays and Sundays, $4 per day; per week, $10. CADDIE FEES: Caddies not available. GOLF CLUB RENTALS: $1 per day. GOLF CART RENTALS: 60¢ per day. MOTORIZED GOLF CART RENTALS: Not available. LESSONS: $3 per hour. CLUBHOUSE FACILITIES: Snacks and refreshments available. Bar, casino, and nightclub located at hotel in Visby. RECOMMENDED ACCOMMODATIONS:

Kronholmensgard (½ mile to course; 50 yards to beach), Visby Stads-hotel.

Wermdö Golf and Country Club

LOCATION: Torpa, Hemmestavik (20 miles by bus or taxi south-east of Stockholm). COURSE SIZE: 18 holes; 6,435 yards; par 71. AVAIL-ABILITY TO VISITORS: Visitors welcome. GREEN FEES: Weekdays, $4; Saturdays and Sundays, $6 per day. CADDIE FEES: Not available. GOLF CLUB RENTALS: $1 per day. GOLF CART RENTALS: Included in green fees. MOTORIZED GOLF CART RENTALS: Not available. LESSONS: $4 per 50 minutes. CLUBHOUSE FACILITIES: Restaurant and bar, gymnasium, sauna, swimming pool, tennis court, boating. RECOMMENDED ACCOM-MODATIONS: See Stockholms Golfklubb listing.

BERMUDA, THE BAHAMAS, AND THE CARIBBEAN

Golf is booming in the Caribbean.

Puerto Rico and Jamaica are flourishing resorts, each having several outstanding courses. Nassau and the surrounding Bahamas have undergone extensive development in the past few years and now boast links on New Providence, Grand Bahama, and Eleuthera that aspire to be the best in the Caribbean. Nassau's Blue Hill Golf Club is a 9-hole, par-3 course which has the unique feature of lights for night play. Even the Virgins have a glorious 18-hole beauty at Fountain Valley.

In the southern Caribbean the 18-hole courses vanish, but there is a sprinkling of 9-hole spreads among the Virgin Islands, Antigua, Barbados, Aruba, Grenada, Monserrat, and St. Vincent. At the southern tip of the island chain, 18 holes reappear at Trinidad, and Trinidad's sister, Tobago, will soon have another one.

Course conditions vary a great deal throughout the Caribbean. Some of the courses are worthy of garden club awards for their fastidious grooming, while others, particularly in the south, lack the equipment and the devoted greenkeepers to maintain top standards. In Trinidad, as on many other islands, fairways and greens are kept by hand. Modern power equipment is rarely seen. The natural beauty of the islands, however, more than compensates for the rough edges of the courses.

Native caddies are excellent, courteous, charge reasonably, and are unusually expert at club selection; they themselves often play quite well.

Clubs can be rented, but it is suggested that the traveling golfer take along his own to insure quality and a complete set.

For the golf widow and children there are plenty of beaches, tennis courts, shops, and other attractions to occupy the day while the man on the links swings away. The Caribbean is an ideal selection for a combination golf-and-family vacation.

SEASON: Year round.

HOW TO GET THERE: Pan Am Jet Clippers depart many times a day for the Caribbean from New York, Baltimore–Washington, Philadelphia, and Miami. Check with the local Pan Am office or travel agent for flights to fit vacation needs.

GOLF EQUIPMENT: Available throughout Caribbean at U.S. prices or slightly higher.

LANGUAGE: English spoken and understood everywhere.

TIME: About the same as U.S. Eastern Standard Time.

Antigua

Antigua, in the Lesser Antilles, has two small 9-hole courses. They both have rather limited facilities and are less than 2,500 yards in length. They provide a nice break from the fabulous fishing, skindiving, sailing, and beaches.

Gambles Golf Club

LOCATION: Hodges Bay. COURSE SIZE: 9 holes; 2,500 yards; par 34. AVAILABILITY TO VISITORS: Visitors welcome. GREEN FEES: Per day, $1.20; per week, $3; per month, $9. CADDIE FEES: 65¢ per 9 holes. GOLF CLUB RENTALS: Not available. GOLF CART RENTALS: Available. MOTORIZED GOLF CART RENTALS: Not available. LESSONS: No professional. CLUBHOUSE FACILITIES: Bar and snack service. RECOMMENDED ACCOMMODATIONS: Antigua Beach Hotel (next to course), White Sands Hotel, Blue Waters Hotel, Anchorage, Caribbean Beach Club, Jolly Beach, and Curtain Bluff. All are within 20 minutes of the course.

Half-Moon Bay

LOCATION: Half-Moon Bay (½-hour ride from St. John's by taxi). COURSE SIZE: 9 holes; 2,410 yards; par 35. AVAILABILITY TO VISITORS: Visitors welcome. GREEN FEES: Per day, $2.50; per week, $10. GOLF CLUB RENTALS: Available.

Bahama Islands

The Bahamas form a chain of 700 beautiful semitropical islands that stretches in an arc from just off the coast of Florida down into the Caribbean. However, there are golf courses on only four of the islands.

New Providence and Grand Bahama have nine good courses between them, including the fabulous King's Inn and Coral Harbour clubs. At Eleuthera, the Cotton Bay Club is open to guests only during the summer; it is well worth a trip to play it. Shell's Wonderful World of Golf staged a match there early in 1968 between Arnold Palmer and Julius Boros. It is testimony enough to say that Cotton Bay is still a proud golf course.

Bahamas Country Club

LOCATION: Nassau, New Providence (4 miles from city). COURSE SIZE: 18 holes; 6,500 yards; par 71. AVAILABILITY TO VISITORS: Visitors welcome. GREEN FEES: Per day, December 15 through April 21, $7; all other times, $6. CADDIE FEES: $3 per round. GOLF CLUB RENTALS: $4 per day. CLUBHOUSE FACILITIES: Restaurant, bar, and lockers. RECOMMENDED ACCOMMODATIONS: Carleton House, Dolphin, Pilot House Club, Mantagu Beach, Sheraton-British Colonial, Emerald Beach, Nassau Beach.

Coral Harbour Golf Club

LOCATION: Coral Harbour, Nassau, New Providence. COURSE SIZE: 18 holes; 6,710 yards; par 70. AVAILABILITY TO VISITORS: Open to guests of Coral Harbour Hotel and Club and to guests of members. GREEN FEES: December to May, $8; May to December, $6. CADDIE FEES: 9 holes, $2; 18 holes, $3. GOLF CLUB RENTALS: $4 per day.

Blasting out of sand in Nassau.

GOLF CART RENTALS: Not available. MOTORIZED GOLF CART RENTALS: 9 holes, $5; 18 holes, $8 (for 2). LESSONS: $5.50 per half hour. CLUBHOUSE FACILITIES: Lunch and light snacks; no social facilities. RECOMMENDED ACCOMMODATIONS: Coral Harbour Club, 2 miles from course, for which free transportation is provided.

Grand Bahama Hotel and Country Club

LOCATION: West End, Grand Bahama Island. COURSE SIZE: 18 holes; 6,800 yards; par 72. AVAILABILITY TO VISITORS: Visitors welcome. GREEN FEES: Included in hotel package, otherwise extra. CADDIE FEES: $3, plus tip. GOLF CLUB RENTALS: Available. CLUBHOUSE FACILITIES: Full facilities.

Cotton Bay Golf Club

LOCATION: Rock Sound, Eleuthera. COURSE SIZE: 18 holes; 7,140 yards (championship); 6,510 (regular); par 72. AVAILABILITY TO VISITORS: Exclusively for members and their guests from Dec. 15 to April 30. Available other times to guests of the Rock Sound Club, which operates off season. GREEN FEES: $5 daily. CADDIE FEES: 9 holes, $1; 18 holes, $2; 2 bags for 18 holes, $3. GOLF CLUB RENTALS: Not available. GOLF CART RENTALS: Not available. MOTORIZED GOLF CART RENTALS: 9 holes, $5; 18 holes, $8. LESSONS: Available. CLUBHOUSE FACILITIES: Full clubhouse facilities. RECOMMENDED ACCOMMODATIONS: Rock Sound Club.

King's Inn and Golf Club

LOCATION: Freeport, Grand Bahama Island. COURSE SIZE: 18 holes; 7,000 yards; par 72. AVAILABILITY TO VISITORS: Visitors welcome. GREEN FEES: December to May, $7.50; May to December, $5. CADDIE FEES: Caddies not available. GOLF CLUB RENTALS: All equipment available on a rental basis. GOLF CART RENTALS: Not available. MOTORIZED GOLF CART RENTALS: December to May, $10 and $6; May to December, $7.50 and $5. Electric golf carts only. LESSONS: 4 professionals available at $10 per half hour. CLUBHOUSE FACILITIES: Restaurant, bar, lounge, and locker facilities available. RECOMMENDED ACCOMMODATIONS: King's Inn, on the premises. Many other hotels and inns available in Freeport.

Lucayan Golf and Country Club

LOCATION: Freeport, Grand Bahama Island. COURSE SIZE: 18 holes; 6,800 yards; par 72. AVAILABILITY TO VISITORS: Visitors limited to guests of the Lucayan Beach Hotel and the Lucayan Harbour Inn and Marina. GREEN FEES: May 1-December 15, $3 daily; December 15-May 1, $5 daily. CADDIE FEES: Caddies not available. GOLF CLUB RENTALS: $5 per round. GOLF CART RENTALS: Not available. MOTOR-IZED GOLF CART RENTALS: $10 per cart per round (two persons). LESSONS: John Schoonmaker, $12 per hour; Craig Wood, $25 per hour. CLUBHOUSE FACILITIES: Complete, modern restaurant, lounge, and locker facilities. RECOMMENDED ACCOMMODATIONS: Lucayan Harbour Inn and Marina, Lucayan Beach Hotel. There are also many fine hotels and inns in Freeport.

Lyford Cay Club

LOCATION: Nassau (by car to the tip of New Providence). COURSE SIZE: 18 holes; 6,832 yards; par 72. AVAILABILITY TO VISITORS: Visitors welcome when accompanied by members.

Nassau Golf Club

LOCATION: Nassau, New Providence (4 miles from city by taxi). COURSE SIZE: 18 holes; 6,700 yards. AVAILABILITY TO VISITORS: Visitors welcome. GREEN FEES: $7.50 daily, December through April; $6 daily, May through November. CADDIE FEES: $3 per bag, 18 holes; $2 per bag, 9 holes. GOLF CLUB RENTALS: $3 daily. MOTORIZED GOLF CART RENTALS: $8 per round (electric carts). LESSONS: Professional available year round. CLUBHOUSE FACILITIES: Bar, lockers. RECOM-MENDED ACCOMMODATIONS: Nassau Beach Hotel, Emerald Beach Hotel, and Balmoral Club are nearby.

Barbados

Barbados is nightclubs, rum, exotic seafoods, sunshine, duty-free perfumes, cameras, and cashmeres, and two golf courses. One, Rockley Golf and Country Club, has just added a back nine to become the island's first full-size course. Barbados even has a church in which George Washington worshiped.

Rockley Golf and Country Club

LOCATION: About 1 mile by taxi from south shore hotels, and 10 or more miles south of the St. James hotel area of Bridgetown. COURSE SIZE: 18 holes. AVAILABILITY TO VISITORS: Visitors welcome. GREEN FEES: Per day, $4. GOLF CLUB RENTALS: Available. GOLF CART RENTALS: Not available. MOTORIZED GOLF CART RENTALS: Not available. LESSONS: Available from December to March, $3.75 per lesson. CLUBHOUSE FACILITIES: Bar and snack lunches available. RECOMMENDED ACCOMMODATIONS: St. Lawrence, Royal-on-Sea, Royal Caribbean, Caribbee, Blue Waters Beach, Colony Club, Miramar, Coral Reef, Sandy Lane, South Winds, Bonnie Dundee, Marine Hotel, Ocean View, Windsor, Accra Beach.

Sandy Lane Hotel Golf Course

LOCATION: St. James (a short ride by taxi from Bridgetown). COURSE SIZE: 9 holes; 3,369 yards; par 36. AVAILABILITY TO VISITORS: Visitors welcome. GREEN FEES: Per day, $5. CADDIE FEES: By arrangement. GOLF CLUB RENTALS: Available. RECOMMENDED ACCOMMODATIONS: St. Lawrence, Royal-on-Sea, Royal Caribbean, Caribbee, Blue Waters Beach, Colony Club, Miramar, Coral Reef, Sandy Lane, South Winds, Bonnie Dundee, Marine Hotel, Ocean View, Windsor, Accra Beach.

Bermuda

Bermuda is truly a golfer's paradise. It has more acres of fairway per square mile than any place in the world. It is playable all year long. And, for the American golfer, it is only 773 miles from New York—just 2 hours by plane. Whether the golfer intends to go for a week or even for just a long weekend, Bermuda offers him outstanding golf facilities.

There are seven good golf courses in Bermuda, including one par-3 course. They are all easy to get to from any hotel. But where the visitor stays in Bermuda will determine to a great extent where he will play his golf. There is only one public course, the Queen's Park Golf Club. The traveling golfer must be introduced at the other clubs by a member, unless he is a guest at a particular hotel. The hotel requirements are not difficult to meet since it is very easy to "trade" with golfers staying at the various affiliated hotels. But two of the private courses, Riddel's Bay and Charles Blair MacDonald's masterpiece at Mid-Ocean, are difficult at peak season and the golfer will have to find a member ahead of time who will supply him with a letter of introduction.

The courses here are some of the world's finest. They are plush and well designed. Many of them have been picturesquely situated by the seashore and offer numerous sand traps and heavy roughs. A classic hole is the eighteenth overlooking the Atlantic at Robert Trent Jones' Castle Harbour. If the player has a tendency to slice, he should bring along a fish net or a shovel. Heavy rough borders the shoreline along the right side and after that nothing but water faces the player. But if the player stays straight, he'll do well—just so long as he stays out of the traps that guard the green.

Caddies are available to help the golfer play the various courses. Most of them are experts regarding their particular course and it is wise for the golfer to have them club for him until he gets the feeling of local terrain and wind conditions.

If the traveling golfer is the competitive type, the Bermuda Golf Association will supply details on major tournaments which he can enter with or without an accredited handicap. Discounts and special golf rates for groups are available on request from the Bermuda Trade Development Board. Any time of year the golfer can expect that the emerald fairways, pink sands (in traps and otherwise), and warm weather will give him an ideal golfing vacation.

SEASON: Year round.

HOW TO GET THERE: By Pan Am Jet Clipper, about 2 hours from New York or Boston; a little more than 1½ days by boat.

GOLF EQUIPMENT: American equipment available at reasonable prices.

LANGUAGE: English.

TIME: One hour later than U.S. Eastern Standard Time.

Belmont Golf and Country Club

LOCATION: Warwick (3 miles by taxi from Hamilton). COURSE SIZE: 18 holes; 5,683 yards; par 68. AVAILABILITY TO VISITORS: Limited to guests of the Belmont Golf and Country Club, the Bermudiana and the Harmony Hall hotels; otherwise, introduction by member is necessary. GREEN FEES: Hotel guests, $5; others, $7. CADDIE FEES: $2 per 9-hole round, single; $7 per 18-hole round, double. GOLF CLUB RENTALS: Half set, $3 per day; full set, $4 per day. GOLF CART RENTALS: $1 per day. MOTORIZED GOLF CART RENTALS: $5 for 9 holes; $9 for 18 holes. LESSONS: $5 per lesson. CLUBHOUSE FACILITIES: Restaurant, bar, and pro shop.

Castle Harbour Golf Club

LOCATION: Castle Harbour (6 miles by taxi from Hamilton). COURSE SIZE: 18 holes; 6,022 yards; par 71. AVAILABILITY TO VISITORS: Limited to guests of the Castle Harbour Hotel; otherwise, introduction by member is necessary. GREEN FEES: Hotel guests, $5; others, $7. CADDIE FEES: $2.50 per 9-hole round, single; $4 double. $4 per 18-hole round, single; $7 double. GOLF CLUB RENTALS: $4 per day. GOLF CART RENTALS: Not available. MOTORIZED GOLF CART RENTALS: $9 per 18-hole round. LESSONS: George Bird, pro. CLUBHOUSE FACILITIES: Full facilities.

Allan Brown

The 5th hole at the famous Mid-Ocean Golf Club.

Mid-Ocean Golf Club

LOCATION: Tuckerstown (8 miles by taxi from Hamilton). COURSE SIZE: 18 holes; 6,519 yards; par 71. AVAILABILITY TO VISITORS: Private club; inquire at club concerning playing privileges. GREEN FEES: House guests, $5 per day; others, $10 per day. CADDIE FEES: $2.15 per 9-hole round, single; $4, double. $4 per 18 holes, single; $7, double. GOLF CLUB RENTALS: $3 per day. LESSONS: Available. CLUBHOUSE FACILITIES: Full facilities.

Princess Golf and Beach Club

LOCATION: Southampton Parish (private bus service from Princess Hotel). COURSE SIZE: 18 holes; 3,000 yards; par 54. AVAILABILITY TO VISITORS: By introduction. GREEN FEES: Princess Hotel guests, $3; guests of other hotels, $5. GOLF CLUB RENTALS: $2.50 per round. GOLF CART RENTALS: $1.50 per round. MOTORIZED GOLF CART RENTALS: $6 per round. CLUBHOUSE FACILITIES: Bar, snack bar, changing rooms, showers. RECOMMENDED ACCOMMODATIONS: Princess Hotel.

Queen's Park Golf Club

LOCATION: Devonshire (2 miles by taxi from Hamilton). COURSE SIZE: 9 holes; 3,081 yards; par 35. AVAILABILITY TO VISITORS: Visitors welcome. GREEN FEES: $4 per day. CADDIE FEES: $1.40 per 9-hole round; $2.80 per 18-hole round. GOLF CLUB RENTALS: $1.40 per day. LESSONS: H. Bascome, pro.

Riddell's Bay Golf and Country Club

LOCATION: Warwick (5 miles by taxi from Hamilton). COURSE SIZE: 18 holes; 5,600 yards; par 68. AVAILABILITY TO VISITORS: Only on introduction by a member. GREEN FEES: $7 daily. CADDIE FEES: $2.50 per round. GOLF CLUB RENTALS: $3 per day. GOLF CART RENTALS: 75¢ per round. LESSONS: Douglas Dalziel, pro. CLUBHOUSE FACILITIES: Full facilities.

St. George Hotel Golf Club

LOCATION: St. George. COURSE SIZE: 9 holes; 2,700 yards; par 34. AVAILABILITY TO VISITORS: Open to guests of all other hotels and guest houses in Bermuda upon presentation of an introduction card. GREEN FEES: Free to St. George Hotel guests; visitors, $3 per day. CADDIE FEES: $2 per round. GOLF CLUB RENTALS: Half set, $2 per round. GOLF CART RENTALS: Not available. MOTORIZED GOLF CART RENTALS: Not available. LESSONS: Grant Lockhead, pro; $5 per hour. CLUBHOUSE FACILITIES: Fully licensed, changing facilities, and golf shop.

Curaçao

A touch of Holland in the Caribbean, Curaçao is a duty-free haven for the bargain shopper and a quiet interlude from the more bustling resort islands to the north. For those who have their clubs along, the Shell Golf Club, with its sand greens, makes a nice afternoon of exercise.

Shell Golf Club

LOCATION: 7 miles from Willemstad. COURSE SIZE: 9 holes; 3,079 yards; par 36. AVAILABILITY TO VISITORS: Visitors welcome. GREEN FEES: $3.50 daily. CADDIE FEES: $1 per 9 holes. GOLF CLUB RENTALS: Only 2 sets available at $1 each. GOLF CART RENTALS: Not available. MOTORIZED GOLF CART RENTALS: Not available. LESSONS: $3 per half hour. CLUBHOUSE FACILITIES: Full facilities of Shell Clubhouse including bar and restaurant. RECOMMENDED ACCOMMODATIONS: Hotel Curaçao Intercontinental, Hotel Country Inn, Hotel Flamboyant, Hotel Curaçao Hilton.

Dominican Republic

The Bella Vista Club in Santo Domingo is currently undergoing renovations and is scheduled to reopen in late 1968. The Santo Domingo Country Club, the only other course on the island, is one of the better bargains in the Caribbean. Full facilities include an air-conditioned clubhouse and modern swimming pool at reasonable prices, and there is seldom any wait on the first tee.

Bella Vista Club *

LOCATION: Santo Domingo (adjacent to the El Embajador Intercontinental Hotel). COURSE SIZE: 18 holes; par 72. AVAILABILITY TO VISITORS: Visitors welcome. GREEN FEES: Per day, $2.50. CADDIE FEES: $2.50 per day. GOLF CLUB RENTALS: Available. CLUBHOUSE FACILITIES: Full facilities. RECOMMENDED ACCOMMODATIONS: El Embajador Intercontinental Hotel.

* NOTE: Club undergoing renovations; opening in late 1968.

Santo Domingo Country Club

LOCATION: Santo Domingo (5 miles from El Embajador Intercontinental Hotel). COURSE SIZE: 18 holes; regulation length; par 72. AVAILABILITY TO VISITORS: Guests of Intercontinental Hotel welcome. GREEN FEES: Per round, $3. CADDIE FEES: $2 per round, plus tip. GOLF CLUB RENTALS: $3 and $4 per day. GOLF CART RENTALS: Not available. CLUBHOUSE FACILITIES: Full facilities, including swimming pool. RECOMMENDED ACCOMMODATIONS: El Embajador Intercontinental Hotel.

Grenada

It has been said of Grenada: "With the many other tropical delights, who needs golf?"

There is one nine-hole course. The fairways and greens are excellent, the latter being of Acapulco grass, which remains green the year round. The course is 350 feet above sea level, delightfully cool, and offers a unique view of both sides of the island.

Grenada Golf Club

LOCATION: St. Georges. COURSE SIZE: 9 holes; 2,780 yards; par 35. AVAILABILITY TO VISITORS: Visitors welcome. GREEN FEES: $3 per day. CADDIE FEES: 60¢ for 9 holes. GOLF CLUB RENTALS: $1.25 per day. GOLF CART RENTALS: Not available. MOTORIZED GOLF CART RENTALS: Not available. LESSONS: Available. CLUBHOUSE FACILITIES: Bar and lounge. RECOMMENDED ACCOMMODATIONS: Silver Sands Hotel, Grenada Beach Hotel, Spice Island Inn, Calabash, The Islander Hotel, The Grand Anse Riviera Hotel, Ross Point Inn, Crescent Inn, St. James Hotel.

Jamaica

Jamaica has excellent golf and all the amenities to go with it. It is the complete resort with all the comforts and luxuries of the world's most exclusive vacation retreats.

It is difficult to find a club more attractive than Tryall, a few miles from Montego Bay. The clubhouse was built in 1834 as a sugar plantation, and sits high on a hill overlooking most of the course and the Caribbean. Behind the seventeenth tee there's a giant old waterwheel still in operation. Below the clubhouse a bar is set up with the stools in the swimming pool—makes it hard to take a tumble after too many tumblers.

Elsewhere on the island there is Runaway Bay, a sprawling resort with private beach, pool, and everything else. The course is long and hard, a place where the big hitters will enjoy themselves.

Half Moon–Rose Hall, on the other side of Montego Bay from Tryall, is a Robert Trent Jones 7,000-yard monster. It is right on the water and attached to a lovely hotel at Half Moon Bay.

At Kingston, the Caymanas Golf Club is as tough as any in the islands. As a matter of fact, wherever one is in Jamaica, there is a good day of golf close by.

Caymanas Golf and Country Club

LOCATION: Spanish Town (by car or taxi 12 miles west of Kingston). COURSE SIZE: 18 holes; 6,844 yards; par 72. AVAILABILITY TO VISITORS: Visitors welcome; $1 daily membership fee. GREEN FEES: $5 per day. CADDIE FEES: 90¢, $1.15, or $1.40 per 18-hole round. GOLF CLUB RENTALS: $2 per day. GOLF CART RENTALS: Not available. MOTORIZED GOLF CART RENTALS: Not available. LESSONS: $3 per lesson. CLUBHOUSE FACILITIES: Bar, restaurant, and swimming pool. RECOMMENDED ACCOMMODATIONS: Sheraton Kingston, Myrtle Bank.

How to beat the high cost of golf carts in Jamaica.

Constant Spring Golf Club

LOCATION: Constant Spring (by car or taxi, 5½ miles north of Kingston). COURSE SIZE: 18 holes; 5,475 yards; par 68. AVAILABILITY TO VISITORS: Visitors welcome. GREEN FEES: Weekdays, $4 per round; weekends and holidays, $7 per round. CADDIE FEES: Included in green fees. GOLF CLUB RENTALS: $2.50 per day. GOLF CART RENTALS: 50¢ per day. MOTORIZED GOLF CART RENTALS: Not available. LESSONS: Teaching, $3; playing, $7.50. CLUBHOUSE FACILITIES: Available. RECOMMENDED ACCOMMODATIONS: Courtleigh Manor, Flamingo, Liguanea Terrace, Terra Nova, Sheraton Kingston.

Half Moon–Rose Hall Club

LOCATION: Montego Bay (9 miles from town by car or taxi). COURSE SIZE: 18 holes; 7,143 yards; par 72. AVAILABILITY TO VISITORS: Visitors welcome. GREEN FEES: Winter, $10 per day; summer, $5 per day. CADDIE FEES: $2.00 for 9 holes; $3.00 for 18 holes, plus tip. GOLF CLUB RENTALS: $3 per day. GOLF CART RENTALS: Not available. MOTORIZED GOLF CART RENTALS: $6 for 9 holes; $10 for 18 holes. LESSONS: $10 per lesson. CLUBHOUSE FACILITIES: Changing rooms, bar. RECOMMENDED ACCOMMODATIONS: Half Moon Hotel.

Montego Bay Country Club

LOCATION: 2 miles west of Montego Bay. COURSE SIZE: 9 holes; 2,642 yards; par 34. AVAILABILITY TO VISITORS: Visitors welcome. GREEN FEES: Winter, $7 per day; summer, $4 per day. CADDIE FEES: $1.25 per round. GOLF CLUB RENTALS: $3 per day. GOLF CART RENTALS: Not available. MOTORIZED GOLF CART RENTALS: Not available. LESSONS: Not available. CLUBHOUSE FACILITIES: Changing rooms, bar, restaurant. RECOMMENDED ACCOMMODATIONS: Fairfield Inn (on premises).

Runaway Bay Golf and Beach Club

LOCATION: Runaway Bay (40 miles by car or taxi west of Montego Bay; 80 miles north of Kingston). COURSE SIZE: 18 holes; 6,518 yards (club tee); par 72. AVAILABILITY TO VISITORS: Visitors welcome. GREEN FEES: Winter, $7.50 per day, $30 per week; summer, $5 per day, $20 per week. CADDIE FEES: Winter, $3 per 18-hole round; summer, $2 per 18-hole round. GOLF CLUB RENTALS: $3 per day. GOLF CART RENTALS: Not available. MOTORIZED GOLF CART RENTALS: $10 per round. LESSONS: Teaching, $5 per half hour; playing, $7 per round. CLUBHOUSE FACILITIES: Full facilities. RECOMMENDED ACCOMMODATIONS: Runaway Bay Hotel, Trelawny Club, both adjacent to the course, special rates for visitors.

Shell's Wonderful World of Golf

Tryall Golf Club.

Tryall Golf Club

LOCATION: Montego Bay (12 miles by car or taxi west of city). COURSE SIZE: 18 holes; par 71. AVAILABILITY TO VISITORS: Make arrangements with club secretary. GREEN FEES: Hotel guests: $10 per round, $50 per week, $75 per week for two. Summer fees included in hotel rate. Visitors: winter, $14 per round; summer, $8. CADDIE FEES: $2 per round. GOLF CLUB RENTALS: $5 per round. MOTORIZED GOLF CART RENTALS: Gasoline, $6 per round; electric, $8 per round. CLUBHOUSE FACILITIES: Beach, bar, cafeteria, and pro shop.

Upton Country Club

LOCATION: Ocho Rios (about 5 miles by taxi from Ocho Rios). COURSE SIZE: 9 holes; 3,070 yards; par 35. AVAILABILITY TO VISITORS: Visitors welcome. GREEN FEES: Per day, $4; per week, $14. CADDIE FEES: $1.50 per round. GOLF CLUB RENTALS: $2.50 per day. RECOMMENDED ACCOMMODATIONS: Sans Souci, Tower, Isle, Jamaica Inn, Plantation Inn, Silver Seas, Arawak, Jamaica Playboy, Falcon Dip, Carib, Ocho Rios, Hibiscus Lodge, Shaw Park Beach Club, Golden Head, Beach Hotel, and Casa Maria.

Puerto Rico

Twenty years ago golf in Puerto Rico was limited to the tiny layout at El Morro, the poorly manicured Berwind Golf Club, and a series of small crude courses on sugar plantations in the south. Grass greens were unknown; putting surfaces were made of sand.

Today in Puerto Rico golf has come of age. There are nearly a dozen good courses available, and many claim there is no better golf in the Caribbean. The Dorado Beach course, designed by the ubiquitous Robert Trent Jones, is one of the finest layouts available anywhere. Its 36 holes curl around the Mata Redonda Lagoon and through a series of small lakes. Palm trees sentry the fairways, and a stray shot is likely to bring down a giant coconut. Several holes along the beach afford fine views, but add more hazards to an already difficult course. For those who have a gloomy round, two or three rum *especiales* at the bar will solve all problems.

Three miles down the road from the Dorado Beach is the Dorado Hilton, which has another spectacular championship course, plus lavish facilities for tennis and water sports.

High on a hillside on the east coast is the new El Conquistador at Las Croabas. This is another superresort with a championship-size monster course, but it has only ten holes with water hazards. The hotel and pool area look like something out of the next century, and they have every resort facility conceivable.

Across the island at the elegant Hotel Ponce Inter-Continental guests are granted privileges on the lovely, manicured nine-hole course at the Ponce Country Club.

Contrary to popular opinion, the temperature in Puerto Rico does not vary more than six degrees throughout the year and it is ideal for a summer vacation; it is cheaper then, too.

SEASON: Year round.

HOW TO GET THERE: By Pan Am Jet nonstop from New York or Newark, 3½ hours; from Miami nonstop, 2¼ hours. Service

163

also from Boston, Philadelphia, and Baltimore–Washington, and direct flights from Europe, and Central and South America.

GOLF EQUIPMENT: American equipment available at American prices.

LANGUAGE: Spanish; but English is spoken and understood throughout the island.

TIME: One hour later than U.S. Eastern Standard Time.

Berwind Country Club

LOCATION: Rio Grande (about 20 miles from San Juan by taxi). COURSE SIZE: 18 holes; championship course. AVAILABILITY TO VISITORS: Limited to guests of following hotels: Americana, El San Juan, Condado Beach, La Concha, Puerto Rico Sheraton, El Conquistador, Holiday Inn, El Miramar. GREEN FEES: Winter, $10 per day; summer, $8 per day. CADDIE FEES: $3.50 per round. GOLF CLUB RENTALS: $3 per day. GOLF CART RENTALS: Not available. MOTORIZED GOLF CART RENTALS: $7 per round. LESSONS: $7.50 per half hour. CLUBHOUSE FACILITIES: Full facilities, including swimming pool, beach, tennis courts, and snack bar on course. RECOMMENDED ACCOMMODATIONS: Wide choice of accommodations in San Juan.

Dorado Beach Hotel and Golf Club

LOCATION: Dorado (45 minutes by car, 15 minutes by air taxi from San Juan). COURSE SIZE: East course: 18 holes; 7,081 yards; par 72. West course: 18 holes; 7,085 yards; par 72. AVAILABILITY TO VISITORS: On request and subject to availability of starting times. GREEN FEES: Hotel guests (per day): winter, $6; summer, $3.50. Visitors (per day): winter, $12; summer, $7.50. CADDIE FEES: Caddies not available. GOLF CLUB RENTALS: Winter, $3 per day; summer, $2 per day. GOLF CART RENTALS: Not available. MOTORIZED GOLF CART RENTALS: $8 per round. LESSONS: Chi Chi Rodriquez, $15 per half hour; resident pro, $10 per half hour in winter, $8 in summer. CLUBHOUSE FACILITIES: Lockers, dining room, pool, bar, and beach. RECOMMENDED ACCOMMODATIONS: Dorado Beach Hotel and Golf Club, Dorado Hilton Hotel (next door), and wide choice in San Juan.

Demanding tee shot at Dorado Beach.

Among the walls of El Morro Castle, San Juan.

Dorado Hilton

LOCATION: Dorado (45 minutes by car, 15 minutes by air taxi from San Juan). COURSE SIZE: 18 holes; 7,300 yards; par 72. AVAILABILITY TO VISITORS: Visitors welcome. Starting times required in season. GREEN FEES: Hotel guests (per day): winter, $6; summer, $3. Visitors: winter, $10; summer, $7. CADDIE FEES: 9 holes, $2; 18 holes, $3. GOLF CLUB RENTALS: $3 per day. GOLF CART RENTALS: Not available. MOTORIZED GOLF CART RENTALS: $8 per round; $6 for 9 holes. LESSONS: Jack Bender, pro: $8 per half hour. CLUBHOUSE FACILITIES: Full facilities including swimming pool and tennis courts. RECOMMENDED ACCOMMODATIONS: Dorado Hilton Hotel, Dorado Beach Hotel and Golf Club, and hotels in San Juan.

El Conquistador Hotel and Golf Club

LOCATION: Las Croabas (about 35-mile drive from San Juan). COURSE SIZE: 18 holes; 6,440 yards; par 71. AVAILABILITY TO VISITORS: Welcome. GREEN FEES: Guests, $6 per day; visitors, $12 per day. GOLF CLUB RENTALS: $5; also shoes, $2. GOLF CART RENTALS: $10.00. LESSONS: $7 per half hour. CLUBHOUSE FACILITIES: Every possible resort facility. RECOMMENDED ACCOMMODATIONS: El Conquistador Hotel.

Fort Buchanan Golf Club

LOCATION: Catano (short distance by car from San Juan). COURSE SIZE: 9 holes. AVAILABILITY TO VISITORS: Visitors welcome. GREEN FEES: Per day: $4.70 for guests, $3.20 if accompanied by a member. CADDIE FEES: $2 for 9 holes; $3 for 18 holes. GOLF CLUB RENTALS: 75¢ per day. GOLF CART RENTALS: $2 per 9 holes. MOTORIZED GOLF CART RENTALS: Available. LESSONS: Available; Ralph E. Barnette, pro. CLUBHOUSE FACILITIES: Lockers, bar, and snack room. RECOMMENDED ACCOMMODATIONS: Wide choice in San Juan.

Ponce Country Club

LOCATION: Ponce (a short cab ride from the hotel area). COURSE SIZE: 9 holes; par 36. AVAILABILITY TO VISITORS: Welcome. GREEN FEES: $5 daily. CADDIE FEES: $2.50 per round. GOLF CLUB RENTALS: $2 per day. GOLF CART RENTALS: 50¢ per round. MOTORIZED GOLF CART RENTALS: 9 holes, $4; 18 holes, $6. LESSONS: Available. CLUBHOUSE FACILITIES: Bar, restaurant, and swimming pool. RECOMMENDED ACCOMMODATIONS: Ponce Inter-Continental.

Trinidad

St. Andrews Golf Club, Trinidad, was built in 1870 by a group of Scottish settlers, as the name implies. The barefooted caddies are excellent "club-toters" as well as good golfers. When invited, many caddies can give even the low handicapper a good match. After a round, take a drive through the 3,000-foot-high mountain range to Maracas Beach. The view is spectacular.

Pointe-à-Pierre Golf Club

LOCATION: Pointe-à-Pierre, Trinidad. COURSE SIZE: 18 holes; 6,398 yards; par 72. AVAILABILITY TO VISITORS: Introduction by member. GREEN FEES: 50¢ per 9 holes. CADDIE FEES: 60¢ per 9 holes; $1.20 per 18 holes. GOLF CLUB RENTALS: Not available. GOLF CART RENTALS: Not available. MOTORIZED GOLF CART RENTALS: Not available. LESSONS: Not available. CLUBHOUSE FACILITIES: Restaurant, bar, lockers available. RECOMMENDED ACCOMMODATIONS: Hilton in Port of Spain.

St. Andrews Golf Club

LOCATION: Maraval (a few minutes from Port of Spain by taxi). COURSE SIZE: 18 holes; 5,611 yards; par 68. AVAILABILITY TO VISITORS: Visitors welcome. GREEN FEES: $3 per round. CADDIE FEES: Range from $1.70 to $2.40 per round. GOLF CLUB RENTALS: $1.30 per day. GOLF CART RENTALS: Not available. MOTORIZED GOLF CART RENTALS: Not available. LESSONS: $1.30 per half hour, $2 for 9 holes, $4 for 18 holes. CLUBHOUSE FACILITIES: Restaurant, bar, and changing rooms. RECOMMENDED ACCOMMODATIONS: Trinidad Hilton.

Virgin Islands

The Virgin Islands offer sun, sand, and seclusion to the vacationer. They do not offer very much in the way of golf. The major exception is the Fountain Valley course. Built with Rockefeller funds, the layout is a tribute to Robert Trent Jones's abilities as an architect. The course is luxurious, as is the clubhouse with its spacious grounds and sumptuous facilities. There is a private bathing beach nearby for an inviting swim. Golf privileges are available on a daily, weekly, or annual basis.

On St. Thomas the Judge Herman E. Moore Course offers nine holes with sand greens, but beware: the local sky-diving club uses the course as a target for early morning jumps.

Fountain Valley Golf Course

LOCATION: In a beautiful valley between Frederiksted and Christiansted, St. Croix. Easily accessible from either place by taxi. COURSE SIZE: 18 holes; 6,340 yards; par 72. AVAILABILITY TO VISITORS: Visitors welcome. GREEN FEES: Per day, $8; per week, $35; annually, $300 for a family membership with $50 extra for beach privileges; $175 for individual membership. An associate membership is available for $50, entitling member to $5-daily and $22-weekly green fees. CADDIE FEES: Caddies not allowed. GOLF CLUB RENTALS: $4 per day. GOLF CART RENTALS: Not available. MOTORIZED GOLF CART RENTALS: $4 for 9 holes; $7 for 18 holes. LESSONS: $7 per half hour, group of five for $30. CLUBHOUSE FACILITIES: Complete facilities. RECOMMENDED ACCOMMODATIONS: Wide choice of luxury hotels, guest houses, and other accommodations throughout the island.

Judge Herman E. Moore Course

LOCATION: St. Thomas (10 minutes by cab from town). COURSE SIZE: 9 holes, par 35. AVAILABILITY TO VISITORS: Visitors always welcome. Caution: local sky-diving club uses course as a target occasionally for early morning jumps. GREEN FEES: $2 daily. CADDIE FEES: $1.50 for 9 holes. GOLF CLUB RENTALS: $2 per 9 holes. GOLF CART RENTALS: 50¢ per day. MOTORIZED GOLF CART RENTALS: Not available. LESSONS: $2.50 per hour. CLUBHOUSE FACILITIES: Light refreshments and beer only. RECOMMENDED ACCOMMODATIONS: Wide choice of accommodations available throughout the island.

CENTRAL AND
SOUTH AMERICA

South America's golf courses are as colorful and distinctive as its music, its dance, and its culture. Most of the courses have been designed by British and American architects who have combined their previously successful ideas with local charm to produce some splendid golf clubs.

The continent has some of the world's finer courses. Although golf is not a national sport in any of the South American countries—that is, it is a game played by the upper classes rather than the masses—there are signs of a new popularity for the sport largely because of the ever-increasing number of South American pros, such as Roberto de Vicenzo, who have been attracting attention in the big tournaments in the United States and elsewhere. De Vicenzo won the British Open in 1967. Successful athletes become national heroes in these Latin American countries. An important tournament victory or two by any one of them could easily set off a prairie fire of interest that would sweep the continent.

Most South American courses tend to be flat, and around the equator the greens are sun-beaten and difficult to keep in good condition. The main reason is a lack of water; the dry season lasts from December through the middle of April in the more tropical areas, and the golf courses suffer heavily during this period. It should be remembered, however, that much of the South American continent is not hot. Southern Brazil, Argentina, and Chile have a temperate climate. In the tropical area, elevation will make a radical difference in the temperature. The touring golfer should keep that in mind when selecting his wardrobe.

Venezuela has every kind of climate and golf courses to match. The Caracas Country Club, one of the finest on the continent, is situated in the middle of this exciting city. Prices in Caracas are generally high, but the bite for golf is not so bad. Green fees run around $7, and an experienced caddie costs $3.50. About a half-hour ride from Caracas is the Lagunita Golf Club in El Hatillo, one of the most beautiful courses in the world. Designed by American architect Dick

Wilson, it is a fine championship course. The hilly nature of the terrain makes a level lie difficult to find, but the ball goes so far off the tee up here (4,000 feet) that an angular lie for the second shot is not really a serious disadvantage. The high elevation also provides a year-round temperate climate which keeps the course in excellent condition. A particularly interesting hole is the tenth, where a good portion of a mountainside was cut away to make way for the fairway.

The Junko Club, about an hour from Caracas, is another mountain course, which has a back nine not fit for a goat. Also worthy of the visitor's attention is the Valle Arriba club, which is the annual site of the Caracas Open. Green fees at these two clubs are the most reasonable in town—from $2.50 to $4.25 on weekdays.

The Jockey Club in Buenos Aires, Argentina, is a course no golfer should miss. Thirty years ago when I played there with Joe Kirkwood, we thought the course was located too far from the city. When I played there again in 1963, I discovered that the course is almost in the middle of the city. That's how Buenos Aires has boomed. The Jockey Club's championship layout is an exciting experience, as is the entire club. Alister MacKenzie, the architect who made the original plans for the Augusta National Golf Club in Georgia, made this course out of a piece of dull, unattractive, flat land. It stands as another tribute to his great skill.

The Canada Cup matches were played at the Jockey Club in 1962, and the international stars had a tough time with the 3,462-yard back nine. Several of the greens are of the punch-bowl variety, with great mounds, some as high as 15 feet, surrounding the backs and sides of the putting surface. There is a smaller eighteen at the Jockey which is not quite as difficult as the big course, but is certainly not a weak sister. After a day on the big course, however, it may be worthwhile to take a tour on this course to get the ego back.

There is only one Rio, and there is hardly another course like the Gavea Golf and Country Club in the city's suburbs. Rio, being in mountainous terrain, really doesn't have enough room for golf courses. To install the 18-hole Gavea layout, the front nine had to be carved out of the hills and the home nine had to be spread along the shore. It makes for some very interesting golf—especially those five par-5 holes on the front nine. This is an intriguing course, and one the visiting golfer will long remember for the orchid-bearing trees and other scenic wonders along the fairways.

In Colombia, the Country Club de Bogotá has two 18-hole courses, one of which should be a regular site for the pro tour. Colombians take pride in the plush clubhouse and big swimming pool.

Central America is not particularly well known for golf. It is still a sport of the few, and there are not many courses. Guatemala has two good clubs, both of which have long, challenging courses. The average temperature here is always in the sixties, and ideal for golf the year round. In Panama, the Club de Golf de Panamá is attractive and reasonably priced. There are also several military courses that will accept visitors. Otherwise Central America is still in the dark ages of golf history.

Many other courses in South America will capture the interest of the touring player—the Golf Club del Uruguay in Montevideo; the Los Leones country club in Santiago, Chile; and the La Paz Golf Club in Mallasilla, Bolivia. The visitor is welcome at most clubs, but he should have with him a letter of introduction from the secretary of his own club. In some cases, an introduction by a member is necessary before the golfer can play, but this is not a problem. South Americans are friendly and well mannered, and English is spoken at most of the better clubs and resorts. The caddies are generally well trained and helpful with club selection. Clubs, incidentally, can be rented at many courses.

One final tip for the nineteenth hole: Don't put ice in the drink. Stick to whiskey and bottled water or soda unless your system is accustomed to the local water supply.

Argentina

SEASON: Year round.

HOW TO GET THERE: By Pan Am's Jet Clipper nonstop to Buenos Aires, 10¾ hours from New York, 17¾ hours from Los Angeles. By ship, 19 days from New York.

GOLF EQUIPMENT: American equipment available, but taxes likely to be very heavy.

LANGUAGE: Spanish; English is spoken to a great extent.

TIME: Two hours later than U.S. Eastern Standard Time.

Club Nautico San Isidro

LOCATION: San Isidro (30 minutes by car from hotels in Buenos Aires). COURSE SIZE: 18 holes; 6,250 yards; par 71. AVAILABILITY TO VISITORS: Visitors welcome on introduction by member. GREEN FEES: Weekdays, $1.50; weekends, $3.75 per day. CADDIE FEES: 70¢ per round, plus tip. GOLF CLUB RENTALS: Not available. GOLF CART RENTALS: Not available. MOTORIZED GOLF CART RENTALS: Not available. LESSONS: Available. CLUBHOUSE FACILITIES: For members and their guests. RECOMMENDED ACCOMMODATIONS: Hotel Plaza, Alvear Palace, Continental, Lancaster, City, Claridge, California, Dora, Nogaró.

Hindu Club

LOCATION: Don Torenato (about 1½ hours by car from downtown Buenos Aires). COURSE SIZE: Two courses available: 18 holes, 6,342 yards, par 71; 18 holes, 6,154 yards, par 70. AVAILABILITY TO VISITORS: Welcome with introduction by a member. GREEN FEES: Weekdays, $1.50; Saturdays, Sundays, and holidays, $3 per day. CADDIE

FEES: $1.25 to $1.50 per round, plus tip of 60¢. GOLF CLUB RENTALS: Not available. GOLF CART RENTALS: Not available. MOTORIZED GOLF CART RENTALS: Not available. LESSONS: Fee varies with professional. CLUBHOUSE FACILITIES: Restaurant, bar, lockers, riding, tennis. RECOMMENDED ACCOMMODATIONS: See listing above.

Hurlingham Club

LOCATION: Hurlingham (about 1 hour from hotel area in Buenos Aires). COURSE SIZE: 18 holes; regulation length. AVAILABILITY TO VISITORS: Visitors welcome on introduction by member. GREEN FEES: Weekdays, $1.10; weekends, $2.20 per day. CADDIE FEES: $1.10 per round, plus tip. GOLF CLUB RENTALS: $2.20 per round (this includes golf cart). MOTORIZED GOLF CART RENTALS: Not available. LESSONS: Available. CLUBHOUSE FACILITIES: For members and their guests. RECOMMENDED ACCOMMODATIONS: See listing above.

Ituzaingo Golf Club

LOCATION: San Antonio de Podera (about 1½ hours by car from downtown Buenos Aires). COURSE SIZE: 18 holes; 6,722 yards; par 73. AVAILABILITY TO VISITORS: Visitors welcome on introduction by a member. GREEN FEES: Weekdays, $1; weekends, $3 per day. CADDIE FEES: 70¢ to 80¢ per round, plus tip of about 65¢. GOLF CLUB RENTALS: Not available. GOLF CART RENTALS: Available. MOTORIZED GOLF CART RENTALS: Not available. LESSONS: Fee varies according to professional. CLUBHOUSE FACILITIES: Complete dining, bar, and locker facilities available. RECOMMENDED ACCOMMODATIONS: See listing above.

Jockey Club

LOCATION: Buenos Aires (about 30 minutes from downtown by car). COURSE SIZE: Red Course: 18 holes; 6,383 yards; par 72. Blue Course: 18 holes; 6,191 yards; par 71. AVAILABILITY TO VISITORS: Visitors welcome on introduction by a member. GREEN FEES: Weekdays, $3; weekends, $7.50 per day. CADDIE FEES: $3 per round. GOLF CLUB RENTALS: Not available. GOLF CART RENTALS: Not available. MOTORIZED GOLF CART RENTALS: Not available. LESSONS: Available. CLUBHOUSE FACILITIES: Tennis, swimming, riding, polo, lawn bowling, lockers, dining rooms, bar, and all conceivable facilities. RECOMMENDED ACCOMMODATIONS: See listing above.

Palermo Park Municipal Golf Course

LOCATION: Buenos Aires (15 minutes from downtown hotel area by car or bus). COURSE SIZE: 18 holes; 6,600 yards; par 72. AVAILABILITY TO VISITORS: Visitors welcome. GREEN FEES: $1 per round. CADDIE FEES: 75¢ to $1, plus 60¢ tip. GOLF CLUB RENTALS: $1.75 per round. GOLF CART RENTALS: Not available. MOTORIZED GOLF CART RENTALS: Not available. CLUBHOUSE FACILITIES: Restaurant, bar, and changing rooms available. Horseback riding and tennis located elsewhere in the park. RECOMMENDED ACCOMMODATIONS: See above.

San Andres Golf Club

LOCATION: San Martin (45-minute drive from downtown Buenos Aires). COURSE SIZE: 18 holes; 6,714 yards; par 72. AVAILABILITY TO VISITORS: Visitors welcome on introduction by Pan American or a member. GREEN FEES: Weekdays, $1.25; weekends, $2.25 per day. CADDIE FEES: 75¢ per round, plus 60¢ tip. GOLF CLUB RENTALS: $1.25 per round. GOLF CART RENTALS: Not available. MOTORIZED GOLF CART RENTALS: Not available. LESSONS: Cost varies with professional. CLUBHOUSE FACILITIES: Restaurant, bar, and changing rooms available. RECOMMENDED ACCOMMODATIONS: See above.

Bolivia

SEASON: All year.

HOW TO GET THERE: By Pan American arrangement to La Paz, 11¼ hours (elapsed time) from New York via Miami. La Paz is 1½ hours from Lima, Peru. La Paz is an hour's flying time from Cochabamba. By ship from New York, 14 days to Arica, Chile, then about 9 hours by Swiss-built diesel train that leaves Arica twice a week for La Paz.

GOLF EQUIPMENT: American equipment available.

LANGUAGE: Spanish; but English is understood in the better hotels, shops, and restaurants.

TIME: One hour later than U.S. Eastern Standard Time.

La Paz Golf Club

LOCATION: Mallasilla (½ hour from downtown La Paz by car). COURSE SIZE: 18 holes; 6,369 yards; par 70. AVAILABILITY TO VISITORS: Visitors welcome. GREEN FEES: $1.80 per round. CADDIE FEES: Caddie is required; about 90¢ per round. GOLF CLUB RENTALS: Not available. MOTORIZED GOLF CARTS: Not available. LESSONS: Available. CLUBHOUSE FACILITIES: Full facilities. RECOMMENDED ACCOMMODATIONS: Crillon, Copacabana, Grand Hotel Sucre Palace.

Oruro Golf Club (highest in the world)

LOCATION: Capachols (by taxi or bus about 8 miles from Oruro). COURSE SIZE: 18 holes; 6,277 yards; par 72. AVAILABILITY TO VISITORS: Visitors welcome. GREEN FEES: 80¢ per round. CADDIE FEES: 50¢ per round. GOLF CLUB RENTALS: Available. GOLF CART RENTALS: Not available. MOTORIZED GOLF CARTS: Not available. LESSONS: Not available. CLUBHOUSE FACILITIES: Restaurant and bar. RECOMMENDED ACOMMODATIONS: Oruro: Hotel Repostero, Hotel Perfectural Oruro.

Brazil

SEASON: All year.

HOW TO GET THERE: By Pan Am Jet Clipper, 9¼ hours from New York to Brasília, 9½ hours to Rio, an hour more to São Paulo. By ship, about 11 days from New York.

GOLF EQUIPMENT: American equipment available, but highly taxed.

LANGUAGE: Portuguese; English is understood in tourist centers.

TIME: Two hours later than U.S. Eastern Standard Time.

NOTE: The value of local currency fluctuates rapidly; be sure to check rates on arrival.

Club de Golfe Campinas

LOCATION: Via Anhanguera, Kilometer 108, Campinas. COURSE SIZE: 9 holes. AVAILABILITY TO VISITORS: Introduction by a member is necessary. GREEN FEES: $3.70 per day. CADDIE FEES: $2.25 for 9 holes. GOLF CLUB RENTALS: Not available. GOLF CART RENTALS: Not available. MOTORIZED GOLF CART RENTALS: Not available. LESSONS: $2.25 per hour. CLUBHOUSE FACILITIES: Complete dining, bar, and locker facilities available. RECOMMENDED ACCOMMODATIONS: Campinas: Hotel Savoy, Hotel Terminus.

Gavea Golf and Country Club

LOCATION: Rio de Janeiro (near city). COURSE SIZE: 18 holes; 6,042 yards; par 68. AVAILABILITY TO VISITORS: Visitors welcome throughout the week provided a Pan American letter of introduction is presented. Otherwise a tourist card for 15 days can be purchased at $1.80. CADDIE FEES: Caddies are required; $1 per round. GOLF

Tricky approach at Gavea Club outside Rio de Janeiro.

The spectacular Gavea course near Rio de Janeiro.

CLUB RENTALS: About $2 per day. GOLF CART RENTALS: Not available. MOTORIZED GOLF CARTS: Not available. LESSONS: $1.80 per half hour; Mario Gonzales, pro. CLUBHOUSE FACILITIES: Restaurant, bar, and locker facilities. RECOMMENDED ACCOMMODATIONS: Copacabana Beach: Copacabana Palace, Miramar, Ouro Verde, Excelsior, Leme Palace, Trocadero, Lancaster, Olinda, California.

Golf Club São Fernando

LOCATION: Estrada Raposo Tavares, Kilometer 28, São Paulo. COURSE SIZE: 18 holes; regulation length. AVAILABILITY TO VISITORS: Introduction by a member is necessary. GREEN FEES: $7.35 per day. CADDIE FEES: $2.50 per round. GOLF CLUB RENTALS: Not available. GOLF CART RENTALS: Not available. MOTORIZED GOLF CART RENTALS: Not available. LESSONS: $2.40 per hour. CLUBHOUSE FACILITIES: Complete restaurant, bar, and locker facilities available. RECOMMENDED ACCOMMENDATIONS: Othon Palace, Samambaia, Jaraquá.

Itanhanga Golf Club

LOCATION: Rio de Janeiro (near city). COURSE SIZE: 18 holes, championship length. AVAILABILITY TO VISITORS: Visitors welcome. GREEN FEES: Weekdays, $3; Sundays, $4. CADDIE FEES: Caddie is required; $1 per round. GOLF CLUB RENTALS: Not available. GOLF CART RENTALS: Not available. MOTORIZED GOLF CARTS: Not available. LESSONS: 3 pros available, approximately $2 per hour. CLUBHOUSE FACILITIES: Full facilities available. RECOMMENDED ACCOMMODATIONS: Copacabana Beach: Copacabana Palace, Miramar, Ouro Verde, Excelsior, Leme Palace, Trocadero, Lancaster, Olinda, California.

São Paulo Golf Club

LOCATION: Largo Dom Francisco Souza, 635 Santa Amaro, São Paulo (10 miles from downtown São Paulo). COURSE SIZE: 18 holes, championship length. AVAILABILITY TO VISITORS: Visitors welcome provided prior arrangements made or if accompanied by a club member. GREEN FEES: Weekdays, $4; weekends, $6 per day. CADDIE FEES: $1.50 per round. GOLF CLUB RENTALS: $1 per bag per day. MOTORIZED GOLF CARTS: Not available. LESSONS: 5 professionals available, $2 per hour. CLUBHOUSE FACILITIES: Full facilities. RECOMMENDED ACCOMMODATIONS: São Paulo: Samambaia, Jaraquá, Othon Palace.

Uninviting water of 9th hole at São Paulo Golf Club.

Tee shot from a hill in Rio.

Chile

SEASON: Year round.

HOW TO GET THERE: By arrangement, Pan American without change of plane down the west coast of South America, 11½ hours (elapsed time) from New York, 10¼ hours from Miami. Stopovers if you wish en route. By Pan Am Jet Clipper down the east coast, 10¾ hours to Buenos Aires from New York. Then Santiago is 1¾ hours from Buenos Aires. From the United States west coast, flights for South America connect at Miami or Panama City. By ship, about 18 days from New York to Valparaiso and about 30 days from the United States west coast.

GOLF EQUIPMENT: Difficult to obtain and likely to be very expensive.

LANGUAGE: Spanish is the official language, but most people in tourist centers speak and understand English.

TIME: Noon in Santiago is 11 A.M. in New York.

Club de Golf Los Leones

LOCATION: Santiago (20 minutes from town by car). COURSE SIZE: 18 holes; 6,625 yards; par 72. AVAILABILITY TO VISITORS: Visitors welcome with introduction. GREEN FEES: $5 per day. CADDIE FEES: $2 per round. GOLF CLUB RENTALS: Available. GOLF CART RENTALS: Not available. MOTORIZED GOLF CART RENTALS: Not available. LESSONS: $2 per hour. CLUBHOUSE FACILITIES: Full facilities including bar, restaurant, swimming pool, tennis courts, and putting green. RECOMMENDED ACCOMMODATIONS: Hotel Carrera and Hotel Crillon.

182

Club de Golf Santo Domingo

LOCATION: Rocas de Santo Domingo (a seaside resort 74 miles from Santiago; 1½ hours from Santiago by car). COURSE SIZE: 18 holes; 6,600 yards; par 72. AVAILABILITY TO VISITORS: Admitted without introduction. GREEN FEES: $2.50 per day. CADDIE FEES: $2 per round. GOLF CLUB RENTALS: Available. GOLF CART RENTALS: Not available. MOTORIZED GOLF CART RENTALS: Not available. LESSONS: $1.50 per hour. CLUBHOUSE FACILITIES: Bar, restaurant, and putting green. RECOMMENDED ACCOMMODATIONS: Rocas de Santo Domingo Hotel.

Club de Golf Sport Français

LOCATION: Vitacura, Santiago (30 minutes from town by car). COURSE SIZE: 18 holes; 6,652 yards; par 72. AVAILABILITY TO VISITORS: Welcome with letter of introduction. GREEN FEES: $3 per day. CADDIE FEES: $2 per round. GOLF CLUB RENTALS: Not available. GOLF CART RENTALS: Not available. MOTORIZED GOLF CART RENTALS: Not available. LESSONS: $2 per hour. CLUBHOUSE FACILITIES: Bar, restaurant, putting green, and swimming pool. RECOMMENDED ACCOMMODATIONS: Hotel Carrera, Hotel Crillon.

Granadilla Country Club

LOCATION: Viña del Mar (90 miles from Santiago; about 2 hours by car). COURSE SIZE: 18 holes; 6,360 yards; par 72. AVAILABILITY TO VISITORS: Welcome with introduction from their home club. GREEN FEES: $3 per day. CADDIE FEES: $2 per round. GOLF CLUB RENTALS: Available. GOLF CART RENTALS: Not available. MOTORIZED GOLF CART RENTALS: Not available. LESSONS: $2 per hour. CLUBHOUSE FACILITIES: Bar, restaurant, putting green, and swimming pool. RECOMMENDED ACCOMMODATIONS: O'Higgins, Miramar, and San Martín hotels.

Prince of Wales Country Club

LOCATION: Tobalaba, Santiago (20 minutes from town by car). COURSE SIZE: 18 holes; 6,753 yards; par 72. AVAILABILITY TO VISITORS:

Visitors permitted limited play when introduced by member or letter. GREEN FEES: Weekends and holidays, $5 per day; weekdays, $2.50 per day. CADDIE FEES: $2 per round. GOLF CLUB RENTALS: Available. GOLF CART RENTALS: Not available. MOTORIZED GOLF CART RENTALS: Not available. LESSONS: $2 per hour. CLUBHOUSE FACILITIES: Full facilities including bar, restaurant, swimming pool, tennis courts, and putting green. RECOMMENDED ACCOMMODATIONS: Hotel Carrera and Hotel Crillon.

Colombia

SEASON: Throughout the year.

HOW TO GET THERE: By Pan Am Jet 4½ hours from New York to Caracas, which in turn is 1½ hours from Bogotá. Miami to Barranquilla is 3¼ hours; Panama to Bogotá, nonstop 1¼ hours; Quito to Bogotá, 1¼ hours; Panama to Barranquilla, 1 hour; Panama to Medellin, 1½ hours; New York to Cali, 8½ hours; Quito to Cali, 50 minutes.

GOLF EQUIPMENT: American equipment available, but may be expensive.

LANGUAGE: Spanish, but English and French are widely spoken.

TIME: Same as U.S. Eastern Standard Time.

Club Campestre de Cali

LOCATION: Cali (a 20-minute drive from downtown, about $1 by taxi). COURSE SIZE: 18 holes; 6,860 yards; par 71. AVAILABILITY TO VISITORS: Visitors are welcome as guests of a regular member. This may be arranged through the Pan American district sales office. GREEN FEES: Weekdays, $1.25; weekends and holidays, $2.50 per day. CADDIE FEES: 75¢ per 18 holes. A tip of 20¢ to 40¢ is customary. GOLF CLUB RENTALS: 30¢ per round. GOLF CART RENTALS: Not available. MOTORIZED GOLF CART RENTALS: Not available. LESSONS: 3 professionals available, charging from $1 to $1.50 for 45 minutes. CLUBHOUSE FACILITIES: Dining room, Turkish baths, barber shop, swimming pool, lake, tennis courts, bowling alley, polo field, riding, etc. RECOMMENDED ACCOMMODATIONS: Cali: Hotel Alferez Real, Hotel Aristi.

Country Club de Bogotá

LOCATION: Bogotá (just a short ride by taxi from the center of town). COURSE SIZE: Two 18-hole courses, one of championship length

Shell's Wonderful World of Golf

Swimming-pool enclosure at Country Club de Bogotá.

(both are 7,500 feet above sea level). AVAILABILITY TO VISITORS: Visitors welcome upon introduction. Check with local Pan American office for details. CADDIE FEES: About $4 per round. MOTORIZED GOLF CART RENTALS: Not available. LESSONS: Available. CLUBHOUSE FACILITIES: Bowling, tennis, Olympic-size pool (glass enclosed), facilities for children, bar and restaurants. RECOMMENDED ACCOMMODATIONS: Hotel Tequendama, Hotel Continental, Cordillera, Presidente, Residencias Santa Fé, Residencias Steves.

Country Club of Barranquilla

LOCATION: The El Prado section of Barranquilla. COURSE SIZE: 18 holes; 6,355 yards; par 72. AVAILABILITY TO VISITORS: Visitors welcome on introduction by a member. At certain times, Pan American may be able to arrange such introduction through the local office. GREEN FEES: 65¢ daily. CADDIE FEES: $1.25 per round. GOLF CLUB RENTALS: $1.25 per day. GOLF CART RENTALS: Not available. MOTORIZED GOLF CART RENTALS: Not available. LESSONS: $1.10 per hour. CLUBHOUSE FACILITIES: Dining room, bar, outdoor pool, tennis courts, lockers. RECOMMENDED ACCOMMODATIONS: Prado Hotel, Vallclaire Apartments (advance reservations necessary).

Guatemala

SEASON: Year round.

HOW TO GET THERE: By Pan American Jet Clipper, 3 hours from New Orleans; 2½ hours from Los Angeles. By ship, 3 days from New Orleans.

GOLF EQUIPMENT: Difficult to obtain and likely to be very expensive.

LANGUAGE: Spanish is the official language but English is spoken in tourist centers.

TIME: Central Standard Time is observed throughout the year.

Guatemala Country Club

LOCATION: 5 miles east of the center of town. COURSE SIZE: 18 holes; 6,820 yards; par 72. AVAILABILITY TO VISITORS: As guest of a member only. GREEN FEES: $10. CADDIE FEES: $2 per round, plus tip if caddie satisfactory. GOLF CLUB RENTALS: $2 per day. GOLF CART RENTALS: Not available. MOTORIZED GOLF CART RENTALS: Not available. LESSONS: $3 for 40 minutes. CLUBHOUSE FACILITIES: Dining room, bar, locker rooms for both men and women, swimming pool. RECOMMENDED ACCOMMODATIONS: Guatemala Biltmore Hotel, Ritz-Continental.

Mayan Golf Club

LOCATION: 14 miles south of Guatemala City in the hill country near Lake Amatitlán. COURSE SIZE: 18 holes; 6,764 yards; par 72. AVAILABILITY TO VISITORS: Visitors welcome. GREEN FEES: Weekdays, $5; weekends and holidays, $10 per day; 50% less with courtesy card obtainable locally from Pan Am. CADDIE FEES: $2 per round. GOLF CLUB RENTALS: $2 per day. GOLF CART RENTALS: Not available.

MOTORIZED GOLF CART RENTALS: Not available. LESSONS: Roberto Galindo, pro; $3 per 40 minutes. CLUBHOUSE FACILITIES: Restaurant, bar, locker room, swimming pool, and bowling alleys. RECOMMENDED ACCOMMODATIONS: Guatemala Biltmore, Ritz-Continental, Maya Excelsior, Motel Plaza, Palace, Pan American, Plaza.

Panama

SEASON: Year round.

HOW TO GET THERE: By Pan Am Jet Clipper from Miami, 2½ hours to Panama City. From Los Angeles nonstop, 6¼ hours, or via Guatemala City. By Pan Am nonstop service, 4½ hours from New York. By ship, about 5 days. By land, via the Inter-American Highway.

GOLF EQUIPMENT: Difficult to obtain and likely to be very expensive.

LANGUAGE: The official language is Spanish, but almost everybody speaks English too.

TIME: Same as U.S. Eastern Standard Time.

Club de Golf de Panama

LOCATION: Panama City. COURSE SIZE: 18 holes; 6,485 yards; par 72. AVAILABILITY TO VISITORS: Visitors welcome. Course is closed on Monday. GREEN FEES: $3.50 daily. CADDIE FEES: 9 holes, $2; 18 holes, $3. GOLF CLUB RENTALS: Not available. GOLF CART RENTALS: Not available. MOTORIZED GOLF CART RENTALS: Not available. LESSONS: $3 per half hour. CLUBHOUSE FACILITIES: Restaurant, bar, lockers, showers. RECOMMENDED ACCOMMODATIONS: Hotel El Panama Hilton and Hotel El Continental both within 15 minutes of the course. Hotel La Siesta, about 30 minutes from the course.

190

Surinam

SEASON: Year round.

HOW TO GET THERE: By Pan American Jet Clipper from New York in 8¾ hours, elapsed time. Taxi fare from the airport into Paramaribo is $2.50 per passenger.

GOLF EQUIPMENT: Difficult to obtain and likely to be very expensive.

LANGUAGE: Dutch is the official language but English is widely spoken.

TIME: Noon in Surinam is 11 A.M. Eastern Standard Time.

Golfclub Paramaribo

LOCATION: Paramaribo. COURSE SIZE: 9 holes, but with a different number 12 and number 17 to make an 18-hole course of 5,625 yards. AVAILABILITY TO VISITORS: All visiting golfers most welcome. GREEN FEES: $2.50 daily. CADDIE FEES: 90¢ for 18 holes. GOLF CLUB RENTALS: 75¢ for 18 holes. GOLF CART RENTALS: Not available. MOTORIZED GOLF CART RENTALS: Not available. LESSONS: $1 per half hour. CLUBHOUSE FACILITIES: Small comfortable clubhouse with bar and open air upper gallery; men's and ladies' lockers. RECOMMENDED ACCOMMODATIONS: Torarico Hotel and Casino, first class and fully air-conditioned; Palace Hotel and Casino, second class and partially air-conditioned.

Uruguay

SEASON: All year.

HOW TO GET THERE: By Pan American Jet Clipper, 12 hours from New York, or 35 minutes from Buenos Aires, which is 10¾ hours from New York by nonstop Clipper. By ship from New York or New Orleans, about 13 days.

GOLF EQUIPMENT: American equipment available.

LANGUAGE: Spanish; English and French are widely spoken.

TIME: Two hours later than U.S. Eastern Standard Time.

Cantegril Country Club

LOCATION: Punte del Este (in town). COURSE SIZE: 18 holes; 6,300 yards: par 70. AVAILABILITY TO VISITORS: Visitors welcome. GREEN FEES: Weekdays and all mornings, $3; Saturdays, Sundays, and holiday afternoons, $6. CADDIE FEES: $1.20 per 18-hole round. GOLF CLUB RENTALS: Not available. GOLF CART RENTALS: Not available. LESSONS: Several pros available, about $3 per hour. CLUBHOUSE FACILITIES: Excellent facilities available. RECOMMENDED ACCOMMODATIONS: Edificio Vanguardia, Cantagril Country Club.

Club de Golf del Cerro

LOCATION: Montevideo (20 minutes from downtown by car or taxi). COURSE SIZE: 18 holes; 6,211 yards; par 73. AVAILABILITY TO VISITORS: Visitors welcome. GREEN FEES: $3. Open for golf Wednesdays, Saturdays, Sundays, and holidays. Visitors staying at Hotel Victoria Plaza exempt from green fees. CADDIE FEES: $1.40 plus tip per 18-hole round. RENTAL OF GOLF CLUBS: $1.50 per game. GOLF CART RENTALS: Not available. MOTORIZED GOLF CART RENTALS: Not available. LESSONS: $2 per hour. CLUBHOUSE FACILITIES: Dressing room, showers, bar, and restaurant. RECOMMENDED ACCOMMODATIONS: Hotel Victoria Plaza, Lancaster Hotel, Columbia Palace.

Golf Club del Uruguay

LOCATION: Montevideo (10 minutes from downtown by car, taxi, or limousine). COURSE SIZE: 18 holes; 6,358 yards; par 73. AVAILABILITY TO VISITORS: Visitors welcome; must be introduced by member or by a tourist agency. GREEN FEES: Weekdays, $1.50; Saturdays, Sundays, holidays, $2.40 per day. Visitors staying at hotels listed below are permitted to play at no charge upon presenting a card provided by the hotel. CADDIE FEES: $1.50 per round. GOLF CLUB RENTALS: $1.80 per game. GOLF CART RENTALS: Not available. LESSONS: $4.80 per hour. CLUBHOUSE FACILITIES: Dressing rooms, showers, and bar and restaurant. RECOMMENDED ACCOMMODATIONS: Columbia Palace, Hotel Victoria Plaza, Lancaster Hotel.

Venezuela

SEASON: All year.

HOW TO GET THERE: By Pan Am Jet Clipper, only 4½ hours from New York to Caracas. Flights from Miami, 2¾ hours. Direct service also from Los Angeles and San Francisco. Caracas is 2 hours from Panama, where connections are made with Pan Am flights from other points. One hour nonstop from Trinidad. By ship, about 5 days from New York.

GOLF EQUIPMENT: American equipment available.

LANGUAGE: Comprehension of English is on the upswing, but still sparsely understood outside cities and resort areas.

TIME: One half hour later than New York; same during Daylight Saving Time.

Carabelleda Golf and Yacht Club

LOCATION: Macuto (less than an hour by car from Caracas). COURSE SIZE: 9 holes; 3,173 yards; par 35. AVAILABILITY TO VISITORS: Visitors welcome. GREEN FEES: $4.50 per 18 holes ($3.50 for guests of Macuto-Sheraton). CADDIE FEES: $2.80 per 18-hole round, plus gratuities. GOLF CLUB RENTALS: $4.50 per 18-hole round. GOLF CART RENTALS: Available. MOTORIZED GOLF CARTS: Not available. CLUBHOUSE FACILITIES: Course is adjacent to the Macuto-Sheraton, which has complete facilities.

Caracas Country Club

LOCATION: Caracas (convenient to all parts of the city). COURSE SIZE: 18 holes; championship length. AVAILABILITY TO VISITORS: Visitors welcome weekdays only, unless accompanied by members. Closed Monday. GREEN FEES: $7 per day. CADDIE FEES: $3.50 per round.

GOLF CLUB RENTALS: Not available. GOLF CART RENTALS: Not available. MOTORIZED GOLF CART RENTALS: Not available. CLUBHOUSE FACILITIES: Available to members only. RECOMMENDED ACCOMMODATIONS: Hotel Avila, Hotel Tamanaco.

The Junko Country Club

LOCATION: Caracas (1 hour from Caracas by car). COURSE SIZE: 18 holes; championship length. AVAILABILITY TO VISITORS: Visitors welcome on weekdays; must be accompanied by member on weekends. GREEN FEES: Weekdays, $2.50; weekends, $5 per day. CADDIE FEES: About $3.50 per round. CLUBHOUSE FACILITIES: Restaurant and bar. RECOMMENDED ACCOMMODATIONS: Hotel Tamanaco, Hotel Avila.

Lagunita Golf Club

LOCATION: El Hatillo (30 minutes from downtown Caracas). COURSE SIZE: 18 holes; championship length. AVAILABILITY TO VISITORS: Visitors welcome weekdays; inquire about weekend play. GREEN FEES: Weekdays, $2.25; weekends, $4.50 per day. CADDIE FEES: About $3.50 per round. MOTORIZED GOLF CARTS: Not available. CLUBHOUSE FACILITIES: Restaurant, bar, swimming pool, tennis courts. RECOMMENDED ACCOMMODATIONS: Hotel Avila, Hotel Tamanaco.

Valle Arriba Golf Club

LOCATION: Caracas (not more than 15 minutes by car from any place in the city). COURSE SIZE: 18 holes; 6,127 yards; par 70. AVAILABILITY TO VISITORS: Recommendation by member or residence at Hotel Tamanaco necessary. Guest play is not allowed Saturdays; club is closed Mondays. GREEN FEES: Weekdays, $4.25; weekends, $5 per round. CADDIE FEES: $1.80 to $3.50 per round. GOLF CLUB RENTALS: Not available. GOLF CART RENTALS: Not available. CLUBHOUSE FACILITIES: Swimming pool, tennis court, Turkish bath, bar, restaurants, and snack bar. RECOMMENDED ACCOMMODATIONS: Hotel Tamanaco, Hotel Avila.

HAWAII AND THE
SOUTH PACIFIC

Australia

For the traveling golfer, playing his favorite sport Down Under offers an exciting challenge as well as a unique experience.

Australia boasts the second largest number of golf courses in the world—about 1,100. At the majority of clubs, there is very little problem about admittance. Most of the private clubs do extend guest courtesies to foreign visitors provided they have references from their home clubs. But even without the proper credentials there are many outstanding public courses for golfers to enjoy.

American golfers will find the Australian climate a little unusual in comparison with their own. Every course in Australia is playable throughout the year. But because the continent is in the Southern Hemisphere, the seasons are reversed; the Australian spring is from September to November and the fall is from March to May. Prime golf seasons vary from locale to locale. In Brisbane, on the east coast, the best time to play golf is from April through October. However, on the southern coast, which includes Melbourne and Sydney, the best golf months are during the spring and fall.

Australian golf courses tend to be long and tough. Almost every course the traveling golfer will consider is more than 6,500 yards long. Since most of the good golf courses are located near the coast, the winds coming off the three oceans surrounding Australia play a great part in any round of golf. It is not uncommon for a golfer to begin his round in the midst of a calm breeze and finish with a strong wind blowing into his face.

The golfer will have his choice of hilly courses as well as flat ones. In Perth, the Lake Karrinyup course is considered one of the hilliest courses on the continent. The Royal Perth club in nearby South Perth is comparatively flat, but well-placed hazards make any golfer work hard to come close to its par 72.

Most Australian golf courses are well maintained, and the local climate keeps the fairways in a condition of prolific growth. The roughs, unfortunately, are in the same state, and they grow into thick, mean monsters, the equivalent of which is hard to find in the United States.

Greens vary in type and texture in Australia according to geography. In Melbourne, Adelaide, and Perth, very fast, English-style "bent" grass is used. In the Sydney area a slightly coarser grass is necessary to withstand the higher average temperature, and in Brisbane the grasses are even coarser than Bermuda grass and require a good solid stroke for successful putting.

The availability of caddies in Australia varies with each locality. Most Australian golfers either carry their own clubs or use "buggies," which are the equivalent of hand golf carts. Where caddies are available, the cost is between 60¢ and 80¢ per round during the week and from 80¢ to $1.40 on weekends and holidays. It would be wise to determine in advance what is available at each club.

Throughout Australia green fees are inexpensive by U.S. standards. On public courses they average from 50¢ to $1. Private courses charge a little more, generally about $1 to $3 per round.

Regarding golf equipment: Pan Am golf travelers may borrow clubs and other equipment free of charge from the Precision Golf Forging Pty., Ltd., a leading Australian golf-equipment manufacturer. For further information, contact the Pan Am Airport Traffic Manager on arrival in Sydney.

SEASON: Year round.

HOW TO GET THERE: By Jet Clipper via Honolulu, and continuing via the Fiji Islands, via Pago Pago, or via Auckland, Sydney is about 18½ hours (elapsed time) from San Francisco and Los Angeles. Melbourne is about 1¼ hours from Sydney by air. By ship, about 21 days from the U.S. west coast.

GOLF EQUIPMENT: American equipment available, plus good local equipment.

LANGUAGE: English.

TIME: Eastern Australia is eighteen hours later than U.S. Pacific Standard Time; three time zones within the country; no Daylight Saving Time.

ADELAIDE AREA

Glenelg Golf Club

LOCATION: 6 miles from Adelaide. COURSE SIZE: 18 holes; 6,640 yards; par 72. AVAILABILITY TO VISITORS: Available to visitors who are members of registered clubs elsewhere. GREEN FEES: $2.75 for men; $1.40 associates. CADDIE FEES: No caddies. GOLF CLUB RENTALS: $1.10 per round. GOLF CART RENTALS: 30¢ per day. MOTORIZED GOLF CART RENTALS: Available only to disabled players. LESSONS: $2.75 per half hour. CLUBHOUSE FACILITIES: Bar and light refreshments available, as well as showers. RECOMMENDED ACCOMMODATIONS: Hotel Australia, Hotel South Australian, Hotel Earl of Zetland, Hotel Oriental.

Grange Golf Club

LOCATION: 8½ miles from Adelaide. COURSE SIZE: Two 18 holes: west course, 6,732 yards; east course, 6,891 yards. AVAILABILITY TO VISITORS: Introduction by member only. GREEN FEES: $2.20 per round. CADDIE FEES: $1.10 per round. GOLF CLUB RENTALS: $1.10 per day. GOLF CART RENTALS: Not available. MOTORIZED GOLF CART RENTALS: Available only to disabled players. LESSONS: $2.20 per half hour. CLUBHOUSE FACILITIES: Club room and facilities available (including bar, etc.). RECOMMENDED ACCOMMODATIONS: See above listing.

Kooyanga Golf Club

LOCATION: Lockleys (5 miles from Adelaide). COURSE SIZE: 18 holes; 6,525 yards; par 73. AVAILABILITY TO VISITORS: Visitors welcome with a letter from own club. MOTORIZED GOLF CART RENTALS: Not available. LESSONS: Available; H. J. Mills, pro. CLUBHOUSE FACILITIES: Full facilities available. RECOMMENDED ACCOMMODATIONS: See above listing.

North Adelaide Municipal Golf Club

LOCATION: ½ mile from city. COURSE SIZE: Three 18 holes: north course, 5,160 yards, par 68; south course, 6,635 yards, par 73; also 18-hole, 1,800-yard course. AVAILABILITY TO VISITORS: Open to the public. GREEN FEES: $1.10 per round. CADDIE FEES: No caddies. GOLF CLUB RENTALS: $1.10 per day. GOLF CART RENTALS: 30¢ per round. MOTORIZED GOLF CART RENTALS: Not available. LESSONS: $2.20 per half hour. CLUBHOUSE FACILITIES: All facilities including licensed restaurant. RECOMMENDED ACCOMMODATIONS: See above listing.

Palawalunga Golf Club

LOCATION: 6½ miles from city. COURSE SIZE: 18 holes; 6,400 yards; par 70. AVAILABILITY TO VISITORS: Visitors welcome. GREEN FEES: 10¢ per round. CADDIE FEES: No caddies. GOLF CLUB RENTALS: 55¢ per round. GOLF CART RENTALS: 55¢ per day. MOTORIZED GOLF CART RENTALS: Not available. LESSONS: $1.95 per half hour. CLUBHOUSE FACILITIES: Full golfing facilities. No clubroom, catering, or bar. RECOMMENDED ACCOMMODATIONS: See above listing.

Royal Adelaide

LOCATION: Seaton Park (4 miles by taxi from Adelaide). COURSE SIZE: 18 holes; 6,714 yards; par 73. AVAILABILITY TO VISITORS: Visitors welcome with a letter from home club. MOTORIZED GOLF CART RENTALS: Not available. LESSONS: Available; Alan Murray, pro. CLUBHOUSE FACILITIES: Full facilities. RECOMMENDED ACCOMMODATIONS: See above listing.

BRISBANE AREA

Brisbane Golf Club

LOCATION: Yerongpilly (5 miles from Brisbane). COURSE SIZE: 18 holes; 6,613 yards; par 73. Subsidiary 9-hole course available.

AVAILABILITY TO VISITORS: Visitors welcome with letter from own club. LESSONS: Mike Stafford, pro. CLUBHOUSE FACILITIES: Full facilities. RECOMMENDED ACCOMMODATIONS: Lennons Hotel, Majestic Hotel, Carlton Hotel, Canberra Hotel, Gresham Hotel.

Gailes Golf Club

LOCATION: Gailes, Brisbane (near city). COURSE SIZE: 18 holes; 6,722 yards; par 73. AVAILABILITY TO VISITORS: Visitors welcome with a letter from own club. MOTORIZED GOLF CART RENTALS: Not available. LESSONS: Available; Jack Coogan, pro. CLUBHOUSE FACILITIES: Full facilities available. RECOMMENDED ACCOMMODATIONS: See Brisbane Golf Club listing.

Indooroopilly Golf Club

LOCATION: Indooroopilly, S.W. 2 (4 miles from Brisbane). COURSE SIZE: 18 holes; regulation length; par 72. AVAILABILITY TO VISITORS: Visitors with a letter from own club are welcome to use the club Monday, Tuesday, and Thursday afternoons, Wednesday mornings, Fridays, and Sundays. GREEN FEES: About $1.10 per round for men; 85¢ for women. CADDIE FEES: About 60¢ per round. GOLF CLUB RENTALS: About $1.10 per day; arrangements should be made in advance. MOTORIZED GOLF CART RENTALS: $3.40 per round for a motor buggy. LESSONS: Available. CLUBHOUSE FACILITIES: Full facilities available. RECOMMENDED ACCOMMODATIONS: See Brisbane Golf Club listing.

Royal Queensland Golf Club

LOCATION: Eagle Farm (6 miles from Brisbane). COURSE SIZE: 18 holes; 6,784 yards; par 74. AVAILABILITY TO VISITORS: Visitors welcome with a letter from home club. MOTORIZED GOLF CART RENTALS: Not available. LESSONS: C. Earp, pro. CLUBHOUSE FACILITIES: Full facilities. RECOMMENDED ACCOMMODATIONS: See Brisbane Golf Club listing.

CANBERRA

Royal Canberra Golf Club

LOCATION: Westbourne Woods, Yarralumla, Canberra (easily accessible by taxi from downtown). COURSE SIZE: 18 holes; 6,883 yards; par 72. AVAILABILITY TO VISITORS: Visitors with a letter from own club are welcome to use the course Monday, Tuesday, and Wednesday except between noon and 1:30 P.M., and Friday and Sunday before 8:15 A.M. and after 1:30 P.M. GREEN FEES: About $1.50 per round. CADDIE FEES: Caddies not usually available except for important tournaments. GOLF CLUB RENTALS: About 80¢ per round. GOLF CART RENTALS: A few hand-pulled buggies available. MOTORIZED GOLF CART RENTALS: Not available. LESSONS: Available. CLUBHOUSE FACILITIES: Full facilities. RECOMMENDED ACCOMMODATIONS: Rex at Canberra, Canberra, Ainslee-Rex.

Royal Canberra Golf Club.

Royal Canberra Golf Club

MELBOURNE AREA

Albert Park Golf Club

LOCATION: 4 miles from Melbourne. COURSE SIZE: 18 holes; 6,038 yards. AVAILABILITY TO VISITORS: Always welcome. GREEN FEES: 80¢ per round. CADDIE FEES: No caddies. GOLF CLUB RENTALS: 55¢; $11 deposit. GOLF CART RENTALS: 35¢ per day. MOTORIZED GOLF CART RENTALS: Not available. LESSONS: $1.95 half hour. CLUBHOUSE FACILITIES: Locker rooms and showers, kiosk, but no lounge or bars. RECOMMENDED ACCOMMODATIONS: Melbourne: Southern Cross Hotel, The Australia, Ress Oriental, Savoy Plaza, Windsor, and Chevron hotels.

Commonwealth Golf Club

LOCATION: Oakleigh (10 miles from Melbourne). COURSE SIZE: 18 holes; 6,616 yards; par 74. AVAILABILITY TO VISITORS: Visitors welcome with a letter from own club. MOTORIZED GOLF CART RENTALS: Not available. LESSONS: Available; Bob Jennings, pro. CLUBHOUSE FACILITIES: Full facilities. RECOMMENDED ACCOMMODATIONS: See Albert Park Golf Club listing.

Huntingdale Golf Club

LOCATION: East Oakleigh (10 miles from Melbourne). COURSE SIZE: 18 holes; 6,941 yards; par 75. AVAILABILITY TO VISITORS: Visitors welcome with a letter from home club. MOTORIZED GOLF CART RENTALS: Not available. LESSONS: Available; Geoff Flanagan, pro. CLUBHOUSE FACILITIES: Full facilities available. RECOMMENDED ACCOMMODATIONS: See Albert Park Golf Club listing.

Kingston Heath Golf Club

LOCATION: Menton (10 miles from Melbourne). COURSE SIZE: 18 holes; 6,807 yards; par 74. AVAILABILITY TO VISITORS: Visitors welcome with a letter from own club. LESSONS: Available; George Cussell, pro. CLUBHOUSE FACILITIES: Full facilities available. RECOMMENDED ACCOMMODATIONS: See Albert Park Golf Club listing.

Kingwood Golf Club

LOCATION: Dingley (16 miles from Melbourne). COURSE SIZE: 18 holes; 6,669 yards; par 74. AVAILABILITY TO VISITORS: Visitors welcome with letter from home club. MOTORIZED GOLF CART RENTALS: Not available. LESSONS: Available; Jack Beazley, pro. CLUBHOUSE FACILITIES: Full facilities available. RECOMMENDED ACCOMMODATIONS: See Albert Park Golf Club listing.

Metropolitan Golf Club

LOCATION: Oakleigh (10 miles from Melbourne). COURSE SIZE: 18 holes; 6,602 yards; par 74. AVAILABILITY TO VISITORS: Visitors welcome with a letter from own club. MOTORIZED GOLF CART RENTALS: Not available. LESSONS: Available; Brian Twite, pro. CLUBHOUSE FACILITIES: Full facilities. RECOMMENDED ACCOMMODATIONS: See Albert Park Golf Club listing.

Royal Melbourne Golf Club

LOCATION: Black Rock (in Melbourne). COURSE SIZE: East Course: 18 holes; 6,546 yards; par 74. West Course: 18 holes; 6,456 yards; par 73. AVAILABILITY TO VISITORS: Visitors welcome with a letter from home club. MOTORIZED GOLF CART RENTALS: Not available. LESSONS: Available; Alex Orr, pro. CLUBHOUSE FACILITIES: Full facilities available. RECOMMENDED ACCOMMODATIONS: See Albert Park Golf Club listing.

Victoria Club

LOCATION: Cheltenham (13 miles from Melbourne). COURSE SIZE: 18 holes; 6,665 yards; par 73. AVAILABILITY TO VISITORS: Visitors welcome with a letter from home club. MOTORIZED GOLF CART RENTALS: Not available. LESSONS: Available; Dennis Denehy, pro. CLUBHOUSE FACILITIES: Full facilities. RECOMMENDED ACCOMMODATIONS: See Albert Park Golf Club listing.

Gary Player exploding from pot bunker at Royal Melbourne.

Yarra Bend Golf Club

LOCATION: 5 miles from Melbourne. COURSE SIZE: 18 holes; 6,262 yards. AVAILABILITY TO VISITORS: Visitors welcome. GREEN FEES: 80¢ per round. CADDIE FEES: No caddies. GOLF CLUB RENTALS: 66¢; $11 deposit. GOLF CART RENTALS: 35¢ per day. MOTORIZED GOLF CART RENTALS: Not available. LESSONS: $1.95 per half hour. CLUBHOUSE FACILITIES: Locker rooms and showers, kiosk, but no lounge or bars. RECOMMENDED ACCOMMODATIONS: See listing for Albert Park Golf Club.

PERTH AREA

Cottesloe Golf Club

LOCATION: North Claremont (on the way from Perth to Freemantle). COURSE SIZE: 18 holes; 6,640 yards; par 72. AVAILABILITY TO

VISITORS: Visitors welcome with letter from own club. LESSONS: R. Draddy, pro. CLUBHOUSE FACILITIES: Full facilities.

Lake Karrinyup Golf Club

LOCATION: Balcatta (10 miles from Perth). COURSE SIZE: 18 holes; 6,517 yards; par 72. AVAILABILITY TO VISITORS: Visitors welcome with a letter from home club; advance arrangements required. GOLF CART RENTALS: About 35¢ per day. MOTORIZED GOLF CART RENTALS: Not available. LESSONS: Available; T. K. Osborn, pro. CLUBHOUSE FACILITIES: Full facilities. RECOMMENDED ACCOMMODATIONS: Travelodge Motor Hotel, Esplanade, Riverside Lodge, Palace, and Adelphi.

The Lakes Golf Links

LOCATION: 14 miles south of Perth. COURSE SIZE: 18 holes; 6,350 yards. AVAILABILITY TO VISITORS: Welcome. GREEN FEES: $1.10 per round. CADDIE FEES: No caddies. GOLF CLUB RENTALS: 90¢ per round. GOLF CART RENTALS: Included in rental of clubs. MOTORIZED GOLF CART RENTALS: Not available. LESSONS: $2.25 per half hour. CLUBHOUSE FACILITIES: All facilities of the Lakes Hotel. RECOMMENDED ACCOMMODATIONS: The Lakes Hotel.

Mt. Lawley Golf Club

LOCATION: 3½ miles north of Perth. COURSE SIZE: 18 holes; 6,671 yards. AVAILABILITY TO VISITORS: Usually as guests of members; however, allowances are made for visitors on application to the secretary and presentation of their club membership card. GREEN FEES: $1.10 daily for men; 85¢ for women. CADDIE FEES: 85¢ per round. GOLF CLUB RENTALS: $1.10 per round. GOLF CART RENTALS: 35¢ per round. MOTORIZED GOLF CART RENTALS: Not available. LESSONS: $2.25 per half hour. CLUBHOUSE FACILITIES: Excellent facilities, including bar. RECOMMENDED ACCOMMODATIONS: Travelodge Motor Hotel, Esplanade, Riverside Lodge, Palace, and Adelphi.

Royal Perth Golf Club

LOCATION: South Perth (3 miles from Perth). COURSE SIZE: 18 holes; 6,543 yards; par 72. AVAILABILITY TO VISITORS: Visitors welcome with a letter from home club. MOTORIZED GOLF CART RENTALS: Not available. LESSONS: Available; Charles Newman, pro. CLUBHOUSE FACILITIES: Full facilities. RECOMMENDED ACCOMMODATIONS: See above listing.

SYDNEY AREA

Australian Club

LOCATION: Kensington (accessible by bus or taxi from downtown Sydney). COURSE SIZE: 18 holes; 6,667 yards; par 72. Additional 9-hole course. AVAILABILITY TO VISITORS: Visitors welcome with a letter from home club. MOTORIZED GOLF CART RENTALS: Not available. LESSONS: Available; Darryl Welch, pro. CLUBHOUSE FACILITIES: Full facilities available. RECOMMENDED ACCOMMODATIONS: Sydney: Hotel Wentworth, Hotel Chevron, Hotel Menzies, Hotel Carlton-Rex, and Hotel Metropole.

Moore Park Golf Club

LOCATION: Anzac Parade, Moore Park (about 2 miles from Sydney; accessible by many bus routes or by taxi for about 50¢). COURSE SIZE: 18 holes; 6,451 yards; par 71. AVAILABILITY TO VISITORS: Welcome except from 8 A.M. to 1 P.M. Saturday and Sunday. Starting times are booked by calling the starter at 663 3724, and overseas visitors are invited to call the club secretary at 663 3791. GREEN FEES: 65¢. CADDIE FEES: No caddies available. GOLF CLUB RENTALS: 55¢ per round. GOLF CART RENTALS: 25¢. MOTORIZED GOLF CART RENTALS: Not available. LESSONS: $2 per half hour. CLUBHOUSE FACILITIES: Bar and restaurant. RECOMMENDED ACCOMMODATIONS: See Australian Club listing.

New South Wales Golf Club

LOCATION: Henry Head, La Perouse, Sydney (11 miles by taxi from downtown Sydney). COURSE SIZE: 18 holes; 6,667 yards; par 72. AVAILABILITY TO VISITORS: Visitors welcome with a letter from home club. CADDIE FEES: Caddies available by arrangement. MOTORIZED GOLF CART RENTALS: Not available. LESSONS: Available; Colin Mcgregor, pro. CLUBHOUSE FACILITIES: Full facilities. RECOMMENDED ACCOMMODATIONS: See Australian Club listing.

Royal Sydney Golf Club

LOCATION: Rose Bay (near Sydney). COURSE SIZE: 18 holes; 6,651 yards; par 72. Also subsidiary 9-hole course. AVAILABILITY TO VISITORS: Visitors must be introduced by and play with members. Those belonging to certain other Australian clubs are eligible, as well as those in the "Distinguished Golfer" category. Make prior arrangements. LESSONS: Alex Merces, pro. CLUBHOUSE FACILITIES: Full facilities. RECOMMENDED ACCOMMODATIONS: See Australian Club listing.

St. Michaels Golf Club

LOCATION: Little Bay (12 miles from Sydney; accessible from downtown by taxi for about $3, or by La Perouse bus). COURSE SIZE: 18 holes; 6,998 yards; par 72. AVAILABILITY TO VISITORS: Open Monday and Tuesday after 12 noon; Wednesday, Friday, Saturday, and Sunday after 2 P.M.; Thursday midweek competition is open to members of affiliated clubs, including overseas. Overseas visitors should call the club secretary, Mr. Longdon, at 661 0621. GREEN FEES: $1.10 throughout the week. CADDIE FEES: No caddies available unless prior arrangements made. GOLF CLUB RENTALS: 55¢ per round. GOLF CART RENTALS: 33¢ per round. MOTORIZED GOLF CART RENTALS: Not available. LESSONS: Available by appointment; $2 per half hour. CLUBHOUSE FACILITIES: Restaurant and bar. RECOMMENDED ACCOMMODATIONS: See Australian Club listing.

TASMANIA

Kingston Beach Golf Club

LOCATION: Kingston, Tasmania (11 miles by car from Hobart). COURSE SIZE: 18 holes; 6,589 yards; par 73. AVAILABILITY TO VISITORS: Visitors welcome with a letter from home club. GREEN FEES: $1.20 per day. CADDIE FEES: No caddies available. GOLF CLUB RENTALS: Available. GOLF CART RENTALS: Available. MOTORIZED GOLF CART RENTALS: Not available. LESSONS: Available. CLUBHOUSE FACILITIES: Full facilities available. RECOMMENDED ACCOMMODATIONS: Hobart: The Wrest Point Hotel, Hadley's Hotel, Travelodge Motel.

Fiji Islands

The Fiji Golf Club is the only course on Suva, and one of the few in the South Seas. It is currently 9 holes, but is being expanded to 18 holes at the present time. Because of the tropical climate and healthy rainfall enjoyed at Suva, the course is at all times in perfect condition, and playable twelve months a year. The Fiji Golf Club welcomes visitors, except as specified below.

> HOW TO GET THERE: By Pan Am Jet Clipper to Nandi from the east or west coast of the United States via Honolulu; 12¾ hours elapsed time from West Coast. Air service between Nandi and Suva (135 miles) by Fiji Airways. By ship, Fiji is reached in 14 days.

Fiji Golf Club

LOCATION: 3 miles from the center of Suva (accessible by taxi for about $1). COURSE SIZE: 9 holes (18 tees); 6,205 yards; par 72. A further 9 holes will be ready by 1968. AVAILABILITY TO VISITORS: Open to visitors every day except Saturday and Tuesday afternoons, when golf competitions are played. GREEN FEES: $1.25 per 18 holes. CADDIE FEES: 65¢ per 18 holes. GOLF CLUB RENTALS: $2.50 per 18 holes. GOLF CART RENTALS: Not available. MOTORIZED GOLF CART RENTALS: Not available. LESSONS: Not available. CLUBHOUSE FACILITIES: Bar facilities, lockers, and showers. RECOMMENDED ACCOMMODATIONS: Suva: Outrigger Motel.

Hawaii

If Scotland is the home of golf, then Hawaii is the playground. The idyllic weather, natural beauty, and casual atmosphere provide the perfect setting for a golfing holiday.

The main island, Hawaii, is the home of one of the most spectacular courses in golfdom. Black sand beaches, roaring white surf, turquoise waters, emerald greens and fairways, and the added attraction of Mauna Loa—the world's most active volcano—erupting in the distance gave Robert Trent Jones a unique setting for his famous Mauna Kea beach golf course. The serious golfer, regardless of handicap, should sample the devilish delights of this golf resort at least once.

Maui—the Valley Isle—boasts a course at least as scenic and difficult as the Mauna Kea. The Royal Kaanapali Golf Course, located on the western tip of the island, plays to a testing 7,179 yards. The kona (trade) breezes must be reckoned with, as well as the many picturesque lagoons that lie in wait for the erring drive. Mt. Haleahala, the world's largest extinct volcano, rises to a height of over 30,000 feet from base to crater and keeps the sun from the eyes of early morning golfers.

Oahu—the Aloha Isle—home of Waikiki, Pearl Harbor, Diamond Head, and the fabled Makaha surf, offers the pressed-for-time golfer several interesting and sporty courses within easy commuting distance from the Waikiki Beach area. The popular Ala Wai Golf Course lies in the shadow of Diamond Head and combines reasonable rates with ease of access to make it the most frequently played course on the island.

For raw beauty, the vacationing golfer should try the Pali Golf Course, a difficult but inexpensive layout located at the base of the towering Pali cliffs on the windward side of Oahu. Legend has it that King Kamehameha once tested the loyalty of his army by marching them over the sheer, 1,000-foot walls. After a round here, the high handicapper may feel the urge to toss his clubs after the unfortunate warriors.

Kauai—the Garden Isle—lies in the northwest portion of the island chain. Green and silent, this little gem of the Pacific easily surpasses the beauty of her rivals to the south. It is not uncommon to see three or four rainbows simultaneously, as the rainfall in the mountains is quite heavy, but the showers seldom fall on the beach courses.

Wailua Golf Course, Kauai's contribution to golfing pleasure, is the best-kept course in the islands. After a round here, the tourist will want to spend an afternoon inspecting the Menehune Fish Ponds. The Menehunes are the leprechauns of the islands, and many a native golfer, facing a penalty for a lost ball, amiably blames the Menehunes and plays on through.

Beauty, atmosphere, and variety await the traveling golfer on his excursion to our fiftieth state.

SEASON: Year round.
HOW TO GET THERE: By Pan American Jet Clipper from San Francisco, Los Angeles, Portland, or Seattle. Flying time from San Francisco 5 hours. By ship from San Francisco, 4½ days.
GOLF EQUIPMENT: Available at reasonable rates.
TIME: Two hours earlier than U.S. Pacific Standard Time.

OAHU

Ala Wai Golf Course

LOCATION: Honolulu. COURSE SIZE: 18 holes; 6,371 yards; par 71. AVAILABILITY TO VISITORS: Visitors welcome. GREEN FEES: Weekdays, $1.50; Saturdays, Sundays, and holidays, $2.50 per day. GOLF CLUB RENTALS: $1.50 per day. MOTORIZED GOLF CART RENTALS: $6 per round. LESSONS: Ted Makalena, pro. CLUBHOUSE FACILITIES: Restaurant, bar, and lockers. RECOMMENDED ACCOMMODATIONS: Royal Hawaiian, Halekulani, Hilton Hawaiian Village, Kahala Hilton, and many other hotels and guest houses available in the Waikiki area.

Francis H. Ii Brown Golf Course

LOCATION: Pearl Harbor Heights (25 minutes from Waikiki by car). COURSE SIZE: 18 holes; 7,200 yards; par 72. AVAILABILITY TO

VISITORS: Visitors welcome. Reservations necessary. GREEN FEES: $6.50 per person weekdays, $8.50 per person weekends and holidays; includes electric carts. CADDIE FEES: No caddies. GOLF CLUB RENTALS: $3.50 for pro-line golf sets. GOLF CART RENTALS: Not available. MOTORIZED GOLF CART RENTALS: Included in the green fees. LESSONS: Available at pro shop; Guinea Kop, pro. CLUBHOUSE FACILITIES: Restaurant, bar. RECOMMENDED ACCOMMODATIONS: See above listing.

International Golf and Country Club

LOCATION: Near Wai Pahu, Oahu (bus or car from Waikiki). COURSE SIZE: 18 holes; 5,755 yards; par 69. AVAILABILITY TO VISITORS: Visitors welcome. GREEN FEES: Weekdays, $1.50; weekends, $4 per day. GOLF CLUB RENTALS: Available. MOTORIZED GOLF CART RENTALS: $6 per round. LESSONS: Red Uldrick, pro. CLUBHOUSE FACILITIES: Snack bar for light refreshments. RECOMMENDED ACCOMMODATIONS: Royal Hawaiian, Hilton Hawaiian Village, Halekulani, Kahala Hilton. (Sprecial package for visitors includes round-trip transportation from Waikiki hotels to the International Golf course, green fees, clubs, balls, lunch, as well as golf snacks—price: $15.) Many additional hotels and guest houses available in the Waikiki area.

Makaha Valley Golf and Country Club

LOCATION: Makaha Valley in West Oahu (an hour by car from Waikiki). COURSE SIZE: 18 holes; 7,252 yards; par 72. AVAILABILITY TO VISITORS: Privately owned; open to public play. GREEN FEES: Weekends and holidays, $6 for 18 holes, $3 for 9 holes; weekdays, $3 for 18 holes, $1.50 for 9 holes. CADDIE FEES: No caddies. GOLF CLUB RENTALS: $2.50 per set. GOLF CART RENTALS: 75¢ for 18 holes. MOTORIZED GOLF CART RENTALS: $7 for 18 holes, $4 for 9 holes. LESSONS: By pro Bruce Fowler. CLUBHOUSE FACILITIES: Snack shop and pro shop. RECOMMENDED ACCOMMODATIONS: Ilikai Hotel.

Mauka-Kai

LOCATION: Honolulu (beyond Koko Head in Hawaii Kai, about 30 minutes by car from Honolulu). COURSE SIZE: 18 holes; 2,285 yards; par 54. AVAILABILITY TO VISITORS: Visitors welcome. GREEN FEES: Weekdays, $2; weekends, $3 per day; ladies' day, Tuesday, $1;

students, $1. CADDIE FEES: Caddies are not available. GOLF CLUB RENTALS: $1 per round. GOLF CART RENTALS: 50¢ per day. MOTORIZED GOLF CART RENTALS: $5 per round. LESSONS: Available. RECOMMENDED ACCOMMODATIONS: Royal Hawaiian, Halekulani, Hilton Hawaiian Village, Kahala Hilton, and many other hotels and guest houses available in the Waikiki area.

Mid-Pacific Country Club

LOCATION: Lanikai, Oahu (about 30 minutes by car from Honolulu). COURSE SIZE: 18 holes; 6,471 yards; par 72. AVAILABILITY TO VISITORS: Visitors welcome; reservations necessary. GREEN FEES: Weekdays, $3; weekends, $8 per day. MOTORIZED GOLF CARTS: $6.20 per round. LESSONS: Chuck Jones, pro. CLUBHOUSE FACILITIES: Restaurant, bar, and lockers. RECOMMENDED ACCOMMODATIONS: Royal Hawaiian, Halekulani, Hilton Hawaiian Village, Kahala Hilton, and many other hotels and guest houses available in the Waikiki area.

Mililani Golf Club

LOCATION: Near Waipio in Central Oahu (30 minutes by car from Waikiki). COURSE SIZE: 18 holes; 6,490 yards; par 72. AVAILABILITY TO VISITORS: Public course. Sunday mornings reserved for group tournaments. GREEN FEES: Weekends and holidays, $5 for 18 holes, $3 for 9 holes; weekdays, $2.50 for 18 holes, $1.50 for 9 holes. CADDIE FEES: No caddies. GOLF CLUB RENTALS: Available. GOLF CART RENTALS: 50¢ per 18 holes. MOTORIZED GOLF CART RENTALS: $6.50 for 18 holes. LESSONS: Available. CLUBHOUSE FACILITIES: Pro shop and snack bar. RECOMMENDED ACCOMMODATIONS: Any Waikiki area hotel.

Moanalua Golf Club

LOCATION: Honolulu (by taxi from city). COURSE SIZE: 9 holes; 3,112 yards; par 36. AVAILABILITY TO VISITORS: Visitors welcome; reservations are advised for weekend play. GREEN FEES: Weekdays, $1.50; weekends, $3 per day. GOLF CLUB RENTALS: $2 per day. MOTORIZED GOLF CART RENTALS: $6 per round. LESSONS: Available; Bill Kim, pro. CLUBHOUSE FACILITIES: Restaurant, bar, and lockers available. RECOMMENDED ACCOMMODATIONS: Royal Hawaiian, Halekulani, Hilton Hawaiian Village, Kahala Hilton, and many other hotels and guest houses available in the Waikiki area.

The 6th hole at Oahu Country Club, Honolulu.

Oahu Country Club

LOCATION: Nuvanu Valley, Honolulu. COURSE SIZE: 18 holes; 5,505 yards; par 71. AVAILABILITY TO VISITORS: Visitors welcome Monday, Tuesday, or Friday afternoon with guest card and reservations with club. GREEN FEES: $10 per day. CADDIE FEES: $3.50 per bag, double; $4 per bag, single. GOLF CLUB RENTALS: $2.50 per day. MOTORIZED GOLF CART RENTALS: $7.25 per day. LESSONS: Ed Sochacki, pro. CLUB-HOUSE FACILITIES: Restaurant, bar, and lockers. RECOMMENDED AC-COMMODATIONS: Royal Hawaiian, Halekulani, Hilton Hawaiian Village, Kahala Hilton, and many other hotels and guest houses available in the Waikiki area.

Pali Golf Course

LOCATION: Honolulu (a few minutes from downtown by car). COURSE SIZE: 18 holes; 6,920 yards; par 72. AVAILABILITY TO VISITORS: Visitors welcome, reservations required. GREEN FEES: Weekdays, $1.50; weekends, $2.50 per day; after 4 P.M., 75¢; student rate, 75¢. CADDIE FEES: Caddies available on weekends. GOLF CLUB RENTALS: $3.50 per bag. MOTORIZED GOLF CART RENTALS: $6. LESSONS: Joe Negatosh, pro. CLUBHOUSE FACILITIES: Restaurant, bar, and lockers. RECOMMENDED ACCOMMODATIONS: Royal Hawaiian, Halekulani, Hilton Hawaiian Village, Kahala Hilton, and many other hotels and guest houses available in the Waikiki area.

Waialae Country Club

LOCATION: Diamond Head, Oahu (a few minutes by bus from Honolulu). COURSE SIZE: 18 holes; 6,608 yards; par 72. AVAILABILITY TO VISITORS: Visitors welcome; reservations required; Wednesdays players must tee off before 10 A.M. GREEN FEES: $10 per day; after 3:30 P.M. $5, but play restricted to 9 holes. CADDIE FEES: By arrangement. GOLF CLUB RENTALS: $3.50 per day. MOTORIZED GOLF CART RENTALS: $6 per day. LESSONS: Tony Anthony, pro. CLUBHOUSE FACILITIES: Restaurant, bar, and lockers. RECOMMENDED ACCOMMODATIONS: Royal Hawaiian, Halekulani, Hilton Hawaiian Village, Kahala Hilton, and many other hotels and guest houses available in the Waikiki area.

HAWAII

Hamakua Country Club

LOCATION: Honokaa, Hawaii (about 40 miles from Hilo). COURSE SIZE: 9 holes; 2,787 yards; par 35. AVAILABILITY TO VISITORS: Visitors welcome. GREEN FEES: Weekdays, 75¢; weekends, $1 per day. GOLF CLUB RENTALS: No charge. CLUBHOUSE FACILITIES: None. RECOMMENDED ACCOMMODATIONS: Hilo Hotel, Naniloa.

Hilo Country Club

LOCATION: Hilo, Hawaii (6½ miles, 20 minutes by car from Hilo). COURSE SIZE: 9 holes, two sets of tees to make variation on 18-hole round; 2,949 yards; par 36. AVAILABILITY TO VISITORS: Visitors welcome; reservations advised. GREEN FEES: Weekdays, $1; weekends, $1.50 per day. CADDIE FEES: $2 per round; available weekends. GOLF CLUB RENTALS: 50¢ per round. CLUBHOUSE FACILITIES: Restaurant and bar. RECOMMENDED ACCOMMODATIONS: Hilo Hotel, Naniloa.

Hilo Municipal Course

LOCATION: Hilo, Hawaii (by taxi from Hilo). COURSE SIZE: 18 holes; 6,467 yards; par 72. AVAILABILITY TO VISITORS: Visitors welcome. GREEN FEES: Weekdays: $1.50 before 3 P.M., $1 after 3 P.M.; Saturdays, Sundays, and holidays, $2.50 before 3 P.M., $1.25 after 3 P.M. CADDIE FEES: $2 per round. GOLF CLUB RENTALS: $3 per round. GOLF CART RENTALS: 50¢ per round. MOTORIZED GOLF CART RENTALS: $7 per round. LESSONS: $4 per half hour. CLUBHOUSE FACILITIES: Restaurant, showers. RECOMMENDED ACCOMMODATIONS: Hilo Hotel, Naniloa.

Mauna Kea

LOCATION: Kamuela, Hawaii (12 miles from Waimea-Kamuela Airport; 1½ hours from Hilo by car; 1 hour from Kona by car). COURSE SIZE: 18 holes; 6,593 yards; par 72. AVAILABILITY TO VISITORS: Visitors welcome. GREEN FEES: Hotel guests, $6; nonguests, $10. CADDIE FEES: $4 per round. GOLF CLUB RENTALS: Available. MOTORIZED GOLF CART RENTALS: Electric and gas carts available. LESSONS: Mrs. Jackie Pung, pro. CLUBHOUSE FACILITIES: Restaurant, bar, and locker rooms. RECOMMENDED ACCOMMODATIONS: Mauna Kea Beach Hotel. (Mauna Kea was designed by Robert Trent Jones and opened in 1965.)

Volcano Golf Course

LOCATION: Hilo, Hawaii (by car, 29 miles from Hilo). COURSE SIZE: 18 holes; 6,187 yards; par 72. AVAILABILITY TO VISITORS: Visi-

Everybody plays golf in Hawaii.

tors welcome; reservations advised. GREEN FEES: Weekdays, $1.50; weekends, $2 per day. GOLF CLUB RENTALS: Available. GOLF CART RENTALS: 50¢ per day. LESSONS: Not available. CLUBHOUSE FACILITIES: Restaurant, bar, and lockers. RECOMMENDED ACCOMMODATIONS: Volcano House (near course).

KAUAI

Kukuiolono Golf Course

LOCATION: Lihue, Kauai (15 miles west of Lihue). COURSE SIZE: 9 holes; 3,400 yards; par 36. AVAILABILITY TO VISITORS: Visitors welcome. GREEN FEES: Weekdays, 50¢; weekends, 75¢ per day; per month, $2. Since there is no clubhouse, green fees are collected via the honor system—a deposit box is located on one of the greens. CLUBHOUSE FACILITIES: None. RECOMMENDED ACCOMMODATIONS: Coco Palms Hotel, Kauai Surf Hotel.

Wailua Golf Course

LOCATION: Lihue, Kauai (4 miles from Lihue). COURSE SIZE: 18 holes; 6,686 yards; par 72. AVAILABILITY TO VISITORS: Visitors welcome. GREEN FEES: Weekdays, $3; weekends, $5 per day. GOLF CLUB RENTALS: $2 per round. MOTORIZED GOLF CART RENTALS: $6 per round. CLUBHOUSE FACILITIES: Restaurant and bar. RECOMMENDED ACCOMMODATIONS: Coco Palms Hotel, Kauai Surf Hotel.

MAUI

Maui Country Club

LOCATION: Sprecklesville, Maui (10 minutes by car from airport). COURSE SIZE: 9 holes; 3,310 yards; par 36. AVAILABILITY TO VISITORS: Visitors welcome, reservations advised. GREEN FEES: Weekdays, $2; weekends, $3 per day, plus 25¢ per 9 holes. CADDIE FEES: Caddies are not available. GOLF CLUB RENTALS: $1.50 per day. GOLF CART RENTALS: 25¢ per round. MOTORIZED GOLF CART RENTALS: $3 per round. LESSONS: Not available. CLUBHOUSE FACILITIES: Restaurant and bar available only to guests of members. RECOMMENDED ACCOMMODATIONS: Hana-Maui, Sheraton-Maui, Royal Lahaina Beach Hotel.

Maui Municipal Course

LOCATION: Waiehu. COURSE SIZE: 18 holes; regulation length; par 72. AVAILABILITY TO VISITORS: Visitors welcome. GREEN FEES: Weekdays, $1.50; weekends, $2.50 per day. CADDIE FEES: Caddies available weekends and holidays. GOLF CLUB RENTALS: Available. MOTORIZED GOLF CART RENTALS: $6 per round. LESSONS: Henry Yogi, pro. CLUBHOUSE FACILITIES: Light refreshments, snack bar, driving range. RECOMMENDED ACCOMMODATIONS: Hana-Maui, Sheraton-Maui, Royal Lahaina Beach Hotel.

Royal Kaanapali Golf Course

LOCATION: Kaanapali, Maui (airstrip for charter planes only 300 yards from course). COURSE SIZE: 18 holes; 7,179 yards; par 72. AVAIL-

ABILITY TO VISITORS: Visitors welcome; reservations advised (priority to Kaanapali Hotel guests). GREEN FEES: $10 per day; special rates for longer stays. CADDIE FEES: $5 per bag. GOLF CLUB RENTALS: $5 per day. MOTORIZED GOLF CART RENTALS: $8 per round. LESSONS: William Schwallie, pro. CLUBHOUSE FACILITIES: Complete dining and hotel facilities, bar, and lockers. RECOMMENDED ACCOMMODATIONS: Kaanapali Hotel, Hana-Maui, Sheraton-Maui, Royal Lahaina Beach Hotel.

New Zealand

For its small size New Zealand offers a great deal of golf. Nearly all the cities and towns, even the little ones, have golf courses. There are 370 courses in the 100,000-square-mile area of the two islands.

Golf is a year-round sport in New Zealand. But, as in other countries in the Southern Hemisphere, the seasons are reversed. The best seasons for golf are the spring (September, October, and November) and fall (March through June).

New Zealand golf courses offer a wide variety of facilities, ranging from seaside links to the mountainous layouts of the interior.

One of the country's most beautiful golf courses is in Heretaunga, home of the Wellington Golf Club. Often the site for New Zealand's national championships, it can humble even the finest golfers. A player viewing the course for the first time may think that it is easy. Its panoramic vistas and immaculate appearance help create a demure impression. But watch out! The 6,217-yard course contains five par-3 holes ranging in length from 123 yards to 202 yards. The short 123-yard fifteenth is the most celebrated hole on the course. When the ground is hard it is extremely difficult to pitch the ball onto the green without having it run off the opposite side. The better players generally try to put the ball on the apron surrounding the green. But don't use that strategy when the ground is soft. Then, a pitching wedge probably will be needed to hit out of the apron. Another serious consideration when playing this deceptive hole is the gentle crosswind that usually sweeps through at the tee. This wind has a tendency to alter the course of a tee shot, pushing it left of the green and into a sand trap.

Another fine golf course is Auckland's Titirangi Golf Club, which has recently undergone extensive renovation to improve facilities. The course teems with treacherous gullies, especially on the second, fourth, eighth, and thirteenth holes. In some cases, a 5-iron can provide the height and distance needed to get out of these unusual hazards. But the golfer should keep his trusty pitching wedge limber. It is the favorite club for such shots. The leading hole on the Titirangi course is the par-3 fourteenth which measures a long 215 yards. Originally laid out as a 176-yarder, this hole is a stumbling block for even the best golfers. A wind generally blows in from the green to the tee and even the top professionals frequently use a 4-wood off the tee rather than an iron. Strategically placed traps catch almost every shot.

Most New Zealand golf courses make good use of the natural growth of the country. Large trees border the fairways, in many cases making them very narrow. Pin placement on the greens usually requires accurate approach shots to "get down in two." Traps and water hazards are planned carefully to hurt the erring golfer. On one course, Rotorua, a warm lake provides a natural hazard for several holes and there are steaming fumaroles gurgling at the golfer, destroying his concentration.

Green fees vary, depending on the time of year. However, they are never very expensive. Except at the better clubs, the golfer will either have to tote his own bag or bring his own caddie cart. Caddies are usually available on weekends but must be requested in advance.

Although most of the clubs in New Zealand are private, the visitor who wants to get on a course has few problems. A letter from his club or permission from one of the club's officials is all he needs.

SEASON: Year round.

HOW TO GET THERE: By Pan Am Jet Clipper from San Francisco, Los Angeles, Seattle, or Portland, to Auckland via Honolulu; or via Tahiti, from San Francisco and Los Angeles, about 15 hours elapsed time. By ship, about 17 days from San Francisco.

GOLF EQUIPMENT: American equipment available.

LANGUAGE: English.

TIME: Twenty hours later than U.S. Pacific Standard Time.

NORTH ISLAND

Auckland Golf Club

LOCATION: Middlemore, Auckland (about a 30-minute drive from Auckland). COURSE SIZE: 18 holes; 6,526 yards; par 71. AVAILABILITY TO VISITORS: Visitors welcome weekdays only with a letter from home club; make arrangements in advance. GREEN FEES: Men: $1.40, weekdays. Women: 90¢ weekdays. CADDIE FEES: Not available. GOLF CLUB RENTALS: Available, but very limited. GOLF CART RENTALS: Available. MOTORIZED GOLF CART RENTALS: Not available. LESSONS: Available. CLUBHOUSE FACILITIES: Locker and dining rooms only. RECOMMENDED ACCOMMODATIONS: Auckland Inter-Continental, White Heron Lodge, Royal International, De Bretts, Great Northern, and Star Hotel.

Miramar Golf Club

LOCATION: Wellington (adjacent to the airport). COURSE SIZE: 18 holes; 6,627 yards; par 71. AVAILABILITY TO VISITORS: Welcome anytime. GREEN FEES: Weekdays, $1; weekends, $1.40 per day. CADDIE FEES: 50¢ per round. GOLF CLUB RENTALS: $1 per round. GOLF CART RENTALS: 50¢ per round. MOTORIZED GOLF CART RENTALS: Not available. LESSONS: $1.50 each. CLUBHOUSE FACILITIES: Changing rooms, snacks, no bar. RECOMMENDED ACCOMMODATIONS: White Heron Lodge in Wellington, approximately a mile from the club.

Paraparaumu Golf Club

LOCATION: About 35 miles north of Wellington by car. COURSE SIZE: 18 holes; 6,507 yards; par 73. AVAILABILITY TO VISITORS: Visitors welcome with a letter from own club. GREEN FEES: $1 per round; $1.50 per day. CADDIE FEES: Not available. GOLF CLUB RENTALS: Not available. GOLF CART RENTALS: 30¢ per day. MOTORIZED GOLF CART RENTALS: Not available. LESSONS: Available. CLUBHOUSE FACILITIES: Full facilities. RECOMMENDED ACCOMMODATIONS: Wellington: White Heron Lodge, Royal Oak, St. George, Grand, and Waterloo.

Rotorua Golf Club

LOCATION: Rotorua (2 miles from the center of town). COURSE SIZE: 18 holes; 6,012 yards; par 70. AVAILABILITY TO VISITORS: Visitors welcome with a letter from own club. GREEN FEES: $1 per round; $1.75 per day. CADDIE FEES: Caddies not available. GOLF CLUB RENTALS: Available. GOLF CART RENTALS: Available. MOTORIZED GOLF CART RENTALS: Not available. LESSONS: Available. CLUBHOUSE FACILITIES: Full facilities. RECOMMENDED ACCOMMODATIONS: Grand Hotel, Brents, Geyserland Motel.

Papaparaumu Beach Golf Club, Wellington.

Taupo Golf Club

LOCATION: About a mile from the center of Taupo in the heart of North Island. COURSE SIZE: 18 holes; 6,145 yards; par 72. AVAILABILITY TO VISITORS: Visitors welcome. GREEN FEES: Weekdays, 85¢ per round, $1.40 per day; weekends and holidays, $1.40 per round. CADDIE FEES: Not available. GOLF CLUB RENTALS: $1.15 per round. GOLF CART RENTALS: 30¢ per round. MOTORIZED GOLF CART RENTALS: Not available. LESSONS: Available; Jim Lelland, pro. CLUBHOUSE FACILITIES: Full facilities. RECOMMENDED ACCOMMODATIONS: Lake Hotel Taupo, Wairakei Hotel, Spa Hotel Taupo, Guestward Ho Motels, Oasis Motel, DeBretts Hotel are among many of excellent standards.

Titirangi Golf Club

LOCATION: About 9 miles from Auckland. COURSE SIZE: 18 holes; 6,258 yards; par 69. AVAILABILITY TO VISITORS: Visitors welcome with a letter from own club; advance reservations recommended. GREEN

Titirangi Golf Club, Auckland.

FEES: Weekdays: Men, $1 per round; women, 75¢ per round. Weekends and holidays: men, $1.25 per round; women, $1 per round. CADDIE FEES: 50¢ per round. GOLF CLUB RENTALS: 80¢ per round. GOLF CART RENTALS: 20¢ per round. MOTORIZED GOLF CART RENTALS: Not available. LESSONS: $1.50 per half hour. CLUBHOUSE FACILITIES: Dining room and lounge facilities. RECOMMENDED ACCOMMODATIONS: See Auckland Golf Club listing.

Waitangi Golf Club

LOCATION: Waitangi, Bay of Islands (approximately 125 miles north of Auckland). COURSE SIZE: 18 holes; 6,070 yards, par 70. AVAILABILITY TO VISITORS: Visitors welcome except Sunday and Wednesday. GREEN FEES: 70¢ per round. CADDIE FEES: Caddies are not usually available. GOLF CLUB RENTALS: Clubs are available for hire to the guests of the Waitangi Hotel. GOLF CART RENTALS: Trundlers (pull carts) also for rent to hotel guests. MOTORIZED GOLF CART RENTALS: Not available. LESSONS: No professional. CLUBHOUSE FACILITIES: Incomplete at present. No completion date was set at this printing. RECOMMENDED ACCOMMODATIONS: Waitangi Hotel alongside the course offers seaside bar and dining facilities. Further accommodations are available at the beach resort of Paihia not far from the course.

Wanganui Golf Club

LOCATION: 3 miles from the center of Wanganui on the southern coast of North Island. COURSE SIZE: 18 holes; 6,239 yards; par 71. AVAILABILITY TO VISITORS: Visitors welcome with a letter from home club. GREEN FEES: Men: 75¢ per round; women, 65¢ per round. Wednesday is ladies' day. CADDIE FEES: Caddies available on previous notice. GOLF CLUB RENTALS: Available. GOLF CART RENTALS: Available. MOTORIZED GOLF CART RENTALS: Not available. LESSONS: Available. CLUBHOUSE FACILITIES: Full facilities.

Wellington Golf Club

LOCATION: Heretaunga (17 miles from downtown Wellington by car; train service from Wellington every half hour to Heretaunga station). COURSE SIZE: 18 holes; 6,217 yards; par 71. AVAILABILITY TO VISITORS: Visitors welcome; advance reservations advisable. GREEN FEES: Weekdays, $1.40; Saturdays, Sundays, and holidays, $2.10 per day. CADDIE FEES: Available weekends and holidays, $1.40 per round. GOLF CLUB RENTALS: $1.40 per round. GOLF CART RENTALS: 30¢ per round. MOTORIZED GOLF CART RENTALS: Not available. LESSONS: About $2 per half hour. CLUBHOUSE FACILITIES: Tennis, swimming pool, and restaurant; no bar. RECOMMENDED ACCOMMODATIONS: See Paraparaumu Golf Club listing.

SOUTH ISLAND

Invercargill Golf Club

LOCATION: Invercargill (at the southern end of South Island on the Faveaux Strait). COURSE SIZE: 18 holes; 6,510 yards; par 72. AVAILABILITY TO VISITORS: Visitors welcome with a letter from home club; advance reservations recommended. GREEN FEES: $1 per round; $1.75 per day; $2.80 per week. CADDIE FEES: Not available. GOLF CLUB RENTALS: Not available, but may be borrowed by previous arrangement. GOLF CART RENTALS: Not available, but may be borrowed. MOTORIZED GOLF CART RENTALS: Not available. LESSONS: Available. CLUBHOUSE FACILITIES: Full facilities.

Nelson Golf Club

LOCATION: 4 miles from Nelson City (on Tasman Bay). COURSE SIZE: 18 holes; 6,400 yards; par 70. AVAILABILITY TO VISITORS: Visitors welcome with letter from home club; advance reservations suggested. GREEN FEES: $1 per round; $1.50 per day. CADDIE FEES: Not available. GOLF CLUB RENTALS: Not available, but clubs may be borrowed by arranging with the secretary in advance. GOLF CART RENTALS: Available. MOTORIZED GOLF CART RENTALS: Not available. LESSONS: Available; K. D. Foxton, pro. CLUBHOUSE FACILITIES: Full facilities.

Otago Golf Club

LOCATION: Dunedin (5 minutes from downtown). COURSE SIZE: 18 holes; 6,083 yards; par 71. AVAILABILITY TO VISITORS: Visitors welcome. Make arrangements in advance. GREEN FEES: $1 per round for men; 80¢ for women. CADDIE FEES: About 70¢ per round; arrangements should be made ahead. GOLF CLUB RENTALS: $1 per day. GOLF CART RENTALS: Not available. MOTORIZED GOLF CART RENTALS: Not available. LESSONS: $1.50 per half hour. CLUBHOUSE FACILITIES: Full facilities. RECOMMENDED ACCOMMODATIONS: Wains Hotel, City Hotel, Grand Hotel.

"The Glen" at Otago Golf Club, Dunedin.

Russley Golf Club

LOCATION: Christchurch (next to the airport). COURSE SIZE: 18 holes; 6,627 yards. AVAILABILITY TO VISITORS: Welcome on weekdays. Sunday sponsorship by a member is required and Saturdays there are no guests at all. GREEN FEES: Weekdays, 70¢; Sundays, $1. CADDIE FEES: No regular caddies available. GOLF CLUB RENTALS: Not available. GOLF CART RENTALS: 70¢ per round. MOTORIZED GOLF CART RENTALS: Not available. LESSONS: $1.40 per half hour. CLUBHOUSE FACILITIES: Lounge and lockers available. RECOMMENDED ACCOMMODATIONS: White Heron Lodge, Russley Hotel.

St. Clair Golf Club

LOCATION: About 10 minutes by car from Dunedin. COURSE SIZE: 18 holes; 6,361 yards; par 71. AVAILABILITY TO VISITORS: Visitors welcome with a letter from home club. GREEN FEES: $1 per round. CADDIE FEES: Difficult to obtain caddies unless prior arrangements are made. GOLF CLUB RENTALS: Available. GOLF CART RENTALS: Available. MOTORIZED GOLF CART RENTALS: Not available. LESSONS: Available. CLUBHOUSE FACILITIES: Full facilities. RECOMMENDED ACCOMMODATIONS: See Otago Golf Club listing.

ASIA AND THE PHILIPPINES

Hong Kong

There are two golf clubs in Hong Kong, the Royal Hong Kong, which has four courses, and the Shek "O" Country Club, which has one.

The Royal Hong Kong operates two 18-hole courses and one 9-hole course on the mainland at Fanling, New Territories, as well as the 9-hole Deep Water Bay course on the Island. The Shek "O" club course is a short, 4,441-yard, 18-hole course also located on the island.

The courses at Fanling are located on 400 acres of land among the hills close by the northern border of the colony. A stray shot here may well land behind the Bamboo Curtain, and it is advisable not to go after it.

The courses are in their best playing condition from September to the end of April. Visitors are entirely welcome, but it is advisable for large groups to make advance arrangements to insure that the courses are not fully booked on arrival.

Green fees are about $5 per day and caddies about $1 for 18 holes. Golf clubs may be rented at a nominal charge, and professionals are available for instruction at both Fanling and the Deep Water Bay courses. Up-to-date clubhouse facilities are also available at both locations.

A club bus meets all trains at Sheung Shui station, which is the last station on the line before Lowo, the border station. Visitors should not alight at Fanling station.

SEASON: Throughout the year.

HOW TO GET THERE: By Jet Clipper from the U.S. west coast about 21 hours (elapsed time) via Honolulu and Tokyo; about 2 hours from Manila; 2½ hours from Bangkok; 4½ hours from Tokyo. Hong Kong is visited twice a day by Pan Am's round-the-world flights. By ship, about 18 days from San Francisco.

CURRENCY: The open market rate of exchange for the Hong Kong dollar is about HK $5.71 to U.S. $1. Legal money exchange houses often give better rates than hotels or banks.

GOLF EQUIPMENT: American equipment available at reduced prices in Hong Kong.

LANGUAGE: The official language is English, but the city is populated almost entirely by Chinese. Cantonese is heard mostly on the streets. English, however, is readily understood in hotels, restaurants, and shops. In Chinese, "Hong Kong" means "fragrant harbor."

TIME: Sixteen hours later than U.S. Pacific Coast Time. Daylight Saving Time from late March to early November.

Royal Hong Kong—Deep Water Bay

LOCATION: Hong Kong Island (7½ miles from Victoria; easily accessible by taxi). COURSE SIZE: 9 holes; 1,736 yards; par 28. AVAILABILITY TO VISITORS: Welcome weekdays. Advance arrangements are suggested. GREEN FEES: $1.75 daily. CADDIE FEES: 75¢ per 18-hole round. GOLF CLUB RENTALS: Not available. GOLF CART RENTALS: Not available. MOTORIZED GOLF CART RENTALS: Not available. LESSONS: Available. CLUBHOUSE FACILITIES: Complete modern facilities. RECOMMENDED ACCOMMODATIONS: Mandarin Hotel and Hilton Hotel, both on the harbor.

Royal Hong Kong—Fanling

LOCATION: 23 miles from Hong Kong; ¾ mile from Sheung Shui Station, New Territories (accessible by train, bus, or taxi from Kowloon). COURSE SIZE: Old Course: 18 holes; 6,390 yards; par 70. New Course: 18 holes; 6,495 yards; par 71. Eden Course: 9 holes; 2,100 yards; par 30. AVAILABILITY TO VISITORS: Visitors are welcome during the week, but arrangements should be made in advance, as the courses are very busy throughout the year. GREEN FEES: $5 per day. CADDIE FEES: $1 per 18-hole round. GOLF CLUB RENTALS: $1 per round. GOLF CART RENTALS: 30¢ per round. MOTORIZED GOLF CART RENTALS: Not available. LESSONS: Not available. CLUBHOUSE FACILITIES: Complete up-to-date facilities. RECOMMENDED ACCOMMODATIONS: Kowloon: Peninsula, Park, Ambassador, Empress, Merlin, and Mirimar hotels.

Shell's Wonderful World of Golf

Caddying Chinese-style, Royal Hong Kong Golf Club.

Fairways at Royal Hong Kong are weeded and maintained by Chinese women.

Allan Brown

Shek "O" Club

LOCATION: Shek "O" (14 miles by car or bus from the city of Victoria on Hong Kong island). COURSE SIZE: 18 holes; 4,441 yards. AVAILABILITY TO VISITORS: Visitors welcome on invitation by a member. GREEN FEES: By arrangement with a member. CADDIE FEES: By arrangement. GOLF CLUB RENTALS: Not available. GOLF CART RENTALS: Not available. MOTORIZED GOLF CART RENTALS: Not available. LESSONS: Not available. CLUBHOUSE FACILITIES: Full facilities, including swimming pool. RECOMMENDED ACCOMMODATIONS: Hotels in Victoria.

India

India is a new experience in golf. Two caddies instead of one, and putting on browns instead of greens.

There are more than 50 courses near the major cities, and most are accessible to the touring golfer. Green fees are nominal, and most facilities are generally quite good. Be sure, however, to carry all the necessary equipment, especially balls and tees—these items are in very short supply throughout the country. Light clothing and rain gear are essential.

At most Indian courses one caddie is required, but it is smart to have two. The second, who costs about a dime, is called a forecaddie. He will guard the ball from thieving birds and hungry monkeys that have been known to snatch balls from greens and devour them. The forecaddie fee is included in the caddie fee in the listings below.

On courses that have browns instead of greens, the golfer finds a putting surface of sand and oil. Sweeping a smooth path from ball to hole is quite legal, and makes the surface similar to grass.

SEASON: All year, but inquire in advance to avoid monsoons.

HOW TO GET THERE: By Pan Am Jet Clipper, through-plane service from New York to Calcutta, 23 hours; to Delhi 22½ hours (elapsed time); Delhi is 1½ hours by air from Karachi, 3 hours from Calcutta. Bombay is 1½ hours from Karachi via Middle East Airlines. By ship, 25 to 45 days.

GOLF EQUIPMENT: American equipment available.

LANGUAGE: India has more than 800 dialects; English is spoken by hotel managers and tour personnel.

TIME: Ten and a half hours later than U.S. Eastern Standard Time.

Bangalore Golf Club

LOCATION: Bangalore (several miles from the center of town by car). COURSE SIZE: 18 holes; regulation length. AVAILABILITY TO VISI-

TORS: Visitors welcome. GREEN FEES: 65¢ per round; $4.25 per month.
CADDIE FEES: 30¢ per round for caddie and forecaddie. GOLF CLUB
RENTALS: Not available. GOLF CART RENTALS: Not available. MOTOR-
IZED GOLF CART RENTALS: Not available. LESSONS: Not available.
CLUBHOUSE FACILITIES: Restaurant and bar. RECOMMENDED ACCOM-
MODATIONS: West End Hotel, opposite race track, not far from course.

Bombay Presidency Golf Course

LOCATION: Chembur (15 miles by taxi or bus from center of
Bombay). COURSE SIZE: 18 holes; 6,127 yards; par 71. AVAILABILITY
TO VISITORS: Visitor must play as guest of a member (see Pan Am
District Sales Manager for assistance). GREEN FEES: Weekdays, $1.25;
Saturdays, Sundays, and holidays, $1.70 per day. CADDIE FEES: 47¢,
including tip, per round. GOLF CLUB RENTALS: Available. GOLF CART
RENTALS: Not available. MOTORIZED GOLF CART RENTALS: Not avail-
able. LESSONS: Available. CLUBHOUSE FACILITIES: Game room, locker
rooms, and dining room. RECOMMENDED ACCOMMODATIONS: Fairway
View (on course). Juhu Beach: Sun 'n' Sand Hotel. Other hotels in
Bombay.

Cochin Golf Club

LOCATION: Bolghatty Island, Ernakulam, Kerala (easily accessible
by boat or launch from Ernakulam jetty). COURSE SIZE: 9 holes; 1,545
yards; par 30. AVAILABILITY TO VISITORS: Visitors welcome; play Saturday afternoons and Sunday mornings restricted to members. GREEN
FEES: About $1 per 18-hole round or part. CADDIE FEES: 25¢ per 18-
hole round; caddies required. GOLF CLUB RENTALS: Not available.
GOLF CART RENTALS: Not available. MOTORIZED GOLF CART RENTALS:
Not available. LESSONS: 40¢ per hour. CLUBHOUSE FACILITIES: Locker
room only; prohibition not in force here. RECOMMENDED ACCOMMODA-
TIONS: Bolghatty Palace Tourist Bungalow. Willington Island: Mala-
bar Hotel. Other hotels in Ernakulam.

Cosmopolitan Club

LOCATION: Saidapet (in Madras). COURSE SIZE: 18 holes; 6,030
yards; par 72 (sand greens). AVAILABILITY TO VISITORS: Visitors welcome. GREEN FEES: 50¢ for first round of the day; 25¢ for any addi-

tional rounds. CADDIE FEES: 35¢ for caddie and forecaddie. GOLF CLUB RENTALS: Not available. GOLF CART RENTALS: Not available. MOTORIZED GOLF CART RENTALS: Not available. LESSONS: Not available. CLUBHOUSE FACILITIES: Soft drinks and snacks available. RECOMMENDED ACCOMMODATIONS: Connemara, Queen's, Claridge's, Oceanic.

Country Golf Club

LOCATION: Faridibad (15 miles from Delhi by car or taxi). COURSE SIZE: 18 holes; regulation length. AVAILABILITY TO VISITORS: Visitors welcome. GREEN FEES: Weekdays, $1; weekends and holidays, $1.20 per day. CADDIE FEES: $1 for caddie and forecaddie (both are necessary). GOLF CLUB RENTALS: $1 per day. GOLF CART RENTALS: Not available. MOTORIZED GOLF CART RENTALS: Not available. LESSONS: 60¢ per hour. CLUBHOUSE FACILITIES: Restaurant; the nearest bar is at the Holiday Inn. RECOMMENDED ACCOMMODATIONS: Holiday Inn.

Delhi Golf Club

LOCATION: New Delhi (in the center of the city). COURSE SIZE: 18 holes; 6,979 yards; par 74. AVAILABILITY TO VISITORS: Visitors welcome. GREEN FEES: Weekdays, $1.40; weekends, $1.80 per day. CADDIE FEES: $1 per day for caddie and forecaddie (both necessary). GOLF CLUB RENTALS: $1 per round. GOLF CART RENTALS: Not available. MOTORIZED GOLF CART RENTALS: Not available. LESSONS: $1 per hour. CLUBHOUSE FACILITIES: Locker rooms, bar, and restaurant. RECOMMENDED ACCOMMODATIONS: New Delhi: Oberoi Inter-Continental, Hotel Rajdoot, Hotel Imperial, Ashoka Hotel, and Claridge's. Delhi: Maidens Hotel, Swiss Hotel.

Gulmarg

LOCATION: Kashmir (28 miles by car and 4 miles by pony from Srinagar, the tourist center of Kashmir). COURSE SIZE: 18 holes; 6,460 yards; par 70. AVAILABILITY TO VISITORS: Visitors welcome.

Gymkhana Club

LOCATION: Guindy (about 7 miles from Madras by car). COURSE SIZE: 18 holes; 6,326 yards; par 72 (sand greens). AVAILABILITY TO

The architecture of the clubhouse of the Delhi Golf Club is in keeping with the beautiful ancient tombs on its course.

VISITORS: Visitors welcome. GREEN FEES: $1 per round. CADDIE FEES: Caddie 25¢, plus 20¢ tip; forecaddie, 15¢, plus 10¢ tip per round. GOLF CLUB RENTALS: Not available. GOLF CART RENTALS: Not available. MOTORIZED GOLF CART RENTALS: Not available. LESSONS: Available; R. N. Atzenqiler, pro. CLUBHOUSE FACILITIES: Bar and locker rooms. RECOMMENDED ACCOMMODATIONS: Connemara, Oceanic, Queen's, Claridge's.

Gymkhana Club

LOCATION: Ootacamund (Nilgiris), South India (3 miles from Ootacamund). COURSE SIZE: 18 holes; regulation length; par 72. AVAILABILITY TO VISITORS: Visitors welcome. GREEN FEES: 65¢ per day. CADDIE FEES: 50¢ for caddie and forecaddie. GOLF CLUB RENTALS: 40¢ per round. GOLF CART RENTALS: Not available. MOTORIZED GOLF CART RENTALS: Not available. LESSONS: Available. CLUBHOUSE FACILITIES: Bar. RECOMMENDED ACCOMMODATIONS: Savoy Hotel, Willingdon House.

High Range Club

LOCATION: Munnar, Kerala, South India (on the outskirts of Munnar; accessible by car or taxi). COURSE SIZE: 9 holes; regulation length. AVAILABILITY TO VISITORS: Visitors welcome on introduction by a member. GREEN FEES: No charge. CADDIE FEES: 10¢ per 18-hole round if available. GOLF CLUB RENTALS: Not available. GOLF CART RENTALS: Not available. MOTORIZED GOLF CART RENTALS: Not available. LESSONS: Not available. CLUBHOUSE FACILITIES: Full facilities, including tennis courts. RECOMMENDED ACCOMMODATIONS: High Range Club, Government Tourist Bungalow.

Kundala Club

LOCATION: Chundavurrai, High Range, Kerala (20 miles from Munnar by car). COURSE SIZE: 9 holes; regulation length; sand greens. AVAILABILITY TO VISITORS: Visitors welcome on introduction by a member. GREEN FEES: No charge. CADDIE FEES: 20¢ per 9-hole round. GOLF CLUB RENTALS: Not available. GOLF CART RENTALS: Not available. MOTORIZED GOLF CART RENTALS: Not available. LESSONS: Not available. CLUBHOUSE FACILITIES: Very limited, lockers only. RECOMMENDED ACCOMMODATIONS: Government Tourist Bungalow, hotels in Munnar.

Proforma Club

LOCATION: Agra (facing the Taj Mahal; accessible by car, taxi, or train). COURSE SIZE: 18 holes; regulation length. AVAILABILITY TO VISITORS: Visitors welcome. GREEN FEES: 40¢ per round. Free to guests of hotels listed below. CADDIE FEES: 70¢ per round for caddie and forecaddie. GOLF CLUB RENTALS: Not available. GOLF CART RENTALS: Not available. MOTORIZED GOLF CART RENTALS: Not available. LESSONS: 60¢ per hour. CLUBHOUSE FACILITIES: Soft drink bar open from 4 to 7 P.M. RECOMMENDED ACCOMMODATIONS: Clark Shieraz Hotel, Lauriz Hotel.

Royal Calcutta Golf Club

LOCATION: Golf Club Road, Tollygunge (4 miles from Calcutta by car or taxi). COURSE SIZE: Old Course: 18 holes, 6,845 yards, par 73; New Course: 18 holes, 6,217 yards, par 70. AVAILABILITY TO VISITORS: Visitors welcome on introduction by a member, or with a letter from the Pan American office in Calcutta. The Old Course is unavailable after noon on Saturday and all day Sunday. GREEN FEES: Old Course: $1.60; New Course: $1. CADDIE FEES: 40¢ per 18 holes; forecaddies 20¢ additional; usual tip for good service is 15¢. GOLF CLUB RENTALS: 75¢ per round. GOLF CART RENTALS: Golf carts not permitted. MOTORIZED GOLF CART RENTALS: Not available. LESSONS: $2 per half hour; $3.50 per hour; J. A. Hardwick, pro. CLUBHOUSE FACILITIES: Bar, air-conditioned cocktail lounge, dining room, and locker rooms. RECOMMENDED ACCOMMODATIONS: Calcutta: Great Eastern, Oberoi Grand, Spence's.

Trivandrum Golf Club

LOCATION: Trivandrum, Kerala State (within the city, can be reached by taxi or bus). COURSE SIZE: 9 holes; 3,775 yards; par 36 (additional 9 holes to be completed in 1968). AVAILABILITY TO VISITORS: Visitors welcome. GREEN FEES: About 50¢ per day for visitors. CADDIE FEES: 30¢ per 18-hole round. GOLF CLUB RENTALS: Available. GOLF CART RENTALS: Not available. MOTORIZED GOLF CART RENTALS: Not available. LESSONS: Not available. CLUBHOUSE FACILITIES: Full facilities; alcoholic beverages available to tourists providing they have a drinking permit; table tennis, billiards, badminton. RECOMMENDED ACCOMMODATIONS: Trivandrum Golf Club, Trivandrum Tennis Club, Mascot Hotel, Government Resthouse.

Wellington Gymkhana Club

LOCATION: Wellington, Madras (10 miles by taxi or bus from Ootacamund). COURSE SIZE: 18 holes; 6,282 yards; par 72. AVAILABILITY TO VISITORS: Visitors welcome; tourists are eligible for local tournaments provided they have proof of handicap. GREEN FEES: 40¢ per round; $6 per month. CADDIE FEES: About 30¢ per round. GOLF CLUB RENTALS: Not available. GOLF CART RENTALS: Not available.

Playing among the monuments of an ancient burial ground in Delhi.

MOTORIZED GOLF CART RENTALS: Not available. LESSONS: Not available. RECOMMENDED ACCOMMODATIONS: Full accommodations available at the club.

Willingdon Sports Club

LOCATION: Bombay (near the center of the city, across from the race track; by taxi or municipal bus). COURSE SIZE: 18 holes; 4,349 yards; par 63. AVAILABILITY TO VISITORS: Private club, visitors must play as guest of member (call Pan Am District Sales Manager for assistance). GREEN FEES: Weekdays, $1.25; Saturdays, Sundays, and holidays, $1.70 per day. CADDIE FEES: 25¢ plus 20¢ tip per round. GOLF CLUB RENTALS: Available. GOLF CART RENTALS: Not available. MOTORIZED GOLF CART RENTALS: Not available. LESSONS: Available. CLUBHOUSE FACILITIES: Swimming pool, locker rooms, game rooms, and tennis courts. RECOMMENDED ACCOMMODATIONS: Taj Mahal, Ambassador, Nataraj.

Indonesia

There are fifteen golf clubs in the Indonesian golf association, with courses located on Java, Sumatra, and Kalimantan. However, only two of these have 18-hole courses. One is at Palembang in southern Sumatra, and rather inaccessible, and one, the Djakarta Golf Club, is just a few minutes from the capital at Rawamangun.

The Djakarta club is rather flat, with several water hazards, but no rough; the many trees on the course are obstruction enough. Best time for play is during the afternoon, when there is usually a soft breeze to cool the course.

The club is purely for golf, and there are no facilities other than a bar and snack bar. The snack bar sells Chinese noodles called "Ba Mi." Tourists staying in the Hotel Indonesia and wishing to play all day long are advised to take sandwiches with them.

SEASON: Year round.
HOW TO GET THERE: By Pan American Jet Clipper across the Pacific, via Singapore to Djakarta. Elapsed time including stopovers about 26½ hours from Los Angeles.
LANGUAGE: Indonesian is the national language, derived from Malay. English is spoken by hotel and restaurant personnel.

Djakarta Golf Club

LOCATION: Rawamangun (at the eastern outskirts of the city, easily reachable by taxi). COURSE SIZE: 18 holes; full length; par 71. AVAILABILITY TO VISITORS: Welcome daily except from Saturday noon until Sunday noon. GREEN FEES: $1.50 per day. CADDIE FEES: 75¢ per day. GOLF CLUB RENTALS: Available at Hotel Indonesia. GOLF CART RENTALS: Not available. MOTORIZED GOLF CART RENTALS: Not available. LESSONS: $1.50 per 18-hole round or per hour. CLUBHOUSE FACILITIES: Bar and snack bar. RECOMMENDED ACCOMMODATIONS: Hotel Indonesia, Djakarta.

Japan

Japan offers an unforgettable golfing experience. Nowhere else in the world is the game growing so rapidly and with such enthusiasm. And no other country, except Britain, has so many facilities for its size. Most of Japan's 350 courses have been built within the past decade, and because the overpopulated island has little unused land along its relatively level coastal areas, the new golf layouts have been carved out of rugged mountainous land. The result is some of the world's most challenging—and most beautiful—golf courses.

A golfer could very easily become spoiled by the condition of Japan's courses. The fairway grass is like the perfectly positioned tufts of a clothes brush, and most courses have two greens at each hole to insure that one will be in top playing condition at all times. Hand-tended care, and this is not an exaggeration, is the reason for the superb fairways and greens. Japanese women laborers actually weed, reseed, and clip the grass by hand, and it is a common sight to see hundreds of them at work in that unique Oriental squat on almost every golf course.

The Japanese classify their courses according to the terrain—flat or hilly. Most of the old courses are in the former category, but they present a stiff test nevertheless. Few layouts are made for the recreational golfer; Japanese architects strive to make every course one of championship caliber. Almost all Japanese courses have length—averaging around 7,000 yards—and the heavy fairway turf, which discourages bounce and roll, makes them play even longer. Most greens are composed of korai grass, which is coarser than Bermuda. As a result, putts must be stroked more firmly. Incidentally, the par-5 holes in Japan will disappoint the average golfer. They are not as challenging as one would expect. A few of the championship courses, however, have managed to overcome this general weakness.

Of all the courses in Japan, the one considered the finest is Hirono Golf Club, which is an hour away from Kobe. Every one of its 18 holes is patterned after an internationally famous hole. The course is far from easy and the golfer should expect to use every club in his bag.

A variety of hills at the 18-hole Nasu Golf Club makes the course's 6,690 yards look shorter than they actually are. The wind is also an important factor. In crosswinds, don't be surprised to find the ball hooking or slicing. After several holes, the golfer learns to play wind to his advantage.

The internationally famous Kawana Fuji course is long and tough, with many hills. Situated between the Pacific Ocean and Fuji, the highest mountain in Japan, the course is actually a corridor for wind coming off the water. Except for the par 3's, almost every tee shot should be hit with a No. 1 or No. 2 iron for the necessary accuracy.

At the Senguku course, the really hazardous holes are the ninth and seventeenth, which are steeply inclined upward. In many instances a normal fairway shot has to be treated as an uphill lie and the golfer has to play the ball more toward his back foot.

The Japanese caddies—attractive and efficient young girls—are talked about by golfers the world over. They are fine examples of what good caddie training can produce. They know the game perfectly, club the golfer perfectly, and even reseed divots from a small bag of seed they carry. And what's more, the Japanese caddie is one of the best golfing luxuries for the money—usually less than $2 per round.

Golf in Japan is not inexpensive, ranging from $3.50 to $10 for weekdays, and from $4.50 to $13 on weekends. The visiting golfer is welcome at all times almost everywhere, but arrangements must be made in advance. Contact club secretaries or members where possible before starting for the course. Some clubs restrict the number of guests on weekends and holidays, and others insist on the accompaniment of a member on certain occasions; so check ahead.

Clubs can be rented at most courses, and almost every course has good clubhouse facilities. Lunch is often served for less than $1, and tipping, where it is permitted, is modest. It is wise to check with the manager before dealing out gratuities.

Incidentally, there are golf driving ranges all over Japan—some on building rooftops—to accommodate the great new interest in the game among the Japanese. Indeed, the visitor will find the golfing atmosphere of Japan stimulating and exciting.

SEASON: All year.

HOW TO GET THERE: By Pan American Jet Clipper from east or

west coast. Tokyo is an important stop on Pan Am's twice daily round-the-world flights.

GOLF EQUIPMENT: American equipment available.

LANGUAGE: English is understood in hotels, good restaurants, and private clubs. If you plan to go on tour, go on a planned package, or take a guide.

TIME: Seventeen hours later than U.S. Pacific Standard Time.

Fuji Country Club

LOCATION: Higashiyama, Gotemba-shi, Shizuoka (2 hours by car from Tokyo). COURSE SIZE: 18 holes; 6,970 yards; par 72. AVAILABILITY TO VISITORS: Prior arrangements necessary to insure starting time. GREEN FEES: Weekdays, $7; Saturdays and Sundays, $9.70 daily. CADDIE FEES: $1 per round. LESSONS: Available. CLUBHOUSE FACILITIES: Restaurant and bar.

Fuji Heigen Golf Club

LOCATION: Midono, Gotemba City (1½ hours by train from Tokyo, plus 10-minute drive from station). COURSE SIZE: Fuji course: 9 holes; 3,463 yards; par 36. Hakone course: 9 holes; 3,501 yards; par 36. Tanzana course: 9 holes; 3,227 yards; par 36. AVAILABILITY TO VISITORS: Visitors welcome on weekdays and Saturdays. GREEN FEES: Weekdays, $4.70; Saturdays, $7. CADDIE FEES: $1.20 per 18-hole round. GOLF CLUB RENTALS: $1.50 per round. GOLF CART RENTALS: Available. MOTORIZED GOLF CART RENTALS: Not available. LESSONS: Available. CLUBHOUSE FACILITIES: Restaurant, bar, and facilities of the hotel. RECOMMENDED ACCOMMODATIONS: Gotemba Hotel.

Hakone Country Club

LOCATION: Sengokuhara, Hakone-Machi, Ashigara-Shimogun, Kanagawa (30 minutes from Yumoto or Odawara station, Tokyo). COURSE SIZE: 18 holes; 7,100 yards; par 73. AVAILABILITY TO VISITORS: Arrangements must be made in advance. GREEN FEES: Weekdays, $8.30; Sundays, $9.70. CADDIE FEES: $1.70 per round. CLUBHOUSE FACILITIES: Restaurant and bar.

Hirono Golf Club

LOCATION: Hirono, Shijimi-cho, Miki, Hyogo (one hour from Kobe by car; 40 minutes by train). COURSE SIZE: 18 holes; 6,950 yards; par 72. AVAILABILITY TO VISITORS: Arrangements must be made with the club in advance. GREEN FEES: Weekdays, $8.30; Saturdays, $9.70; Sundays, $11. CADDIE FEES: $1 per round. CLUBHOUSE FACILITIES: Restaurant and bar.

Kasumigaseki Country Club

LOCATION: Kasahata Kawagoe-shi, Saitama (just over 2 hours by car from Tokyo). COURSE SIZE: East Course: 18 holes; 6,913 yards; par 72. West Course: 18 holes; 6,590 yards; par 72. AVAILABILITY TO VISITORS: Arrangements must be made with the club in advance. GREEN FEES: Weekdays, $9.70; Saturdays, $12.50; Sundays and holidays, $13.90. CADDIE FEES: $1 per round. LESSONS: Available. CLUBHOUSE FACILITIES: Restaurant and bar. RECOMMENDED ACCOMMODATIONS: No resort hotels nearby.

Kawana Hotel Golf Courses

LOCATION: Kawana, Ito-city (2 hours by train from Tokyo plus 15-minute drive from Ito station). COURSE SIZE: Fuji course: 18 holes; 6,691 yards; par 72. Oshima course: 18 holes; 5,711 yards; par 70. AVAILABILITY TO VISITORS: Visitors are welcome, but arrangements must be made in advance. GREEN FEES: Weekdays, $8.30; Saturdays, Sundays, and holidays, $12.50 per day. CADDIE FEES: $1.30 per round. GOLF CLUB RENTALS: $1.40 per day. GOLF CART RENTALS: Available. MOTORIZED GOLF CART RENTALS: Not available. LESSONS: Available. CLUBHOUSE FACILITIES: All facilities of the hotel. RECOMMENDED ACCOMMODATIONS: Kawana Hotel on course. Ito-city: Ryokans.

Koganei Country Club

LOCATION: Kodaira-Machi, Kitatama-gun, Tokyo (45 minutes from downtown). COURSE SIZE: 18 holes; 6,755 yards; par 72. AVAILABILITY TO VISITORS: Playing arrangements must be made with the

Shell's Wonderful World of Golf

Tony Lema knocks one toward the ocean at Kawana Fuji Country Club.

club in advance. GREEN FEES: Weekdays, $8.30; Saturdays, $9.70; Sundays and holidays, $11.10. CADDIE FEES: $1 per round. CLUBHOUSE FACILITIES: Restaurant and bar.

Kyoto Golf Club

LOCATION: Motoyama, Kamigama, Kita-Ku (10 minutes outside Kyoto by car). COURSE SIZE: East Course: 18 holes; 6,015 yards; par 68. West Course: 18 holes; 5,529 yards; par 66. AVAILABILITY TO VISITORS: Visitors welcome, but arrangements should be made in advance. GREEN FEES: Weekdays, $8.30; Saturdays, Sundays, and holidays, $9.70 per day. CADDIE FEES: $1 per round. CLUBHOUSE FACILITIES: Restaurant and bar.

Nasu Golf Club

LOCATION: Nasu-Machi, Tochigi (3 hours by train from Ueno Station, Tokyo; 30 minutes by car from Kuroiso Station). COURSE SIZE: 18 holes; 6,690 yards; par 72. AVAILABILITY TO VISITORS: Arrangements must be made with the club in advance. GREEN FEES:

Weekdays, $8.30; Saturdays, Sundays, and holidays, $11.10 per day. CADDIE FEES: $1 per round. CLUBHOUSE FACILITIES: Restaurant and bar.

Nikko Country Club

LOCATION: Nikko, Tochigi (about 2 hours by train from Tokyo, then 10 minutes from the station). COURSE SIZE: 18 holes; 6,875 yards; par 72. AVAILABILITY TO VISITORS: Arrangements must be made with the club in advance. GREEN FEES: Weekdays, $7; Sundays and holidays, $9.70 per day. CADDIE FEES: $1 per round. CLUBHOUSE FACILITIES: Restaurant and bar.

Oarai Golf Club

LOCATION: Oarai-Machi, Ibaraki (2½ hours by car from the center of Tokyo; 1½ hours by train from Ueno Station, Tokyo, to Miro Station; then 20 minutes by car). COURSE SIZE: 18 holes; 7,190 yards; par 72. AVAILABILITY TO VISITORS: Prior arrangements must be made with the club. GREEN FEES: Weekdays, $5.60; Saturdays, Sundays, and holidays, $9.70 per day. CADDIE FEES: $1 per round. CLUBHOUSE FACILITIES: Restaurant and bar.

Osaka Golf Club

LOCATION: 31 Tempozan, Fuke, Misaki-cho, Sennan-gun, Osaka (1½ hours from Osaka by car; about an hour by train on Nankai Line). COURSE SIZE: 18 holes; 6,435 yards; par 72. AVAILABILITY TO VISITORS: Arrangements must be made in advance. GREEN FEES: Weekdays, $9.50; Sundays and holidays, $11 per day. CADDIE FEES: $1 per round. CLUBHOUSE FACILITIES: Restaurant and bar.

Sapporo Golf Club

LOCATION: Sapporo, Hokkaido (30 minutes by car from the center of Sapporo). COURSE SIZE: 18 holes; 7,100 yards; par 72. AVAILABILITY TO VISITORS: Prior arrangements must be made with the club. GREEN FEES: Weekdays, $7; Saturdays, Sundays, and holidays, $9.70 per day. CADDIE FEES: $1 per round. CLUBHOUSE FACILITIES: Restaurant and bar.

Japan's attractive, excellently trained female caddies are among the best in the world.

Senguku Golf Club

LOCATION: Hokone-Machi Sengukubara, Kanagawa (40 minutes by car from Odawara; 30 minutes by car from Yumoto, just south of Tokyo). COURSE SIZE: 18 holes; 6,338 yards; par 72. AVAILABILITY TO VISITORS: Arrangements must be made in advance. GREEN FEES: Weekdays, $5.50; Saturdays, $7; Sundays and holidays, $8.30. Hotel guests: weekdays, $2.20; Sundays and holidays, $4.10. CADDIE FEES: 75¢ per round. LESSONS: Available. CLUBHOUSE FACILITIES: Restaurant and bar at Fujiya Hotel. RECOMMENDED ACCOMMODATIONS: Fujiya Hotel.

Takanodai Country Club

LOCATION: Chiba (2-hour drive from Tokyo). COURSE SIZE: 18 holes; 7,070 yards; par 72. AVAILABILITY TO VISITORS: Prior arrangements must be made with the club. GREEN FEES: Weekdays, $9.70; Sundays and holidays, $11.10. CADDIE FEES: $1 per round. CLUBHOUSE FACILITIES: Restaurant and bar.

Tokyo Golf Club

LOCATION: Sayama City, Saitama (1½-hour drive from downtown Tokyo). COURSE SIZE: 18 holes; summer greens (July-November), 6,810 yards; winter greens, 6,488 yards; par 72. AVAILABILITY TO VISITORS: Prior arrangements must be made with the club. GREEN FEES: Weekdays, $9.70; Saturdays, $12.50; Sundays and holidays, $13.90. CADDIE FEES: $1 per round. CLUBHOUSE FACILITIES: Restaurant and bar.

Tokyo Tomin Golf Course

LOCATION: Fuji Course, 8 Miyagi-cho Adachi-ku, Tokyo (15 minutes by car from Tabata station or Ooji station). COURSE SIZE: 18 holes; 3,975 yards; par 59. AVAILABILITY TO VISITORS: Prior arrangements must be made with the club. GREEN FEES: Weekdays, $3.50; Sundays and holidays, $4.50. CADDIE FEES: $1 per round. CLUBHOUSE FACILITIES: Restaurant and bar.

Tokyo Tomin Golf Course II

LOCATION: Tsukubu Course, Adachi-ku, Tokyo (35 minutes by car from Tokyo; 10 minutes by car from Oji station). COURSE SIZE: 18 holes; 6,110 yards; par 69. AVAILABILITY TO VISITORS: Prior arrangements must be made with the club. GREEN FEES: Weekdays, $3.30; Sundays and holidays, $6.10. CADDIE FEES: $1 per round. CLUBHOUSE FACILITIES: Restaurant and bar.

Unzen Golf Course

LOCATION: Unzen, Obama-Nachi, Nagasaki (less than 2 hours by bus or car from Isahaya City). COURSE SIZE: 9 holes; 3,324 yards; par 37. AVAILABILITY TO VISITORS: Arrangements must be made with the club in advance. GREEN FEES: $3.30 per day. CADDIE FEES: 50¢ per round. CLUBHOUSE FACILITIES: Restaurant and bar.

Malaysia and Singapore

Malaysia is the land of perpetual summer. The average temperature does not vary more than 2 degrees throughout the year, hovering just above 80. There is no distinct wet or dry season, and any time of year is a good time for a visit. Scattered through Malaysia, within commuting distance of the larger cities, are many fine golf courses.

Seven miles from Singapore, the extravagant Singapore Island Country Club offers three excellent 18-hole courses. As if this were not enough, the fourth course is now under construction. In addition, bowling, swimming, a restaurant and bar are among the many other facilities available to guests. To play here, the traveling golfer needs an introductory letter from his home club, or an introduction from Pan Am, Malaysia-Singapore Airlines, or a regular club member. Such a guest will then be entitled to all the privileges of the club upon payment of the prescribed fees. Incidentally, the managers of the leading hotels in Singapore are members of the club, and they may introduce visitors as their guests once in any calendar month. Visitors on extended stay in Singapore who wish to enjoy the facilities of the club on more than one occasion may become Visiting Members.

Excellent golfing is also featured at Kuala Lumpur, the Federal capital of Malaysia, and Penang, a resort and free port island.

SEASON: Year round.

HOW TO GET THERE: By Pan American Jet Clipper, Singapore is 23¼ hours from San Francisco, including stopovers. There are regular domestic flights to Malacca, Kuala Lumpur, and Penang in Malaysia; to Kuching, Jesselton, Sondkan, and Brunei Town in Borneo.

GOLF EQUIPMENT: American equipment is for sale, but equipment should be taken along.

LANGUAGE: The official language is Malay, but English is widely understood. Singapore policemen who are especially fluent in English wear red shoulder tabs.

TIME: Fifteen and one half hours later than U.S. Pacific Standard Time. Tuesday noon in Singapore is 8:30 P.M. on Monday in San Francisco.

Penang Golf Club

LOCATION: Penang (3½ miles by taxi or charter bus from the center of town). COURSE SIZE: 9 holes; 3,150 yards; par 36. AVAILABILITY TO VISITORS: Visitors welcome with a letter from own club or Malaysian Airways. GREEN FEES: $1.70 per 18-hole round or $8.30 per week. CADDIE FEES: 70¢ for 18-hole round. MOTORIZED GOLF CART RENTALS: Not available. CLUBHOUSE FACILITIES: Restaurant and bar. RECOMMENDED ACCOMMODATIONS: Eastern and Oriental Hotel, The Town House.

Perak Turf and Sports Club

LOCATION: 2½ miles from downtown Ipoh. COURSE SIZE: 18 holes; 6,804 yards; par 73. AVAILABILITY TO VISITORS: Visitors welcome with letter from own club, or introduction by a member. GREEN FEES: 35¢ per day. CADDIE FEES: 70¢ per round. GOLF CLUB RENTALS: Not available. GOLF CART RENTALS: Not available. MOTORIZED GOLF CART RENTALS: Not available. LESSONS: Available. CLUBHOUSE FACILITIES: Full facilities, including bar, restaurant, bowling alleys, billiards, tennis, and badminton. RECOMMENDED ACCOMMODATIONS: Station Hotel, Kowloon Hotel.

Royal Selangor Golf Club

LOCATION: 3 miles from Kuala Lumpur. COURSE SIZE: Old Course: 18 holes; 6,793 yards; par 72. New Course: 18 holes; 6,536 yards; par 70. Suleiman Course: 9 holes; 1,394 yards; par 27. AVAILABILITY TO VISITORS: Visitors welcome with a letter from own club. GREEN FEES: $1.70 per day. CADDIE FEES: 85¢ per round. GOLF CLUB RENTALS: $1 per day. GOLF CART RENTALS: 65¢ per round. MOTORIZED GOLF CART RENTALS: Not available. LESSONS: $2 per hour. CLUBHOUSE FACILITIES: Bar, restaurant, tennis courts, and swimming pool. RECOMMENDED ACCOMMODATIONS: Hotel Federal, Hotel Merlin, Hotel Malaysia.

Phil Rogers tees off at Singapore Island Country Club in Shell's Wonderful World of Golf Tournament.

Singapore Island Country Club

LOCATION: Singapore (7 miles by taxi from downtown). COURSE SIZE: Island Course: 18 holes; 6,455 yards; par 72. Bukit Course: 18 holes; 6,584 yards; par 71. Sime Course: 18 holes; 6,333 yards; par 69. AVAILABILITY TO VISITORS: Visitors welcome with a letter from home club or Pan American Airways; inquire in advance. GREEN FEES: Weekdays, $3.25; weekends and holidays, $6.50 per day; per week, $13; per month, $33. CADDIE FEES: $1 per round. GOLF CART RENTALS: 25¢ per round. MOTORIZED GOLF CART RENTALS: Not available. LESSONS: Available. CLUBHOUSE FACILITIES: Island Course: Full facilities, including bowling alley, swimming pool, bar, and restaurant. RECOMMENDED ACCOMMODATIONS: Singapore: Singapura Intercontinental, Raffles, Goodwood Park, Adelphi.

Pakistan

In this country of over 100,000,000 people, there are only 300 golfers playing on 19 courses. Most of the courses are located in West Pakistan, and no major city is without a course or two nearby.

Because of the shortage of local golfers, conditions are matchless for visitors. Nearly all the clubs welcome foreign players any time other than tournament days. Green fees are low, and caddies and forecaddies are readily available at a small price. There are no cart rentals of any kind, but many of the courses do rent clubs of various qualities at nominal rates. For the serious golfer, it is suggested that he take his own set along.

SEASON: Year round. Best season varies by locality.
HOW TO GET THERE: By Pan Am Jet Clipper, about 19½ hours elapsed time from New York; 32½ hours from San Francisco. Karachi is on Pan Am's round-the-world jet routes. By ship, about 23 days.
LANGUAGE: English is used extensively in government and generally in commerce, and is also widely understood and spoken throughout Pakistan. Other languages widely used are Urdu, Bengali, Pushtu, Gujarati, Punjabi, and Baluchi.
TIME: Time in Karachi and West Pakistan is 10 hours later than Eastern Standard Time. East Pakistan is 11 hours later.

Dacca Golf Club

LOCATION: Two courses in separate locations, one downtown at Ramna green opposite the Dacca Club, and one in the Dacca contoument area about 12 miles from town. Both are easily accessible from downtown Dacca. COURSE SIZE: Both courses are full-length, 18-hole layouts. AVAILABILITY TO VISITORS: Visitors welcome on introduction by a member. GREEN FEES: 75¢ per round. CADDIE FEES: 50¢

per round for caddie and forecaddie. GOLF CLUB RENTALS: Not available. GOLF CART RENTALS: Not available. MOTORIZED GOLF CART RENTALS: Not available. LESSONS: 50¢ per hour. CLUBHOUSE FACILITIES: The clubhouse of the Dacca Club to which these courses are attached offers bar, restaurant, lockers, and full club facilities. RECOMMENDED ACCOMMODATIONS: Dacca Intercontinental, Shahbagh Hotel, and Dacca Club.

Karachi Golf Club

LOCATION: Karachi. COURSE SIZE: 18 holes, sand course with no greens. AVAILABILITY TO VISITORS: Always. GREEN FEES: $2 per day. CADDIE FEES: 55¢ for 18 holes. GOLF CLUB RENTALS: Not available. GOLF CART RENTALS: Not available. MOTORIZED GOLF CART RENTALS: Not available. LESSONS: $2 per hour. CLUBHOUSE FACILITIES: Bar and light refreshments available. RECOMMENDED ACCOMMODATIONS: Karachi Intercontinental, Metropole, Beach Luxury, and Palace hotels.

Lahore Gymkhana Golf Course

LOCATION: Upper Mall, Lahore. COURSE SIZE: 18 holes; 6,609 yards; par 73. AVAILABILITY TO VISITORS: Welcome anytime. GREEN FEES: 65¢ daily for members of all clubs affiliated with Pakistan Golf Union. All others, $1. CADDIE FEES: 9 holes, 40¢; 18 holes, 65¢. This includes a forecaddie. GOLF CLUB RENTALS: $1 per day. GOLF CART RENTALS: Not available. MOTORIZED GOLF CART RENTALS: Not available. LESSONS: $1 per half hour. CLUBHOUSE FACILITIES: Bar with soft drinks, snacks; swimming pool. RECOMMENDED ACCOMMODATIONS: Lahore Intercontinental, Falettis Hotel, Park Luxury Hotel, Ambassador Hotel, International Hotel.

Peshawar Golf Club

LOCATION: Peshawar Cantonment, on the northern fringes of the old city. COURSE SIZE: 18 holes; 6,490 yards; par 72. AVAILABILITY TO VISITORS: Welcome. GREEN FEES: $1.50 per day. CADDIE FEES: 20¢ per round for caddie and 10¢ for forecaddie. GOLF CLUB RENTALS: 20¢ per round. GOLF CART RENTALS: Not available. MOTORIZED GOLF CART RENTALS: Not available. LESSONS: $1 per hour. CLUBHOUSE FACILITIES: Light refreshments and drinks available from dawn to dusk.

RECOMMENDED ACCOMMODATIONS: Peshawar Cantonment: Dean's Hotel.

PWR Golf Course

LOCATION: Mogulpura, Lahore. COURSE SIZE: 18 holes; 6,218 yards; par 71. AVAILABILITY TO VISITORS: Always welcome. GREEN FEES: 65¢ for all members of clubs affiliated with the Pakistan Golf Union. All others, $1. CADDIE FEES: 9 holes, 25¢; 18 holes, 45¢, including forecaddie. GOLF CLUB RENTALS: $1 per day. GOLF CART RENTALS: Not available. MOTORIZED GOLF CART RENTALS: Not available. LESSONS: From 50¢ to $1 per half hour depending on professional. CLUBHOUSE FACILITIES: Bar, light refreshments, card room, and swimming pool. RECOMMENDED ACCOMMODATIONS: Lahore Intercontinental Hotel, Falettis Hotel, Park Luxury Hotel, International Hotel.

Rawalpindi Golf Club

LOCATION: Jhelum Road, Rawalpindi. COURSE SIZE: 18 holes; 6,351 yards; par 70. AVAILABILITY TO VISITORS: Always welcome. GREEN FEES: $1 daily. CADDIE FEES: 40¢ per round. GOLF CLUB RENTALS: $1 per round. GOLF CART RENTALS: Not available. MOTORIZED GOLF CART RENTALS: Not available. LESSONS: $1 per half hour. CLUBHOUSE FACILITIES: Bar and light snacks available. RECOMMENDED ACCOMMODATIONS: Intercontinental Hotel, Flashman Hotel, Sherazad Hotel.

Philippines

There are more than 7,000 islands in the Philippine group. Some 50 golf courses are scattered among them. In design they are equal to, if not ahead of, standard American golf courses.

One of the most charming courses in Asia is the posh Wack-Wack Golf and Country Club on Luzon within half an hour of Manila. The courses at Wack-Wack are long and tough, but one cannot complain because they are manicured to perfection. Players in the Philippine Open, which is played here every February, praise the condition of the course. If the golfer stays on the fairway most of the time, his score will make him smile. If not, keep the ladies out of hearing distance when he gets into the dense underbrush in the rough.

Sand traps average five per hole, so approach shots must be precise or the wedge will get a workout. Large acacia trees also lurk along the fairways, and their sprawling limbs snag many an otherwise perfect shot. There is little as frustrating as the sweet click of the perfectly hit shot followed by the bang of the ball as it hits an overhanging branch and finishes up thirty yards down the fairway in the wrong direction. The greens, once reached, are large with sharp undulations, and it is rare to find a straight putt on any of them. The nature of the grass makes Wack-Wack a course for the "lag" putter.

In the suburb of Makati there are two courses for tourists. One, the Fort Bonifacio Golf Course, is located on a military reservation and maintained by the Philippine army. Not only are visiting golfers welcome to play, but two tournaments are held every fall that visitors can enter if they have accepted handicaps. The other in Makati is the Manila Golf Club, somewhat shorter, but more scenic than Fort Bonifacio.

In Manila itself, the Municipal Golf Links is within walking distance of major hotels. Situated against the walls of the old city, it is truly more of an obstacle course than a golf course since its total length is less than 4,000 yards. By American standards, the golfer would have to consider it a short "executive course." One of the more interesting features of the course can be found on the sixteenth hole, where a golfer's drive must carry between ancient walls only 30 feet apart. If nothing else, the Municipal course is an excellent place to sharpen up a short game and putting before taking on the rigors of the longer layouts in the suburbs.

The Philippine Islands are ideal for Christmas vacations. At that time the temperature is between 75 and 80 degrees and perfect for golf and the many other attractions in the islands. If a Christmas vacation is not possible, try to schedule the trip during the rainy season from June to November. Although it gets pretty wet during these months, there are still plenty of sunny days to make a golf vacation worthwhile.

Surprisingly, there is very little tourist traffic in the Philippines. Prices are reasonable and access to courses, hotels, restaurants, and other attractions is no problem. The hotels are good, and the public transportation system is efficient. The Philippines is a very pleasant experience in the blending of the cultures of East and West.

SEASON: Year round.

HOW TO GET THERE: By Pan Am Jet Clipper from Los Angeles via Honolulu, about 18½ hours (elapsed time) to Manila. Saigon is 2½ hours away and Singapore is another 1¾ hours farther. By ship from San Francisco, 17 to 21 days.

GOLF EQUIPMENT: The Philippine Amateur Golf Association now sells golf clubs and balls free of taxes; prices, however, are slightly higher than in the U.S.

LANGUAGE: Tagalog is the national language, but English is spoken everywhere, as is Spanish.

TIME: Sixteen hours later than U.S. Pacific Standard Time. Tuesday noon in Manila is 8 P.M. Monday in San Francisco.

Fort Bonifacio Golf Course

LOCATION: Makati (30 minutes from hotel area in Manila). COURSE SIZE: 18 holes; 6,445 yards; par 72. AVAILABILITY TO VISITORS: Visitors welcome. GREEN FEES: Weekdays, $1.25; weekends and holidays, $3 per day. CADDIE FEES: 50¢ per 9-hole round; 90¢ per 18-hole round. GOLF CLUB RENTALS: Not available. GOLF CART RENTALS: Not available. MOTORIZED GOLF CARTS: Not available. LESSONS: $1.25 per half hour; reservations should be made a day in advance. CLUBHOUSE FACILITIES: Full facilities. Putting green, driving range, and Putt-putt course. RECOMMENDED ACCOMMODATIONS: Manila: Hotel El Presidente,

Hotel Hilton, Manila Hotel, Bay View Hotel, Filipinas Hotel, Shelbourne Arms Hotel, Swiss Inn.

Holiday Hills

LOCATION: San Pedro Tunasan, Laguna (an hour's drive from Manila). COURSE SIZE: 18 holes; 6,915 yards; par 72. AVAILABILITY TO VISITORS: Introduction by a member is necessary. GREEN FEES: Weekdays, $2.50; weekends, $5 per day. CADDIE FEES: $1.25 per round. GOLF CLUB RENTALS: Not available. GOLF CART RENTALS: Not available. MOTORIZED GOLF CART RENTALS: Not available. LESSONS: $2.50 per hour. CLUBHOUSE FACILITIES: Full clubhouse facilities including picnic grove. RECOMMENDED ACCOMMODATIONS: See above listing.

Manila Golf Club

LOCATION: Makati (30 minutes by car from Manila). COURSE SIZE: 18 holes; 6,108 yards; par 70. AVAILABILITY TO VISITORS: Visitors welcome when introduced by a member; no women allowed Wednesday, Thursday, and Saturday. GREEN FEES: Weekdays, $2.50; weekends, $5 per day. CADDIE FEES: $1 per round. GOLF CART RENTALS: Available at no charge. MOTORIZED GOLF CARTS: Not available. LESSONS: Available. CLUBHOUSE FACILITIES: Full facilities. RECOMMENDED ACCOMMODATIONS: See above listing.

Municipal Golf Links

LOCATION: Manila (within walking distance of the major hotels). COURSE SIZE: 18 holes; 3,985 yards; par 65. AVAILABILITY TO VISITORS: Visitors welcome. GREEN FEES: Weekdays, 40¢; weekends, 75¢ per day. CADDIE FEES: Weekdays, 40¢ per 9-hole round; 65¢ per 18-hole round. GOLF CLUB RENTALS: Available. GOLF CART RENTALS: Not available. MOTORIZED GOLF CARTS: Not available. LESSONS: $2.50 per hour; advance notice required. CLUBHOUSE FACILITIES: Full facilities, including driving range; open days and evenings. RECOMMENDED ACCOMMODATIONS: See Fort Bonifacio Golf Course listing.

Modern clubhouse at Wack Wack Golf and Country Club outside Manila.

Valley Golf Club

LOCATION: Antipolo, Rizal (about an hour's drive from most hotels in Manila). COURSE SIZE: 18 holes; 7,150 yards; par 72. AVAILABILITY TO VISITORS: Introduction by a member is necessary. GREEN FEES: Weekdays, $2.50; weekends, $7.50 per day. CADDIE FEES: $1 per 18 holes. GOLF CLUB RENTALS: Not available. GOLF CART RENTALS: Not available. MOTORIZED GOLF CART RENTALS: Not available. LESSONS: $2.50 per hour. CLUBHOUSE FACILITIES: Full clubhouse facilities, including swimming pool. RECOMMENDED ACCOMMODATIONS: See Fort Bonifacio Golf Course listing.

Wack-Wack Golf and Country Club

LOCATION: Manila (1-hour drive from city). COURSE SIZE: East Course: 18 holes; 6,900 yards; par 72. West Course: 18 holes; shorter than East; par 72. AVAILABILITY TO VISITORS: Visitors welcome when accompanied by a member. GREEN FEES: East Course: weekdays, $5; weekends, $10 per day. West Course: weekdays, $2.50; weekends, $5 per day. CADDIE FEES: $1 per round. GOLF CLUB RENTALS: Not available. MOTORIZED GOLF CART RENTALS: Not available. LESSONS: Available. CLUBHOUSE FACILITIES: Full facilities, including swimming pool, pitch and putt course, six bowling alleys, and a driving range open days and evenings. RECOMMENDED ACCOMMODATIONS: See Fort Bonifacio listing.

Shell's Wonderful World of Golf

Beautifully groomed fairway of course on Luzon.

Thailand

Popularly known as the "Land of Smiles," Thailand is a haven for the sport-minded. Fine fishing, grass court tennis, and squash are all available around Bangkok. Visitors are welcome at the three Royal Thai service clubs, the Royal Bangkok Sports Club, and the Dusit Golf Club division of the Royal Turf Club, but guest cards are necessary. The Bangphra Golf Course has 18 holes open to the public.

The Royal Bangkok Sports Club is unusual in that it is built through the middle of a race track. Twelve of the holes cross the track itself, and red and green warning flags must be observed to avoid being cut down by the local thoroughbreds. Furthermore, there is so much water, in little ditches called klongs, that some of the caddies wear bathing gear to retrieve lost balls. And if that's not enough, try to concentrate on a delicate pitch shot while the crowd is urging the favorite down the home stretch: it's not exactly like playing with the Royal Company of Edinburgh Golfers.

The Royal Thai Air Force Club and Bangphra are the only full-size courses in Bangkok. The Air Force course is laid out between the civil and military runways of the airport, and it has long fairways and tricky greens. Hua Hin, the best sea resort in Thailand, has an 18-hole golf course, as well as a fine beach, tennis, and sailing. At the resort of Kao Yai, 60 miles from Bangkok, a new course is opening, and should be ready for play in late 1968.

Most courses in Thailand are plush and rich in vegetation. Caddies are always available, and green fees are inexpensive. Be sure to carry all equipment, as local rental and purchase may be difficult. And don't be surprised to see six or seven or more golfers playing together. Foursomes have the right-of-way, but these larger groups, called alligators, are allowed.

The best time for golf in Thailand is the "cold season," December through February, when temperatures are in the 70's and 80's, but humidity is low. March through May is the hot season, and uncomfortable for golf except in the early morning or late afternoon. From June through October, monsoons prevent play most of the time.

SEASON: December through February, but may extend through May.

HOW TO GET THERE: By Pan Am Jet Clipper, Bangkok is 2½ hours from Hong Kong, about 25 hours eastbound from New York. By ship, 50 to 60 days.

CURRENCY: The baht (also called tical) is divided into 100 satangs, and is worth about 5¢, or 20-21 to U.S. $1.

GOLF EQUIPMENT: American equipment available, but may be difficult to obtain.

LANGUAGE: Thai (pronounced "tie") is the national lauguage. Personnel in first-class hotels and some shops understand some English, so don't worry about not speaking Thai.

TIME: Fifteen hours later than U.S. Pacific Standard Time.

Bangphra Golf Course

LOCATION: Bangphra, Cholburi, on Gulf of Thailand (2 hours from Bangkok by car). COURSE SIZE: 18 holes; 6,417 yards; par 72. AVAILABILITY TO VISITORS: Visitors welcome. GREEN FEES: Weekdays, 50¢; weekends and holidays, $1.75 per day. CADDIE FEES: $1 per round. GOLF CLUB RENTALS: Not available. GOLF CART RENTALS: Not available. MOTORIZED GOLF CART RENTALS: Not available. LESSONS: $2 per hour. CLUBHOUSE FACILITIES: Full facilities. RECOMMENDED ACCOMMODATIONS: Bang Saen: Hotel and bungalows 7 miles from course.

Dusit Golf Club

LOCATION: Royal Turf Club of Thailand (in Bangkok). COURSE SIZE: 18 holes; 5,050 yards. AVAILABILITY TO VISITORS: Visitors welcome on introduction by member. GREEN FEES: $1 per day. CADDIE FEES: $1 per round. GOLF CLUB RENTALS: Available at pro shop. GOLF CART RENTALS: Not available. LESSONS: Available. CLUBHOUSE FACILITIES: Bar, changing room only. Royal Turf Club bar, billiards, card room, etc., which are adjacent, may be used with a guest card from the Turf Club. RECOMMENDED ACCOMMODATIONS: Bangkok: Siam Inter-Continental, Erawan, Oriental Hotel, Trocadero Hotel.

Hua Hin Golf Course

LOCATION: Hua Hin, on Gulf of Thailand (4 hours by car, 5 hours by train from Bangkok). COURSE SIZE: 18 holes; 6,760 yards; par 72. AVAILABILITY TO VISITORS: Visitors welcome. GREEN FEES: $1.25 per day; no charge for guests of Hua Hin Railway Hotel. Tournaments are open to all qualified competitors. CADDIE FEES: $1 per round; caddie required. GOLF CLUB RENTALS: Not available. LESSONS: Not available. CLUBHOUSE FACILITIES: Small clubhouse with restaurant and bar. RECOMMENDED ACCOMMODATIONS: Hua Hin Railway Hotel and bungalows.

Royal Bangkok Sports Club

LOCATION: Bangkok (in Bangkok). COURSE SIZE: 18 holes; 5,010 yards. AVAILABILITY TO VISITORS: Visitors welcome on introduction by member. GREEN FEES: $1.75 per round. CADDIE FEES: $1 per round. GOLF CLUB RENTALS: Available at pro shop. GOLF CART RENTALS: Not available. LESSONS: Available. CLUBHOUSE FACILITIES: Restaurant, bar, locker rooms, swimming pool, badminton, squash, billiards, and card room. RECOMMENDED ACCOMMODATIONS: See Dusit Golf Club listing.

Royal Navy Golf Club

LOCATION: Bank Na, about 7 miles from downtown Bangkok. COURSE SIZE: 9 holes; 3,200 yards; par 34. AVAILABILITY TO VISITORS: Visitors welcome, but must be cleared by Royal Thai Navy personnel at the clubhouse. GREEN FEES: $1 for 9 holes. CADDIE FEES: 50¢ per 9 holes. GOLF CLUB RENTALS: Not available. GOLF CART RENTALS: Not available. MOTORIZED GOLF CART RENTALS: Not available. LESSONS: Not available. CLUBHOUSE FACILITIES: Bar and refreshments. RECOMMENDED ACCOMMODATIONS: See Dusit Golf Club listing.

Royal Thai Air Force Golf Club

LOCATION: Within the Royal Thai Air Force Area at Bangkok Airport (by car 30 to 40 minutes from Bangkok). COURSE SIZE: 18 holes; 6,875 yards; par 72. AVAILABILITY TO VISITORS: Visitors welcome on introduction by member, but must also be cleared by Royal Thai Air Force personnel. GREEN FEES: $1.25 per round. CADDIE FEES: $1 per round. GOLF CLUB RENTALS: Available at pro shop. GOLF CART RENTALS: Not available. MOTORIZED GOLF CARTS: Not available. LESSONS: Available. CLUBHOUSE FACILITIES: Snack bar, bar, locker rooms, and swimming pool. RECOMMENDED ACCOMMODATIONS: See Dusit Golf Club listing.

Royal Thai Army Golf Club

LOCATION: 40-minute drive from Bangkok in Minburi. COURSE SIZE: 18 holes; 7,100 yards; par 72. AVAILABILITY TO VISITORS: Visitors welcome, but must be cleared by Royal Thai Army personnel at the clubhouse. GREEN FEES: $1 for 9 holes. CADDIE FEES: 50¢ per 9 holes. GOLF CLUB RENTALS: Not available. GOLF CART RENTALS: Not available. MOTORIZED GOLF CART RENTALS: Not available. LESSONS: Not available. CLUBHOUSE FACILITIES: Bar service and refreshments. RECOMMENDED ACCOMMODATIONS: See Dusit Golf Club listing.

Israel

Occupied with many vital projects during its early growth, this new nation still found time to launch a golf program. Israel has only one course, but it must be considered unique. Where else could a golfer easily uncover an ancient relic while blasting out of a sand trap?

Two thousand years ago Herod the Great made Caesarea an important Mediterranean port. In 1960, when golf-course engineers began to carve fairways and greens out of the sand dunes that covered the buried city, they struck an archaeologist's treasure. Roman and Byzantine vases, old coins, and statues were uncovered. Golfers continue to make frequent discoveries on this historic land.

The Caesarea Golf and Country Club course is a green island in the middle of a desert. Grass had to be imported—Bermuda for the fairways, and a fine-bladed Bermuda hybrid, developed in Georgia, U.S.A., for the greens. Trees, other than the giant carobs, which have been there for more than five hundred years, had to be planted. And an irrigation system was installed to prevent the grass from completely burning out. The result has given Israel an excellent, year-round golf course.

Caesarea's fairways are wide, but they are springy and do not permit very much roll. Tantalizing rough will severely punish the errant tee shot, and the lightning-fast greens must be read carefully. There are two par-5 holes on the front nine and another pair on the incoming nine. The course, originally planned for 7,200 yards, was shortened to 6,671 yards when it seemed to play too long for a holiday layout. Caesarea members still talk about Sam Snead's performance during the match that officially opened the course in 1961. Sam took the short way home on the 455-yard, dogleg sixth hole and left himself with an easy 8-iron shot to the green.

Caesarea has a fine, modern clubhouse overlooking the Mediterranean and the ancient ruins of Caesarea. Superb facilities include a restaurant, bar, pro shop, putting green, and driving range.

Israel Government Tourist Office

Clubhouse for Israel's first 18-hole golf course which is near the ruins of the ancient community of Caesarea.

SEASON: Year round.

HOW TO GET THERE: By Pan American Jet Clipper to London, Paris, Rome, Vienna, or Istanbul. Then by connections; elapsed time New York to Tel Aviv via Rome 12 hours. By ship, about 15 days.

GOLF EQUIPMENT: American equipment available.

LANGUAGE: Whatever it is, you will have no language problem.

TIME: Seven hours later than U.S. Eastern Standard Time.

Caesarea Golf and Country Club

LOCATION: Caesarea (20 miles south of Haifa; 25 miles north of Tel Aviv). COURSE SIZE: 18 holes; 6,600 yards; par 72. AVAILABILITY TO VISITORS: Visitors welcome. Course closed on Monday. GREEN FEES: Daily, $7 single, $10 double; weekly, $20 single, $30 double. CADDIE FEES: $2 per round, single. GOLF CLUB RENTALS: $2.50 per day (7

Caesarea Golf and Country Club.

clubs); $10 per week. GOLF CART RENTALS: $1 per day. MOTORIZED GOLF CART RENTALS: Not available. LESSONS: Available by appointment, $2.50 per half hour. CLUBHOUSE FACILITIES: Locker room, showers, restaurant, and bar. RECOMMENDED ACCOMMODATIONS: Caesarea Golf and Beach Hotel.

Lebanon

This tiny country, lying at the eastern tip of the Mediterranean, is developing rapidly as the golfing center of the Middle East. Though golf has been played here for many years, it has generally been considered a game for foreign residents from America, the Commonwealth, and Europe. Until two years ago there was little organized local interest in the game, and play was restricted to two 9-hole courses: The Zahrani Country Club grass course at Saidon, some thirty-five miles south of Beirut, and the infamous all-sand course at Beirut.

Now the picture has changed; today's visiting golfer can play over three different grass courses. The Zahrani Country Club, the oldest in the country, remains the same sporty, rugged layout it has always been. The grass greens here are especially good for this part of the world, where sand is all-pervading.

The Golf Club of Lebanon has replaced the old Beirut sand course with a new 9 holes which is spectacular for its color and vegetation when compared with its surroundings. It has been developed from barren, rolling sandscape just a few hundred yards from the sea, and lies against a pleasant backdrop of the lower Lebanon Mountains. Although there is still work to be done, this property shows promise of becoming a first-class golfing facility.

The Delhamyah Country Club course, also 9 holes, located 15 miles south of Beirut, near Damour, is built high on a hillside overlooking the Mediterranean. The fairways and greens have been cut out of rocky terrain and seeded with varieties of grass most suitable to the climate and soil. The clubhouse and related facilities are modern and imposing.

Plans are under way for the eventual development of full 18-hole courses both at Beirut and at Delhamyah. In the interim, alternate tees on some of the holes provide back-9 variety to make play more interesting. The Zahrani course also uses some alternate tees on the back side.

Lebanon affords good golfing weather nine or ten months out of the year beginning in March and running through December. Generally speaking, the most favorable times for play are spring and fall. July and August are also good, but play is restricted to the early mornings and late afternoons because of midday heat. Winter offers some good golfing days, too, but there is considerable rain from the usually glowering skies.

SEASON: March through December.

HOW TO GET THERE: By Pan Am Jet Clipper from New York via Paris and Rome, or via London, Frankfurt, and Istanbul. Elapsed time, approximately 13½ hours.

GOLF EQUIPMENT: American, British, and Australian equipment available at reasonable prices.

LANGUAGE: English, French, and Arabic are the three prime languages spoken in Lebanon. Others are also spoken to the extent that language need never be a problem for visitors.

TIME: Seven hours later than U.S. Eastern Standard Time.

The Delhamyah Country Club

LOCATION: Delhamyah, near Damour (15 miles south of Beirut). COURSE SIZE: 9 holes; 3,000 yards; par 34. AVAILABILITY TO VISITORS: Visitors welcome. GREEN FEES: Daily, $3; Saturdays, Sundays, and holidays, $5 per day. CADDIE FEES: 35¢ per 9-hole round. GOLF CLUB RENTALS: Limited supply available. GOLF CART RENTALS: Not available. MOTORIZED GOLF CART RENTALS: Not available. LESSONS: $2.50 per half hour. CLUBHOUSE FACILITIES: Restaurant and bar. RECOMMENDED ACCOMMODATIONS: Phoenicia Hotel, and a wide variety of other hotels in Beirut.

The Golf Club of Lebanon

LOCATION: North of the Beirut International Airport; a 20-minute drive from the hotel area. COURSE SIZE: 9 holes; 3,369 yards; par 36. AVAILABILITY TO VISITORS: Visitors welcome. GREEN FEES: Weekdays, $4.80; weekends and holidays, $8 per day. CADDIE FEES: $1 per 18 holes. GOLF CLUB RENTALS: 9 holes: $1; 18 holes: $1.75. GOLF CART RENTALS: Not available. MOTORIZED GOLF CART RENTALS: Not available. LESSONS: $3.30 per half hour. CLUBHOUSE FACILITIES: Restaurant, bar, locker rooms, tennis, swimming, squash. RECOMMENDED ACCOMMODATIONS: See above listing.

Zahrani Country Club

LOCATION: Saidon (30 miles south of Beirut). COURSE SIZE: 9 holes; 2,687 yards; par 34. AVAILABILITY TO VISITORS: Visitors welcome, but must play with a member. GREEN FEES: $1.75 daily; Saturdays, Sundays, and holidays, $2.30 per day. CADDIE FEES: 35¢ for 9 holes. GOLF CLUB RENTALS: Not available. GOLF CART RENTALS: Not available. MOTORIZED GOLF CART RENTALS: Not available. LESSONS: Not available. CLUBHOUSE FACILITIES: Snack bar and bar available. RECOMMENDED ACCOMMODATIONS: See above listing.

Turkey

There are 440 mosques in Istanbul and one golf course. Needless to say that the sight-seeing is a little more interesting than the golf. Istanbul is rapidly becoming a popular tourist stop as people discover the wonderful weather, the moderate prices, and the exotic, sophisticated culture of the Turks. The courses are not exactly on a par with the culture, but the Turks have done an admirable job with what they have. The Istanbul Golf Club, for example, has been cut out of tough, rocky land, and the golfer is given leeway by local rule to improve his lie anywhere on the course, including fairways and greens.

In addition to Istanbul, there are 18-hole courses near Izmir on the Mediterranean and at Ankara. Visitors are welcome, but bring your own clubs, as they are difficult to obtain locally.

SEASON: Year round.

HOW TO GET THERE: By Jet Clipper from New York to Istanbul, 13 hours; 45 minutes more to Ankara, which is also served by Middle East Airlines—routings via London, Paris, Frankfurt, Munich, Belgrade, Vienna, and Rome. By ship, about 15 days. Airport bus fare is 35 cents.

GOLF EQUIPMENT: American makes available at reasonable prices.

LANGUAGE: English is spoken in hotels and principal shops and restaurants. Turkish is the official language. French is also spoken in most circles in Istanbul and Ankara.

TIME: When it's noon in New York, it's 7 P.M. in Istanbul.

Ankara Golf Club

LOCATION: 3 miles north of Ankara on the road to the airport. COURSE SIZE: 18 holes; 6,121 yards; par 71. AVAILABILITY TO VISITORS: Always welcome. GREEN FEES: Weekdays, $2; weekends, $3 per day.

270

CADDIE FEES: $1 per round. GOLF CLUB RENTALS: Not available. GOLF CART RENTALS: Not available. MOTORIZED GOLF CART RENTALS: Not available. LESSONS: No professional. CLUBHOUSE FACILITIES: Lockers, shower, bar, restaurant, and outdoor pool. RECOMMENDED ACCOMMODATIONS: Hotel Kent, Hotel Balin, and others.

Bornova Golf Club

LOCATION: Bornova (10-mile drive from Izmir). COURSE SIZE: 18 holes; 5,586 yards; par 71. AVAILABILITY TO VISITORS: Always welcome. GREEN FEES: $2.50 daily. CADDIE FEES: $1.50 per round. GOLF CLUB RENTALS: Not available. GOLF CART RENTALS: Not available. MOTORIZED GOLF CART RENTALS: Not available. LESSONS: Not available. CLUBHOUSE FACILITIES: Changing rooms, drinks, tea and homemade cakes. RECOMMENDED ACCOMMODATIONS: Grand Hotel Ephesus, Hotel Kismet, Hotel Kilim.

Istanbul Golf Club

LOCATION: Dördüncü Levent (6 miles north of Istanbul). COURSE SIZE: 18 holes; 5,270 yards; par 72. AVAILABILITY TO VISITORS: Welcome. GREEN FEES: $3 daily. CADDIE FEES: $1.50 per round. GOLF CLUB RENTALS: Available. GOLF CART RENTALS: Not available. MOTORIZED GOLF CART RENTALS: Not available. LESSONS: $2.50 per hour. CLUBHOUSE FACILITIES: Locker rooms, bar serving soft drinks and local liquors. RECOMMENDED ACCOMMODATIONS: Istanbul Hilton, The Divan, Park, Kennedy, Santral, King, Opera, and others.

The Congo

The independent Republic of the Congo is very much on the business-man's agenda again, and is hoping to attract tourists, too.

The capital city of Kinshasa, formerly Léopoldville, has a most colorful native market which is bustling with local bargain hunters from about 7 to 10 each morning. For the sportsman, there are tennis courts and swimming pools available, as well as the Golf Club de Kinshasa.

The local hotels are attractive, and offer European-style meals complemented by superb locally grown fruits.

SEASON: Golf can be played year round, but June through September is the driest time, with cool evenings.

HOW TO GET THERE: Via Pan Am Jet Clipper, Kinshasa is about 18 hours elapsed time from New York.

TIME: Six hours later than Eastern Standard Time.

Golf Club de Kinshasa

LOCATION: Kinshasa. COURSE SIZE: 18 holes; 6,235 yards; par 72. AVAILABILITY TO VISITORS: Welcome upon introduction by a member. GREEN FEES: None. CADDIE FEES: $1 per round. GOLF CLUB RENTALS: Provided without charge by the club. GOLF CART RENTALS: Provided free by the club. MOTORIZED GOLF CART RENTALS: Not available. LESSONS: $3 per half hour. CLUBHOUSE FACILITIES: Restaurant, bar, tennis, and bridge. RECOMMENDED ACCOMMODATIONS: Hotel Regina, Hotel Memling.

Egypt

Egypt offers the traveling golfer five golf courses in the Alexandria and Cairo vicinity. Three are 18-hole layouts.

The Egyptian courses are maintained in first-class condition and have received favorable comments from some of the world's finest professionals. A golfing trip to Egypt combines the game at its best with a sight-seeing tour of some of the great historical sites in the world.

At the 18-hole Gezira Sporting Club, a course on an island in the Nile River, the touring player will enjoy excellent fairways and well-manicured greens made of Uganda grass. When cut well and close, these greens are fast, At the Mena House Golf Club, an 18-hole course in the shadows of the Pyramids, springy fairways usually provide excellent lies. Both courses are quite flat but tricky. As expected in a desert nation, sand traps are plentiful and thick. Don't even try to get out of these traps with any club other than a sand wedge. Because of the dry atmosphere, the sand is loose and will not offer any firmness to the golfer's shot. It is always wise first to get out of the sand and then work toward the green.

A golf trip to Egypt is best during the winter and early spring months when the climate is warm but not hot and humid. Rain gear is never necessary but bring along some heavier clothes since temperatures have been known to drop to as low as 40 degrees.

Accommodations for the visiting golfer in Egypt are delightful. At the courses themselves there are swimming pools, tennis courts, and other facilities to be enjoyed. There are no limitations for admittance, but prior arrangements for play should be made through the Pan Am office.

SEASON: Year round; winter is preferable.

HOW TO GET THERE: By Pan American Jet Clipper to Rome, about 8 hours from New York. Then by connecting airline, about

2¾ hours to Cairo. For Middle East travelers, Cairo is one hour via Middle East Airlines from Beirut, and may be included at no extra cost if you purchase a ticket in advance covering your full itinerary. By ship to Alexandria, 13 to 17 days from New York.

GOLF EQUIPMENT: American equipment available.

LANGUAGE: The tourist can make himself understood in all parts of Egypt in English or French.

TIME: Seven hours later than U.S. Eastern Standard Time. Daylight Saving Time is observed from May 1 to October 31.

Gezira Sporting Club

LOCATION: Gezira Island, Cairo (2 miles from Cairo railway station; 30 minutes from Cairo International Airport). COURSE SIZE: 18 holes; 5,803 yards; par 69. AVAILABILITY TO VISITORS: Visitors welcome. GREEN FEES: About 40¢ per day. CADDIE FEES: $1.25 per round. GOLF CLUB RENTALS: About 40¢. GOLF CART RENTALS: Not available. MOTORIZED GOLF CART RENTALS: Not available. LESSONS: $2 per half hour. CLUBHOUSE FACILITIES: Bar, restaurant, swimming pool, squash, tennis. RECOMMENDED ACCOMMODATIONS: Nile Hilton, Omar Khayyam, Shepheards, Semiramis.

Mena House Golf Club

LOCATION: Giza, near the Pyramids (10 miles from Cairo railway station; 45 minutes by car from Cairo International Airport). COURSE SIZE: 18 holes; 6,000 yards; par 72. AVAILABILITY TO VISITORS: Visitors welcome. GREEN FEES: About $1 per day. CADDIE FEES: About 60¢ per round. GOLF CLUB RENTALS: Available. GOLF CART RENTALS: Not available. MOTORIZED GOLF CART RENTALS: Not available. LESSONS: Available. CLUBHOUSE FACILITIES: Restaurant and bar. RECOMMENDED ACCOMMODATIONS: Mena House Hotel (facing course). Cairo: Omar Khayyam, Nile Hilton, Shepheards, Semiramis.

The New Sport Club

LOCATION: Smouha City, Ramleh, Alexandria (½ mile from Sidi Gaber railway station; 15 minutes by car from Alexandria harbor).

COURSE SIZE: 18 holes; 6,293 yards; par 72. AVAILABILITY TO VISITORS: Visitors welcome. GREEN FEES: 75¢ per day. CADDIE FEES: 60¢ per round. GOLF CLUB RENTALS: Available. GOLF CART RENTALS: Not available. MOTORIZED GOLF CART RENTALS: Not available. LESSONS: Available. CLUBHOUSE FACILITIES: Restaurant and bar. RECOMMENDED ACCOMMODATIONS: Cecil, Windsor, San Stefano.

Ghana

Ghana, otherwise known as the Gold Coast, after the precious metal found there, is cooler than other tropical countries. The weather is warm enough for swimming, but rarely too hot for a round of golf at Achimota or one of the other clubs.

The coastline offers a resortlike atmosphere of waving palms, superb beaches, and gorgeous multicolored flora. The Achimota Club is known locally as the "fairways of flowers" because of the flame trees, frangipanis, and other bright plants that grow around the course. Here is a place where even a nongolfing wife can become entranced with the beauty of the game.

SEASON: Year round. The rainy months are May, June, and October.

HOW TO GET THERE: By Pan Am Jet Clipper about 13 hours elapsed time from New York.

TIME: Five hours later than U.S. Eastern Standard Time.

Achimota Golf Club

LOCATION: Achimota (4 miles north of Accra). COURSE SIZE: 9 holes (with alternate tees for 18); 6,109 yards; par 67. AVAILABILITY TO VISITORS: Welcome except during competitions. GREEN FEES: Mornings, $1.40; full day, $2.80. CADDIE FEES: 70¢ or 55¢ for 9 holes. GOLF CLUB RENTALS: Not available. GOLF CART RENTALS: Not available. MOTORIZED GOLF CART RENTALS: Not available. LESSONS: $2.80 per hour or round of 9 holes. CLUBHOUSE FACILITIES: Table tennis, bridge, billiards, snacks, bar. RECOMMENDED ACCOMMODATIONS: Accra: Hotel Ambassador, Hotel Continental.

Kumasi Golf Club

LOCATION: Kumasi (about 100 miles north of Accra). COURSE SIZE: 9 holes; 6,415 yards (off alternate tees); par 72. AVAILABILITY TO VISITORS: Always welcome. GREEN FEES: 70¢ per round. CADDIE FEES: 30¢ per 9 holes. GOLF CLUB RENTALS: None available. GOLF CART RENTALS: Not available. MOTORIZED GOLF CART RENTALS: Not available. LESSONS: No professional. CLUBHOUSE FACILITIES: Bar, locker rooms, and showers. RECOMMENDED ACCOMMODATIONS: City Hotel.

Tema Golf Club

LOCATION: Tema (20 miles east of Accra near the end of the motorway to Togo and Dahomey). COURSE SIZE: 9 holes (with alternate tees for 18); 2,903 yards; par 35. AVAILABILITY TO VISITORS: Welcome. GREEN FEES: $1.75 per day. CADDIE FEES: 35¢ per 9 holes. GOLF CLUB RENTALS: Not available. GOLF CART RENTALS: Not available. MOTORIZED GOLF CART RENTALS: Not available. LESSONS: No professional. CLUBHOUSE FACILITIES: Restaurant, bar, and locker rooms. RECOMMENDED ACCOMMODATIONS: See Achimota Golf Club, above.

Kenya

Kenya was once an exotic mystery land reserved for the rich man's safari. Today it is still exotic, but it is within the means of the average traveler. Safaris are primarily taken in national parks now, and the animals are shot with cameras instead of guns. In addition, other sports have developed, such as deep-sea fishing, skin diving, tennis, and golf.

There are 33 courses in Kenya, and it would be superfluous to say that in a country such as this they are beautiful. They are rugged and usually hilly, and there are no golf carts anywhere to aid an aching afterpart. It is well to be physically fit before playing here, and also to have a sound game because there are only three pros available at the present time.

Kenya rides astride the equator, and it is hot, particularly along the coast. Elevations above 5,000 feet, and this includes Nairobi, are cool the year round and perfect for golf. The long rains come from March to May, and the coolest days are from June through August.

Nairobi is a city of handsome, modern buildings set in a gorgeous wilderness. There are still reports of leopards and hyenas stealing to the edge of town to raid unsuspecting homeowners of chickens and pet dogs. For the animal lover the Nairobi National Park is just outside the city and affords fine views of elephants, lions, zebra, and other big game.

SEASON: Year round.

HOW TO GET THERE: By Pan Am Jet Clipper, 21½ hours to Nairobi; 4-5 weeks by ship to Mombasa.

LANGUAGE: English is spoken in tourist centers, but Swahili is used by most tribes.

TIME: Noon in Nairobi is 4 A.M. Eastern Standard Time. It is dark in Nairobi by 7 P.M. the year round.

278

Karen Country Club

LOCATION: Karen (11 miles from Nairobi). COURSE SIZE: 18 holes; 6,750 yards; par 72. AVAILABILITY TO VISITORS: Welcome except on those weekends when competitions or tournaments are held. GREEN FEES: Weekdays, 70¢; Saturdays, 80¢; Sundays, $2.10. CADDIE FEES: 70¢ per round. GOLF CLUB RENTALS: Not available. GOLF CART RENTALS: Not available. MOTORIZED GOLF CART RENTALS: Not available. LESSONS: No professional. CLUBHOUSE FACILITIES: Lawn bowling and tennis now available, with a swimming pool soon to be built. Lunch, snacks, and afternoon tea served daily. Showers also available. RECOMMENDED ACCOMMODATIONS: Nairobi hotels. There are no hotels in Karen of first-class standard, but Westwood Park Country Club, about four miles away, is moderately good and offers swimming and riding.

Kiambu Club

LOCATION: 10 miles from Nairobi by taxi. COURSE SIZE: 9 holes; 3,292 yards. AVAILABILITY TO VISITORS: Welcome anytime except Thursday and Saturday afternoons, when the company of a member is required. GREEN FEES: Weekdays, 70¢; weekends, $1.40 per day. CADDIE FEES: 35¢ for each 9 holes. GOLF CLUB RENTALS: Not available. GOLF CART RENTALS: Not available. MOTORIZED GOLF CART RENTALS: Not available. LESSONS: No professional. CLUBHOUSE FACILITIES: Snacks and showers available; no lockers. RECOMMENDED ACCOMMODATIONS: Nairobi hotels.

Kitale Club

LOCATION: Kitale, at the foot of Mt. Elgon (some 245 miles from Nairobi; accessible by tarmac road, or by air to Eldoret and then 50-mile drive). COURSE SIZE: 18 holes; championship length. AVAILABILITY TO VISITORS: Welcome always unless a competition is in progress. GREEN FEES: $1 per day. CADDIE FEES: At discretion of player; there is no set fee. As a guide, caddie fees around Nairobi are 70¢ for 18 holes. GOLF CLUB RENTALS: Not available. GOLF CART RENTALS: Not available. MOTORIZED GOLF CART RENTALS: Not available. LESSONS: No professional. CLUBHOUSE FACILITIES: Bar and dining room are intended for members and their guests only; however, if you stay at the club for a night, a temporary membership may be obtained with the payment of $5.40 for the night's lodging. RECOMMENDED ACCOMMODATIONS: The hotel in Kitale is not recommended. The closest good accommodations are 30 miles away on the road to Eldoret at the residential Soy Club, which has good food and service as well as a 4-hole golf course.

Limuru Country Club

LOCATION: In the foothills 15 miles from Nairobi (easily accessible by taxi; elevation is 7,000 feet). COURSE SIZE: 18 holes; 6,561 yards. AVAILABILITY TO VISITORS: Welcome at all times upon application to the secretary, Mr. Peter Knight, telephone 737351. GREEN FEES: 70¢ per round. CADDIE FEES: Not available. GOLF CLUB RENTALS: Not available. GOLF CART RENTALS: Not available. MOTORIZED GOLF CART RENTALS: Not available. LESSONS: No professional. CLUBHOUSE FACILITIES: Snacks and light meals daily, showers, a few lockers. RECOMMENDED ACCOMMODATIONS: Nairobi hotels.

Muthaiga Golf Club

LOCATION: Nairobi (3 miles from town). COURSE SIZE: 18 holes; 6,513 yards. AVAILABILITY TO VISITORS: Welcome except Saturday afternoon and Sunday morning. GREEN FEES: Weekdays, 80¢; Saturday mornings and Sunday afternoons, $2.10 daily. CADDIE FEES: 70¢ per round. GOLF CLUB RENTALS: Very limited. Occasionally available at $1.40 per set. GOLF CART RENTALS: Not available. MOTORIZED GOLF CART RENTALS: Not available. LESSONS: $2.10 per half hour when professional is available. CLUBHOUSE FACILITIES: Bar offering light snacks, showers but no lockers. RECOMMENDED ACCOMMODATIONS: Nairobi hotels.

Railway Golf Club

LOCATION: On the edge of Nairobi (can be reached on foot from the center of town). COURSE SIZE: 9 holes; 3,112 yards. AVAILABILITY TO VISITORS: Welcome until 4 P.M. on weekdays only, unless in the company of a member. GREEN FEES: Weekdays, 70¢; weekends, $1.40 per day. CADDIE FEES: 35¢ each 9 holes. GOLF CLUB RENTALS: Not available. GOLF CART RENTALS: Not available. MOTORIZED GOLF CART RENTALS: Not available. LESSONS: No professional. CLUBHOUSE FACILITIES: Snacks not usually available—may be if pressed! RECOMMENDED ACCOMMODATIONS: Nairobi hotels.

Royal Nairobi Golf Club

LOCATION: Nairobi (2½ miles from town). COURSE SIZE: 18 holes; 6,819 yards. AVAILABILITY TO VISITORS: Welcome until 4 P.M. weekdays, Saturday morning, and Sunday afternoon. Play Saturday afternoon and Sunday morning with a member only. GREEN FEES: $2.10 per round on weekdays when unaccompanied by a member, 70¢ when accompanied; $1.40 per day with a member on weekends. CADDIE FEES: 70¢ per round. GOLF CLUB RENTALS: Not available. GOLF CART RENTALS: Not available. MOTORIZED GOLF CART RENTALS: Not available. LESSONS: Available. CLUBHOUSE FACILITIES: Snacks served throughout the day, showers, lockers occasionally, bar. RECOMMENDED ACCOMMODATIONS: Nairobi hotels.

Sigona Golf Club

LOCATION: 12 miles from Nairobi by taxi (7,000 feet above sea level). COURSE SIZE: 18 holes; 6,759 yards. AVAILABILITY TO VISITORS: Welcome all the time. GREEN FEES: Weekdays, $1 without a member, 55¢ with; weekends, $1.40 per day without a member, 55¢ with. CADDIE FEES: 70¢ per round. GOLF CLUB RENTALS: Not available. GOLF CART RENTALS: Not available. MOTORIZED GOLF CART RENTALS: Not available. LESSONS: No professional. CLUBHOUSE FACILITIES: Light meals and snacks available at all times; no showers; no lockers. RECOMMENDED ACCOMMODATIONS: Nairobi hotels.

Morocco

Morocco is an unusual combination of fascinating, comfortable resorts and good golf.

During a stay in Casablanca, for example, one can choose between exploring the sights of a countryside that has not changed for centuries, relaxing on the sandy white beaches of the Atlantic coast, and playing a round of golf at the seaside course at Fédala. The course and grounds here are well landscaped, and the clubhouse has full restaurant and locker facilities. Visitors are most welcome.

Marrakech, which used to be a favorite playground of Winston Churchill, is famous as a resort the year round: skiing in the winter, and golf and gambling anytime. The golf course is an oasis of evergreen from which each fairway has been methodically contoured. No two fairways adjoin anywhere on the course, and at 6,500 yards, if the shots are not true, it's a long way from tee to green. From green to tee, the golfer must follow narrow paths through the trees.

At Tangier the hills curve around a lovely bay at the entrance to the Mediterranean, where beaches match those of the Riviera. The golf course here welcomes foreign guests and often allows them to play in local tournaments. Although the course is only 5,515 yards, it is difficult enough, and the climate makes it an ideal place for a relaxing round and a quiet vacation.

SEASON: Year round.

HOW TO GET THERE: By Pan Am Jet Clipper from New York to Rabat near Casablanca in 11 hours.

LANGUAGE: French and Spanish in addition to Arabic, but English is understood almost everywhere.

TIME: Noon in Casablanca is 7 A.M. Eastern Standard Time.

Country Club de Tanger

LOCATION: On outskirts of Tangier. COURSE SIZE: 18 holes; 5,515 yards; par 70. AVAILABILITY TO VISITORS: Welcome. GREEN FEES: Daily, $3. CADDIE FEES: 9 holes, 65¢; 18 holes, $1.10. GOLF CLUB RENTALS: 90¢ per day. No left-handed sets. GOLF CART RENTALS: Not available. MOTORIZED GOLF CART RENTALS: Not available. LESSONS: $2 per half hour. CLUBHOUSE FACILITIES: Bar, locker facilities, light El Minzah.

meals available. RECOMMENDED ACCOMMODATIONS: Hotel Rif, Hotel

Golf Club de Fédala

LOCATION: Casablanca (approximately 15-minute drive from downtown). COURSE SIZE: 18 holes; 6,000 yards; par 73. AVAILABILITY TO VISITORS: Always welcome. GREEN FEES: Daily, $4; free to guests of Hotel Miramar. CADDIE FEES: 9 holes, $1; 18 holes, $1.60. GOLF CLUB RENTALS: $2 per day. GOLF CART RENTALS: Not available. MOTORIZED GOLF CART RENTALS: Not available. LESSONS: $2 per half hour. CLUBHOUSE FACILITIES: Restaurant, bar, and full locker facilities. RECOMMENDED ACCOMMODATIONS: Hotel Miramar near course; Hotel El Mansour in Casablanca.

Golf Club de Marrakech

LOCATION: 5 miles outside Marrakech (about 15 minutes by taxi). COURSE SIZE: 19 holes; 6,500 yards. AVAILABILITY TO VISITORS: Welcome. GREEN FEES: Daily, $3; weekly, $14. CADDIE FEES: 9 holes, $1; 18 holes, $1.50. GOLF CLUB RENTALS: $1. GOLF CART RENTALS: Not available. MOTORIZED GOLF CART RENTALS: Not available. LESSONS: $1.50 per half hour. CLUBHOUSE FACILITIES: Bar and lockers. RECOMMENDED ACCOMMODATIONS: Hotel Mamounia, Es Saadi Hotel, Menara Hotel.

Senegal

For a short interlude from a business or sight-seeing trip through Africa, there is an attractive 9-hole course in Dakar. The club is only a short ride from town, and clubs can be rented there for $1.25 for the day. There is a clubhouse that includes a restaurant and bar.

SEASON: November through June.
HOW TO GET THERE: By Pan American Jet Clipper.
TIME: Four hours later than U.S. Eastern Standard Time.

Golf Club de Dakar

LOCATION: Camberene, Dakar (local bus Number 17 every hour from town to the golf course). COURSE SIZE: 9 holes; 2,976 yards; par 36. AVAILABILITY TO VISITORS: Visitors welcome. GREEN FEES: Weekdays, $2 for the day; Saturdays, Sundays, holidays, $4 per day. CADDIE FEES: 45¢ for 9 holes. GOLF CLUB RENTALS: $1.25 for 18 holes. GOLF CART RENTALS: Not available. MOTORIZED GOLF CART RENTALS: Not available. LESSONS: Professional lessons from October to June. ½ hour, $1.75; 1 hour, $2.85. CLUBHOUSE FACILITIES: Restaurant, bar, showers, lockers; clay pigeon shooting and, shortly, a tennis court. RECOMMENDED ACCOMMODATIONS: Dakar: Croix de Sud, Majestic. Outside Dakar on the Atlantic beach: The Grand Hotel de N'Gor.

South Africa

The Republic of South Africa has more than 250 golf courses, some rated among the finest in the world. There are links that stretch along the coastline as well as exotic layouts hidden in the remote valleys and plateaus in the interior. The natural landscape of Africa, preserved in all its wild beauty, offers exciting and challenging golf.

Since South Africa is in the Southern Hemisphere, its seasons are opposite to those in the Northern Hemisphere. The best time for golf in the northern part of the country is during the winter months of June, July, and August. In the south, the golf climate is excellent throughout the year.

South African golf clubs have several special features that will offer the traveling golfer an enjoyable challenge. Great use is made of trees along the fairway borders, causing the fairways in many instances to seem narrow. Their psychological effect on the golfer usually results in controlled drives rather than maximum distance shots. But don't underestimate those trees. A ball landing in their midst may cost several strokes. Trees also are used extensively to hide greens on short holes. The golfer either has to play over the trees or straight through them in order to get on the green in regulation.

Another characteristic of South African courses is the use of a mixture of sand and oil for greens. Although a great many of the courses have Kimberley bluegrass, an excellent plush grass that holds the line of a putt very well, the visiting golfer had better be prepared for fast putts when he gets to the sand-oil greens.

South African golf courses also have other distinctive features. Water is used ingeniously for hazards. It is possible to play on a course with as many as 8 water holes directly in front of the golfer and several other water hazards bordering fairways.

Most of the courses feature four par-3 holes. But after that, there are very few holes less than 400 yards in length. Expect to make effective use of fairway woods to score well in South Africa.

South African rough is particularly difficult since it generally is allowed to become very heavy in the tropical climate. And there is always the unique problem of monkeys that emerge from the local bush to plague players by stealing their balls.

SEASON: Year round.

HOW TO GET THERE: By Pan Am Jet, 22 hours from New York to Johannesburg. By South African Airways, about 2 hours from Johannesburg to Cape Town and ¾ hour to Durban. Inquire about latest jet schedules. By ship, about 17 days from New York.

GOLF EQUIPMENT: American equipment available.

LANGUAGE: Population is bilingual, speaking English and Afrikaans.

TIME: Seven hours later than U.S. Eastern Standard Time.

JOHANNESBURG

Johannesburg is the ideal city from which to start a South African golf tour. There are 20 courses to choose from in the immediate vicinity. The high veld on which Johannesburg is located enjoys the best climate in the country and is ideal for golf throughout the year. Golfing costs are fairly uniform throughout the country. Green fees are less than $1 a day and caddie fees are 50¢ or less per 18 holes.

Among the finer golf courses available in Johannesburg are those listed below.

Germiston Golf Club

LOCATION: Germiston (10 miles east of center of Johannesburg by car or taxi). COURSE SIZE: 18 holes; 6,995 yards; par 72. AVAILABILITY TO VISITORS: Visitors welcome on introduction by a member or by making advance arrangements with the secretary. GREEN FEES: Weekdays, $1.40; weekends, $2.10 per day. CADDIE FEES: $1.60 per round, including tip. GOLF CLUB RENTALS: Not available. GOLF CART RENTALS: Not available. MOTORIZED GOLF CART RENTALS: Not available. LESSONS: Available; D. Proctor, pro. CLUBHOUSE FACILITIES: Full facilities. RECOMMENDED ACCOMMODATIONS: Johannesburg: Hotels Langham, Waldorf, Criterion, Whitehall, Ambassador, Astor, Skyline, Park Royal, and Dawson's.

Glendower Club

LOCATION: Bedfordview (8 miles east of the center of Johannesburg by car or taxi). COURSE SIZE: 18 holes; 7,060 yards; par 72. AVAILABILITY TO VISITORS: Visitors welcome on introduction by a member or by making advance arrangements with the secretary. GREEN FEES: Weekdays, $1.05; weekends, $1.75 per day. CADDIE FEES: $2.10 per round, including tip. GOLF CLUB RENTALS: Not available. GOLF CART RENTALS: Not available. MOTORIZED GOLF CART RENTALS: Not available. LESSONS: Available; V. Pallett, pro. CLUBHOUSE FACILITIES: Full facilities. RECOMMENDED ACCOMMODATIONS: See Germiston Club listing above.

Houghton Golf Club

LOCATION: Lower Houghton (3 miles north of center of Johannesburg by car or taxi). COURSE SIZE: 18 holes; 7,100 yards; par 72. AVAILABILITY TO VISITORS: Visitors welcome on introduction by a member or by making advance arrangements with the secretary. GREEN FEES: 70¢ for visitors. CADDIE FEES: $1.40 per round, including tip. GOLF CLUB RENTALS: Not available. GOLF CART RENTALS: Not available. MOTORIZED GOLF CART RENTALS: Not available. LESSONS: Available; S. Brews, pro. CLUBHOUSE FACILITIES: Full facilities. RECOMMENDED ACCOMMODATIONS: See Germiston Club listing above.

Kensington Golf Club

LOCATION: Kensington (3½ miles east of center of Johannesburg by car or taxi). COURSE SIZE: 18 holes; 6,774 yards; par 72. AVAILABILITY TO VISITORS: Visitors welcome on introduction by a member or by making advance arrangements with the secretary. GREEN FEES: Weekdays, 70¢; weekends, $1.40 per day. CADDIE FEES: $1.50 per round, including tip. GOLF CLUB RENTALS: Not available. GOLF CART RENTALS: Not available. MOTORIZED GOLF CART RENTALS: Not available. LESSONS: Available; S. Childs, pro. CLUBHOUSE FACILITIES: Full facilities. RECOMMENDED ACCOMMODATIONS: See Germiston Club listing above.

Killarney Golf Club

LOCATION: Killarney (5 miles north of center of Johannesburg by car or taxi). COURSE SIZE: 18 holes; 6,791 yards; par 72. AVAILABILITY TO VISITORS: Visitors welcome on introduction by a member or by making advance arrangements with the secretary. GREEN FEES: $1.10 per round, including tip. CADDIE FEES: Not available. GOLF CLUB RENTALS: Not available. GOLF CART RENTALS: Not available. MOTORIZED GOLF CART RENTALS: Not available. LESSONS: Available; D. Black, pro. CLUBHOUSE FACILITIES: Full facilities. RECOMMENDED ACCOMMODATIONS: See Germiston Club listing above.

Parkview Golf Club

LOCATION: Parkview (3 miles north of Johannesburg by car or taxi). COURSE SIZE: 18 holes; 6,930 yards; par 72. AVAILABILITY TO VISITORS: Visitors welcome on introduction by a member or by making arrangements with the secretary. GREEN FEES: Weekdays, 70¢; weekends, $1.40 per day. CADDIE FEES: $1.55 per round, including tip. GOLF CLUB RENTALS: Not available. GOLF CART RENTALS: Not available. MOTORIZED GOLF CART RENTALS: Not available. LESSONS: Available; A. N. Thomas, pro. CLUBHOUSE FACILITIES: Full facilities. RECOMMENDED ACCOMMODATIONS: See Germiston Club listing above.

Reading Country Club

LOCATION: Alberton (5 miles southeast of center of Johannesburg by car or taxi). COURSE SIZE: 18 holes; regulation length. AVAILABILITY TO VISITORS: Visitors welcome on introduction by a member or by making advance arrangements with the secretary. GREEN FEES: Weekdays, 70¢; weekends, $1.05 per day. CADDIE FEES: $1.55 per round, including tip. GOLF CLUB RENTALS: Not available. GOLF CART RENTALS: Not available. MOTORIZED GOLF CART RENTALS: Not available. LESSONS: Available; I. Hay, pro. CLUBHOUSE FACILITIES: Full facilities. RECOMMENDED ACCOMMODATIONS: See Germiston Club listing above.

Royal Johannesburg Golf Club

LOCATION: Linksfield (7 miles east of center of Johannesburg by car or taxi). COURSE SIZE: 36 holes, two courses; championship length. AVAILABILITY TO VISITORS: Visitors welcome on introduction by a member or by making advance arrangements with the secretary. GREEN FEES: Weekdays, $1.05; weekends, $1.40 per day. CADDIE FEES: $1.40 per round, including tip. GOLF CLUB RENTALS: Not available. GOLF CART RENTALS: Not available. MOTORIZED GOLF CART RENTALS: Not available. LESSONS: Available; R. W. Dunn, pro. CLUBHOUSE FACILITIES: Full facilities. RECOMMENDED ACCOMMODATIONS: See Germiston Club listing above.

Wanderers Golf Club

LOCATION: Kent Park (6 miles north of Johannesburg by car or taxi). COURSE SIZE: 18 holes; 6,832 yards; par 72. AVAILABILITY TO VISITORS: Visitors welcome on introduction by a member or by making advance arrangements with the secretary. GREEN FEES: Weekdays, 70¢; weekends, $1.40 per day. CADDIE FEES: $1.75 including tip. GOLF CLUB RENTALS: Not normally available; arrange with pro. GOLF CART RENTALS: Not available. MOTORIZED GOLF CART RENTALS: Not available. LESSONS: Available; M. MacDonald, pro. CLUBHOUSE FACILITIES: Full facilities. RECOMMENDED ACCOMMODATIONS: See Germiston Club listing above.

PRETORIA

Pretoria lies somewhat north of Johannesburg, and is in the same climate zone. The best time to visit the city is in October, when the jacaranda trees are in full bloom, draping the town in purple and blue. There are two superb clubs in the area:

Wingate Park Country Club

Eleven miles from town. In addition to golf, the club offers bowling on the green, swimming, a polo field, and a children's playground. Visiting golfers are eligible for temporary membership.

Zwartkop Country Club

Near the city. It also provides facilities for several other sports in addition to its championship golf layout. Tourists are eligible for temporary membership.

CAPE TOWN

Cape Town is located on the west coast of Africa, and has the temperate climate of the Mediterranean. Golf is fine throughout the year and there are ample facilities for tennis, fishing, polo, swimming, even mountain climbing. Some of the outstanding clubs in the Cape Town area are:

Millnerton Golf Club

On the shore of Table Bay. Many of the holes run along the edge of the bay or the lagoon. The setting is splendid and the play diffi-

Course at George on the Cape "Garden Route."

African Tourist Corp.

cult. Additional sports facilities are available, including bowling on the green.

Mowbray Golf Club

Near the city, on the Cape Peninsula, it is situated in most picturesque surroundings. The 6,576-yard layout is harassed by a prevailing crosswind which makes low scoring an achievement. Caddies are mandatory here, but only cost about 75¢ a round. Green fees are $1 on weekdays and $1.50 weekends, and rental equipment is available. The clubhouse has full locker and dining facilities. For the ladies: No shorts, please.

Rondebosch Golf Club

A championship course of 6,408 yards, par 74. Facilities include a dining room for luncheon and tea.

Royal Cape Town Golf Club

On the outskirts of the city, easily reached by bus or taxi. Visitors are allowed to play during the week, and weekend matches sometimes can be arranged in advance with the club secretary. The club has full facilities, including a dining room for lunch and tea.

Westlake Golf Club

About 14 miles from Cape Town, off the main road to Muizenberg. It has an 18-hole course of 6,535 yards and par 74. Visitors welcome.

GEORGE

The town of George, midway along the garden route between Cape Town and Port Elizabeth, has one of the finest courses in the country. This entire route is dotted with many resorts and courses that welcome visitors.

PORT ELIZABETH

Port Elizabeth is a sportsman's paradise. Ten miles of superb coastline on the Indian Ocean offer sandy white beaches, fishing, swimming, tennis, archery, golf, and racing facilities. Among the best golf clubs are:

Humewood Golf Course

Only 5 miles from town. This attractive 18-hole layout is strung out along the shores of the Algoa Bay. At 6,777 yards, this course is a tough par 75. The terrain is windswept dune land including the traps, all but two of which are natural. The great Walter Hagen has praised this as one of the finest courses in the world.

Port Elizabeth Hill Course

This course (known as the "Old Course") is not quite as spectacular as the other courses in this area, and is best played in the winter months (June, July, August).

Walmer Golf Club

This is a new club in the area. Eighteen holes, 6,700 yards, par 74.

Wedgewood Park Country Club

Eighteen holes, 6,500 yards.

EAST LONDON

East London is another seaside resort area offering a championship course:

African Tourist Corp.

Scenic links course at East London overlooking the Indian Ocean.

East London Golf Club

Both the South African Amateur and the Open Championship have been played here. Views over the Indian Ocean are spectacular.

DURBAN AND NATAL

The province of Natal, farther north on the Indian Ocean, is the recreational capital of South Africa. The mountain resorts of the Drakensburg Range bordering Natal and the Orange Free State are popular tourist stopovers. The climate is excellent—warm days and cool nights. Hiking, riding, fishing, swimming, and horse racing are at their best. There is also a wild-game reserve at Hluhluwe, home of the white rhino. The hotels in this area are modern and have swimming pools, movies, and *braaivleis* (barbecues). Most resorts along the 300 miles of Natal coast have golf clubs, and visitors are most welcome. Durban offers the following courses:

Beachwood Golf Club

An 18-hole layout, par 73. Guests are welcome at all times.

Royal Durban Golf Club

Located inside the Grayville Race Course; has an 18-hole course, par 74.

Umbogintwini Club

A fine par-72, 18-hole course. The club also offers tennis, bowling, and other popular sports.

Windsor Park Golf Course

An 18-hole, 6,497-yard, par-72 course, with an adjoining 9-hole pitch-and-putt course. It is a municipal course, open to the public at all times.

NORTH AMERICA

Canada

A year-round playground, Canada has some of the most beautiful golf courses in the world.

The park systems throughout the eastern provinces of Nova Scotia, New Brunswick, and Quebec have fine public course facilities. Around Montreal, the Laurentian Mountains are dotted with many golf courses. From mid-September through October, when the trees are most colorful, golf is truly spectacular (as long as the golfer doesn't lose his ball in the leaves).

Farther west are the prairie provinces—Ontario, Manitoba, and Saskatchewan. The Niagara Parks Golf Course, just a few miles from the falls, has an excellent layout with an impressive stone clubhouse overlooking the Niagara River whirlpool.

Farther north into Manitoba is Riding Mount National Park, 1,150 square miles of thick evergreen woods and a marvelous golf course. Here there are few people, but plenty of moose and buffalo wander close by the wooded fairways. After golf, try some fishing: there's an abundance of trout, northern pike, whitefish, and perch. For those less inclined to rough it in the woods, there are several good courses within a short drive of the hotel district in Winnipeg.

Moving toward the Pacific, the five national parks of British Columbia and Alberta offer every outdoor sport imaginable. At some points, black bears and grizzlies outnumber people—be sure to be up on the ways of the wilderness.

The handsome 18-hole course in Banff National Park is set among silver glaciers with fairways carved from magnificent forest evergreens. Farther north, Jasper National Park also offers fine golfing and delightful scenery. Although not quite so spectacular as Banff, Jasper has a remote and primitive charm all its own which is truly an escape from city life.

British Columbia, on the Pacific coast, has the best weather in Canada. In Victoria, on Vancouver Island, the temperature changes only about 20 degrees from summer to winter, and the golfer may be able to find a game in January. Both the McCleery Golf Club on the mainland and the Uplands Club on Vancouver Island are excellent, and there are plenty of other layouts strung along this Pacific seascape to lure the tourist to an unforgettable vacation.

SEASON: April through November, depending on location.

HOW TO GET THERE: By car, train, boat, bicycle, or bus from the U.S.A. Pan Am Jets serve Canada from all parts of the world by connecting carriers through gateway cities of New York, Boston, Detroit, and Seattle.

GOLF EQUIPMENT: American equipment available at standard U.S. prices.

LANGUAGE: English and French are the official languages. There is also a third language called Americanese.

TIME: Same time zones as in the United States, except Newfoundland, which is ½ hour earlier than U.S. Eastern Standard Time.

Algonquin Golf Club

LOCATION: St. Andrews, New Brunswick (by train to McAdam, N.B., by bus or taxi from McAdam; by air to St. John, N.B., by bus or taxi from St. John). COURSE SIZE: "A" 18 holes; 6,314 yards; par: men, 71; women, 76; "B" 9 holes; 2,935 yards; par 35. AVAILABILITY TO VISITORS: Visitors welcome. GREEN FEES: $4 per day. CADDIE FEES: "A" caddies, $2 per round. "B" caddies, $1.50 per round. GOLF CLUB RENTALS: $1.50 half set; $3 full set. GOLF CART RENTALS: $8 per round. LESSONS: Clayton Van Tassel, pro. CLUBHOUSE FACILITIES: Full facilities. RECOMMENDED ACCOMMODATIONS: Algonquin Hotel.

Cape Breton Highlands Golf Course

LOCATION: Ingonish Beach, Cape Breton Highlands National Park, Nova Scotia (Air Canada to Sydney, then 75 miles by car to Ingonish; also bus tours from New York City). COURSE SIZE: 18 holes; 6,600 yards; par: men, 72; women, 74. AVAILABILITY TO VISITORS: Visitors welcome. GREEN FEES: $2 per round; $3 per day. CADDIE FEES: $2 per round. GOLF CLUB RENTALS: Available. GOLF CART RENTALS: Available. MOTORIZED GOLF CART RENTALS: Not available. LESSONS: Not available. CLUBHOUSE FACILITIES: Limited. RECOM-

MENDED ACCOMMODATIONS: Keltic Lodge, Cape Breton Highlands Bungalows, Skyline Cottages, The Point, Ingonish Motel, Glenghorm Cottages and Motel.

Chantecler Golf and Country Club

LOCATION: Ste. Adele, Quebec (through Montreal, car, bus, or train; about 1½ hours). COURSE SIZE: 9 holes; 3,250 yards; par 36. AVAILABILITY TO VISITORS: Visitors welcome. GREEN FEES: $3 and $4 per day. CADDIE FEES: $1.25 for 9 holes; $2.50 for 18 holes. GOLF CLUB RENTALS: $2.50 per day for 18 holes, right-handed and left-handed. GOLF CART RENTALS: 50¢ per 9- or 18-hole round. MOTORIZED GOLF CART RENTALS: $4 per 9-hole round; $7 per 18-hole round. LESSONS: James Arnold, pro. CLUBHOUSE FACILITIES: Locker rooms, light snack bar, lounge, bar. RECOMMENDED ACCOMMODATIONS: Chantecler Golf and Country Club.

Digby Pines Golf Club

LOCATION: Digby, Nova Scotia (daily car ferry service between Saint John, New Brunswick, and Digby. Car ferry from Bar Harbor, Maine, to Yarmouth, Nova Scotia, then along scenic shore to Digby; trains from Montreal to Saint John, then ferry to Digby; by plane to Yarmouth and Halifax). COURSE SIZE: 18 holes; 6,140 yards; par: men, 71; women, 77. AVAILABILITY TO VISITORS: Visitors welcome. GREEN FEES: $4 per day. CADDIE FEES: $2 per round. GOLF CLUB RENTALS: Available. GOLF CART RENTALS: 75¢ per round. LESSONS: "Nick" Nickerson, pro. CLUBHOUSE FACILITIES: Full facilities. RECOMMENDED ACCOMMODATIONS: Digby Pines Motor Hotel.

Don Valley Golf Course

LOCATION: Willowdale, Ontario (about 2 miles north of Toronto city limits). COURSE SIZE: 18 holes; 6,446 yards; par 72. AVAILABILITY TO VISITORS: Visitors welcome. GREEN FEES: Weekdays and after 3 P.M. Saturdays, Sundays and holidays, $1.75; before 3 P.M. Saturdays, Sundays, and holidays, $2.75. CADDIE FEES: $2 and $2.50 per round. GOLF CLUB RENTALS: $1.55 per round. GOLF CART RENTALS: 60¢ per round. LESSONS: $4 per ½ hour; Joe MacNaughton, pro. CLUBHOUSE FACILITIES: Locker rooms, showers, and snack bar. RECOMMENDED ACCOMMODATIONS: Inn on the Park Motel, Royal York Hotel,

Shell's Wonderful World of Golf

Shooting down to a well-trapped green in Nova Scotia.

The Canadian Rockies rise above this course in Banff.

One of many scenic layouts around Quebec.

King Edward Motel, Four Seasons Motel, Westbury Hotel, Park Plaza Hotel.

Fundy National Park Golf Links

LOCATION: Fundy National Park, New Brunswick (¼ mile off highway 14). COURSE SIZE: 9 holes; 3,095 yards; par 35. AVAILABILITY TO VISITORS: Visitors welcome. GREEN FEES: Per 9-hole round, $1.25; per 18-hole round, $1.75; per week, $10. CADDIE FEES: By arrangement. GOLF CLUB RENTALS: Available from the golf pro; fee set by pro. GOLF CART RENTALS: Available from the golf pro; fee set by pro. LESSONS: Available. CLUBHOUSE FACILITIES: Dining room, beach and pool swimming, tennis, playgrounds, bowling green, boat rental, fishing, and riding.

Gray Rocks Golf and Winter Club

LOCATION: St. Jovite, Quebec (by plane, private airport at club; about 2 hours from Montreal). COURSE SIZE: 18 holes; 6,140 yards; par 71. AVAILABILITY TO VISITORS: Visitors welcome. GREEN FEES: Weekdays, $4; Saturdays, Sundays, and holidays, $5 per day. CADDIE FEES: $1.50 per round. GOLF CLUB RENTALS: $2 per day. GOLF CART RENTALS: $1 per day. LESSONS: Phil Laliberte, pro. CLUBHOUSE FACILITIES: Locker rooms, bar. RECOMMENDED ACCOMMODATIONS: Gray Rocks Inn.

Green Gables Golf Club

LOCATION: Prince Edward Island National Park, Cavendish, P.E.I. (an hour by car from airports and both boat terminals to the park). COURSE SIZE: 18 holes; 6,410 yards; par 72. AVAILABILITY TO VISITORS: Visitors welcome May 15 to October 15. GREEN FEES: Per round, $2; per day, $3; per week, $12; per month, $35. CADDIE FEES: $1.25 for 9 holes; $2 for 18 holes. GOLF CLUB RENTALS: $1.50 per set per day. GOLF CART RENTALS: 75¢ per day. LESSONS: W. Errol Nicholson, pro. CLUBHOUSE FACILITIES: Canteen, lounge, locker room, showers.

Jasper Park Lodge Golf Course

LOCATION: Jasper National Park, Alberta, on the shores of Lac Beauvert. COURSE SIZE: 18 holes; 6,590 yards; par 71. AVAILABILITY TO VISITORS: Welcome. GREEN FEES: $7 per day. CADDIE FEES: $5 per round. GOLF CLUB RENTALS: $5 per full set. GOLF CART RENTALS: $1 per round. MOTORIZED GOLF CART RENTALS: $9 for 18 holes. LESSONS: By arrangement. CLUBHOUSE FACILITIES: Dining room, cocktail lounge, pro shop, recreation room, locker rooms, showers. RECOMMENDED ACCOMMODATIONS: Jasper Park Lodge.

Kildonan Park Golf Course

LOCATION: Winnipeg, Manitoba (3½ miles north of city). COURSE SIZE: 18 holes; 5,556 yards; par 69. AVAILABILITY TO VISITORS: Visitors welcome, reservations required on weekends. GREEN FEES: $1.50 per round; juniors (16 years and under), 75¢ per round, seniors (65 years and over), 60¢ per round; twilight (daily, 2 hours before sunset), 75¢. Junior and senior rates do not apply on holidays. CADDIE FEES: Caddies are not available. GOLF CLUB RENTALS: 75¢ per round. GOLF CART RENTALS: 50¢ per round. MOTORIZED GOLF CART RENTALS: $5 per round. LESSONS: Not available. CLUBHOUSE FACILITIES: Snack bar and lockers. RECOMMENDED ACCOMMODATIONS: Airline Motor Hotel, Charter House Motor Hotel, Gordon Downtowner Motor Hotel, International Inn, St. Regis Hotel.

McCleery Golf Club

LOCATION: Vancouver, British Columbia (2 blocks from bus line, or 20 minutes from downtown by car). COURSE SIZE: 18 holes; 6,320 yards; par 72. AVAILABILITY TO VISITORS: Visitors welcome; reservations required weekends (phone on Friday). GREEN FEES: Weekdays, $1.50; weekends and holidays, $2 per day. CADDIE FEES: Caddies not normally available. GOLF CLUB RENTALS: $1 per day. GOLF CART RENTALS: 50¢ per day. LESSONS: Roy M. Heisler, pro. CLUBHOUSE FACILITIES: Lockers and showers; coffeeshop serves full dinners. RECOMMENDED ACCOMMODATIONS: Hotel Vancouver, Bayshore Inn, Georgia Hotel, Georgian Towers.

The Manor Richelieu

LOCATION: Murray Bay, Quebec, north shore of the St. Lawrence (by car 90 miles east of Quebec City, on route 15). COURSE SIZE: 18 holes; 6,070 yards; par 70. AVAILABILITY TO VISITORS: Visitors welcome. GREEN FEES: Hotel guests, $3 per day; nonresidents, $5. CADDIE FEES: $2 and $2.50 per round. GOLF CLUB RENTALS: $3 per day. GOLF CART RENTALS: (electric) $8. LESSONS: Maurice LeBlanc, pro. CLUBHOUSE FACILITIES: Cold buffet luncheon. RECOMMENDED ACCOMMODATIONS: Murray Bay: Manor Richelieu, Les Trois Canards, Auberge.

The Niagara Parks Golf Course

LOCATION: Niagara Falls, Ontario (3 miles by car from Falls on the Niagara Parkway). COURSE SIZE: 18 holes; 6,945 yards; par 72. AVAILABILITY TO VISITORS: Visitors welcome; reservations required on weekends and holidays up to 12 noon. GREEN FEES: Weekdays, $2; weekends and holidays, $3 per day; twilight (2 hours before sunset): weekdays, $1; weekends and holidays, $1.50. CADDIE FEES: $3 per round. GOLF CLUB RENTALS: $1 per day. GOLF CART RENTALS: 50¢ per day. LESSONS: Not available. CLUBHOUSE FACILITIES: Snack bar, pro shop. RECOMMENDED ACCOMMODATIONS: Park Motor Hotel, Clifton Motor Inn, Sheraton Foxhead, Sheraton Brock, Fallsway Motor Inn.

Uplands Golf Club

LOCATION: Victoria, British Columbia (Fort St. to Cadboro Bay Rd.). COURSE SIZE: 18 holes; 6,215 yards; par 70. AVAILABILITY TO VISITORS: Visitors welcome; reservations required on weekends. GREEN FEES: Weekdays, $4 per round; Saturdays and Sundays, $5 per round. CADDIE FEES: $2.50. GOLF CLUB RENTALS: $2 per day. GOLF CART RENTALS: 75¢ per day. LESSONS: J. Wren, E. Wright, pros. CLUBHOUSE FACILITIES: Bar, dining room, coffeeshop, lockers. RECOMMENDED ACCOMMODATIONS: Empress Hotel, Colony Motel, Redwood Motel, Crest Motel, Crystal Court Motel, Belle Isle Motel, Tally-Ho Motel.

Shell's Wonderful World of Golf

The 175-yard 8th hole in Banff, Alberta.

Upper Canada Golf Course

LOCATION: Upper Canada Village, Ontario (7 miles east of Morrisburg; 20 miles west of Cornwall). COURSE SIZE: 18 holes; 6,740 yards; par 72. AVAILABILITY TO VISITORS: Visitors welcome. GREEN FEES: Weekdays, $2.50; weekends, $3.00 per day (under 16 years, $1.50 during the week, no play allowed on weekends). GOLF CLUB RENTALS: $1 per day. GOLF CART RENTALS: 50¢ per day. LESSONS: Len Elliot, pro.

Waterton Park Golf Club

LOCATION: Waterton Park, Alberta (highway 6 north-south, highways 5 and 3 east-west). COURSE SIZE: 18 holes; 6,175 yards; par 71. AVAILABILITY TO VISITORS: Visitors welcome. GREEN FEES: $2 per round, $3 per day. CADDIE FEES: $3 per round, $6 per day. GOLF CLUB RENTALS: $1.50 per set. GOLF CART RENTALS: Not available. LESSONS: Available. CLUBHOUSE FACILITIES: Available. RECOMMENDED ACCOMMODATIONS: Prince of Wales Hotel, Bay Shore Motel, Emerald Bay Motel, El Cortez Motel.

Windsor Park Golf Course

LOCATION: Winnipeg, Manitoba (3 miles south of City Hall, 1 block off highway 1 east). COURSE SIZE: 18 holes; 5,367 yards; par 69. AVAILABILITY TO VISITORS: Visitors welcome; reservations required on weekends. GREEN FEES: Per day, $1.50 per 18-hole round; juniors (16 years and under), 75¢ per 18-hole round; seniors (65 years and over), 60¢ per 18-hole round; twilight (daily, 2 hours before sunset), 75¢. CADDIE FEES: Caddies are not available. GOLF CLUB RENTALS: 75¢ per round. GOLF CART RENTALS: 50¢ per round. MOTORIZED GOLF CART RENTALS: $5 per round. LESSONS: Not available. CLUBHOUSE FACILITIES: Snack bar and lockers. RECOMMENDED ACCOMMODATIONS: See Kildonan Park listing.

Mexico

The golfer visiting Mexico for the first time will be pleasantly surprised at the wide variety of climates to choose from. The warm, tropical areas bordering the Pacific and Caribbean offer courses noted for their lushness and their tricky layouts. The monsters in and around mile-high Mexico City, however, stress length over finesse. The average duffer will be amazed at his ability to pound out 270-yard drives with little effort. The catch here is a preponderance of fairway traps and bunkers which penalize the erring drive.

Two of the best-known courses, Club de Golf Chapultepec and La Hacienda, are both some 7,600 yards long. The problem for the visitor is overexertion. Both of these fine layouts are enjoyable to play but the tourist should take care to pace himself for the first couple of days. In other words, golf in Mexico should be played with the same cheerful indolence that characterizes the natives.

Since golf in Mexico is limited to the wealthy and to the tourist trade, the traveling golfer should expect to pay fairly high green fees. Caddies are very inexpensive, however, and can offer welcome advice on proper club selection. Take along extra balls as urchins abound in the rough and make a game of "finding" lost balls—whether they're still rolling or not.

Accommodations in Mexico City and other resort areas are excellent. Drinking unbottled water is not advisable.

SEASON: Year round. There is a rainy season during July and August, but play is possible in the morning.

HOW TO GET THERE: By Pan Am or connecting airlines, Mexico City is 1¾ hours from Houston, 3¾ hours from Los Angeles. Nonstop service from New York and Chicago, 4½ and 3½ hours, respectively. Mérida is 1½ hours from New Orleans and 1¾ hours from Miami. By train, Mexico City is 3 days and 3 nights from New York.

GOLF EQUIPMENT: American equipment available at all clubs.

LANGUAGE: Spanish is the official language, but all the stores and hotels have English-speaking employees.

TIME: Same as U.S. Central Standard Time, except in the northwest where Mountain or Pacific time applies.

Club de Golf Bellavista

LOCATION: Calacoaya, Estado de México (short distance by car, bus, or taxi from Mexico City). COURSE SIZE: 18 holes; regulation length. AVAILABILITY TO VISITORS: Visitors welcome. GREEN FEES: Weekdays, $10; weekends, $20 per day. CADDIE FEES: $1 per 9 holes; $2 per 18 holes. LESSONS: Available. CLUBHOUSE FACILITIES: Available only to residents. RECOMMENDED ACCOMMODATIONS: Reforma Intercontinental, Continental Hilton.

Club de Golf Campestre de la Ciudad de México

LOCATION: Mexico City (short distance by car, bus, or taxi from Mexico City). COURSE SIZE: 18 holes; regulation length. AVAILABILITY TO VISITORS: Visitors welcome. GREEN FEES: Weekdays, $8; weekends, $24 per day. CADDIE FEES: $1 per 9 holes. LESSONS: Available. CLUBHOUSE FACILITIES: Available only to residents. RECOMMENDED ACCOMMODATIONS: Mexico City: Reforma Intercontinental, Continental Hilton.

Club de Golf Chapultepec

LOCATION: Lomas de Chapultepec (short distance by car, bus, or taxi from Mexico City). COURSE SIZE: 18 holes, 7,600 yards; par 72. AVAILABILITY TO VISITORS: Visitors welcome. GREEN FEES: Weekdays, $8; weekends, $16 per day. CADDIE FEES: $1.60 per 9-hole round. GOLF CART RENTALS: Not available. LESSONS: Available. CLUBHOUSE FACILITIES: Available only to residents. RECOMMENDED ACCOMMODATIONS: Mexico City: Reforma Intercontinental, Continental Hilton.

Club de Golf de Acapulco

LOCATION: Acapulco (280 miles by car from Mexico City, 1 hour by plane). COURSE SIZE: 9 holes; 3,089 yards; par 37. AVAILABILITY TO VISITORS: Visitors welcome. GREEN FEES: $4.80. CADDIE FEES: $2 per 18-hole round. GOLF CLUB RENTALS: Available. LESSONS: Available. CLUBHOUSE FACILITIES: Restaurant and bar. RECOMMENDED ACCOMMODATIONS: Acapulco Hilton, El Presidente, El Cano, Las Brisas.

Club de Golf de México

LOCATION: Tlalpam (short distance by car, bus, or taxi from Mexico City). COURSE SIZE: 18 holes; regulation length. AVAILABILITY TO VISITORS: Visitors welcome. GREEN FEES: Weekdays, $8; weekends, $24 per day. CADDIE FEES: $1 per 9-hole round. GOLF CART RENTALS: Not available. LESSONS: Available. CLUBHOUSE FACILITIES: Available only to residents. RECOMMENDED ACCOMMODATIONS: Mexico City: Reforma Intercontinental, Continental Hilton.

Club de Golf la Hacienda

LOCATION: Ex-Hacienda San Mateo Tecoluapán (short distance by car, bus, or taxi from Mexico City). COURSE SIZE: 18 holes; 7,616 yards; par 72. AVAILABILITY TO VISITORS: Visitors welcome. GREEN FEES: Weekdays, $8; weekends, $24 per day. CADDIE FEES: $1 per 9-hole round. GOLF CART RENTALS: Not available. LESSONS: Available. CLUBHOUSE FACILITIES: Available only to residents. RECOMMENDED ACCOMMODATIONS: Mexico City: Reforma Intercontinental, Continental Hilton.

APPENDIX

United States

A brief guide to courses and tournaments for visiting golfers

For the American golfer traveling from one part of the country to another as well as for the foreign visitor, the United States is the land where golf flourishes in all its glory. The United States now has nearly nine thousand golf courses, and every year the number increases by about four hundred.

Golf courses in the United States belong to one of several groups. Private clubs are usually open only to members and sometimes to their guests. Semi-private courses allow the public to play either at certain times during the week or under some other restriction such as higher green fees. Public courses, which are open to all, are operated in many cases by cities, counties, states, or other governmental agencies. There are also resort courses which will accommodate the tourist. Kept in excellent condition, most of these belong to the finest resorts in the United States.

Wherever the golfer travels he can find courses to suit his taste. However, where he plays will be determined by the season. In the Northeast and Midwest, the golf season lasts seven months, from April through October. In the Pacific Northwest, the player might get in some good golf in March and November also. But in the South, from Florida to California, there is great golf throughout the year.

At a golf resort there really is no problem getting on the resort's course. When staying at a motel or hotel near a golf course, check to see whether the place you choose has made arrangements with private or semi-private courses to allow its guests to play. This will save hours of waiting time in some parts of the country.

Public courses in the United States are numerous—but they are generally crowded, particularly around the larger cities such as New York, Chicago, Los Angeles, and San Francisco. It is not unusual to wait five hours to start at one of New York City's municipal courses and then spend an entire day finishing 18 holes. It is wise to check with a public course to find out if they reserve starting times.

Nearly all private clubs admit guests of members. Also, many clubs will welcome the traveling golfer if he has proof of membership in another established club. In southern California, many private clubs admit members of other clubs affiliated with the Southern California Golf Association. Foreign golfers should write the managers of private clubs in advance, telling them when they will be visiting and requesting permission to play their courses. At many private clubs, this letter of introduction will do the trick.

Many of the golf courses in the United States are rated among the finest in the world. Municipal courses such as Rancho Park and Harding Park in California, both tested PGA tournament courses, are available for public play. The Desert Inn Country Club in Las Vegas, a championship resort course, is the home of the Tournament of Champions. In the Midwest, the resort course at the French Lick-Sheraton was the site of Walter Hagen's 1924 victory in the PGA Championship. In the East, the golfer can play both 18-hole Doral courses which have attained championship recognition as the home of the Doral Open. And there are others that are ready to test the visiting golfer's skill along with that of today's finest professional golfers.

Course design in the United States offers an excellent combination of hazards and length. American golf-course construction has accented distance. The newer courses require a golfer to be able to use his woods both off the tee and on the fairway. Doglegs are commonplace and in many instances courses are designed so that the front nine punishes a slicer and the back nine punishes a hooker, or vice versa. There are hilly courses that can test the golfer's stamina as well as his golfing ability. At the Sullivan County Golf Course in the heart of New York's Catskill resort area, the entire course is built on a hill. When playing there, be careful not to let out a full shaft on most of the holes. The course is so hilly that motorized transportation is provided to some of the holes.

The costs of green fees and course facilities range from very high to very low. A resort or private course may cost as much as $15, a municipal course may charge as little as 50¢. If economy is an important factor, the golfer should find out what the green fees are before be goes out to the course. There are usually enough courses in each area for him to choose one that best fits his pocketbook. At most clubs, he will be able to take his pick of caddies and golf carts. Motorized golf carts are available at the more luxurious clubs. Some private clubs will not allow play without a caddie or golf cart, but most public courses will even let the player carry his own bag if he wants to do it.

One of the big attractions of the American golf scene is the many major professional tournaments held every year. The PGA Tour travels throughout the country, featuring the world's finest golfers playing some of the world's finest courses. Every enthusiastic golfer has heard of the Masters, which is played on the tricky Augusta National Golf Course in Georgia (not open to the public), and such rotating tournaments as the U.S. Open, and the PGA Championship. The Ladies' PGA schedule has also become an exciting and crowd-pleasing attraction throughout the country.

Facts about the United States for Foreign Visitors

SEASON: Year round, depending on locality.

HOW TO GET THERE: Pan American Airways has a variety of money-saving travel plans. The "Extra Cities" Bonus Plan operates to any gateway city: Seattle, Portland, San Francisco, or Los Angeles, on the West Coast; Houston, New Orleans, or Dallas in the South; Boston, New York, Philadelphia, Baltimore–Washington, D.C., in the East; Chicago or Detroit in the Midwest. For the price of a single round-trip ticket to his most distant destination, the golfer can tour the country on domestic airlines and see any number of U.S. cities. Group fares, family fares, and excursion fares also offer appreciable savings on flights. Travel agents can help plan a trip that best fits the golfer's time, taste, and budget.

LANGUAGE: English, although foreign language groups can be found in many communities.

TIME: There are four time zones across the continental U.S.A. Six P.M. European Time is noon Standard Time in New York; 11 A.M. in Chicago; 10 A.M. in Denver; 9 A.M. in San Francisco; 7 A.M. in both Fairbanks, Alaska, and Honolulu, Hawaii.

U.S. Courses Open to the Public

It is impossible, within the scope of this volume, to list all of the courses available for play in the United States. Those listed below are merely a representative sample. Additional information may be obtained by writing to any of these places.

Legend: R—resort course; SP—semi-private; MU—municipal; PR—private course extending privileges to guests of hotels or motels.

These listings are from 1968 *Golf Digest* "Places to Play" section and are reproduced by permission.

SOUTH

Course Location—Type	Holes/Par Length	Comment
ARKANSAS		
Belvedere C.C. Hot Springs—PR	18/72 6,700	Rolling, interesting course.
Cherokee Village G.C. Cherokee Village—R	18/72 7,016	Championship course flanked by river in Ozark retirement village.
Dawn Hill C.C. Resort Siloam Springs—PR	18/72 6,500	Enjoyable, fairly flat; runs through valley in Ozarks; creek, many trees.
Hot Springs G. & C.C. Hot Springs—R	45 holes	Famous health spa; wide choice in courses. Arlington Hotel adjoins.
LOUISIANA		
Webb Memorial G.C. Baton Rouge—MU	18/72 7,024	Former country club now owned by city.
MISSISSIPPI		
Broadwater Beach G.C. Biloxi—R	18/72 6,100	Fairways watered. Excellent condition. Wooded. Also lighted par-3.
Edgewater Gulf Hotel & C.C. Edgewater Park—R	18/72 6,318	Tree-lined course. Year-round play. No water, few bunkers.
Gulf Hills Dude Ranch C.C. Ocean Springs—R	18/72 6,294	Beautiful woodland setting. Gently rolling fairways.
Hickory Hill C.C. Gautier—MU	18/72 7,049	Water, including two large lakes, dominates 8 holes.

Course Location—Type	Holes/Par Length	Comment
Pass Christian Isles G.C. Pass Christian Isles—PR	18/72 6,710	Handsome facilities on water. Runs through heavy pine woods.
Sunkist C.C. Gulfport—SP	18/72 6,379	Delightful, rolling test.

ALABAMA

Course Location—Type	Holes/Par Length	Comment
C.C. of Mobile Mobile—PR	27/72-32 6,517-2,399	Scenic, well-manicured course cut among rolling wooded hills.
Driftwood G. & C.C. Bayou La Batre—SP	18/70 6,261	Rolling terrain. Eleven doglegs. Visitors allowed on weekends.
Isle Dauphin C.C. Dauphin Island—PR	18/72 6,295	Championship course overlooks Gulf of Mexico; sand dunes, water.
Lakewood G.C. Point Clear—R	27/70-36 6,713-3,215	Tree-lined course with 12 dogleg holes. Grand Hotel owns course.
Langan Park Public G.C. Mobile—MU	18/72 6,383	Fine municipal course. Opening 9 hilly, second 9 fairly level. No water.
Skyline C.C. Mobile—PR	18/72 6,573	Front 9 narrow, hilly, wooded; back 9 open and flat.
Spring Hill G.C. Mobile—PR	18/72 6,253	Small greens and rolling fairways. Welcome visitors.

FLORIDA

Course Location—Type	Holes/Par Length	Comment
Atlantis C.C. Lantana—R	27/72-36 6,945-3,540	Scenic, tree-lined course with new accommodations at Atlantis Inn.
Belleview Biltmore G.C. Clearwater—R	36 holes	East, West courses. Many trees, traps. Overlooks Gulf.

Course Location—Type	Holes/Par Length	Comment
Biltmore G.C. Coral Gables—R	18/71 6,563	Picturesque home of Junior Orange Bowl Tournament.
Boca Raton Hotel G.C. Boca Raton—SP	18/71 6,775	Refurbished hotel on 3,500-acre estate. Also par-3 course.
Breakers G.C. Palm Beach—PR	18/71 6,008	Short but loaded with trouble. Elevated greens.
Cape Coral C.C. Cape Coral—PR	27/72-30 6,827-1,895	Good course in large waterfront community. Motels nearby.
C.C. of Miami Miami—PR	36/72-72 6,800-7,000	Fine layout; water hazards; many sand traps, pine trees. Par-3.
Crystal Lake C.C. Pompano Beach--SP	36/72-72 6,560-6,454	Flat course brightened by numerous water hazards. Driving range.
Cypress Creek C.C. Boynton Beach—R	18/72 6,808	Excellent course in resort area.
Daytona Beach G.C. Daytona Beach—SP	36 holes	Four par-36 nines, interesting and tricky. Motels nearby.
Delray Beach C.C. Delray Beach—SP	27/72-36 6,987-3,270	Courses suit both long and short hitters.
DeSoto Lakes G. & C.C. Sarasota—PR	18/72 6,902	Large greens, well trapped. Lodge nearby.
Diplomat Resort & C.C. Hollywood—R	45 holes	Two championship courses, Presidential and Diplomat. Par-3.
Doral Hotel & C.C. Miami—R	63 holes	Three 18-hole courses. Blue course site of PGA tourney. Par-3.
Harder Hall Hotel Sebring—R	18/72 6,723	Dick Wilson course with 7 lakes, many trees. Open to Harder Hall guests.

Course Location—Type	Holes/Par Length	Comment
Hollywood Beach C.C. Hollywood—R	36/70-72 6,479-7,000	On ocean, excellent adjoining hotel. New 18 has island green.
King's Bay Yacht & C.C. Miami—PR	18/72 6,824	Challenging scenic course open to members and guests.
Lehigh Acres C.C. Lehigh Acres—R	18/71 6,670	In large home development area. Daily green fees.
Longboat Key G.C. Sarasota—PR	18/72 6,890	Club is affiliated with various hotels and motels in Longboat and Lido Beach areas.
Lost Tree Club Singer Island—PR	18/72 6,482	Beautiful course, 9 holes on ocean. Open to accredited club members.
Miami Lakes Inn C.C. Miami—SP	18/72 7,039	Large lakes on course. Several elevated greens.
Mirror Lakes C.C. Lehigh Acres—R	9/36 3,345	Daily green fees.
Naples G. & Beach C. Naples—R	18/72 6,470	Testing course with 8 out-of-bounds. Inn adjoins.
North Palm Beach C.C. North Palm Beach— SP	18/72 6,575	Rolling terrain. Recently improved. Olympic-size swimming pool.
Oak Ridge C.C. Fort Lauderdale—SP	18/72 6,517	Pleasing course, 5 years old. Modern hotels nearby.
Ocean Ranch & Villas Pompano Beach—MU	36/72-72 6,753-6,275	Championship layouts; one designed for low handicapper, other easier.
Ocean Reef C.C. Key Largo—SP	18/72 6,503	Fine golf layout in luxury community setting.

Course Location—Type	Holes/Par Length	Comment
Palm Aire C.C. Pompano Beach—R	18/72 7,160	Well-groomed course with water hazards. Adjoins 48-room lodge.
Palm Beach Lakes G. Center West Palm Beach— MU	18/68 5,475	Short but interesting layout in convenient location.
Perdido Bay C.C. & Estates Pensacola—R & PR	18/72 6,871	Opened in 1963. Pro Doug Ford part owner.
PGA National G.C. Palm Beach Gardens —PR	36 holes	Two new courses at site of Professional Golfers' Association headquarters.
Plantation Hotel & C.C. Crystal River—R	18/72 6,985	Adjoins 100-room Hotel Plantation. Course open to visitors.
Ponce de Leon C.C. St. Augustine—PR	18/71 6,545	Championship links. Hotel guests may obtain golf privileges.
Ponte Vedra Club Ponte Vedra Beach —PR	27/36-36-36 3,398-3,337- 3,618	Beautiful course meanders gracefully between the ocean and lagoons.
Rolling Hills Lodge & C.C. Ft. Lauderdale—R	18/72 7,018	Lush, landscaped facility also has swimming, riding; 70-unit lodge.
Royal Palm Beach C.C. Royal Palm Beach —SP	18/72 7,042	With 32-room motel and restaurant. Open to public.
St. Lucie C.C. & Villas Port St. Lucie—R	36 holes	Saints and Sinners courses both great. Water, tree-lined fairways.
Southern Manor C.C. Boca Raton—SP	18/71 6,835	Canal system crosses 15 holes. Three tees each hole.

Course Location—Type	Holes/Par Length	Comment
University Park C.C. Boca Raton—SP	18/71 7,240	Canals and lakes add to sporty character of this fine course.
West Palm Beach G. & C.C. West Palm Beach—MU	18/72 6,745	Good public course with big traps, elevated greens.

GEORGIA

Bobby Jones G.C. Atlanta—MU	18/71 6,300	Tough and hilly. Creek crosses course 5 times.
Callaway Gardens Pine Mountain—R	36/72-70 7,040-6,006	Good course adjoining Holiday Inn. Also new par-3.
Jekyll Island G.C. Jekyll Island—R	18/72 6,926	Excellent turf, tree-lined fairways. Daily fees or package at 5 motels.
Mystery Valley G.C. Atlanta—MU	18/72 7,200	Gently rolling terrain amid thick pine forest.
Savannah Inn & C.C. Savannah—R	18/72 7,009	Championship course with water and plenty of trees.
Sea Island G.C. Sea Island—R	27/36-36-36 3,506-3,321-3,371	Spectacular site on old plantation; accommodations at Cloister Hotel.
Sea Palms G. & C.C. St. Simons Island—PR	18/72 6,700	Very scenic; water holes; beautiful oaks, tall pines.

SOUTH CAROLINA

Adventure Inn G.C. Hilton Head Island—R	18/54 1,850	Alligators in lagoons add to tropical charm of night-lighted course.

Course Location—Type	Holes/Par Length	Comment
Camden C.C. Camden—SP	18/72 7,100	One of the best and most difficult courses in the state.
Dunes G. & Beach C. Myrtle Beach—R	18/72 7,128	Tough, seaside course in resort area. Sixty bunkers.
Latai Inn G. & C.C. Fripp Island—R	18/72 7,000	New resort complex; seaside course; lagoons, many trees.
Litchfield G.C. Litchfield Beach—R	18/72 6,886	Exacting course; water, elevated greens. Resort area.
Midland Valley C.C. Aiken—SP	18/72 6,823	Rolling fairways, big tees and greens. Motels nearby.
Myrtlewood G.C. Myrtle Beach—R	18/72 6,320	On intracoastal waterway; large greens, trees, water hazards.
Palmetto C.C. Aiken—SP	18/72 7,100	Fine, long course. Quite hilly with many elevated tees and greens.
Pine Lakes C.C. Myrtle Beach—R	18/71 6,680	Tight and long, well maintained. Fifty motels within a mile radius.
Port Royal Plantation G.C. Hilton Head Island —R	18/72 7,022	Additional 9 holes will be opened in late summer.
Sea Gull G.C. Pawleys Island—R	18/72 7,100	Championship course open to motel guests; 51 bunkers; much water.
Sea Pines Plantation G.C. Hilton Head Island—R	36/72-72 6,617-6,413	Fine resort; 2 championship courses. William Hilton Inn adjoins.
Surf G.C. Ocean Drive Beach —R	18/72 6,720	Carved out of forest on ocean, 15 natural lakes.

Course Location—Type	Holes/Par Length	Comment
Wellman C.C. Johnsonville—SP	9/36 3,550	Challenging, with 5 water holes.

MIDEAST

TENNESSEE

Course Location—Type	Holes/Par Length	Comment
Audubon G.C. Memphis—MU	18/72 6,121	Relatively flat and easy.
Brainerd G.C. Chattanooga—MU	18/72 6,800	Many trees on long, rolling terrain. Tough par-4s.
Gatlinburg C.C. Gatlinburg—MU	18/72 6,440	At foot of Great Smoky Mts. Hilly terrain with big greens.
Henry Horton State Park Chapel Hill—MU	18/72 7,065	Fine public-owned course.

KENTUCKY

Course Location—Type	Holes/Par Length	Comment
Paxton G.C. Paducah—MU	18/70 6,125	Slightly rolling, few bunkers. Many nearby hotels.
Village Greens C.C. Kentucky Dam Village—SP	18/72 6,745	Rolling, tree-lined layout. Village and Holiday Inns near.

WEST VIRGINIA

Course Location—Type	Holes/Par Length	Comment
The Greenbrier White Sulphur Springs—R	54 holes	Three scenic, interesting courses. Sam Snead head pro.
Oglebay Park G.C. Wheeling—MU	18/71 6,300	Rolling hills, wide fairways. Beautiful landscaping. Lodge nearby.

MARYLAND

Course Location—Type	Holes/Par Length	Comment
All View G.C. Ellicott City—SP	18/72 6,365	Puts premium on short game with small greens, bunkers.
Great Oak Lodge Chestertown—R	18/65 4,821	Not difficult, but sporty. Wooded with lakes, well trapped.

Course Location—Type	Holes/Par Length	Comment
Mt. Pleasant G.C. Baltimore—MU	18/72 6,802	Hilly scenic course. Holiday Inn nearby.
Northwest Park G.C. Wheaton—MU	18/72 7,320	Rolling, narrow, wooded course, 68 bunkers.
Pine Ridge G.C. Lutherville—MU	18/72 6,820	Challenging course with water visible on every hole.
Washingtonian G.C. Gaithersburg—PR	18/72 6,874	Rolling, wooded, 4 large lakes. Motel has 100 rooms.

DISTRICT OF COLUMBIA

Course Location—Type	Holes/Par Length	Comment
Rock Creek Park G.C. Washington—MU	18/64 4,806	Short course is hilly, narrow in spots, has good greens.

DELAWARE

Course Location—Type	Holes/Par Length	Comment
Rock Manor G.C. Wilmington—SP	18/68 5,680	In excellent condition at all times.

VIRGINIA

Course Location—Type	Holes/Par Length	Comment
The Cavalier G. & Y.C. Virginia Beach—R	18/69 6,065	Well-groomed course, water holes, elevated tees.
Golden Horseshoe G.C. Williamsburg—R	18/71 6,743	Fine championship course owned by Williamsburg Inn.
The Homestead Hot Springs—R	54 holes	Three great courses of varying difficulty. 1967 Women's Open site.
Spotswood C.C. Williamsburg—R	9/31 1,865	Very sporty 9-hole test; adjoins Golden Horseshoe course.
The Tides Inn G.C. Irvington—R	18/72 6,482	Tree-lined, narrow fairways, large greens; also par-3 course.

Course Location—Type	Holes/Par Length	Comment

NORTH CAROLINA

Beaver Lake G.C. Asheville—SP	18/72 6,556	One of South's finest. Has longest par-5 in country at 690 yards.
Blair Park G.C. High Point—MU	18/72 6,500	Well-kept course. Clubhouse offers all services.
Blowing Rock C.C. Blowing Rock—SP	18/70 6,100	Tricky, windy mountain course with small greens, narrow fairways.
Boone G.C. Boone—R	18/71 6,325	Frequent tourney site. Hotels, motels nearby.
Foxfire G. & C.C. Pinehurst—SP	18/71 7,000	Gently rolling course, many water hazards. Adjoins airstrip.
Green Valley G.C. Greensboro—SP	18/71 6,200	Lush course. Fine clubhouse with hotels, motels nearby.
High Hampton Inn & C.C. Cashiers—R	18/71 5,904	Gently rolling with beautiful mountain views.
High Meadows G.C. Roaring Gap—R	18/72 7,110	Rolling terrain and lakes characterize this mountain layout.
Hound Ears Lodge C.C. Blowing Rock—R	18/72 6,300	Unusually flat terrain for mountain course with streams, lakes.
Lexington G. & C.C. Lexington—MU	18/70 5,703	Short but tricky. Motels nearby.
Linville G.C. Linville—R	18/71 6,634	Fine championship course high in mountains. Eseeola Lodge adjoins.
Mid-Pines C.C. Southern Pines—R	18/72 6,400	Great Ross-designed layout. Julius and Ernie Boros are professionals.

Course Location—Type	Holes/Par Length	Comment
Pinehurst C.C. Pinehurst—R	90 holes	Outstanding golf complex. Open to guests of nearby inns.
Pine Needles Lodge & C.C. Southern Pines—R	18/71 6,905	Beautiful, rolling course for guests only. For low or high handicappers.
Raleigh Golf Ass'n Raleigh—SP	18/71 6,955	Has 9 more holes for stock-holders and guests. Main course hilly.
Roaring Gap G. & C.C. Roaring Gap—PR	18/71 6,500	Scenic course, for guests of Graystone Inn.
Shamrock Park G.C. Burlington—SP	18/72 6,250	Challenging and demanding course.
Southern Pines C.C. Southern Pines—SP	27 holes	Two Ross-designed courses, an 18 and a 9.
Tanglewood Park G.C. Clemmons—MU	18/71 6,400	Also has par-3 lighted course. Lodge in parklike setting.
Waynesville C.C. Inn Waynesville—SP	18/71 6,014	Hotel and dining room open May—October.
Whispering Pines G.C. Pinehurst—SP	27/72-36 7,151-3,385	Championship 27-hole layout on 2,000-acre community development.

NORTHEAST

PENNSYLVANIA

Course Location—Type	Holes/Par Length	Comment
Bedford Springs Hotel & G.C. Bedford Springs—R	18 6,200	Scenic layout in Allegheny Mountains. Also pitch 'n' putt course.
Buck Hill G. C. Buck Hill Falls—R	27 holes	Tough layouts in mountains.
Cedarbrook G.C. Belle Vernon—SP	18/72 6,710	Fairly level, lush course. Motels nearby.

Course Location—Type	Holes/Par Length	Comment
Championship Lakes G.C. Ligonier—SP	18/71 6,870	Championship course; 7 lakes; trees; 7 mi. north of Ligonier on route 711.
Cobbs Creek G.C. Philadelphia—MU	18/70 5,943	Hilly, few traps. Scene of pro tourneys. Well-kept layout.
Hershey C.C. Hershey—R	18/73 6,928	Large greens, well-maintained course.
Malvern G.C. Downingtown—SP	18/71 6,365	Open all year, golf carts. Accommodations nearby at Downingtown Inn.
Manada G.C. Harrisburg—SP	18/72 6,840	Rolling fairways, large greens, bunkered.
Pleasant Valley G.C. Stewartstown—SP	18/72 6,451	Large trees and normal-size greens. Three water hazards.
Pocono Manor G.C. Pocono Manor—R	36 holes	Fine golf course. Bunkers, hills, and trees.
Shawnee Inn & C.C. Shawnee-on-the-Delaware—R	27 holes	Fred Waring's pleasant golf spa. Mountain scenery surrounds.
Skytop Lodge Skytop—PR	18/71 6,370	Gently rolling, fully irrigated; open to members and lodge guests.
Sportsman's G.C. Harrisburg—SP	18/71 6,715	Challenging layout, 3 lakes, mature trees.
Tamiment-in-the-Poconos Tamiment—R	18/72 7,110	Challenging Robert Trent Jones course.

NEW YORK

Beaver Island State Park Grand Island—MU	18/72 7,100	Generally flat, fine condition.
Bethpage State Park Farmingdale, L.I. —MU	90 holes	Variety of state-owned courses. Black course toughest.

Course Location—Type	Holes/Par Length	Comment
Brighton Park G.C. Tonawanda—MU	18/72 6,481	One of 2 public courses.
Concord Hotel Kiamesha Lake—R	45 holes	Championship 18 stretches to 7,600 yards. Fine entertainment.
Dyker Beach G.C. Brooklyn—MU	18/70 6,307	Most famous of New York's public courses.
Francourt Farms G.C. Horseheads—SP	18/71 6,850	Tough course. Open to public.
Genesee Valley G.C. Rochester—MU	36 holes	East and West offer contrast.
Grossinger Hotel & G.C. Grossinger—R	18/72 6,270	Year-round mountain resort.
Lima G. & C.C. Lima—MU	18/72 7,000	New course in fourth season. Long par-4 holes.
Loon Lake G.C. Loon Lake—R	18/70 5,600	Sporty course with resort accommodations in Adirondack Mts.
The Otesaga Cooperstown—R	18/72 6,372	Interesting course adjoining resort facilities with inn and cottages.
Sara Spa G.C. Saratoga Springs— MU	18/72 7,090	Championship course in fine condition.
Sullivan County G. & C.C. Liberty—SP	9/36 3,036	Hilly course in heart of Catskills. Green fees $3, $5.
Tennanah Lake G.C. Roscoe—R	18/71 6,750	Hotel resort course.
Thousand Islands Club Alexandria Bay—R	18/73 6,140	In St. Lawrence vacation area. Atmosphere relaxed.

Course Location—Type	Holes/Par Length	Comment
Whiteface Inn G.C. Whiteface Inn—R	18/72 6,445	Rolling, hilly course in Adirondacks. Site of many tourneys.

NEW JERSEY

Course Location—Type	Holes/Par Length	Comment
Atlantis C.C. Tuckerton—R	18/72 7,085	Long, narrow fairways, big greens, 4 water holes.
Flanders Valley G.C. Flanders—MU	18/72 6,950	Front 9 wooded, back 9 open. Owned by county.
Golden Pheasant C.C. Medford—SP	18/72 6,252	Hilly, water on 12 holes. Close to Philadelphia.
High Mountain G.C. Franklin Lakes—SP	18/72 6,727	Oak-lined fairways, ponds, and stream give mountain layout zest.
Mays Landing C.C. Atlantic City—SP	18/72 6,857	Long, lined with pines and oaks. Near resort area.
Park Vale C.C. River Vale—MU	18/71 6,313	Rolling, tree-lined, interesting course, modern facilities.

CONNECTICUT

Course Location—Type	Holes/Par Length	Comment
Norwich Inn G.C. Norwich—R	18/71 6,425	Challenging course adjoins inn.
Shennecossett C.C. Groton—MU	18/72 6,512	One of northeast's oldest courses. Adjoins Griswold Hotel.
Tunxis Plantation C.C. Farmington—SP	18/72-9/36 6,585-3,197	Scenic, gently rolling course; 9 new holes just added. Motel nearby.

RHODE ISLAND

Course Location—Type	Holes/Par Length	Comment
Louisquissett G.C. North Providence—SP	18/70 6,340	Hilly, narrow fairways, close to city accommodations.
Triggs Memorial G.C. Providence—MU	18/72 6,850	Outstanding public-owned course. Long and rolling.

Course Location—Type	Holes/Par Length	Comment
Winnapaug G.C. Westerly—SP	18/72 6,375	Somewhat hilly links overlooking Atlantic. No adjacent fairways.

MASSACHUSETTS

Course Location—Type	Holes/Par Length	Comment
Blue Rock G.C. South Yarmouth—R	18/54 2,803	Tough par-3 layout; 36 traps. Greens average 8,000 square feet.
Clauson's Inn & Golf Resort North Falmouth—R	18/72 6,507	Pine tree-lined irrigated fairways, large lake, wind blows often.
Colonial C.C. Lynnfield—SP	18/71 6,825	Tree-lined. Many water hazards. First long public course with lights.
Coonamesset G.C. Hatchville—R	18/72 6,507	Pine-studded course with strong lake breezes, watered fairways.
C.C. of New Seabury Mashpee—SP	36 7,175-5,170	Tough test. First 9 of championship course on ocean.
Dennis Pines G.C. East Dennis—MU	18/72 7,029	Championship course with rolling fairways, many pine trees.
Edgewood G.C. Southwick—SP	18/71 6,800	Second 9 opened in 1964.
Fiddler's Green Hyannis—R	18/54 2,904	Championship par 3; 11 water holes. Undulating greens. On Atlantic.
The Island C.C. Martha's Vineyard—R	18/70 6,018	USGA-rated course overlooking Nantucket Sound. Sporty with breezes.
Miacomet G.C. Nantucket—R	9/37 3,337	Gently rolling moors reminiscent of Scotland. Sea view and breezes.
Northfield Hotel G.C. East Northfield—R	9/35 2,930	Short 9-holer not difficult to play, but fun.

Course Location—Type	Holes/Par Length	Comment
Swansea C.C. North Swansea—SP	18/72 6,855	Challenging course in scenic country.
Taconic G.C. Williamstown—SP	18/71 6,630	Picturesque, rolling championship course. Site of past national events.
Trull Brook G.C. Tewksbury—SP	18/72 6,250	Picturesque course bordered by river, located on 1757 king's grant.
Waubeeka Springs Links Williamstown—SP	18/72 6,620	Moderately wooded, water in play on 10 holes, 6,000-square-foot greens.
Wycoff Park C.C. Holyoke—SP	18/71 6,800	Scenic, hilly course.

VERMONT

Basin Harbor G.C. Vergennes—R	18/72 6,500	Rolling course bordering woodland and Lake Champlain.
Equinox C.C. Manchester—R	18/72 6,690	Fine course in mountains. Top facilities in Equinox Hotel.
Lake Morey C.C. Fairlee—R	18/69 5,485	Rolling fairways, beautiful view. Special rates for Lake Morey Inn guests.
Rutland C.C. Rutland—SP	18/70 6,400	Rolling terrain, 3 water holes. Fine clubhouse facilities. Near town.
Sugarbush G.C. Warren—R	18/72 7,050	Robert Trent Jones championship course. Inns and motels nearby.
Williston G. & C.C. Williston—MU	18/69 5,800	Old front 9 tight, newer back 9 open; 6 mi. east of Burlington.

Course Location—Type	Holes/Par Length	Comment
Woodstock C.C. Woodstock—PR	18/69 6,250	Course rebuilt in 1964. Has fine facilities in clubhouse, good food.

NEW HAMPSHIRE

Course Location—Type	Holes/Par Length	Comment
The Balsams Hotel G.C. Dixville Notch—R	18/72 7,200	Long, championship course in Switzerland-like vacation area.
Bethlehem Municipal G.C. Bethlehem—MU	18/72 6,900	Long, challenging course.
Five Chimneys G.C. Province Lake—R	9/36 2,928	Lakeside course crossing Maine border.
Hanover C.C. Hanover—SP	9/36-18/70 2,880-6,000	Carved in rugged terrain of birch and pine.
Jack O'Lantern C.C. Woodstock—R	9/34 2,700	Nine holes under construction will extend course to over 6,000 yards.
Lake Tarleton Club Pike—R	18/72 6,226	One of New England's first courses. Five lakes on 5,500-acre resort.
Maplewood C.C. Bethlehem—SP	18/72 6,209	In vacation area with other recreation facilities nearby.
Mt. Washington G.C. Bretton Woods—PR	18/71 6,189	Championship course with fairways surrounding resort hotel.
The Waumbek G.C. Jefferson—R	18/72 6,100	Set in unspoiled wilderness. Site of top amateur tournaments.
Wentworth-by-the-Sea Portsmouth—R	18/71 6,420	Excellent new seaside course. Also has enjoyable short course.
Woodbound Inn G.C. Jaffrey—R	18/54 2,224	Short par-3, but interesting. Regulation courses nearby.

Course Location—Type	Holes/Par Length	Comment
MAINE		
Bangor Municipal G.C. Bangor—R	18/72 6,500	Large tees, greens, and watered fairways; 4-hole children's course.
Bethel Inn G.C. Bethel—R	9/34 2,431	Short 9-hole layout in picturesque country. Full facilities.
Kebo Valley C. Bar Harbor—SP	18/72 6,700	Narrow, tree-lined course, small greens. Big clubhouse, restaurant.
Poland Spring G.C. Poland Spring—R	18/71 6,764	First hotel-owned course in country. Beautiful views.
Riverside Municipal G.C. Portland—MU	18/72 6,309	Site of Maine Open. One of best courses in New England.
Squaw Mountain Inn Greenville Junction —R	9/34 2,563	Sporty. Set on wooded tract of New England's largest lake.
Webhannet G.C. Kennebunk Beach —SP	18/70 6,200	Lush seaside links. Level fairways. Adjoins Atlantis Hotel.
York G. & Tennis C. York Harbor—PR	18/70 6,203	Fine seaside course. For guests of nearby Marshall House.

MIDWEST

NORTH DAKOTA

Bois de Sioux C.C. Wahpeton—SP	18/72 6,200	Wide open on front 9, narrow on back.
Edgewood G.C. Fargo—MU	18/72 6,300	Narrow, tree-lined, big greens. Motels nearby.
Grand Forks C.C. Grand Forks—SP	18/72 7,000	Long and tricky. Westward Ho guests may play.

Course Location—Type	Holes/Par Length	Comment
SOUTH DAKOTA		
Elmwood G.C. Sioux Falls—MU	27/72-36 7,100-3,486	Long, tree-lined, tough city-owned course.
Watertown G.C. Watertown—MU	18/72 6,000	Sporty, rolling course.
NEBRASKA		
Alliance Municipal G.C. Alliance—MU	18/72 6,812	Long, rolling challenge.
Holmes Park G.C. Lincoln—MU	18/72 6,812	Rolling, well-trapped greens. Motel facilities nearby. Driving range.
KANSAS		
Lawrence C.C. Lawrence—MU	18/72 6,357	Hilly, tree-lined.
MINNESOTA		
Bemidji C.C. Bemidji—SP	18/72 6,309	Hilly, wooded. All out-of-town guests may play.
Enger Park G.C. Duluth—MU	18/72 6,105	Pine-surrounded hilly course. Many accommodations nearby.
Francis Gross G.C. Minneapolis—MU	18/70 6,361	Tree-lined. National Publinx Championship once held here.
Keller G.C. St. Paul—MU	18/72 6,557	Twice site of PGA Championship. Well-trapped, long par-4 holes.
Madden G.C. Brainerd—R	18/72 6,400	Gentle hills; plenty of trees. Also two 9-hole par-3's.
Madden Pine Beach G.C. Brainerd—SP	36/72-35-28 5,934-2,200- 1,341	Rolling terrain; short 9 adjoins 18-hole course.

Course Location—Type	Holes/Par Length	Comment
Maple Valley G. & C.C. Rochester—SP	18/72 6,975	Scenic, challenging course in Root River Valley.
Meadowbrook G.C. Hopkins—MU	18/72 6,474	Rolling, well-trapped course with many dogleg holes.

IOWA

Ellis Park G.C. Cedar Rapids—MU	18/72 6,515	Outstanding city-owned course.
Okoboji Vu G.C. Spirit Lake—R	18/71 6,215	Opened in 1963. Has par-3 19th hole for playoffs.
U. of Iowa Finkbine G.C. Iowa City—SP	18/72 6,905	Hilly, well-trapped college course.

MISSOURI

Excelsior Springs G.C. Excelsior Springs—SP	18/72 6,418	Rolling terrain, elevated greens. Sheraton-Elms Hotel nearby.
Minor Park G.C. Kansas City—MU	18/70 6,200	New course with lighted driving range.
Paddock C.C. Florissant—SP	18/72 6,300	Hilly, well-trapped, many trees.
Swope Park.G.C. Kansas City—MU	36 holes	One long, one par-65 course. Both tree-lined.

WISCONSIN

Brown Deer Park G.C. Milwaukee—MU	18/71 7,021	Tough public course. Hilly, tree-lined.
Fox Hills C.C. Mishicot—MU	18/71 6,500	Large rolling greens, four holes over water.
Lake Lawn G.C. Delavan—R	18/70 6,100	Rolling course, good greens. Many nearby accommodations.

Course Location—Type	Holes/Par Length	Comment
Lawsonia G.C. Green Lake—SP	18/72 6,600	Tree-lined, elevated multi-level greens. Closed Sundays.
Naga-Waukee Park G.C. Hartland—MU	18/72 6,565	Wooded, scenic, rolling course, well trapped, with water holes.
Nemadji G.C. Superior—SP	18/71 6,298	Plays tough although short. Fine greens.
Odana Hills G.C. Madison—MU	18/72 6,769	Long, rolling, well groomed, tough.
Peninsula State Park Ephraim—MU	18/70 5,800	Hilly and wooded state-owned course. Not too rough, but fun.
Petrifying Springs G.C. Kenosha—MU	18/71 6,170	Wooded, overlooking scenic lake.
Playboy Club-Hotel G.C. Lake Geneva—R	18/72 7,100	A Robert Bruce Harris championship course; excellent greens interestingly trapped.

ILLINOIS

Chicago		The Chicago—Cook County area contains more semi-private courses available to golfers on a green-fee basis than any major city in the U.S.
Cog Hill G. & C.C. Lemont—SP	72 holes	All four courses wooded. Fourth hole has 101 bunkers.
Indian Hills G.C. Mt. Vernon—MU	18/72 6,034	Course is rolling, wooded, with large greens.
Indian Lakes C.C. Bloomingdale—SP	18/72 6,995	Plays long. Good test of skill with 5 lakes, large sand traps.
Macktown G.C. Rockton—R	18/72 5,935	Annual site of ladies' PGA event. Wagon Wheel Lodge nearby.

Course Location—Type	Holes/Par Length	Comment
Midlane Farm C.C. Wadsworth—SP	18/72 7,130	Rolling with big tees and greens, 65 large bunkers.
Pheasant Run Lodge St. Charles—R	18/72 6,826	Lodge is convention center. Has own shops, entertainment.

MICHIGAN

Course Location—Type	Holes/Par Length	Comment
Boyne Highlands G.C. Harbor Springs—R	18/72 7,200	Robert Trent Jones course opening July 30; heavily wooded, well trapped.
Byron Hills G.C. Byron Center—SP	27 holes	Main 18 is tough, wooded. Shorter 9 is tricky. Motels nearby.
Eastern Hills G.C. Kalamazoo—MU	27/72-37 6,680-3,200	Tough course with modern clubhouse.
Forest Akers G.C. East Lansing—SP	27/71-34 6,834-2,826	Stern test of all shots. Course owned by Michigan State U.
Hampshire C.C. Dowagiac—SP	18/72 7,110	Course 5 years old, heavily wooded, rolling.
Raisin River C.C. Monroe—SP	18/68 6,275	Adjoins motel-restaurant. Tough course, watered fairways.

INDIANA

Course Location—Type	Holes/Par Length	Comment
Avalon Lakes G.C. Warren—MU	18/71 7,001	Challenging course; well trapped; water hazards.
Beechwood G.C. La Porte—MU	18/72 6,674	Long course, well trapped. Not far from Chicago.
Coffin G.C. Indianapolis—MU	18/70 6,825	Toughest public course in area. Hilly, narrow, with water hazards.
Elkhart Lodge & C.C. Elkhart—SP	18/72 6,345	Scenic course with 14 water crossings.

Course Location—Type	Holes/Par Length	Comment
French Lick-Sheraton Hotel French Lick—R	36 holes	One tough, one easier course. Free to hotel guests; 600 rooms.
Helfrich Hills G.C. Evansville—MU	18/72 6,086	Hilly with wide fairways.
North Eastway G.C. Castleton—MU	18/70 6,655	Long tees and large rolling greens. New $300,000 clubhouse.
Tri-County G.C. Middletown—MU	18/72 6,709	Greens average 8,000 square feet; wide fairways.
Wicker Park Memorial G.C. Highland—MU	18/72 6,550	Tough course with 8 out-of-bounds chances.

OHIO

Course Location—Type	Holes/Par Length	Comment
Blackhawk G.C. Galena—SP	18/72 6,851	Located in scenic area 15 miles from Columbus. Overlooks lake.
Granville Inn G.C. Granville—SP	18/71 6,417	Superb, rolling course with Granville Inn.
Hinckley Hills G.C. Cleveland—SP	18/72 6,575	Rolling and scenic; 4 years old.
Shelby Oaks C.C. Sidney—SP	18/72 6,553	Contoured, rolling, with large greens, trees, and traps.
Tannenhauf G.C. Alliance—SP	18/72 7,000	Tree-lined, big greens, tough test.

SOUTHWEST

UTAH

Course Location—Type	Holes/Par Length	Comment
Ben Lomond G.C. Ogden—MU	18/72 6,200	Relatively flat and easy course.
Logan G. & C.C. Logan—SP	18/71 5,711	Short but interesting course. Beautiful scenery.

Course Location—Type	Holes/Par Length	Comment
Meadow Brook G.C. Salt Lake City—MU	18/72 6,900	Flat but narrow, lush course. Motels nearby.
Timpanogos G.C. Provo—SP	18/72 6,400	Flat with tree-lined fairways.

ARIZONA

Course Location—Type	Holes/Par Length	Comment
Apache Wells Mesa—R	18/70 6,905	Championship course situated in beautiful Arizona desert.
Arizona Biltmore C.C. Phoenix—R	18/72 6,370	Mountain and desert setting for fine course.
Desert Forest G.C. Carefree—PR	18/72 6,925	Championship course puts emphasis on strategy; Carefree Inn nearby.
The Forty-Niners C.C. Tucson—R	18/72 6,900	Rolling terrain, trees, 4 water holes. Complete resort, dude ranch.
Golden Hills C.C. Mesa—R	18/70 6,483	Accommodations on course; rates include golf; extra-large greens.
Goodyear G. & C.C. Litchfield Park—R	36/70-72 6,120-7,220	Well trapped; many lakes. For club members and Wigwam guests.
Indian Bend C.C. Scottsdale—SP	18/71 6,483	On Indian reservation near Casa Blanca Inn.
Mountain Shadows C.C. Scottsdale—PR	18/56 2,950	Executive course run by Mountain Shadows Resort.
Papago Park G.C. Phoenix—MU	18/72 6,690	Outstanding municipal course opened in 1963.
Paradise Valley C.C. Scottsdale—PR	18/71 6,341	Beautiful championship course open to guests of Camelback Inn.

Course Location—Type	Holes/Par Length	Comment
San Marcos G.C. Chandler—R	18/72 6,775	Plush resort course, bordered by tall tamarack trees.
Scottsdale C.C. Scottsdale—R	18/70 6,500	Course not difficult but tricky; 4 water holes.
Skyline C.C. Tucson—R	18/70 6,344	Cottage colony in Catalina Mts. with real estate development.
Sun City G.C. Sun City—SP	54 holes	Three layouts in senior retirement area include 6,944-yard par-71. Sun City also in California and Florida.

COLORADO

Broadmoor G.C. Colorado Springs—R	36/72-72 7,036-7,144	Both 18's at Broadmoor Hotel resort are championship courses.
Foothills G.C. Boulder—SP	18/69 6,900	Tough test. Valleys and small hills.
Hiwan G.C. Evergreen—SP	18/70 7,114	Long, narrow, rolling course in high Rockies setting.
Los Verdes G.C. Denver—SP	18/72 7,000	Finely conditioned course. Large greens. Many trees.
Vail G.C. Vail—MU	9/36 3,480	Challenging course; near Arnold Palmer Golf Academy.
Walsenburg G.C. Walsenburg—SP	9/36 3,135	Gently contoured fairways; overlooks Culebra Mts.

NEW MEXICO

Cloudcroft Lodge G.C. Cloudcroft—R	18/68 4,693	Highest course in America at 9,200 feet. Hilly.
Los Alamos G.C. Los Alamos—MU	18/72 6,596	Hilly, narrow, big greens. Altitude 7,300 feet.

Course Location—Type	Holes/Par Length	Comment
New Mexico State U. G.C. Las Cruces—MU	18/72 7,200	All 18 holes can be seen from clubhouse, site of 1968 NCAA.
U. of New Mexico G.C. Albuquerque—SP	18/72 7,258	Championship course; desert terrain; driving range. Open to public.

OKLAHOMA

Course Location—Type	Holes/Par Length	Comment
Lake Hefner G.C. Oklahoma City—MU	36/70-70 6,885-6,580	Gently rolling terrain looking over lake. Motels nearby.
Lincoln Park G.C. Oklahoma City—MU	36/70-70 6,508-6,508	Renovated, sporty public courses; well trapped; rolling terrain.
Shamrock C.C. Tulsa—PR	18/72 7,245	Championship course; 7 lakes, many trees. Doug Sanders, pro. Open to members of other clubs.
U. of Oklahoma G.C. Norman—SP	18/72 6,574	Open to public, tough test, rolling terrain, deep traps, water, rough.

TEXAS

Course Location—Type	Holes/Par Length	Comment
Brackenridge Park G.C. San Antonio—MU	18/71 6,490	Closed for remodeling until Sept. 1, 1968.
Casa Blanca G.C. Laredo—MU	18/72 6,850	Flat, wide fairways, 5 water holes. Near Mexican border.
Corpus Christi C.C. Corpus Christi—SP	18/72 7,115	Large greens, long course. Also driving range.
Fairway Farm G.C. San Augustine—PR	18/71 7,352	Brutal course from back tees. No parallel fairways.
Great Southwest G.C. Arlington—SP	18/71 6,986	Thickly wooded, gently rolling terrain. Well trapped. Lighted par-3.
Lake Arlington G.C. Arlington—MU	18/71 7,000	Front 9 flat, back 9 rolling. Four lakes as hazards.

Course Location—Type	Holes/Par Length	Comment
Meadowbrook Municipal G.C. Lubbock—MU	27/72-35 6,696-3,254	In wooded canyon. Requires accurate shots. Many bunkers.
Memorial Park G.C. Houston—MU	18/72 7,122	Wooded course, 5 water hazards.
Memorial Park G.C. Uvalde—MU	9/36 3,113	Wooded course; no water hazards.
Morris Williams G.C. Austin—MU	18/72 6,597	Rolling terrain, wooded, big greens. Motels nearby.
Pecan Valley C.C. San Antonio—PR	18/71 7,150	Always open. Challenging, wooded layout. Site of '68 PGA Championship.
Valley Inn & C.C. Brownsville—PR	18/72 7,006	New championship course.

NORTHWEST

WASHINGTON

Course Location—Type	Holes/Par Length	Comment
Birch Bay G.C. Blaine—R	18/68 5,400	Just 4 miles from Canadian border.
Capitol City G.C. Olympia—MU	18/71 6,438	Monthly rates available.
Cedarcrest G.C. Marysville—SP	18/69 5,165	Rolling hills with bent greens and tees. Very sporty. Motels nearby.
Downriver G.C. Spokane—MU	18/70 6,087	Interesting layout.
Indian Canyon G.C. Spokane—MU	18/72 6,227	One of three city-owned layouts.
Jefferson Park Municipal G.C. Seattle—MU	27/70-28 6,315-1,450	Tree-lined, hilly. Built in 1915. Site of 1967 Publinx Championship.
Meadow Park G.C. Tacoma—MU	27/72-31 6,158-1,775	Narrow, hilly, tree-lined course. Extra 9 is short, sporty.

Course Location—Type	Holes/Par Length	Comment
Moses Lake G. & C.C. Moses Lake—PR	18/71 6,173	Nonmember must be guest of member or member of another club.
Spanaway G.C. Tacoma—MU	18/72 6,825	Opened spring 1967.
Tyee Valley G.C. Seattle—MU	18/71 6,070	Opened June, 1967.

OREGON

Bowman's Mt. Hood G.C. Wemme—SP	18/70 6,433	Beautiful, hilly resort at foot of Mt. Hood, which has winter skiing.
Eastmoreland G.C. Portland—MU	18/71 6,283	Outstanding of several public courses in area. Many hazards.
Gearhart G.C. Gearhart—R	18/72 6,125	Seaside links built in 1890s, flat, windy. Hotel adjoins; beaches near.
McNary G.C. Salem—SP	18/72 6,718	Fairly new course has huge, smooth greens. Luxurious facilities.
Meriwether National G.C. Hillsboro—SP	18/72 7,042	Long, hazard-filled course.
Salishan Golf Lodge Gleneden Beach—R	18/72 6,437	Narrow, well landscaped. Course overlooks Pacific Ocean.

IDAHO

Pinecrest Municipal G.C. Idaho Falls—MU	18/70 6,823	Toughest public course in the region; 9 out-of-bounds chances.
Plantation G.C. Boise—SP	18/72 6,500	Well-kept course made tough by many trees.
Sun Valley G.C. Sun Valley—R	18/71 6,499	Ski Mecca has 18-hole course for May to October season.

Course Location—Type	Holes/Par Length	Comment

MONTANA

| Lake Hills G.C.
Billings—SP | 18/72
7,140 | Long, tough course. Great summer outdoor area. |

WYOMING

| Airport G.C.
Cheyenne—MU | 18/72
6,400 | Flat but fun, open about 7 months. |

FAR WEST

CALIFORNIA

Alameda G.C. Alameda—MU	18/71 6,020	Completely renovated North Course; 5 artificial lake hazards.
Alisal G.C. Solvang—R	18/72 6,600	Tree-lined, 9 fairways cross river. Combined ranch-hotel facility.
Almaden G.C. San Jose—PR	18/72 7,035	Rolling hills, large greens, well trapped.
Apple Valley Inn Apple Valley—R	18/71 6,765	Sprawling resort course, open year around.
Azusa Greens G.C. Azusa—SP	18/70 6,463	Privately owned course open to public.
Canyon Club Inn Palm Springs—R	18/72 7,000	Two large lakes, 140 traps make this course a challenge.
Chimney Rock G.C. Napa—SP	18/72 6,537	Overlooking vineyards and orchards, course has two 5-acre lakes, many trees.
Del Monte G.C. Pebble Beach—MU	18/72 6,338	Former site of Bing Crosby Pro-Am. Near Mark Thomas Inn.
Dry Creek Ranch G.C. Galt—SP	18/72 6,487	New course south of Sacramento. Play all year.

Course Location—Type	Holes/Par Length	Comment
Harding Park G.C. San Francisco—MU	18/72 6,722	Outstanding championship muni course. Narrow, tree-lined.
Hesperia G. & C.C. Hesperia—SP	18/72 7,136	Course lies between two mesas. Country club open all year.
Hillview G.C. San Jose—MU	18/72 6,430	Flat course, tree-lined, small greens. Good clubhouse.
La Costa C.C. Carlsbad—R	18/72 7,157	New championship course. Site of American Airlines As-trojet event.
La Quinta C.C. La Quinta—PR	18/72 6,900	Closed during summer. Hotel La Quinta nearby.
Las Positas G.C. Livermore—MU	18/72 6,790	Good test; fairly long front 9, rolling back 9. Water haz-ards.
Lew Galbraith G.C. Oakland—MU	18/72 6,750	Well laid out course on roll-ing, tree-lined fairways.
Los Verdes G.C. Palos Verdes—MU	18/71 6,520	View of ocean from every hole on course. Accommoda-tions nearby.
Massacre Canyon Inn & Golf Resort Gilman Hot Springs —R	27/36-35-33 3,588-3,447 2,960	Flat and long, 2 lakes, many trees. At foothills of moun-tain range.
Oakmont C.C. Santa Rosa—SP	18/72 6,760	New course with plenty of motels nearby.
Oak Ridge G.C. San Jose—SP	18/72 6,382	Rolling fairways; driving range.
Ojai Valley C.C. Ojai—R	18/71 6,351	Fine course circles Ojai Inn.
Pala Mesa Inn & G.C. Fallbrook—R	18/71 6,500	Championship course; dis-tinctly separate 9's—one hilly, other woody.

Course Location—Type	Holes/Par Length	Comment
Palo Alto G.C. Palo Alto—MU	18/72 6,418	Flat with elevated tees, well trapped.
Pasatiempo G.C. Santa Cruz—MU	18/71 6,245	Old course, rolling fairways. Good test.
Pebble Beach G.C. Pebble Beach—R	18/72 6,747	Borders ocean, one of world's best. Del Monte Lodge guests only.
Rancho Park G.C. Los Angeles—MU	18/71 6,620	Busy course in heart of L.A.
Rancho San Joaquin Newport Beach—SP	18/72 6,500	Slightly rolling. Excellent greens. Three holes play over water.
Silverado C.C. Napa—PR	36/72-72 6,849-6,602	Tough championship courses. Open to guests staying on premises.
Soboba Springs C.C. San Jacinto—PR	18/72 6,661	Muirhead creation is flat but challenging, with huge rolling greens.
Spy Glass Hill G.C. Pebble Beach—MU	18/72 6,972	Robert Trent Jones course opened in 1966. Site of Bing Crosby Pro-Am.
Torrey Pines Inn & G.C. La Jolla—R	36 holes	Choice of two challenging championship courses.

NEVADA

Desert Inn C.C. Las Vegas—R	18/72 7,209	Championship resort course.
Dunes Hotel C.C. Las Vegas—R	18/72 7,240	Longest course in Nevada. Built to meet tournament standards.
Las Vegas G.C. Las Vegas—MU	18/72 6,700	Lots of traps, many trees, wide fairways.

Spectators watch Jack Nicklaus putt the famous 7th hole at Pebble Beach. Probably no spot in golf is more photogenic—or more photographed— than this hole. From an elevated tee, the player must shoot directly for the tiny green ringed by bunkers on a little thumb of land stuck into the Pacific. The test is great in a dead calm; but there's usually a wind off the sea, demanding the ultimate in judgment and skill. Evidence of the numbers who don't quite pass is the harvest of balls scuba divers find in the water around the point.

Course Location—Type	Holes/Par Length	Comment
Paradise Valley C.C. Las Vegas—R	18/72 7,069	Large greens. Site of Sahara Invitational.
Stardust G.C. Las Vegas—R	18/71 6,625	Many doglegs. Site of '68 Tournament of Champions.
Tropicana C.C. Las Vegas—R	18/70 6,502	Sporty course across street from hotel. Lagoons on 5 holes.
Winterwood G.C. Las Vegas—MU	18/71 6,395	A Dick Wilson championship course; fairly flat, well trapped.